ATTITUDES *De Se*

CSLI Lecture Notes Number 208

ATTITUDES *De Se*

Linguistics, Epistemology, Metaphysics

edited by

Neil Feit & Alessandro Capone

CSLI PUBLICATIONS

Center for the Study of
Language and Information
Stanford, California

Center for the Study of Language and Information
Leland Stanford Junior University
Printed in the United States
17 16 15 14 13 1 2 3 4 5

Library of Congress Cataloging-in-Publication Data

Attitudes de se : linguistics, epistemology, metaphysics / edited by Neil Feit, Alessandro Capone.
pages cm. – (CSLI Lecture Notes ; 208)

Summary: "In English, we use the word 'I' to express thoughts that we have about ourselves, and we use the reflexive pronouns 'himself' and 'herself' to attribute such thoughts to others. Philosophers and linguists call such thoughts, and the statements we use to express them, "*de se*." *De se* thoughts and statements, although they appear often in our day-to-day lives, pose a series of challenging problems for both linguists and philosophers. This interdisciplinary volume examines the structure of *de se* thought, various issues concerning the semantics and pragmatics of our discourse about it, and also what it reveals about how humans think about themselves and the world around them." – Provided by publisher.

ISBN 978-1-57586-665-9 (hardback) –
ISBN 978-1-57586-664-2 (paperback) –
ISBN 978-1-57586-666-6 (electronic)
1. English language–Pronoun. 2. English language–Reflexives.
3. English language–Semantics. 4. English language–Grammar.
5. Generative grammar. I. Feit, Neil. II. Capone, Alessandro.

PE1261. A88 2013
425–dc23

2013019453

CIP

∞ The acid-free paper used in this book meets the minimum requirements of the American National Standard for Information Sciences—Permanence of Paper for Printed Library Materials, ANSI Z39.48-1984.

CSLI was founded in 1983 by researchers from Stanford University, SRI International, and Xerox PARC to further the research and development of integrated theories of language, information, and computation. CSLI headquarters and CSLI Publications are located on the campus of Stanford University.

CSLI Publications reports new developments in the study of language, information, and computation. Please visit our web site at
http://cslipublications.stanford.edu/
for comments on this and other titles, as well as for changes and corrections by the author and publisher.

Contents

Contributors

DARREN BRADLEY: Philosophy Department, The City College of New York, 160 Convent Ave., New York, NY 10031, USA.
dbradley@ccny.cuny.edu

ALESSANDRO CAPONE: Department of Linguistics, University of Palermo, Piazza Marina, 61 - 90133 Palermo, Italy.
alessandro.capone@istruzione.it

EROS CORAZZA: Department of Philosophy, Carleton University, 1125 Colonel By Drive Ottawa, ON K1S 5B6, Canada.
eros_corazza@carleton.ca

WAYNE A. DAVIS: Department of Philosophy, Georgetown University, 37th and O Streets, N.W., Washington D.C. 20057, USA.
davisw@georgetown.edu

DENIS DELFITTO: Department of Linguistics, University of Verona, Via dell'Artigliere 8, 37129 Verona, Italy.
Denis.delfitto@univr.it

MICHAEL DEVITT: Philosophy Program, Graduate Center, City University of New York, 365 Fifth Ave., New York, NY 10016, USA.
mdevitt@gc.cuny.edu

IGOR DOUVEN: Faculty of Philosophy, University of Groningen, Oude Boteringestraat 52, 9712 GL Groningen, The Netherlands.
i.e.j.douven@rug.nl

NEIL FEIT: Department of Philosophy, SUNY Fredonia, Fredonia, NY 14063, USA.
Neil.Feit@fredonia.edu

GAETANO FIORIN: Department of Linguistics, University of Verona, Via dell'Artigliere 8, 37129 Verona, Italy.
gaetano.fiorin@gmail.com

JAMES HIGGINBOTHAM: School of Philosophy, University of Southern California, 3709 Trousdale Parkway, Los Angeles, CA 90089.
higgy@usc.edu

YAN HUANG: Department of Applied Language Studies and Linguistics, University of Auckland, Private Bag 92019, Auckland 1142, New Zealand.
yan.huang@auckland.ac.nz

KASIA M. JASZCZOLT: Department of Theoretical and Applied Linguistics, University of Cambridge, Sidgwick Avenue, Cambridge, CB3 9DA, UK.
kmj21@cam.ac.uk

MICHAEL NELSON: Department of Philosophy, University of California, Riverside, 900 University Ave, Riverside, CA 92521, USA.
michael.nelson@ucr.edu

PIETRO PERCONTI: Department of Cognitive Science, University of Messina, Piazza Pugliatti, 1 - 98122 Messina, Italy.
pietroperconti@gmail.com

JOHN PERRY: Department of Philosophy, University of California, Riverside, 900 University Ave, Riverside, CA 92521, USA.
john.perry@ucr.edu

MICHAEL G. TITELBAUM: Department of Philosophy, University of Wisconsin, 5185 Helen C. White Hall, 600 N. Park St., Madison, WI 53706, USA.
titelbaum@wisc.edu

The Problem of *De Se* Attitudes

An Introduction to the Issues and the Essays

NEIL FEIT AND ALESSANDRO CAPONE

If Smith says ‘I am hungry’, then she makes a *de se* assertion and expresses a *de se* belief, that is, an assertion and a belief that are irreducibly about the way she herself is. If Jones says ‘Smith believes that she herself is hungry’, he attributes a *de se* belief to Smith. More generally, *de se* attitudes are those that we express with ‘I’ or other first-person pronouns, and those that we attribute to others with emphatic reflexives such as ‘she herself’ and ‘he himself’ (and with certain other constructions where appropriate). *De se* attitudes do not merely lurk at the margins of our psychology and our discourse about it, they are everywhere. And yet they raise challenging problems concerning the nature of the content of our attitudes, and the proper analysis of belief reports and other attitude attributions. This volume collects together new essays, by linguists and philosophers, examining these problems. Although the division is to a certain extent arbitrary, the book is divided into two parts: the first has to do with a cluster of issues in linguistics and the philosophy of language, and the second with issues in the epistemology and metaphysics of attitude content. In this introduction, we discuss the problem of *de se* attitudes and several of the classic papers devoted to it, and so we hope that this book might serve as a stand-alone volume on the topic.

Attitudes De Se: Linguistics, Epistemology, Metaphysics.
Neil Feit and Alessandro Capone (eds.).

1 The Problem of *De Se* Attitudes

There are at least two interconnected problems associated with *de se* attitudes. One of them is a semantic, or broadly linguistic, problem. Consider the following:

(1) Obama believes that Obama is tall.

(2) Obama believes that the president of the USA is tall.

(3) Obama believes that he is tall.

(4) Obama believes that he himself is tall.

Suppose that Obama is suffering from temporary amnesia, so that in some ordinary sense he does not realize that he is Obama, does not realize that he is the president of the USA, and does not realize that he is tall. Suppose also that, while amnesic, Obama looks at a photograph of a group of people, among them a tall man who is identified by the caption as Barack Obama, the president of the USA.

In the imagined scenario, utterances of (1) and (2) would be true. But an utterance of (4) would clearly not be true. Moreover, while it might be the case that an utterance of (3) has a reading on which it is equivalent to an utterance of (4), that is, a *de se* reading, such a reading is not obligatory even in cases where 'he' is anaphoric to the subject, 'Obama'. For example, in uttering (3) a speaker might be reporting that Obama has a belief about a certain man, who, unbeknownst to Obama happens to be Obama himself – and in virtue of looking at the photograph, he does indeed have such a belief. So, there is at least a sense in which (3) also does not entail (4). The non-entailment goes the other way as well. We can imagine scenarios in which (4) is true, but in which (1), (2), and (3) on its non-*de se* reading are false. The main linguistic problem, then, is to account for the semantic difference between *de se* attitude reports like (4), on the one hand, and reports like (1)-(3) on the other.

One way to summarize this problem is to ask: How does the meaning of an emphatic reflexive like 'he himself' in the complement of an attitude report differ from that of a co-referential proper name, definite description, or pronoun? (A related problem, or perhaps a different face of the same problem, concerns the difference in meaning between the first person pronoun and other co-referential terms.) The problem is challenging for several reasons, perhaps the strongest being the fact that whatever we take the realm of meanings of subject terms to be, it would seem to be *exhausted* by the meanings we assign to proper names, definite descriptions, and pronouns. If this is the case, then it seems there is nothing else the emphatic reflexive can mean.

The linguistic problem of *de se* attitudes just sketched is sharpest when set within a particular framework for belief, which will set the stage for the psychological version of the problem. (Indeed some would argue that in the absence of such a framework, *de se* attitudes do not constitute a *problem* at all.) According to this framework, a cognitive attitude such as belief is a two-place relation between a subject and a proposition, the truth or falsehood of which does not vary from person to person or from time to time. When such a relation is instantiated, the relevant proposition is the content of the attitude.

With this framework in mind, let's reconsider (4) above:

(4) Obama believes that he himself is tall.

The framework of propositional attitudes, unless it is adorned with additional machinery, cannot easily make sense of the belief that is attributed to Obama in an utterance of (4). This is because it seems plausible that Obama could believe the proposition *that Obama is tall* without believing that he himself is tall. He might, as in the amnesia example above, fail to realize that he himself is Obama. Moreover, it is plausible that for any property *F*, Obama could believe the proposition *that the F is tall* without believing that he himself is tall. He might not believe that he himself is the one and only individual who has *F*, for example, even if he is that individual. Every candidate for content available on the framework seems to misrepresent or fail to pin down the content of Obama's belief.

To summarize the main psychological problem: if Obama does not realize that he himself is Obama, then he can believe *de se* that he is tall without believing that Obama is tall; and if he does not realize that he himself is the *F*, for any property *F*, then he can believe *de se* that he is tall without believing that the *F* is tall. As a result, it seems that Obama's *de se* belief cannot be identified with any belief of the form *x is tall*, where *x* is any name or definite description that designates Obama, and so his belief must have a different content than any belief of that form. The problem, in general, is to identify the content of a given *de se* belief and thereby distinguish it from beliefs that are not *de se*.

Before turning to some classic discussions of *de se* attitudes in the literature, we would like briefly to consider one more problem about *de se* belief. This problem is probably the first to be explicitly posed, by Peter Geach (1957). Geach formulates it like this: "if we say of a number of people that each of them believes that he himself is clever, what belief exactly are we attributing to all of them? Certainly they do not all believe the same proposition, as 'proposition' is commonly understood by philosophers" (1957: 23). The imagined belief report seems to attribute the same belief to each of the people, and certainly the predicate 'believes that he himself is clever' is true of each of them. But the intuitive sense in which different people can share the same *de se* belief seems difficult to capture, especially given the propositional framework discussed above.

2 Some Classic Sources on *De* Se Attitudes

2.1 Castañeda

In the middle to late 1960s, Hector-Neri Castañeda published a series of papers focusing on the use of indexicals and demonstratives in attitude reports, and in particular focusing on attributions of self-knowledge and other *de se* attitudes. In his seminal 1966 paper, '"He": A Study in the Logic of Self-Consciousness', Castañeda discusses uses of the pronominal 'he' in attributions of self-knowledge, which normally have the following linguistic structure: *S knows that she herself (he himself) is F*. Castañeda introduces the term 'he*' – a so-called *quasi indicator* – to abbreviate 'he' as it occurs in attributions of self-knowledge and the like, which he labels "the *S-use* of 'he'" (1966: 130). 'He*' thus disambiguates 'he', identifying the cases in which a *de se* reading is required. So, for example, Castañeda would render (4) above, and the *de se* reading of (3), as follows:

(5) Obama believes that he* is tall.

Using several clever and engaging examples, Castañeda forcefully argues that 'he*' is an essential indexical in that it cannot be replaced in an attribution like (5) by any of the following: (a) a pronominal that refers to Obama, (b) a description that denotes Obama, (c) a proper name for Obama, (d) a deictic, (e) the pronominal 'I'. What should be emphasized, and what is perhaps most important to Castañeda's project, is that in attributions of *de se* attitudes 'he*' cannot be replaced with a definite description or with a demonstrative pronoun.

Let's take a look at one of Castañeda's own examples. Consider (6) below:

(6) The Editor of *Soul* knows that he* is a millionaire.

In an utterance of (6), the token of 'he*' is not a proxy for the description 'the Editor of *Soul*'. To show this, Castañeda imagines the following: "The Editor of *Soul* may know that he himself is a millionaire while failing to know that he himself is the Editor of *Soul*, because, say, he believes that the Editor of *Soul* is poverty-stricken Richard Penniless" (1966: 134-35). So, the Editor of *Soul* can believe that he himself is a millionaire without believing that the Editor of *Soul* is a millionaire. The converse entailment also fails. "To see this," writes Castañeda, "suppose that on January 15, 1965, the man just appointed to the Editorship of *Soul* does not yet know of his appointment, and that he has read a probated will by which an eccentric businessman bequeathed several millions to the man who happens to be the

Editor of *Soul* on that day" (1966: 135). Here, the Editor believes that the Editor of *Soul* is a millionaire, but does not believe that he himself is.

Analogously, we should not be inclined to use (7) below, or (8) with a deictic use of 'he', to express (6):

(7) The Editor of *Soul* knows that this man is a millionaire.

(8) The Editor of *Soul* knows that he is a millionaire.

In one of Castañeda's examples (1966: 130), the Editor of *Soul* knows something about the man whose photograph lies on a certain table, but he does not know that he himself is the man in the photograph. In such a case, we can imagine the Editor looking at himself in the photograph, assenting to 'This man is a millionaire' and 'He is a millionaire', but failing to be disposed to assent to 'I am a millionaire'. (We could also imagine the case with a mirror instead of a photograph.) It is clear that a speaker can utter (7) or (8), making reference to the Editor of *Soul*, without also committing herself to (6). So, 'he*' as it occurs in (6) cannot be replaced with 'this man' or with the deictic 'he'. Neither (7) nor (8) entails (6). The extension of Castañeda's reasoning to similar conclusions about proper names and genuine pronominals is straightforward.

With respect to the linguistic problem of *de se* attitudes, Castañeda uses these considerations to motivate the view that occurrences of 'he*' are "unanalyzable; they constitute a peculiar and irreducible mechanism of reference to persons" (1968: 447). The idea is that 'he*' cannot be analyzed, even partly, in terms of the semantics associated with definite descriptions, demonstratives, other pronouns, and the like. (Strictly speaking, only occurrences of 'he*' that Castañeda labels *degree 1* are unanalyzable. In certain iterated attitude attributions, there are occurrences of higher degree. However, these are analyzed partly in terms of degree 1 occurrences, and so every attribution of a *de se* attitude will have at least one unanalyzable occurrence of 'he*'.)

Castañeda's early account addresses the problem of *de se* attitudes, but it leaves several questions unanswered. We will not go into much detail here, but it is plausible to attribute to him a broadly Fregean view of the workings of 'I' and 'he*'. Some support for this comes from the following:

> [W]hen Privatus asserts "The Editor of *Soul* believes that he* is a millionaire", Privatus does not attribute to the Editor the possession of any way of referring to himself aside from his ability to use the pronoun 'I' or his ability to be conscious of himself. The latter ability is the only way of referring to himself that Privatus must attribute to the Editor for his statement to be true. (1966: 138)

This and other passages seem to suggest that each person grasps a special sense, a special first-personal mode of referring to himself. When the Editor of *Soul* says 'I am a millionaire', the pronoun 'I' expresses the Editor's special first-personal sense. When Privatus says 'The Editor of *Soul* knows that he* is a millionaire', the reflexive pronoun 'he*' expresses a sense such that the reference of this sense is the Editor's special first-personal sense.

This sort of view solves the linguistic problem of *de se* belief from within the framework of propositions – in particular, within the framework of the view that *belief and other cognitive attitudes are simply two-place relations between conscious subjects and propositions*. It distinguishes attributions of self-knowledge (and *de se* attributions more generally) from others by postulating a class of special senses associated with the pronoun 'I', every one of which differs from the senses of co-referential terms that do not contain 'I'. Reference is made to such senses by devices like 'he*' when they occur in the complement sentences of attitude reports.

This sort of view solves the psychological problem by identifying the sort of proposition to which a given subject is related when she has a *de se* attitude. We cannot express a proposition of this sort by uttering a sentence that contains a proper name or definite description (that does not itself contain a first person pronoun), but it was wrong to look to such propositions for a solution to the problem. The content of a *de se* attitude is simply a proposition that one would express if one were to say 'I am such-and-such', which is constituted by the speaker's special first-personal sense. One might object that this sort of view cannot solve Geach's problem of shared *de se* belief, since – in virtue of a difference in reference – the belief that the Editor of *Soul* expresses by saying 'I am a millionaire' is a different proposition than the belief that Obama expresses by saying 'I am a millionaire'. But perhaps good sense might be made of the idea that, although the two propositions are different, they are tokens of the same *type* of proposition, which accounts for the intuitive sameness of the beliefs.[1]

2.2 Perry

In his extremely insightful and influential 1979 paper 'The Problem of the Essential Indexical', John Perry presents the case of the messy shopper. Like Castañeda's examples, this case poses a challenge for the view that belief is irreducibly a two-place relation between a conscious subject and a proposition. Perry describes the example as follows:

> I once followed a trail of sugar on a supermarket floor, pushing my cart down the aisle on one side of a tall counter and back along the aisle on the other, seeking the shopper with the torn sack to tell him he was making a mess. With each trip around the counter, the trail became thicker. But I seemed unable to catch up. Finally it dawned on me. I was the shopper I was trying to catch. (1979: 3)

---

[1] For an excellent exposition and critical discussion of Castañeda's work, see Perry (1983).

The challenge is to pick out two propositions: first, the one Perry believed before the truth dawned on him (the content of the belief he would have expressed by saying something like 'The shopper who left this trail of sugar is making a mess'); and second, the one he later comes to believe (the content of the belief he would express by saying 'I am making a mess'). Perry makes this need more vivid by noting that the second belief has a special sort of motivational force. It explains a change in his behavior, a change that the first belief cannot even partly explain:

> I believed at the outset that the shopper with a torn sack was making a mess. And I was right. But I did not believe that I was making a mess. That seems to be something I came to believe. And when I came to believe that, I stopped following the trail around the counter, and rearranged the torn sack in my cart. (1979: 3)

We explain why Perry stopped to rearrange the bag of sugar in part by conveying information about the relevant change in his beliefs. Since the change in belief explains his behavior, it seems that we must be able to provide the propositions to give an account of the change. However, as we have already seen, identifying the proposition that Perry believes when he finally says '*I* am making a mess', is not a trivial task. The argument lurking around the case of the messy shopper, then, is something like this. Although the change in Perry's behavior is partly explained by his acquiring a new belief, there is no *proposition* such that Perry's coming to believe it even partly explains the change. As a result, belief is not (or is not simply) a matter of a two-place relation between a believer and a proposition.

Why think that there is no proposition such that his coming to believe it explains Perry's behavior? Let's note first that the use of 'I' or 'he himself' seems essential to explaining Perry's behavior. For this reason, Perry (1979: 8) claims that propositions lack an "indexical ingredient" that his belief must have, given its explanatory role. We have already touched on the reasoning here, in the discussion of the problem of *de se* belief. Consider the singular or purely descriptive propositions that a theory of propositions might have to offer. It seems that believing any one of them is consistent with lacking the *de se* belief that the explanation of Perry's behavior requires.

Let's take purely descriptive (non-singular, non-object dependent) propositions first. Suppose that we identify a purely descriptive proposition, *P*, and claim that Perry's coming to believe *P* explains his clean-up behavior. We know a bit about what *P* must be like, given that it is alleged to be both purely descriptive and the content of Perry's *de se* belief that he himself is making a mess. Proposition *P* must somehow pick out Perry by means of some property (set of properties, uniquely satisfiable condition), and associate this with the concept or property of making a mess. So, for some property *F*, *P* is true if and only if exactly one thing has *F*, and whatever has *F* is making a mess. In a nutshell, then, on the current proposal the belief that explains Perry's clean-up behavior is his belief in the proposition *that the F is making a mess*. But it is extremely implausible that such a belief could explain why he begins to clean up. Perry makes this point as follows:

> even if I was thinking of myself as, say, the only bearded philosopher in a Safeway store west of the Mississippi, the fact that I came to believe that the only such philosopher was making a mess explains my action only on the assumption that I believed that I was the only such philosopher, which brings in the indexical again. (1979: 8)

The point here is that it seems quite clear that Perry could believe the proposition *that the only bearded philosopher in a Safeway west of the Mississippi is making a mess* without believing that he himself is making a mess, since he could fail to believe himself to be the only bearded philosopher in a Safeway store west of the Mississippi. The same goes for any purely descriptive proposition. So, belief in such a proposition cannot play the explanatory role of Perry's *de se* belief that he himself is making a mess.

Can we say that what explains Perry's behavior is his coming to believe a singular or object-dependent proposition, where truth conditions are not determined descriptively? For example, can we say that Perry's clean-up behavior is explained by his coming to believe the singular proposition *that Perry is making a mess*? There are several reasons why this seems unsatisfactory. First, the most common views according to which people believe singular propositions entail that Perry believed this proposition *before* the truth finally dawned on him. When he started following the trail of sugar, for example, he believed that the shopper who was leaving the trail was making a mess. Since he was this shopper, he had a belief about himself, to the effect that he was making a mess. This, on the most common views allowing belief in singular propositions, means that he believed the proposition *that Perry is making a mess*. Even views on which it is more difficult to believe a singular proposition are in trouble here. This is because we can imagine that Perry perceived himself in some way and took the person he perceived to be making a mess, without believing that he himself was making one. In fact, Perry imagines just this:

> Suppose there were mirrors at either end of the counter so that as I pushed my cart down the aisle in pursuit I saw myself in the mirror. I take what I see to be the reflection of the messy shopper going up the aisle on the other side, not realizing that what I am really seeing is a reflection of a reflection of myself. I point and say, truly, "I believe that he is making a mess." (1979: 12)

Of course, if Perry believed the singular proposition *that Perry is making a mess*, and he believed it *before* the truth finally dawned on him, then his coming to believe it cannot explain his clean-up behavior. Moreover, if following a person's trail of sugar, or seeing him in a mirror, are sufficient for believing a singular proposition, then someone with merely a third-person perspective on Perry could believe the singular proposition *that Perry is making a mess*. And if this is the case, Perry could believe this proposition without believing *de se* that he himself is making a mess. So belief in this proposition could not play the explanatory role of that *de se* belief.

This brings us to what Perry calls "propositions of limited accessibility" (1979: 15-16). It seems that the attempt to explain Perry's behavior in terms of his belief in the relevant singular proposition implies that *only* Perry could believe it, and in general, that any given person can believe propositions that no other person can believe. Perry gives some reasons to resist propositions of limited accessibility. Their relation to genuine *de se* belief is also less than fully clear. For example, why is it impossible for Perry to believe the proposition *that Perry is making a mess* without believing that he himself is making one? If Perry does not know who he is, it seems he could know exactly which individual is making a mess, and know every bit of information about this individual down to the last detail – and thereby, it seems, believe *that Perry is making a mess* – but not believe *himself* to be this individual.

We have focused on the singular proposition *that Perry is making a mess*, but we will briefly consider another. For example, we might want to identify some token sensory or perceptual experience of Perry's, call it 'E', and say that he believes the proposition *that the subject of E is making a mess*.[2] This is a singular proposition about E, not Perry. In addition to sharing some of the difficulties just discussed, there is good reason to think this suggestion lacks an important sort of psychological realism. Certainly, Perry can think to himself 'I am making a mess' without identifying himself as the unique person who is having a particular experience. So, this sort of proposition is also ill-suited to play the explanatory role that Perry's *de se* belief in fact plays.

We might try to solve the problem along explicitly Fregean lines. When Frege discussed the sense of the word 'I', he maintained that "every one is presented to himself in a special and primitive way in which he is presented to no one else" (1918 [1988]: 42). Applied to Perry's *de* se belief, this suggests that the content is a proposition that only Perry could believe, in virtue of its containing a sense that only Perry could grasp. This in turn seems to suggest that the sense, or mode of presentation, does not contribute purely descriptive information to the proposition. (If the proposition were purely descriptive, we would have the problems for that view discussed above.)

---

2 Cf. Higginbotham (2003 [2009]).

So, on this account, what Perry believes is a proposition that contains his *self concept* – i.e., a non-qualitative mode of presentation that presents or determines Perry, but not in virtue of any descriptive fit – and the sense of 'is making a mess'. In addition to postulating first-person propositions, which Perry wishes to avoid,[3] this strategy requires a clear account of non-descriptive modes of presentation and how they determine subjects as their referents.

We turn now to Perry's solution to the puzzle. Perry makes a distinction between *what* he believed, and the *belief state* in virtue of which he believed it, one that led him to examine the sack of sugar in his cart, and one we might individuate by using the sentence 'I am making a mess'. In the case of the messy shopper, what explains Perry's clean-up behavior is his coming to be in *this belief state*. Before the truth dawned on him, Perry might have believed the proposition *that Perry is making a mess*, but only in virtue of being in a different belief state (perhaps one individuated by 'He is making a mess', if Perry had pointed to the man in the supermarket mirror). What explains Perry's behavior, then, is a change in his belief state, and not his coming to believe a new proposition.

Perry's account solves the psychological problem of *de se* belief by rejecting the presumption that we need to identify a proposition that can serve as *de se* content. On his view, this role is played by belief states rather than propositions. The account also gives an answer to Geach's problem about shared *de se* belief. People who share *de se* beliefs are in the same belief state – for example, the belief state that might lead each one to say 'I am clever' – despite believing different propositions. Perry (1979) does not explicitly address the linguistic problem, but his view suggests an answer. A *de se* attribution of belief – such as an utterance of 'Perry believes that he himself is making a mess' – might be claimed to contain information not only about the alleged object of belief, but about the belief state as well. For example, it might contain the information that the belief state is one that is individuated by the sentence 'I am making a mess'.[4]

2.3 Lewis

In his seminal 1979 paper 'Attitudes *De Dicto* and *De Se*', David Lewis argues that the belief relation and, more generally, the relations that comprise our cognitive attitudes, relate us to properties instead of propositions. Properties are akin to what Perry (1979) calls *relativized propositions*, which are not true or false *simpliciter* but are true or false at-a-person (-and-time). For example, the property of making a mess is true at, or true of, each

---

3 See also Perry (1977).

4 See Richard (1983) for an account like this, which employs sentence-meanings instead of sentences.

person who is making a mess. Perry argued cogently that relativized propositions cannot serve as *de se* contents, but he presupposed the traditional conception of belief as something like inward assent to a proposition. Lewis, however, takes the belief relation to be in a way necessarily reflexive – to believe something is to take-yourself-to-have some property. He calls this relation *self-ascription*. So, for example, when Perry believes that he himself is making a mess, what he does is self-ascribe the property of making a mess.[5]

Lewis uses the extraordinary case of the two gods to motivate his account:

> Consider the case of the two gods. They inhabit a certain possible world, and they know exactly which world it is. Therefore they know every proposition that is true at their world. Insofar as knowledge is a propositional attitude, they are omniscient. Still I can imagine them to suffer ignorance: neither one knows which of the two he is. They are not exactly alike. One lives on top of the tallest mountain and throws down manna; the other lives on top of the coldest mountain and throws down thunderbolts. Neither one knows whether he lives on the tallest mountain or on the coldest mountain; nor whether he throws manna or thunderbolts. (1979: 520-21)

It does seem that the gods "inhabit a certain possible world," i.e., that this is a metaphysically possible scenario. How could the gods suffer ignorance? Well, we can imagine that the gods always have qualitatively identical experiences. Lewis suggests that the gods might lack the beliefs that they do because "they have an equally perfect view of every part of their world, and hence cannot identify the perspectives from which they view it" (1979: 521). This seems possible, and if it were the case, then neither perspective would allow its subject to identify his own spatial location. Since the gods believe every proposition that is true at their world but could still truly believe more than they in fact do, the contents of the missing beliefs could not be propositions. They must instead be properties that the gods are unable to self-ascribe. It might seem plausible to think that if the content of a belief is not a proposition, then it is a property (or something *very* much like a property). One way to have a true belief is to take yourself to have a property that you do in fact have. On Lewis' view, if the god on the tallest mountain were somehow to come to believe that he himself lived on the tallest mountain, his belief would consist in his self-ascribing the property of living on the tallest mountain. We have in this case a kind of "property ignorance" despite propositional omniscience.

On Lewis' account, the belief relation exhibits a kind of necessary reflexivity, and the verb 'believes' can roughly be paraphrased by 'believes oneself to have'. The account is extended from *de se* belief to *de se* attitudes

---

5 Chisholm (1979, 1981) argues for and develops a view very close to that of Lewis.

in general. For example, the desire to be a millionaire is understood in terms of the subject bearing the appropriate cognitive relation – the analogue of self-ascription for desire – to the property of being a millionaire (of the subject's wanting-to-have this property). Moreover, the account is also extended away from paradigm examples of *de se* attitudes, so that *de dicto* beliefs, for example, are also treated as self-ascriptions of properties. For instance, believing the proposition that all squares are rectangles is viewed as self-ascribing the corresponding property of being such that all squares are rectangles. So, *de dicto* attitudes are subsumed under *de se* ones.

On the view proposed by Lewis, then, to have a cognitive attitude is to bear the psychologically appropriate relation to a property. To believe something is to self-ascribe a property, to desire something is to want-to-have a property, and so on. The property is the content of the attitude. The content of Perry's *de se* belief that he himself is making a mess, for example, is simply the property of making a mess. There is no *de se* element, indexical ingredient, or self-concept in the content of the belief. What makes the attitude *de se* is built into the attitude instead of the content of the attitude. Here the attitude is self-ascription, and it is in virtue of self-ascribing the property of making a mess that Perry's belief is *de se*.

Like Perry, Lewis solves the psychological problem of *de se* belief by rejecting the presumption that we need to identify a proposition that can serve as *de se* content. Unlike Perry, he retains the idea that belief is ultimately analyzable in terms of a two-place relation. Lewis' account also offers a straightforward solution to Geach's problem of shared *de se* belief. Every person who believes himself to be clever self-ascribes the property of being clever, and so all such people have beliefs with the very same content.

The account provides the resources to solve the linguistic problem. Consider (1) and (4) from section 1 above, repeated here:

(1) Obama believes that Obama is tall.

(4) Obama believes that he himself is tall.

Lewis can say that an utterance of (4) is true if and only if Obama self-ascribes the property of being tall. The that-clause in (4) might be taken to denote this property.[6] But (1) does not have Obama self-ascribing the property of being tall. Instead, we might take an utterance of (1) to be true if and only if Obama self-ascribes the property of being such that Obama is tall. Lewis himself would take an utterance of (4) to assert that there is some relation of acquaintance *R* – looking at, reading about, remembering, looking at a photograph of – such that Obama stands in *R* to Obama, and Obama self-ascribes the property of standing in *R* to someone who is tall.[7] We can-

---

6 See Chierchia (1989).

7 The non-*de se* reading of (3) above receives the same treatment.

not go into these details here, but either way there is a semantic difference between (1) and (4).

2.4 Stalnaker

Robert Stalnaker, in his 1981 paper 'Indexical Belief', defends the idea that belief is simply a two-place relation between subjects and propositions from arguments based on cases of *de se* belief (and indexical belief more generally). Like Lewis, Stalnaker takes propositions to be sets of worlds, but Stalnaker rejects Lewis' analysis of the case of the two gods. To get clear on Stalnaker's view, it will be helpful to consider his analysis of this case. Remember that this is a case of ignorance of *de se* information, in that neither god knows his location in ordinary space. According to Stalnaker, if we suppose that the gods really are ignorant in this way, we must reject Lewis' stipulation that they know every proposition that is true at their world. As Stalnaker sees it, the two gods case is

> a case of ignorance of which of two indiscernible possible worlds is actual. One of these possible worlds is the actual world (assuming that the theologian's story is true), while the other is like it except that the god who is in fact on the tallest mountain is instead on the coldest mountain, with all the properties which the god on the coldest mountain in fact has. (1981: 143)

Let's call the world that Lewis describes '*W*'. Let's also use '*TM*' and '*CM*' as names for the god on the tallest mountain in *W*, and the god on the coldest mountain in *W*, respectively. According to Stalnaker, there is a world that is qualitatively exactly like *W*, but differs in that the gods have swapped places and properties. Let's call this world '*V*'. So, in *V*, *TM* is on the coldest mountain and *CM* is on the tallest mountain. If *TM* is ignorant in *W* about his location, then he does not know which of *W* or *V* is actual. On Stalnaker's view, then, he is ignorant of at least one proposition (one that is true at *W* but false at *V*). The upshot is Lewis cannot claim both that the gods are ignorant about their locations, and also that they are omniscient with respect to *all* propositions.

Stalnaker's account uses a doctrine called 'haecceitism' and a technique called 'diagonalization'. Haecceitism, roughly, is the view that objects have non-qualitative essences, but do not have any qualitative properties essentially. This allows *TM* to inhabit world *V* with all the qualitative properties and relations that *CM* has in *W*: living on the coldest mountain, throwing thunderbolts, and so on. What makes him *TM* there is his non-qualitative haecceity, the property of being TM.

Diagonalization can be illustrated by considering the following sentence:

(9) I live on the tallest mountain.

In world *W*, an utterance of (9) by *TM* would express a proposition that is true at *W* but false at *V*, since his token of 'I' rigidly designates himself and he lives on the tallest mountain in *W* but not in *V*. In world *V*, too, an utterance of (9) by *TM* would express a proposition that is true at *W* but false at *V*. Supposing that *W* and *V* are the only worlds relevant to attributing attitudes to *TM* in the present context, we can form a matrix, or *propositional concept*, of (9) like this:

	W	*V*
W	T	F
V	T	F

Here, the *diagonal proposition* is true at *W* but false at *V*. (The same goes for the horizontal propositions here, but we will soon see an example where they differ from the diagonal proposition.) According to Stalnaker, this diagonal proposition is the belief that *TM* would express by uttering a token of (9). It is the belief that we would attribute to *TM* if we were to say he believes that he himself lives on the tallest mountain. On Stalnaker's view, if *TM* can distinguish *W* from *V*, he would know this proposition and hence know his location. In this way, Stalnaker argues that Lewis cannot assume both that *TM* knows he is in *W* rather than *V*, and that he is ignorant of his location.

The example above might not make the point of diagonalization clear. So let's consider another example. Suppose that in *W*, *TM* looks upon the world and somehow demonstrates the god on the tallest mountain, and while doing so utters a token of

(10) He lives on the tallest mountain.

What belief does *TM* express? By diagonalizing, Stalnaker arrives at the result that the content of this belief is the proposition that contains both *W* and *V*. In *W*, *TM*'s utterance of (10) expresses a proposition that is true at *W* but false at *V*, since his token of 'he' rigidly designates *TM*, who lives on the tallest mountain in *W* but not in *V*. But his utterance of (10) occurs in *V* as well. In *V*, the utterance expresses a proposition that is true at *V* but false at *W*, since this token of 'he' rigidly designates *CM*, who lives on the tallest mountain in *V* but not in *W*. On this view, then, the content of the belief that *TM* expresses in uttering (10) is the diagonal proposition represented in the propositional concept below, which is true at *W* and *V*:

	W	*V*
W	T	F
V	F	T

Stalnaker thus objects to the two gods argument and defends the adequacy of propositions as contents for indexical belief. Stalnaker puts it like this: "One cannot just stipulate that the god knows that he is in *W* and not in *V*, for on the proposed explanation, that amounts to the assumption that he knows which mountain he is on" (1981: 144). We might balk at the kind of haecceitism that is presupposed here. We might also wonder, with Lewis, how *TM's* knowledge of the proposition containing *W* but not *V* gives him the *de se* knowledge that he himself is on the tallest mountain. We might think, for example, that *TM's* knowing that *TM* rather than *CM* is on the tallest mountain would give *TM* the relevant *de se* knowledge only if he also knows that he himself is *TM*. But we shall not pursue these issues here.[8]

Stalnaker's view does provide a way of solving the problems of *de se* attitudes. On the linguistic side, Stalnaker accounts for the semantic difference between a *de se* attitude attribution and a non-*de se* attribution. (With the case of the two gods, we have been supposing that only possible worlds *W* and *V* need to be taken into account, which might be an oversimplification. In general, context (broadly construed) will determine which possible worlds need to be countenanced.) An utterance of '*TM* believes that he himself is on the tallest mountain', for example, would express (in the imagined context) the proposition that is true at *W* but not *V*. But an utterance of '*TM* believes that he is on the tallest mountain', given a non-*de se* reading associated with *TM's* utterance of (10), would express the diagonal proposition that is true at both *W* and *V*.[9]

On the psychological side, Stalnaker holds that it is a mistake to think that no proposition adequately captures the content of a given *de se* attitude. In the context relevant to our discussion of the two gods case, for example, the proposition that is true at *W* but not *V* serves as the content of the *de se* information that *TM* lacks. In some sense, Stalnaker is reducing *de se* content to mere *de re* content, without the trappings of modes of presentation, guises, or the like.[10] Perry's *de se* belief that he himself is making a mess, for example, is true at a given world if Perry is making a mess there, and false otherwise (that is, if someone else is making a mess, or nobody is). This might give Stalnaker a way to approach Geach's problem of shared *de se* belief – two people who intuitively have the same *de se* belief do not believe the same proposition, but each believes a proposition that depends for its truth on the very subject of belief, and not on whatever happens to satisfy some description or to be picked out by some mode of presentation.

---

8 See Lewis (1979), Stalnaker (1981) and Feit (2008: 34-42) for more discussion.

9 See Stalnaker (1981) for a discussion of his treatment of attributions with the proper name of the subject in an embedded context, for example 'Lingens believes that Lingens is a cousin of a spy'. An utterance of this sentence, via diagonalization, has Lingens believing a proposition that is true if and only if 'Lingens is a cousin of a spy' expresses a truth.

10 See, for example, Higginbotham (2003 [2009]) for some discussion of this point.

This volume collects together sixteen new papers on *de se* attitudes. The papers in Part I deal primarily with issues concerning the linguistic problem of *de se* attitudes. The papers in Part II deal with issues concerning the psychological problem, or with closely related issues concerning the nature of *de se* attitudes and their place in our psychological lives. In the next section, we present short summaries of the collected papers.

3 Summaries of the Essays

3.1 Part One: Linguistics and Philosophy of Language

The problem of *de se* attitudes, according to Wayne Davis, is the problem of the essential indexical, an instance of Frege's problem, as applied to 'I'. It is both semantic (How does the meaning of 'I' differ from that of a coreferential proper name or definite description?) and psychological (How do the mental states we use 'I' to express differ from those we use coreferential names or descriptions to express?).

In his contribution to this volume, Davis reviews the limitations of character, self-attribution, and event-subject analyses. He then sketches a solution within the general theory that words are conventional signs of mental states, principally thoughts and concepts, and that meaning consists in their expression. On Davis' view, indexicals express thought parts ("indexical concepts") that are distinctive in the way they link to other mental events ("determinants"), either presentations or other concepts. Indexicals are distinguished in part by the pattern of uses they allow, which on his account are differentiated principally by determinants. Used deictically, 'I' expresses the speaker's self-concept, whose determinant is the speaker's introspective self-awareness. *De se* attitudes are those whose objects contain the subject's self-concept.

In his contribution, James Higginbotham begins by considering the view he defended on the issue of the first person pronoun. This view appeals to Donald Davidson's hypothetical event position (extending it to all predications, not just action sentences). On Higginbotham's view, we should say that a speaker using the first person refers to him/her self *as* the speaker $s(u)$ of his/her very utterance u (this view was earlier suggested in passing by John Perry). Under that circumstance, it makes no sense for one to ask of oneself, "But is it I who am speaking?" (*modulo* a couple of concessions in other work). This view requires giving up the idea that the content of a person's belief, as reported in 'John believes that *p*' can be properly discriminated in purely modal terms – but Higginbotham suggests that it is not at all clear that anything is thereby lost.

However, the semantic issues in the context of speech and interpretation of speech come forward also in the context of belief, desire and the rest. Castañeda's examples (see section 2.1 above) extend to our steady cognitive states: so your desire to eat a hamburger may not be the same as your desire that x eat a hamburger, even if x=you. This leads Higginbotham to consider a problem with his view and others: speech is deliberate action, so that we can ask of a person's reference to anything, how was it secured? But our doxastic, or epistemic, or desiderative states do not involve action at all. It follows, then, that if we are to take the first person in thought along the lines that he adumbrated for speech, we must conclude that many ordinary thoughts we have about ourselves must involve the capacity for thinking of ourselves as the possessors of these thoughts. But isn't that too fancy? After all, we mammals do pretty well in general in thinking about ourselves (and we have no problem in saying that the dog wants to eat the hamburger).

Higginbotham argues that Lewis' account faces the same problem. Lewis proposed that a first-person belief involved the self-ascription of a property. For instance, if you know that you are sitting down in an ordinary way, then you self-ascribe the property of inhabiting a possible world where you are sitting down. Well, Higginbotham asks, when a dog wants a hamburger, does it thereby prefer to inhabit a world in which it gets a hamburger? Higginbotham strives to make some progress on the problem raised by these questions.

In her contribution to this volume, Kasia Jaszczolt notes that early discussions of *de se* belief ascription focused on the status of the objects of attitudes and stemmed out of consolidated attempts to exorcise propositions and introduce properties and 'relations to oneself' instead. Propositions were revindicated via various rescue plans but the problem of compositional semantics of belief reports, including *de se* attributions, has remained a testing ground for semantic theories to this day. In her essay, Jaszczolt looks at *de se* belief reports in the light of the current debate between minimalism and contextualism in semantics. She argues that the differences in the reference-securing functions between *de re* and *de se* occur on the level of semantic content itself where the latter has to be understood as on contextualist accounts. The contextualist orientation is required for the essential ingredient of self-awareness to be included in the semantic representation. This representation, on Jaszczolt's account, is regarded as compositional in the contextualist sense of compositionality of meaning. In the course of her discussion Jaszczolt proposes some amendments to Chierchia's (1989) claim of the systematicity of retrieval of the cognitive access to oneself from the types of grammatical expressions, and discusses the different roles that the concepts of self-ascription, self-attribution, and self-awareness play in a contextualist semantic theory of *de se* belief reports.

Expression of self-awareness does not require a specific grammatical marker in English such as 'I' in *oratio recta* or (coreferential) '(s)he' in *oratio obliqua*, neither do such expressions come with guaranteed expression of self-awareness. There does not seem to be a lexical or grammatical 'peg' on which to hang the property of expressing self-awareness. On Jaszczolt's view, sometimes the property is externalized through the grammar, at other times by default interpretations of this grammatical form, and at yet others by pragmatic resolution of the genuinely underspecified representation. The contextualist framework and pragmatic compositionality embraced by Default Semantics (Jaszczolt 2005, 2010) allow for this diversity.

In his contribution, Neil Feit develops an account of the truth conditions and propositions expressed by cognitive attitude reports, with a focus on belief reports in particular. Feit's account makes use of the property theory of mental content, which denies the traditional view that the contents of our beliefs and other attitudes are propositions. Instead, the property theory takes such contents to be properties, that is, entities without truth values that are constant across persons and other objects, places, and times. The property theory is built for *de se* belief. For example, if Feit believes that he himself is a philosopher, the content of his belief is simply the property of being a philosopher. On this account, there is no *de se* element in the content of the belief. What makes the belief *de se* is a matter of the attitude itself and not its content. The attitude is self-ascription, and it is in virtue of self-ascribing the property of being a philosopher that Feit's belief is *de se*. To self-ascribe a property is, roughly, to reflexively believe-oneself-to-have that property.

The first section of Feit's essay has to do with *de se* belief reports, the second with belief reports that contain embedded proper names or natural kind terms, and the third with what might be described as reports of purely *de dicto* belief. In the fourth section, Feit suggests some ideas for unifying the accounts offered in the first three sections, and turns to the logical form of belief reports and the sort of proposition they express. The result is a contextualist account according to which *that*-clauses merely characterize (rather than specify) belief content, but on which their semantic contents enter into logical form along with contextually-supplied information about how the subject is related to certain salient semantic values.

As the existence of this volume and most of its essays indicate, the received wisdom is that *de se* thoughts and their ascriptions are particularly problematic. In his contribution, however, Michael Devitt argues that this is a myth, an artifact of misguided philosophical approaches to the mind and semantics, particularly the positing of Platonic propositions. A theory of thoughts and a theory of their ascriptions, Devitt argues, must be related. Appealing to Quinean naturalism and Occam, he argues for the explanatory priority of the theory of thoughts. Assuming the Representational Theory of the Mind, he takes mental representations, not propositions, to be the "objects of thoughts". From this basis, he offers suggestions about thoughts in standard and "puzzle" situations: Kripke's Paderewski, Richard's phone booth, and the *de se*. These suggestions are far from a complete theory of thoughts, Devitt concedes, but he stresses that they are sufficient to show that there is nothing particularly problematic about *de se* thoughts.

In light of this, Devitt considers ascriptions of thoughts. He concludes that there is nothing particularly problematic about the ascription of *de se* thoughts either. Throughout his essay, he emphasizes that both languages and minds are parts of the natural world, interacting causally with other parts of that world. Devitt argues that it is hard to see how Platonic propositions, the root of the myth, could be a part of that world. In any case, he finds no need to posit them.

In their contribution to this volume, Denis Delfitto and Gaetano Fiorin argue for a certain sort of descriptive account of indexicals. They note that in the tradition initiated by Kaplan, two main claims are associated with indexicality: (i) indexicals cannot be treated as concealed descriptions ('I' is not equivalent to 'the speaker in the context of utterance', or any other suitable description) and (ii) indexicals are referentially rigid (in the sense that they refer to the same object in all possible worlds). It follows from these two facts that the *subjective* meaning of indexicals cannot be expressed propositionally: the sentences 'his pants are on fire' and 'my pants are on fire' express the very same singular proposition as long as 'I' and 'he' refer to the same object. The case against a descriptive analysis of indexicals is that, if indexicals were treated as descriptions, the sentence 'If I were not speaking, then p' would be predicted to be truth-conditionally equivalent to the sentence 'If the speaker were not speaking, p', contrary to facts.

According to Delfitto and Fiorin, however, the price to pay for abandoning the descriptive analysis of indexicals is high. Meaning is no longer propositional in nature, in the sense that sentences containing indexicals cannot be reduced to functions from worlds to truth-values. They argue that indexicals can be treated as descriptions as long as their descriptive content is treated presuppositionally. As a consequence, the informativeness of indexical sentences can be expressed in terms of (partial) propositions. They go on argue that indexical presuppositions are special in that their scope is constrained by independently motivated syntactic factors. The main result of their proposal is an account of shifted indexicals. It has been shown that, in a number of languages, the first person pronoun in an indirect report such as 'John said that I am a hero' can be interpreted as referring to the subject of the reported speech act and that, on such a reading, the report is unambiguously *de se*. On their approach, the *de se* interpretation of shifted indexicals is the result of a syntax-driven process of "local" resolution of the presupposition of 'I', which forces the descriptive content of 'I' to remain within the scope of the verb of speech. Finally, they extend the presupposititional analysis of indexical terms to definite descriptions and show that it accounts for attitudes *de re* in general.

Yan Huang, in his contribution, considers the pragmatics of attributions of *de se* beliefs from a third-person point of view. As we have seen above, Castañeda created an artificial pronoun *he*/she*/it** to encode the attribution of a *de se* belief from a third-person perspective. He called this artificial pronoun a 'quasi-indicator' and claimed that it is the only device that allows the marking of *de se* belief from a third-person viewpoint. Huang's essay has two goals. First, he examines two types of linguistic expressions: (i) logophoric expressions in West African languages, and (ii) long-distance reflexives in East, South, and Southeast Asian languages, showing that both can function as quasi-indicators in Castañeda's sense. Second, given that quasi-indicators are largely a pragmatic phenomenon, Huang provides a formal pragmatic analysis of the marking of *de se* attribution by logophoric expressions in West African languages and long-distance reflexives in East, South, and Southeast Asian languages (and the related use of regular expressions/pronouns in these languages) in terms of the version of the neo-Gricean pragmatic theory of anaphora developed by Huang, using the three general pragmatic principles proposed by Levinson (2000), namely the Q-, I- and M-principles.

In his contribution, Eros Corazza begins by discussing some linguistic data favoring the *de re / de se* distinction. In so doing he focuses on the different way epithets (e.g., 'the bastard', 'the imbecile') and quasi-indicators (e.g., 's/he her/himself') behave when they appear in psychological characterizations. He argues that they often work like attributive anaphors. The quasi-indicator 'she herself' in 'Jane$_1$ believes that *she (herself)*$_1$ is rich' inherits its value from 'Jane' and *attributes* an 'I'-thought to Jane. The epithet 'the bastard' in 'Jane planned to marry Jon$_1$, but *the bastard*$_1$ ran away' also inherits its value from 'Jon' and *attributes* the property of being a bastard to Jon. Corazza shows how the ungrammaticality of sentences like '*Jon$_1$ claimed/ said/ thinks/... that *the bastard*$_1$ was honest') does not threaten the view that epithets can be understood as anaphoric pronouns. Their ungrammaticality rests on the fact that the epithet is embedded in what should be a *de se* attribution (e.g. 'Jon$_1$ claimed/ said/ thinks/... that *he (himself)*$_1$ was honest') while its nature is to contribute to the expression of a *de re* attribution. This also helps to understand the ungrammaticality of '*Jane$_1$ said/ thinks/ promised/... that *the imbecile*$_1$ will come' *vs.* the grammaticality of 'Jane$_1$ said/ thinks/ promised/... that *she (herself)*$_1$ will come' on the one hand, and the ungrammaticality of '*Jon$_1$ ran over a man who was trying to give *him (himself)*$_1$ directions' *vs.* the grammaticality of 'Jon$_1$ ran over a man who was trying to give *the idiot*$_1$ directions' on the other hand.

These linguistic data, on Corazza's view, can be accounted for by referring to discourse consideration involving the notions of point of view, perspective and empathy. He argues that empathy is central to the distinction between *de se* and *de re* construals, and that the difference in behavior between an epithet and a quasi-indicator is best accounted for by focusing on such a notion. When the reporter empathizes with the attributee s/he is unlikely to use an epithet in characterizing the attributee. Empathy is also important to Corazza's defense of the view that in a psychological characterization an epithet forces the *de re* reading, while a quasi-indicator triggers the *de se* one.

Finally, in his contribution, Alessandro Capone discusses various philosophical theories of *de se* attitudes and explores a bifurcation of the ideas of two major theorists on them. He defends the idea that the ego-concept is an essential element of *de se* thoughts. Furthermore, Capone defends the claim that pragmatic intrusion is involved in *de se* constructions: the ego-concept being a component of the *de se* thought. He defends this idea from a number of objections. He then explores the related notion of immunity to error through misidentification, and argues that this too depends on pragmatic intrusion. After defending this view from obvious objections, Capone arrives at the conclusion that immunity to error through misidentification is both an epistemological and a semantic phenomenon, and also that its semantics has interesting epistemological implications.

3.2 Part Two: Epistemology and Metaphysics

In his contribution, Igor Douven begins with the observation that the distinction between beliefs held about oneself *de se*, and beliefs held about oneself merely *de re*, has led some theorists to abandon the traditional conception of propositions as sets of possible worlds, and has led others to deny that belief is a two-place relation between a subject and a proposition. Like Devitt, Douven argues that *de se* beliefs do not pose any special problems with respect to theorizing about cognitive attitudes. Unlike Devitt, however, Douven suggests that we can account for *de se* attitudes within the traditional framework of propositions. Douven argues that the *de se* / *de re* distinction warrants revision neither of the concept of proposition nor of that of belief, and that the distinction can be fully captured in terms of differences in the kinds of evidence needed to warrant reports of the distinct types of belief. On Douven's account, the distinction between *de se* attitudes and those that are merely *de re* depends on the justification conditions that attach to certain attitude-ascribing propositions.

In his contribution, Darren Bradley argues along several lines that beliefs can be characterized in one way that allows their truth values to change over time, and in another way that does not. Suppose for example that you previously believed it was Sunday, and now believe it is Monday. What are the implications of this truism for the philosophy of mind, and in particular, for the question of whether beliefs have eternal truth-values? Eternalists hold that beliefs have eternal truth values, temporalists hold that they do not (Bradley calls both of these *one-dimensional theories*). On the other hand, two-dimensionalists (e.g., Perry 1979, Chalmers 2002) hold that we need not choose – beliefs have both eternal and temporal components. Bradley defends two-dimensionalism over one-dimensionalism, and specifically, over temporalism.

Two-dimensionalism is a more complex and less unified theory, and as a result the burden is on the two-dimensionalist to show that the extra complexity is worth the cost. Bradley argues that two-dimensionalism buys us an ontology of *dynamic beliefs*. These are beliefs that survive as time passes, even though their linguistic expression might change. This allows us to say that the earlier belief that it *is* Sunday, and the later belief that it *was* Sunday, are the very same belief. Two-dimensionalism offers a less unified theory, but it offers more unified beliefs, and Bradley argues that these unified beliefs are needed to give a natural account of belief retention.

Bradley appeals to certain tensions within Frege's writings, as he struggled to find a single object of belief that played all the roles beliefs are supposed to play. He defends two-dimensionalism from a criticism that can be extrapolated from Lewis (1980b). Finally, he argues that two-dimensionalism is independently motivated by considerations from confirmation theory – the two dimensions correspond to two rules of belief update – and so he argues that this is a case where epistemology informs philosophy of mind.

Michael Titelbaum, in his contribution, argues that while *de se* degrees of belief create special problems for traditional Bayesian updating, these problems can be resolved without first committing to a particular theory of *de se* content. He does this by outlining a new credence-updating scheme that, instead of working directly with the contents of an agent's doxastic attitudes, works with the agent's willingness to affirm linguistic sentences in contexts. This approach utilizes an element (truth-values of linguistic sentences in contexts) common to all theories of *de se* content. Crucial to Titelbaum's strategy is a new, epistemic notion of context-sensitivity. He argues that epistemically context-sensitive sentences are the ones that cause trouble for traditional Bayesian Conditionalization.

Having identified the troublemakers for the traditional Bayesian updating rule, Titelbaum describes a new updating scheme that solves various decision-theoretic conundrums like the Sleeping Beauty Problem. Finally, Titelbaum suggests that although he has made no assumptions about the theory of content in constructing his updating scheme, the answers that scheme gives to problems like the Sleeping Beauty Problem may leave some theories of content looking more plausible than others. In particular, there may be trouble for Lewisian theories on which 'I'm awake today' has the same content on Tuesday as it does on Monday.

In his contribution, Pietro Perconti argues that first-person beliefs have an essentially indexical nature, and moreover that only such beliefs can have a genuine motivational force in our behavior. Perconti distinguishes the motivational power that a given belief might have, and its causal role in behaviour. He goes on to argue that the motivational power of a belief is, in a certain way, a linguistic state of affairs.

If we take into account justifications people have for their actions, according to Perconti, we can see that only first-person beliefs are endowed with motivational force. In order to achieve this power, all the other kinds of beliefs must be transformed into first-person beliefs. The reference of first-person beliefs depends on a specific mode of presentation of first-person bodily perspective, which is specifically realized in the human brain. On Perconti's view, the brain represents the body in a direct and specific way, without any attribution of a property to oneself or the mastery of a self-concept. The word 'I' and similar "pure" indexicals are taken to be the linguistic counterparts of the cognitive processes that the human brain uses to shape bodily self-representation.

Michael Nelson, in his contribution, argues for a relativist account of temporal thought and a contextualist account of first-personal thought. Time, on this sort of view, serves as an index of truth. One thinks the same thought yesterday that one thinks today in saying to oneself, 'It is Monday'. That same thought is true at the date that is yesterday and false at the date that is today. A proposition is true or false at a time, and can have different truth values at different times. Person, on the other hand, enters into the content of the proposition thought. Susan and Sally think different thoughts when each says to herself, 'I am hungry', Susan thinking a thought about herself and Sally a thought about herself. These propositions are then true or false indifferently across different people. On Nelson's view, time serves as a parameter of truth, but persons do not.

Nelson argues that the existent linguistic and psychological arguments for and against contextualist and relativist accounts are unpersuasive. He then argues that there are metaphysical reasons for thinking that the constitution of reality is time relative, but person absolute. A fact obtains, Nelson argues, at a time but not at a person. The truth and falsity of propositions should mirror the obtaining of facts. So, he concludes, propositional truth is time but not person relative.

In the final contribution, John Perry uses self-locating beliefs to argue against a simple account of belief, according to which belief consists merely in an agent at a time believing a proposition. Perry argues that a more complex view makes better sense of self-locating beliefs among other phenomena. On this view, a belief is an internal mental representation – a particular structure of ideas in the mind – with a certain proposition as its content but also with truth-conditions that are distinct from those of the proposition.

A belief is self-locating provided that its truth constrains the location or features of the believer. On Perry's version of the complex view, certain ideas of objects – called *notions* – are sensitive to information about those objects and the roles they play in our cognitive lives. This helps to explain the self-locating nature of the beliefs of which these notions are a part. In the case of *de se* belief, our self-notions are sensitive to information about ourselves in a way that accounts for the sort of belief about oneself that ordinary self-knowledge requires. Perry argues that one cannot have a belief of this sort without a role-based idea of oneself (i.e., a self-notion). This serves as the basis for an objection to the Lewisian view, on which a self-notion need not be part of a *de se* belief.

References

Castañeda, H. N. 1966. 'He': A Study in the Logic of Self-Consciousness. *Ratio* 7: 130-57.

Castañeda, H. N. 1968. 'On the Logic of Attributions of Self-Knowledge to Others', *Journal of Philosophy*, 65: 439-459.

Chalmers. D. 2002. 'The Components of Content' in *Philosophy of Mind: Classical and Contemporary Readings*. Oxford University Press.

Chierchia, G. 1989. Anaphora and Attitudes *De Se*. In *Semantics and Contextual Expression*, edited by R. Bartsch, J. van Benthem and P. van Emde Boas, 1-31. Dordrecht: Foris Publications.

Chisholm, R. 1979. 'The Indirect Reflexive', in C. Diamond and J. Teichman (eds.), *Intention and Intentionality: Essays in Honour of G. E. M. Anscombe* (Brighton: The Harvester Press), 39-53.

Chisholm, R. 1981. *The First Person* (Minneapolis: University of Minnesota Press).

Feit, N. 2008. *Belief about the Self: A Defense of the Property Theory of Content.* New York: Oxford University Press.

Frege, G. 1918. 'Der Gedanke'. Translated as 'Thoughts' in N. Salmon and S. Soames, eds., *Propositions and Attitudes* (New York: Oxford University Press, 1988), 33-55.

Geach, P. 1957. 'On Beliefs about Oneself', *Analysis*, 18: 23-24.

Higginbotham, J. 2003. 'Remembering, Imagining, and the First Person', in A. Barber (ed.), *Epistemology of Language* (Oxford: Oxford University Press), 496-533. Reprinted in J. Higginbotham, *Tense, Aspect, and Indexicality*. (New York: Oxford University Press, 2009) 212-245.

Jaszczolt, K. M. 2005. *Default Semantics: Foundations of a Compositional Theory of Acts of Communication*. Oxford: Oxford University Press.

Jaszczolt, K. M. 2010. 'Default Semantics', in B. Heine and H. Narrog (eds)., *The Oxford Handbook of Linguistic Analysis*, 193-221.

Levinson, S. C. 2000. *Presumptive Meanings*. Cambridge, MA: MIT Press.

Lewis, D. 1979. 'Attitudes *De Dicto* and *De Se*', *Philosophical Review*, 87: 513-545.

Lewis, D. 1980. 'Index, Context and Content', in S. Kanger and S. Ohman (eds.), *Philosophy and Grammar*. (Dordrecht: Reidel).

Perry, J. 1977. 'Frege on Demonstratives', *Philosophical Review*, 87: 474-497.

Perry, J. 1979. 'The Problem of the Essential Indexical', *Nous*, 13: 3-21.

Richard, M. 1983. 'Direct Reference and Ascriptions of Belief', *Journal of Philosophical Logic*, 12: 425-452.

Stalnaker, R. 1981. 'Indexical Belief', *Synthese*, 49: 129-151.

Part I

Linguistics and Philosophy of Language

1

Indexicals and *De Se* Attitudes

WAYNE A. DAVIS

1 Introduction

The problem of *de se* attitudes is the problem of the essential indexical, an instance of Frege's problem, as applied to 'I'. It is both semantic (How does the meaning of 'I' differ from that of a coreferential proper name or definite description?) and psychological (How do the mental states we use 'I' to express differ from those we use coreferential names or descriptions to express?). After reviewing limitations of character, self-attribution, and event-subject analyses, I sketch a solution within the general theory that words are conventional signs of mental states, principally thoughts and concepts, and that meaning consists in their expression. Indexicals express thought parts ("indexical concepts") that are distinctive in the way they link to other mental events ("determinants"), either presentations or other concepts. Indexicals are distinguished in part by the pattern of uses they allow, which on my account are differentiated principally by determinants. Used deictically, 'I' expresses the speaker's self-concept, whose determinant is the speaker's introspective self-awareness. *De se* attitudes are those whose objects contain the subject's self-concept.

2 *De Se* Attitudes and Expressions

The propositions and propositional attitudes expressed using the first-person pronoun differ markedly from those expressed using any non-indexical terms. Consider Ronald Reagan, actor and 40th president of the United States, who contracted Alzheimer's disease. One symptom is progressive amnesia. Short-term memory is affected first, long-term memories later.

Attitudes De Se: Linguistics, Epistemology, Metaphysics.
Neil Feit and Alessandro Capone (eds.).

At one time, Reagan remembered that Ronald Reagan had been president of United States, but not that he himself had been. Consider now the marked differences in meaning among the sentences in (1) as used by Reagan at that forgetful time. Imagine (1)(c) used while pointing at the familiar photograph of Reagan standing at a lectern displaying the presidential seal.

(1) (a) Reagan was president.
(b) The man named 'Ronald Wilson Reagan' was president.
(c) He was president.
(d) I was president.

The sentences in (1) are all true because Reagan was president. But they differ markedly in meaning, and consequently in what they express. Reagan believed what is expressed by (1)(a)-(c), but not what is expressed by (1)(d). He was therefore in a position to use (1)(a)-(c) sincerely and truthfully, but not (1)(d). When his memory loss worsened, Reagan might have believed what is expressed by (1)(c) (because of the presidential seal) but not what is expressed by (1)(a) (because his memories of Ronald Reagan became restricted to old movies). What a declarative sentence expresses is commonly called a *proposition*. The proposition expressed by (1)(d) differs from the others because 'I' differs in meaning from the other subject terms. A problem for linguistics is to account for this difference in meaning, thereby explaining how the sentences express different propositions.

A problem for psychology is to identify and differentiate the objects of propositional attitudes. What is it that (2)(c) and (d) say Reagan believes? How does it differ from what (2)(a) says he believes?

(2) (a) Reagan believes that Reagan was president.
(b) Reagan believes that he was president.
(c) Reagan believes that he himself was president.
(d) Reagan believes "I was president."

Sentences (2)(c) and (d) say that Reagan believes the proposition expressed by (1)(d) in the imagined context. What then are propositions, and what kind could be expressed by the complement of (2)(d)? These differences in what a person believes result in significant differences in the causes and effects of the beliefs. If Reagan knows that all former presidents have been summoned to the White House, he not will start preparing go unless (2)(d) is true, even if (2)(a) is true.

The first-person pronoun is exceptional in another way. Typically, we can describe what a person believes either by prefixing a sentence expressing what he believes with 'that,' or by enclosing it in quotation marks. Thus the *oratio recta* form (3)(a) is just a stylistic variant of the *oratio obliqua* form (2)(a).

(3) (a) Reagan believes "Reagan was president."
(b) Reagan believes that I was president.

But (2)(d) is not equivalent to (3)(b), which ascribes to Reagan a belief about the speaker (me). That would make him delusional as well as amnesic. The use of 'I' in (2)(d) is anaphoric, with 'Reagan' its antecedent. Because this use is necessarily *de se*, it is *"logophoric."*[1] Note that (2)(d) and (3)(a) are no more metalinguistic than (2)(a) and (3)(b) are. None of these sentences entails that Reagan is an English speaker, nor even that some translation of the subordinate clauses occurred in Reagan's external or inner speech.

The sentences in (2) reveal further complexity in the linguistic *de se* problem. Speakers can use (2)(b) to mean what (2)(d) means. But it is also possible to use (2)(b) differently, as illustrated above. (2)(c), however, always entails (2)(d); a *de se* interpretation is obligatory, conveyed here by the reflexive morpheme 'self' rather than the first-person pronoun. In some cases, moreover, *de se* attitudes are expressed without using any pronouns. Whatever is expressed logophorically by 'I' in (4)(b) is implicit in (4)(d). Sentence (4)(d) has an obligatory *de se* interpretation, and thus is always equivalent to (4)(b) with logophoric 'I.' (4)(c) can be used to express a *de se* attitude, but it can also be used with the pronoun referring to someone other than Reagan.

(4) (a) Reagan is thinking the thought "Reagan was president."
(b) Reagan is thinking the thought "I was president."
(c) Reagan is thinking of his having been president.
(d) Reagan is thinking of having been president.

The sentences in (4) also illustrate that belief is not the only propositional attitude with a *de se* form. In the sense expressed by (4), thinking is independent of believing. People often believe what they are not currently thinking (as when asleep or preoccupied with other matters) and can think thoughts they do not believe (as when reading novels or daydreaming). The sentences in (5) show that *de se* attitudes can be found even among states that appear not to be *propositional* attitudes.

---

[1]Hagége 1974; Schlenker 2003; Bhat 2004: 33, 58-78; Huang 2006: 235-7. Schlenker (2003: 31) takes logophoric uses to be "monstrous," violating the thesis that "The semantic value of an indexical is fixed solely by the context of the actual speech act, and cannot be affected by any logical operators [or attitude verbs]." This thesis is not well-defined however, given that the sentential context is part of the context determining the referent of pronouns. Curiously, Schlenker (2003: 38, 74) and Bhat (2004: 61, 58) fail to recognize logophoric uses of 'I' in English despite recognizing them in other languages and providing instances in their own writing.

(5) (a) Reagan remembers Reagan being president.
(b) Reagan remembers his being president.
(c) Reagan remembers himself being president.
(d) Reagan remembers being president.

The objects of memory seem more situational (or event-like) than propositional. Can the same account be given of *de se* memory as for *de se* belief and thought? The equivalence of (5)(d) and (c) suggests that the distinction between situational and propositional attitudes may be more apparent than real, an illusion fostered by the obvious surface-syntactic difference.

The problem of the essential indexical also arises with other indexicals and the attitudes they express. A busy vice-president might believe "I have a meeting at noon" without believing "I have a meeting *now*," with the result that she misses an important meeting. A pilot may know that flying in Iranian airspace is prohibited without realizing that flying *here* is prohibited, with fatal consequences.

According to Higginbotham (2009: §12.4), a characteristic of *de se* beliefs is "immunity to error through misidentification." He recalls Wittgenstein's discussion.

> [I]f I feel that I am in pain, although I might conceivably ask whether it is really pain that I am in (perhaps others would consider it merely mild discomfort), I can't ask whether it is *I* who am in pain if anybody is, or think correctly that somebody is in pain, and wonder whether it is me. (Higginbotham 2009: 221)

Higginbotham is certainly on to something. With amnesia, Reagan can wonder whether Ronald Reagan is in pain without wondering whether he himself is. But Higginbotham overstates the difference. First, if I misidentified the sensation I am experiencing as pain, so that I mistakenly believe that I am in *pain*, then I also mistakenly believe that *I* am in pain. Second, the Wittgensteinian passage assumes, contentiously, that *de se* attitudes are necessarily conscious. If Freud was correct, however, then Otto may want to kill his father without knowing it. He may know that someone wants to kill his father while mistakenly believing that it is not him. Otto's psychoanalyst may, after many costly sessions, make Otto wonder whether '*I* want to kill my father' is true. What can safely be said is this: *De se* attitudes are generally introspectible, but other attitudes are never introspectible. Assuming that his mental states are conscious, a subject will know introspectively whether or not he himself is in them. This special property of *de se* attitudes is also shared by other indexical attitudes. I can know introspectively that I am thinking of coffee *here* and *now* even though introspection alone does not suffice for me to know that I am at 9:36 am in Springfield Virginia thinking of coffee. A complete solution to the *de se* problem must explain how the difference in what is expressed by 'I' and other indexicals can make such a difference in epistemological access.

3 Limitations of Alternative Accounts

The problem posed by the nonequivalence of the sentences in (1), (2), (4), and (5) for referential theories of meaning and Russellian theories of propositional attitudes is a special case of Frege's problem. The subject terms in (1) do not have the same meaning when they have the same referent. And if propositions are taken to consist of the objects, properties, and relations that make them true—"states of affairs" or "situations"—then beliefs are not individuated by their propositional objects. For the sentences in (2) can ascribe up to three different beliefs to Reagan even though all are made true by Reagan's having been president. A possible worlds semantics that identifies the meaning of a sentence with the set of worlds in which it is true, and treats belief as a relation to a world-set, faces the same difficulties. That Reagan might believe "I am not Reagan" is problematic for any theory taking belief-objects to be sets of n-tuples with a possible-world coordinate.[2]

Triadic Relation Theory. Kaplan (1977: 532) and Perry (1979: 17-8) take belief to be a relation between a subject, a state of affairs (or set of possible worlds), and a particular "way of believing" it. On this theory, the different sentences in (2) say that Reagan believes the same thing in three different ways. The triadic relation theory has as much trouble with Russell's problem as dyadic Russellian theories: believing that Santa Claus is coming cannot involve any relation to Santa Claus since he does not exist. The major issue for us, however, is that triadic relation theory merely relocates the problem of *de se* belief. The psychological question now is this: What are ways of believing things? How do the ways of believing expressed using 'I' differ from those expressed using other terms? And the linguistic question remains: How do we account for the differences in meaning among the sentences in (1)?

Character Theory. The principal linguistic problem is to account for the semantics of indexicals: their meaning and reference, and their contributions to the truth conditions of sentences. David Kaplan (1977) developed a very attractive framework for solving this problem. Kaplan represents the meaning of an indexical by assigning it a *character*, which is a function from a *context* to an *intension* (or "content"). The intension in the case of personal, demonstrative, or locative pronouns is a function from worlds to an object existing in them. For 'I,' Kaplan proposed a function satisfying the following condition: *i(c) is the intension whose value in any world w is the speaker uttering 'I' in c*. Thus the value of *i*(c) in any context in which Reagan used 'I' is the constant function RWR(w) whose value is Reagan for

[2] E.g. Schlenker 2003: 32, 37.

every world. The value of *i*(c) in any context in which Bill Clinton used 'I' is the constant function WJC(w) whose value is Clinton for every world. Proper names, in contrast, are assigned constant characters. The relevant sense of 'Ronald Reagan' would be represented by the function *rwr*(c) whose value at any context is RWR(w), whose value in any world is Ronald Wilson Reagan. Pure definite descriptions like 'the 40th U. S. president' are also assigned constant characters, but their intensions typically have different values at different worlds. The difference between (2)(d) and (3)(b) shows that the character function for 'I' must be more complex than Kaplan imagined. For in (2)(d) 'I' is used anaphorically like 'he' is in (2)(c). So in contexts in which (2)(d) is used by a speaker other than Reagan, the value of the character function for 'I' must be an intension whose value is Reagan, not the speaker.

Character theory can account for the fact that the four sentences in (1) have different meanings, and thus provides some account of why Reagan can use (1)(a)-(c) but not (1)(d). It can also account for the different interpretations of (2)(b) and the univocity of (2)(d). But it provides no account of how (2)(b) can have different truth conditions from (2)(d) even when both 'he' and 'I' are interpreted anaphorically with 'Reagan' as their antecedent. For in such contexts they have not only the same referent, Reagan, but the same intension (assigning Reagan to every world). Kaplan suggests that belief is a relation to objective states of affairs "under a character." But why should Reagan be capable of believing something under one character rather than another when Reagan is in a context in which the two characters have the same "content" as their value? What is it to believe something "under" a character? Without an answer to these questions, the character theory provides no explanation of immunity to misidentification.

Pro Theory. A final problem for character theory is that it provides no account of the meaning of the (d) sentences of (4) or (5), and hence no account of why (4)(d) has the meaning of (4)(b) and is equivalent to (4)(c) on only one of the latter's interpretations. Character theorists might introduce "PRO."

> I represent the understood subject by the element PRO, as in Chomsky (1981). PRO is an expression having an interpretation (in fact, necessarily anaphoric to the main clause subject), but no phonetic realization. (Higginbotham 2009: 213)

PRO theorists take the meaning of (4)(d) to be given by (6):

(6) Reagan is thinking of PRO having been president.

Character theorists can thus assign the sort of character to 'PRO' that 'I' has in logophoric contexts like (2)(d).

This suggestion presents several problems. Whatever PRO might be, it is not an *expression* in (4). (4) has one less word in it than (6), and is thus a shorter sentence. The expression 'PRO' in (6), moreover, does have a phonetic realization. (6) is not an English sentence because it contains an expression English speakers do not use. It makes more sense to take the term 'PRO' to *represent* a theoretically postulated entity—an "understood subject." Chomsky took it to represent an element in deep structure or LF. But that raises the question of what the element is, how it gets a character, and how its postulation explains immunity to misidentification. Even if these foundational questions have answers, a further problem is this: if 'PRO' (or PRO) has a character function, it is necessarily going to be different from the character function for 'I.' For 'PRO' cannot be used in the deictic way that is characteristic of 'I.' That is, 'PRO was president' has no interpretation as an independent clause. So even with PRO, character theory cannot account for the fact that (4)(d) has the meaning of (4)(b).

Self-Attribution Theory. Developing an idea of Loar (1976: 358), Lewis (1979), Chisholm (1981), and Chierchia (1989) take belief to involve *self-attributing* properties or attributes. On Lewis's account:

(7) (a) S believes that he himself is F iff S self-attributes being F.
(b) S believes that N is F iff S self-attributes being such that N is F, when 'N' is not reflexive.[3]

Given that the property *having been president* is distinct from the property *being such that Reagan was president* (everyone has the latter but only forty-five people so far have had the former), it is possible to self-attribute one without the other. In this way, the self-attribution theory accounts for the independence of (2)(a) and (b) from (2)(c) and (d). Other attitudes can be handled similarly, as can sentence complements of forms other than 'N is F.' Self-attribution theory differentiates between 'S expects to F' and 'S expects S to F' without postulating the understood subject PRO.

Despite advantages over theories taking belief to be a relation between subjects and states of affairs or world-sets, self-attribution theory has its own defects.[4] First, it maintains that believing oneself to be F is fundamentally different from believing N to be F, involving a relation to different objects with little in common. Yet those beliefs seem very similar, differing only in who one believes to be F—in the subject of what is believed. Second, by denying that belief is a propositional attitude, self-attribution theory must deny that *Reagan believes "I was president"* entails that Reagan believes what is expressed by *I was president* as used by Reagan. Self-attribution theory cannot say that a man who infers someone was pres-

[3] Count 'I' as reflexive when it is also the subject.

[4] See for example Stalnaker 1981: 147; Sosa 1983: 135-7; Castañeda 1987: 426-3, 434.

ident from the fact that he himself was president and a man who infers it from the fact that Reagan was president engage in the same structure-driven cognitive process. Third, to account for the distinctive character of attitudes expressed using other indexicals like 'now' and 'here,' self-attribution theories must also postulate relations of *now-attributing* and *here-attributing* properties. Accounting for the meaning of 'now' in independent clauses will not provide an account of the special character of believing that one has a meeting *now*. Parallel postulates, moreover, are needed for every attitude. Fourth, Lewis's self-attribution theory entails that every attitude entails a *de se* attitude—that no matter what people are thinking about, they are thinking about themselves. For example, it entails most implausibly that (8)(a) entails (b) and (c).[5]

(8) (a) David believes that Angelina Jolie is sexy.
(b) David believes that he himself is such that Angelina Jolie is sexy.
(c) David believes "I am such that Angelina Jolie is sexy."

While (8)(b) and (c) might conceivably be true when talking about a philosopher like David Lewis, it is hard to imagine an ordinary teenage boy with such a belief. It is doubtful that he even has the concept of being such that p. Fifth, sometimes there are no properties corresponding to what we believe about ourselves. I believe I am not a property, and so not a self-possessing property. But there is no property of not being a self-possessing property for me to self-ascribe (by a variant of Russell's paradox).

Finally, self-attribution theory provides little insight into what is special about *de se* attitudes. When Reagan self-attributes both being such that Reagan is famous and being this man (focusing on himself), why is he not thereby self-attributing being famous? What else is involved in the latter? Chierchia (1989: 8ff) suggests "the cognitive access that we have to ourselves." But Reagan does have that cognitive access to Reagan: he is aware of himself. Requiring Reagan to know that he himself is self-aware of Reagan would beg the question. Chierchia suggests defining K(x,x) as "x is disposed to describe the relevant belief by referring to x by means of the first person pronoun"—presumably intending a non-logophoric and non-demonstrative description. This is problematic, he notes, in implying that individuals without a first-person pronoun or a language cannot have beliefs about themselves. A more fundamental problem is the presupposition that we can characterize the meaning of 'I' without saying that it is used to express *de se* attitudes.

---

[5]Applying (b) to (a) yields *David self-attributes being such that AJ is sexy*. Applying (a) to that yields *David believes that he himself is such that AJ is sexy* (let 'F' be 'such that AJ is sexy'). Loar and Chierchia avoid this problem by taking *de se* beliefs to be attributional and other beliefs to be propositional, exacerbating the first problem.

Event-Subject Theory. Following Davidson, Higginbotham (2009, 2010) takes propositional attitude reports to involve quantification over events and takes propositions to be sets of possible worlds.

> An assertion of the sentence 'John loves Mary' is an assertion:
>
> (∃e)love(John, Mary, e)
>
> to the effect that there is at least one event of (as we may say) John loving Mary. Any sentence that may be asserted may occur also as a finite complement (hosted by a complementizer such as 'that'), in which case it will refer to a proposition. Following Richard Montague's (1960[: 160]) notation, the reference of the finite complement is
>
> ^(∃e)love(John, Mary, e)
>
> where the circumflex '^' represents λ-abstraction over possible worlds. (Higginbotham 2009: 219)

^(∃x)love(John, Mary, e) is the set of worlds with an event of John loving Mary. Let 'he' in (9)(b) to be anaphoric on 'John,' with no implicit 'himself.'

(9) (a) John expects to win.
(b) John expects he [John] will win.

Taking the infinitival complement of (9)(a) to have an understood subject, represented in *John expects PRO to win,* Higginbotham (2009: 228) suggests that "we identify as the peculiar semantic contribution of PRO that it presents the subject as *the subject (or experiencer) of the event or state e* as given in the higher clause, or σ(e) for short." He thus represents the logical form of (9)(a) and (b) as follows:

(10) (a) (∃e)expect[John, ^(∃e′)win(σ(e), e′), e].
(b) (∃e)expect[John, ^(∃e′)win(John, e′), e].[6]

Logical form (10)(b) says that John is the subject of an expecting event whose object is *the set of worlds in which John wins.* (10)(a) says that John is the subject of an expecting event whose object is *the set of worlds in which the event's subject wins.* However, given that John *is* the event's subject, these two world-sets are identical. So while Higginbotham assigns different logical forms to (9)(a) and (b), they represent the same truth conditions. Consequently his logical forms do not capture the difference between *de se* expectations and expectations about someone who turns out to be oneself. The problem of *de se* belief is precisely that (9)(a) and (b) do *not* have the same truth conditions.

---

[6] I simplified Higginbotham's formulas, writing '(∃e)expect[John, ...]' instead of '(For John = x)(∃e)expect[x, ...].'

Higginbotham nevertheless maintains that the propositional objects mentioned in (10)(a) and (b) are different.

> The thought
>
> $^\wedge(\exists e')\text{win}(\sigma(e), e')$
>
> is distinct from
>
> $^\wedge(\exists e')\text{win}(x,e')$
>
> (for given values of x and e), even if they are not intensionally different; or so I would submit. (Higginbotham 2009: 229)

The world-sets $^\wedge(\exists e')\text{win}(\sigma(e), e)$ and $^\wedge(\exists e')\text{win}(x,e')$ differ when $x \neq \sigma(e)$. But given Higginbotham's stipulation that e is an event consisting of x's expecting something, $x = \sigma(e)$. Assuming that no one else could be the subject of x's expecting something, it follows that $^\wedge(\exists e')\text{win}(\sigma(e), e')$ and $^\wedge(\exists e')\text{win}(x,e')$ are the same world-sets. Higginbotham grants this point, but does not believe it proves that the *thoughts* are different.

> Are the thoughts attributed in the two cases intensionally different? In other words, could anyone other than [John] have been the subject or experiencer of [John's] individual state? This is not a trivial question; but I shall proceed here on the assumption that the answer is negative. If that is so, then there are no grounds upon which the intensionally individuated contents of [(10)(a) and (b)] may be distinguished: they will coincide in truth value in any actual or counterfactual situation. Even if they do coincide, it does not follow that they are the same thought.... (Higginbotham 2009: 230)

If Higginbotham takes the world-sets $^\wedge(\exists e')\text{win}(\sigma(e), e')$ and $^\wedge(\exists e')\text{win}(x,e')$ to *be* thoughts, then he has to conclude that they are the *same* thought. I believe Higginbotham is correct if he is suggesting that thoughts cannot be identified with the sets of worlds where they are true. But then we need an account of what thoughts are. And to solve the *de se* problem, we need to detail what is distinctive about *de se* thoughts. I will sketch such a theory below.

Higginbotham's suggestion that 'PRO' represents the subject as $\sigma(e)$ implies that the two sentences in (11) have the same truth conditions, logical form, and meaning.

(11) (a) John expects to win.
(b) John expects the subject of e to win.

These are not equivalent, however, no matter how 'e' is interpreted. If 'e' is a free variable, (11)(b) is just an open sentence, which is neither true nor false. If 'e' is a constant, then (11)(a) and (b) have distinct truth conditions no matter what 'e' refers to. In most cases, (11)(b) can be true while (a) is false because John might not realize that he himself is σ(e). This substantive knowledge is not just the tautological knowledge that σ(e) is σ(e). The difference between (11)(a) and (b) is made particularly clear by observing that whereas (12)(c) follows routinely from (12)(a) and (b), no instance of (13)(c) follows from (13)(a) and (b) without the additional premise that John believes one individual is the subject of both e and f.

(12) (a) John expects to win
(b) John expects to celebrate.
(c) John expects to win and celebrate

(13) (a) John expects σ(e) to win.
(b) John expects σ(f) to celebrate.
(c) John expects x to win and celebrate.

Deleting 'x' makes the inference even worse.

Higginbotham's (2009: 227) invocation of Prior suggests interpreting 'e' in (11)(b) as a *demonstrative* element with a *reflexive* reference, as in (11)(c):

(11) (c) John expects the subject of this expecting to win.

'This expecting' here most naturally refers to the expectation expressed by (11)(c). So interpreted, its subject is clearly John. However, (11)(c) will not then be equivalent to (11)(a) unless John realizes "*I* am the subject of this expecting" or at least "*I* am John."

Higginbotham officially takes 'e' in (11)(b) to be a variable bound by an existential quantifier. Given his analysis, (11)(b) means (d):

(11) (d) John expects the subject of a winning expectation of John's to win (i.e., there is some e such that e is an expecting by John of the subject of e's winning).

But (11)(d) is even more obviously distinct in meaning from (11)(a) = (9)(a) than (9)(b) is. If John does not realize "*I* am the subject of John's expectation,"[7] then (11)(d) may be true while (11)(a) is false.

As noted in §I, Higginbotham thinks a theory of *de se* attitudes must account for their special epistemological status. One explanation he offers is

[7]Higginbotham (2009: 233) asks "could a person x be in a state e of imagining being F without *recognizing* that x = σ(e)?" and answers "it seems safe to assume that any such condition would be pathological." But there need be no pathology if the world's oldest man fails to recognize that the world's oldest man = σ(e), even if e is a conscious experience of the oldest man. And pathologies such as amnesia make the problem of *de se* attitudes more than an academic curiosity. *Reagan recognizes that Reagan* = σ(e) is false for many of Reagan's conscious experiences. Higginbotham seems to be making the question-begging assumption that 'x recognizes that x = σ(e)' is true only if x recognizes that *he himself* = σ(e).

that in the *de se* case:

> [The subject's expectation] cannot in the nature of the case be the conclusion of an inference wherein the bearer of the thought or action is identified in some way, for the experience or state e, whose subject is given as [σ(e)] in the thought or action, isn't around until the reflexive thought is had. (Higginbotham 2010: 271)

This claim is not warranted by Higginbotham's event analysis, even if we grant that inferences must take time. (11)(d) will be true as long as there is an expectation e meeting two conditions: (i) e is John's expectation; (ii) e is an expectation of the subject of e's winning. Consider the following case: e is the strongest expectation of winning anyone has ever had; John is amnesic, but infers that the subject of the strongest expectation of winning is John because the Guinness book of records said so; since John has inside information that the subject with the strongest expectation of winning is going to win, he comes to expect John to win. (11)(d) is true in this case, but not (11)(a).

Higginbotham elsewhere offers a different explanation of the special status of *de se* beliefs.

> What is the reason for immunity to error through misidentification in the case of thinking, on the basis of a present perception, "I hear trumpets?" I will assume it is this: that when I am in the relevant perceptual state, what I think is *that the subject of that state hears trumpets*. Hence there can be no question of my *identifying* myself as the subject of that state. (Higginbotham 2009: 221)

The antecedent of 'that state' here appears to be 'a present perception' (see also Higginbotham 2010: 276). But if the case is to support Higginbotham's theory of *de se* attitudes, it must refer to 'thinking,' suggesting that the object of a *de se* attitude is given as the subject of *one's own* attitude, as in (11)(e).

(11) (e) John expects the subject of an expectation he himself has to win (i.e., John expects "The subject of an expectation I myself have will win").

So interpreted, (11)(e) entails (11)(a) because John cannot fail to recognize "I am the subject of an expectation I myself have." But (11)(e) cannot be expressed using just bound quantificational variables; any such formula loses the *de se* element. As an analysis of *de se* expectation, (11)(e) itself is circular. And while (11)(e) entails (11)(a), the converse fails. Someone who expects to win—a young boy perhaps—need not have the sophisticated tautological thought that he himself is the subject of an expectation he himself has. Non-philosophers rarely have such thoughts.

Higginbotham's trumpet passage may be suggesting that an expectation is given to us in introspection like a pain or an auditory sensation, and that as such we cannot fail to recognize that it is ours. This is implausible for expectations, except when they happen to be occurrent. But suppose John is aware of one of his expectations in this way, and is thinking of it demonstratively as *this expectation.* Then John surely realizes that he himself is the subject of the expectation he is thinking about. If 'this expecting' in (11)(c) is interpreted as referring to the expectation John is thinking about in this way, then (11)(c) will be true and will entail (11)(a). But the converse entailment fails. It is highly implausible that whenever anyone expects to win, they such have a complex occurrent thought. And unlike (11)(a), (11)(c) will have such a demonstrative interpretation only when John's expectation is occurrent. In sum, whether e is a constant or a bound variable, the marked difference between (11)(a) and (b) is another illustration of the problem of *de se* attitudes.

There is one more problem. Higginbotham's analysis of the *de se* meaning of 'I' in the subordinate clauses of sentences like (2)(d), and of the understood subject in sentences like (9)(a), cannot apply when 'I' is the subject of an independent sentence like (1)(d). For then there is no "material supplied from a higher context"—no existential quantifier over events to bind the 'e' in 'σ(e).' Higginbotham (2010: 261) suggests that a sentence like (1)(d) expresses a thought in which the speaker "is given as the bearer of some superordinate experience e." It is not clear what 'superordinate' could mean given that (1)(d) is not a subordinate clause. And no matter how it is interpreted, 'The bearer of some experience e was president' will not be equivalent to 'I was president.' An adequate analysis of *de se* attitudes should be a consequence of the general semantics of the first-person pronoun. For the difference between *Reagan believes "I will win"* and *Reagan believes that he will win,* which parallels the difference between *Reagan expects to win* and *Reagan expects that he will win,* is what we would expect given the difference between *I will win* and *He will win* as used by Reagan.[8]

[8]Higginbotham (2009: 229) appears to be rejecting this when he says that "whereas I can sensibly ask myself whether, after all, I have identified myself correctly in expecting that I will win, I cannot ask myself whether I have identified myself correctly in expecting to win." But the contrast he sees here is illusory. In both cases, I can ask whether I am correct in believing that the winner will be me, and the answer might be no. And in both cases, it makes little sense to ask whether I am correct in believing that the person I expect to win is me. When Higginbotham does find a genuine difference between the first-person pronoun and PRO, it is because the pronoun is not used to report a *de se* attitude, despite being first-personal. One is the contrast between 'remember my doing A' and 'remember doing A' (see Higginbotham 2009, examples (21) and (22)): the former is not *de se* unless it is interpreted as "remember *me*

4 The Expression Theory and Non-Descriptive Meaning

I adopt the view that words are conventional signs of mental states, principally thoughts and ideas, and that meaning consists in their expression. In Davis (2003), I explain what it is for words to have meaning and express ideas in terms of speaker meaning and expression, and what it is for a speaker to mean or express something in terms of intention.

I focus on *thinking the thought that p* as a propositional attitude distinct from believing that p. One can think the thought that the moon is made of green cheese without believing it, and one can believe that bats fly without thinking that thought at the moment. Thinking in this sense differs from believing in being an *event* in the narrow sense of an *occurrence* or *activity* rather than a dispositional state. We retain our beliefs when we are asleep or unconscious, but thoughts are something actively going on. Thoughts, on my view, are structured events, and a particular kind of mental representation. They are similar in many ways to sentences, but fundamentally different. We think when thoughts occur to us. For S to think a thought T is for T to occur to S. I define *propositions* as thoughts with a declarative structure, or equivalently, as objects of belief and desire. Thought plays a role in the explanation and prediction of action and emotion different from belief and desire, but equally important. For example, no matter how much a man wants beer, and how certain he is that he will get beer if he goes to the supermarket, he will not actually get any beer unless he thinks about beer at the right moment in the store. I argue at length that thoughts have constituent structure—specifically, a phrase-structure syntax. Unlike the familiar "language of thought" hypothesis, what is structured on my view are not hypothetical "vehicles" of thought, but thoughts themselves.

I define *ideas* (or *concepts*) as thoughts or parts of thoughts, and distinguish them carefully from conceptions (belief systems) and sensory images (structures of sensations). Conceptions and images are important forms of mental representation, but meaning cannot be defined in terms of them. In addition to occurring and being parts of thoughts, concepts can be acquired and possessed, and may become associated with each other. We customarily refer to ideas using what I call "ideo-reflexive reference," whereby noun phrases containing an expression refer to the idea it expresses. Thus we use *the idea "vixen,"* or equivalently, *the idea of a vixen*, to refer to the idea of a female fox when we use 'vixen' therein to express that idea. We similarly use *the thought "Reagan was president"* or *the thought that Reagan was president* to refer to the thought expressed by 'Reagan was president' on that occasion. Referring to an idea is different from expressing it.

---

myself doing A," in which case it is equivalent to "remember doing A." Compare the difference between (2) (b) and (c) above and (5) (b) and (c).

Unlike Grice (1989), who assumed that meaning entails attempting to communicate and produce a belief in an audience (false when talking to our pets, writing individual words, or telling stories), I take expressing a thought, belief, or other mental state to involve performing an observable action as an indication that it is occurrent. Thus S expressed the idea and meant *female fox* by uttering 'vixen' only if S uttered 'vixen' as an indication that the idea *female fox* is occurring to him. Since indication is a weaker relative of what Grice called natural meaning, my account is more Aristotelian or Lockean.

Grice focused on *meaning that p* ("cognitive" speaker meaning), which can be defined as expressing the *belief* that p. *Implying* involves expressing one belief by expressing another. If one writes 'Mars exploded' in a work of fiction, however, one is expressing the *thought* but not the *belief* that Mars exploded. Similarly, one expresses the *idea* of Mars by writing 'Mars,' not a belief. Meaning "Mars exploded" by a sentence, or "Mars" by a word or phrase, is a distinct kind of speaker meaning, which I call "cogitative." It can be defined as the direct expression of thoughts or thought parts. As Schiffer (1972: 2-3) observed, when Mark says "Bush is brilliant" ironically, Mark means "Bush is brilliant" by the sentence he uttered, but did not mean that Bush is brilliant by uttering it. While this distinction is easy to miss given that quotation and 'that' subordination are normally just alternative ways of referring to a proposition, it is easy to see that what Mark did was express the belief that Bush is not brilliant by expressing the thought that he is.

On my definition, the meaning of individual words, as well as the non-compositional meaning of idioms, is given in terms of what ideas they are conventionally used to directly express. The meaning of compositional compounds is provided by a recursion clause, based on conventions to use certain expression structures to express certain idea structures. Conventions are common practices that are socially useful, self-perpetuating, and arbitrary.[9] The common goal served by language is preeminently communication. Conventions are self-perpetuating in a number of ways: precedent plays a role, as does habit, transmission of tradition, and normative criticism. Conventions are arbitrary in that other regularities could have served the same purposes and perpetuated themselves in the same ways.

The expression theory is not circular or regressive because thoughts and ideas do not themselves have linguistic meaning. Ideas and thoughts do have intentional *content*, but as a part of their identity, not by either convention or intention. For an idea to have the content "red" is simply for it to *be*

[9] This is a development of David Lewis's (1975: 4-5) characterization, which was inspired by Hume (1739: 490). Lewis's formulation was theoretically fascinating (see especially Lewis 1969), but much too strong, failing to apply to paradigm linguistic conventions.

the idea "red." The referential properties of words are determined by the referential properties of the ideas they express, which in turn are determined by the contents of the ideas and facts about the world.

Defining meaning as idea expression rather than reference enables natural solutions to Frege's and Russell's problems. People do think about Santa even though Santa does not exist, and such thoughts have a part conventionally expressed by the name 'Santa.' So 'Santa' has a meaning even though it has no referent. The thought "ammonia is poisonous" is distinct from the thought "NH_3 is poisonous" even though ammonia is NH_3. Since 'ammonia' and 'NH_3' express different thought parts, they have different meanings, even though their extensions are identical. The states of affairs Russellians take to be propositions are on my vew one kind of extension for thoughts—the entities that make thoughts true. The sets of worlds in which a thought is true is its intension. Ideas and thoughts can naturally serve as the modes of representation and ways of believing introduced in triadic theories.

My theory is thus Fregean in important respects, but not all. First, I do not claim that meanings *are* concepts. In one sense, meanings are properties of words; in another, meanings are what words mean. Neither are true of concepts (thought parts). Words express concepts, and mean what the concepts are of. Second, I do not believe that terms in indirect discourse *refer to* their senses. Third, Frege took thoughts and propositions to be abstract objects independent of the mental realm, making it mysterious how they could play an important role in human mental life. For me, thoughts and their parts are abstract because they are *types*—specifically, *mental event types*. Different people can think the same thought because the same mental event type can occur to different people. Frege denied that thoughts are "ideas," but he used 'Vorstellungen' to denote mental event *token*s, usually images, which necessarily occur to just one individual. Fourth, and most important for our purposes here, I reject the Fregean assumption that senses and concepts must be *descriptive* (see especially Davis 2005). We clearly use 'Mars' to express the common component of the thought that Mars is a planet, the thought that Mars is smaller than Jupiter, and so on. Kripkean arguments show that a name cannot be defined exclusively in descriptive terms. 'Mars' does not have a meaning like that of 'the fourth planet from the sun.' Indeed, standard names appear to be among the primitive or undefinable terms of a language. 'Mars' has a nondescriptive sense because it expresses a nondescriptive concept, as do syncategorematic terms (prepositions, logical constants, and the like)—and indexicals.

5 Indexical Meaning and Concepts

The paradigm indexicals include the personal pronouns *I, you, he, she,* and *it*; the demonstrative pronouns *this* and *that*, plus noun phrases with them as determiners; and the locative pronouns *now, here, there,* and *then.* These expressions contrast markedly with proper names like *Mars* and definite descriptions like *the fourth planet from the sun* in the way their reference is determined by an element of the context of use. Indexicals have different referents in different contexts even when used in the same sense and evaluated with respect to the same circumstances.

Indexicals not only have contextually variable referents, but different ways of being used. Imagine that Thomas Jefferson utters sentence (14) while in a room with George Washington, Alexander Hamilton, and Benjamin Franklin.

(14) Washington became president after he led the Continental Army to victory.
  (a) *Anaphoric*: 'Washington' is the antecedent of 'he.'
  (b) *Demonstrative*: The speaker is pointing at Hamilton.
  (c) *Deictic*: The speaker is visually focusing on Franklin.

On the most natural interpretation of (14), the name 'Washington' is the *antecedent* of 'he,' and the pronoun refers to George Washington. This use is *anaphoric.* But it is also possible that the speaker is using 'he' while pointing at Alexander Hamilton, with the result that the pronoun refers to Hamilton rather than Washington. This use is *demonstrative.* Finally, it is possible that the speaker is using 'he' without using it anaphorically, and without pointing at anything. The speaker might simply be visually focusing on Benjamin Franklin, with the result that the pronoun refers to Franklin rather than Hamilton or Washington. I call this the *deictic* use.[10] The indexical 'he' is used in the same sense (linguistic meaning) in all three uses. But the referent is determined in different ways.

The same three uses can be observed with demonstratives like 'this patriot' and even "pure" indexicals like 'I.' The most typical interpretation of the pronoun in (15) is the deictic, on which it refers to the speaker who uttered it. But it is also possible to use 'I' demonstratively or anaphorically, as illustrated.

(15) I am guilty.
  (a) *Deictic*: The speaker uttered the sentence focusing on himself.
  (b) *Demonstrative*: The speaker wrote the sentence on an arrow-shaped card pointing at a picture of O. J. Simpson.

---

[10]Lyons (1977: 660) observed that when 'he' is anaphoric in sentences like , it is uttered with normal stress. When deictic or demonstrative, it has heavier contrastive stress. The terms 'anaphoric,' 'demonstrative,' and 'deictic' are common in linguistics, but there is little consensus on their usage. There are many ways of classifying the great variety of indexical uses.

(c) *Anaphoric*: The speaker embedded the sentence in *Sam Sheppard thought "___."*

In (15)(b), 'I' would refer to Simpson, whose picture is pointed at. In (15)(c), 'I' would refer back to the subject of the main clause, and thus refer to Sheppard. There are other uses of indexicals, and many distinct species of anaphoric, deictic, and demonstrative uses.

An ideational theory may seem patently absurd for pronouns. Whereas it seems tautological to say that 'Mars' expresses the idea of Mars, and that 'the fourth planet from the Sun' expresses the concept of the fourth planet from the Sun, we cannot say in general that 'I' expresses the idea of I or of me. But our inability in this case is due, I believe, to a fact about noun phrases with the prepositional form *the idea of φ*. When 'φ' therein is a pronoun, it must have the objective case (*me* vs. *I*) and a particular referent. Being indexical, 'me' does not express a concept with a fixed referent. So *'I' expresses the idea of me* is either used improperly without a referent for 'me,' or else it is not generally true. When we use instead the quotational form *the idea "I,"* an ideo-reflexive reading is forced. *'I' expresses the idea "I"* is not obviously incorrect, but does presuppose that 'I' expresses a thought part, which remains to be shown.

Another possible reason for rejecting an ideational theory of indexical meaning is that pronouns do not have enough descriptive content to determine their referents or discriminate between indexicals like 'it' and 'that.' But this argument falsely assumes that all concepts are descriptive.

In the plus column, it is evident that sentences like (14) and (15) do express complete thoughts on any given occasion, and that the pronouns express components of those thoughts. It is not obvious, though, that they express the same thought part on every occasion. It is conceivable that 'I' expresses the concept of Simpson on one occasion, and the concept of Sheppard on another, without any one concept being expressed on both occasions. However, 'I' does not express the concept of any particular person in contexts like (16):

(16) No one can say or believe "I am not me."

Furthermore, example (1) makes it plausible that even Reagan uses (1)(d) to express a different thought than (1)(a)-(c) express, one that differs because the subject-concept Reagan uses 'I' to express differs from the concepts expressed by the other coreferential singular terms. My main argument is an abduction: the hypothesis that pronouns express the same thought part on different occasions, suitably developed, enables us to provide the best explanation of their behavior, and to solve the problems confronting other theories. This hypothesis receives analogical support from the fact that terms other than pronouns express the same thought part when used with the same linguistic meaning, even indexical terms like 'enemy' and 'neighbor.' The hypothesis thus enables a highly uniform account of word meaning.

Evans (1985: §6) observed that there was nothing in Frege's general theory requiring the assumption that the sense of a singular term must be given by a description. "All that a Fregean needs," Evans would say, "is an acknowledgment that those thoughts about ourselves which we typically express with the use of 'I' do involve a particular way of thinking about ourselves." This common "way of thinking of ourselves" would be the sense of 'I.'[11] While Evans's line of thought has the right direction, it does not explain how two people using 'I am guilty' could express different propositions, with different truth values, if the same "way of thinking" is expressed by both. If different "ways of thinking" (Zemach 1985) or "special senses" (Perry 1983: 19) are expressed, how can 'I' have the same meaning on both occasions?

Peacocke (1981, 1983) proposed that there is a single mode of presentation SELF that everyone uses 'I' to express, and also that each individual S uses 'I' to express a special mode of presentation SELF_S. This raises a number of questions. How can 'I' always express SELF if S uses 'I' to express SELF_S? What is the relation between SELF and SELF_S? Peacocke says that SELF_S is a *token* of SELF, which means that everyone expresses the same type of representation while expressing different token representations. But if SELF_S is a thought part, it cannot be a token. For the thought "I am hungry" occurs to me on many different occasions. So there must be many tokens of what I use 'I' to express, making SELF_S a type rather than a token. If SELF_S is some other abstract object, how is it involved in thinking? Even if metaphysical questions about SELF and SELF_S can be answered, linguistic questions remain: How can this theory accommodate anaphorical and demonstrative uses of 'I.' Can it be generalized to other pronouns?

I come at the *de se* problem from the other direction. I develop a general theory of indexical meaning and concepts, and then ask what is special about the *de se* case. I argue that the personal, demonstrative, and locative pronouns express *primary* indexical concepts, ones that do not contain other indexical concepts. They are like the concepts expressed by proper names and definite descriptions in serving as subject concepts in propositions. Primary indexical concepts are like syncategorematic concepts, however, and markedly unlike proper name and definite description concepts, in that they do not themselves represent particular objects and therefore have no reference of their own. Something external to the concepts gives them an extension and intension on particular occasions. I hypothesize that one of

[11]Cf. Peacocke 1981: §1; 1983: 119-20; Sosa 1983: esp. 329; Forbes 1989: §2, esp. p. 469; Künne 1997: §2; Newen 1997: §2.

the distinctive features of primary indexical concepts is that their occurrences are typically connected in a particular way with other representational mental events, including sensory experiences and other subject-concepts, whose objects become their referents. Primary indexical concepts are capable of being *linked* to a *determinant*.

Consider a sentence like (17), which has at least two different interpretations and logical forms because either 'Obama' or 'Clinton' can be the antecedent of 'he.'

(17) Obama admires Clinton because he is liberal.

What makes one noun the antecedent rather than another on a given occasion of use? I hypothesize that 'he' expresses the same thought part whenever it is used with its third-person masculine sense. Let us use '*c(he)*' to refer to that concept (i.e., as short for *the concept "he"*). Let '*c(Obama)*' and '*c(Clinton)*' refer in the same way to the concepts expressed by 'Obama' and 'Clinton.' It seems evident that (17) is ambiguous because it can express either a thought in which *c(he)* is linked to *c(Obama)* or one with *c(he)* linked to *c(Clinton)*. Which thought is expressed depends on the speaker's intentions. The antecedent of 'he' could also be a noun phrase used before (or after) (17) is uttered, perhaps 'Kennedy.' In that case, (17) expresses an unlikely thought in which *c(he)* is linked to *c(Kennedy)*. The speaker S cannot think that thought unless *c(he)* and *c(Kennedy)* both occur to S and do so in the right relationship, which I call indexical linkage.

Let '℞' be a variable for any primary indexical concept and 'δ' for any determinant. On my view, concepts are event types that can occur at different times as parts of different thoughts. Let '℞$^{\delta}$' stand for the subtype of ℞ that consists of its occurrence linked to δ. Hence:

(18) ℞$^{\delta}$ occurs to S iff ℞ and δ occur to S and their occurrences are linked.

℞$^{\delta}$ is thus a more specific event type than ℞. ℞$^{\delta}$ is to ℞ as *driving with friends* is to *driving*, and *striking in anger* to *striking*. For a neural model, suppose ℞ is a circuit whose activation is the occurrence of ℞. Let ℞ be capable of being activated by other neural circuits, including δ. Then ℞$^{\delta}$ might represent the activation of ℞ by δ over a specific type of neural pathway.

From a semantic standpoint, the most important rule governing ℞$^{\delta}$ is the derived reference rule:

(19) ex{℞$^{\delta}$} = ex{δ}.

Thus the extension of $c(he)^{c(Obama)}$ is Obama, and the extension of $c(he)^{c(Clinton)}$ is Clinton. So when 'he' has 'Obama' as its antecedent, it refers to Obama. For 'Obama' is the antecedent of 'he' when the indexical concept expressed by 'he' has the concept expressed by 'Obama' as its determinant. The speaker uses 'he' to express the generic concept *c(he)*, thus meaning "he" by 'he.' The speaker also expresses the more specific concept $c(he)^{c(Obama)}$, thereby referring to Obama. Similarly, the intension of ℞$^{\delta}$ is the intension of δ. The character function for ℞ and indexicals expressing it is the function assigning to any context c the intension of the determinant δ linked to ℞ in c. Indexical terms are characterized by a "double triangle of signification": the reference of a term is in general that of the idea it expresses, and the reference of an indexical idea is that of the determinant it is linked to.

6 Deictic and Demonstrative Occurrence

Returning to example (14), the pronoun 'he' is used anaphorically to refer to George Washington, on my theory, when 'he' is used to express an occurrence of *c(he)* linked to the concept *c(Washington)* expressed by the proper name 'Washington' on that occasion. When the pronoun is used demonstratively, the determinant is related in a particular way to the speaker's pointing gesture. But in the deictic usage, there is no antecedent or demonstration. What then is the determinant? I believe what is distinctive about the deictic occurrence of indexical concepts is that they are linked to perceptual, introspective, memory, or even hallucinatory experiences—what I call collectively *presentations*. When Jefferson used 'he' deictically, he was referring to Franklin because he was visually attending to Franklin, and *c(he)* was linked to that perception. Had Jefferson instead been using 'he' to express an occurrence of *c(he)* linked to his perception of Hamilton, 'he' would have referred deictically to Hamilton. Had he been using 'he' to express an occurrence of *c(he)* linked to an occurrent memory of John Adams, Jefferson would have been referring to Adams. Note that Jefferson could also have been using 'he' to express an occurrence of *c(he)* linked to his visual or auditory perception of Washington. In that case, Jefferson would have referred deictically rather than anaphorically to Washington. And conceivably, Jefferson might not realize that *he* is Washington.

By 'presentation,' I mean a non-epistemic awareness or memory of something, or a similar non-veridical state of consciousness. *Seeing a lemur* differs markedly from *seeing that it is a lemur*. The latter entails knowing and therefore believing that the object is a lemur, which in turn entails having the concept of a lemur. Since seeing-that entails knowing-that, Dretske (1969) called it "epistemic" perception. Seeing a lemur is "non-epistemic" perception. There is a similar distinction between remembering the lemur's jumping and remembering that the lemur jumped. Because the deictic use of indexicals is based on non-epistemic awareness or memory, it enables us to refer to objects we have not yet conceptualized. In this respect it resembles the demonstrative use and differs markedly from the anaphoric (cf. Lyons 1977: 673). Because deictic reference is determined by a presentation and not a concept, it is naturally thought of as more "direct" (cf. Saxena 2006: 131). In both cases, though, the reference of the indexical concept is determined by a determinant.

I characterized the determinant as a *separate* mental event. The externality is particularly clear when an indexical concept is linked to a sensory presentation. Mary's perception of Washington may cause her to think "He's tall," but is not part of the thought it caused.[12] *Indexical concepts connect the conceptual realm of experience to the nonconceptual.* Something must if thought and intentional action are to be effectively coordinated with events in the world. Suppose that a subject wants a cup of coffee, and that seeing one causes him to think "A cup of coffee is within grasping distance of Wayne Davis." Even if I am that subject, such thoughts are not sufficient to guide my hand to the cup. I have to think "*That* is a cup of coffee" looking at it.

Attention is an essential element of the process whereby sense-perceptions or introspections become linked with indexical concepts.[13] Suppose we are looking at the grid of letters in Fig. 1.

c f c
r u b
m i r
w b c

Figure 1

We see all the letters in this grid. There is a sensory presentation of the 'c,' a sensory presentation of the 'f,' and so on. While remaining aware of all the letters, we can attend to a subset. We can mentally single out any two and think *"This is the same as that."* Let brackets and braces indicate which letters we are focusing on, and what we are referring to by which words.

c f c
r u [b]
m i r
w {b} c

c f c
r [u] b
m {i} r
w b c

Fig. 2: "[This] is the same as {that}." Fig. 3: "[This] is different from {that}."

Go back to Fig. 1 and attend to the two letters indicated in Fig. 2, then attend to the two letters indicated in Fig. 3. This shift in attention does not

[12] Compare and contrast Vendler 1972: 73-6; D. W. Smith 1982a: 202ff; Böer 1995: 349.

[13] Cf. Schiffer 1978: 196; Levine 1988: 233.

change what we are perceiving, or the way things look. The array of letters in Fig. 1 looks the same whether we are attending to [b] and {b} or [u] and {i}. The difference between these two attentional processes is non-sensory. Go back to Fig. 1 again and think the two thoughts indicated in Figs. 2 and 3. We can now observe that thinking the thought in Fig. 2 requires not just seeing but attending to [b] and {b}. Thinking the thought in Fig. 3 requires attending to [u] and {i}.

We perceive an object by perceiving some of its parts. If Mary is looking at the *Enterprise*, she may be seeing its bow or its stern. Suppose now that Mary sees the aircraft carrier in virtue of seeing its stern and nothing else (she is looking at it directly from the rear). Even though they may coincide for a while, the process of perceiving the stern is different from the process of perceiving the ship. Moreover, Mary may be attending to the ship rather than the stern even though all she can see is the stern. The purely sensory component of the process may be the same as if she were attending to the stern. But attending to something has an additional non-sensory component that differs in the two cases. In virtue of the different non-sensory components, the subject has different dispositions to respond to changes in the stimulus. If Mary is attending to the stern, and the ship turns so that more of the ship is in view, she is liable to keep the stern in her focal point. But if Mary is attending to the ship, she is liable to shift her focal point away from the stern to a more central part of the ship. Because the processes of perceiving and attending to the ship differ from those of perceiving and attending to the stern, the indexical concept *c(that)* can be linked to a perception that is focused on the ship rather than on the stern, even if her sense-impression of the ship is a sense-impression of the stern. Consequently, she can truly say "That is thousands of feet long," referring to the whole ship rather than just the stern. Sense-impressions (the complexes of sensations involved in seeing, hearing, feeling, tasting, or smelling) are only part of the process of perceiving or attending to an object.

The non-sensory element in attending does not appear to be conceptual. A person can attend to a ship or its stern without having either the concept of a ship or the concept of a stern. Someone might acquire the concept of an aircraft carrier by looking at one. Animals with very limited conceptual abilities can attend to a vast range of objects. Even among humans, attending to an object and thinking of it as *that* does not seem to entail concurrently thinking of it in any other way. Hence the linking of an indexical concept to a perception focused on the ship is not plausibly another case of linkage to a concept.

Attention can also be directed upon objects of introspective awareness. I can work with a pain in my foot without attending to it. But I must be attending to it when I think "It is still there." A similar process is involved when indexical concepts are linked to memory presentations, but is not called attention. Suppose we are remembering a wedding, and have a vivid image of the scene in which the groom kissed the bride. We think *"He kissed her."* We may be remembering the priest too. But our memory presentations of the bride and the groom are mentally highlighted, just as the sense-impressions of [u] and {i} are mentally highlighted when we attend to those letters in Fig. 1. We cannot say that we are literally attending to the bride and the groom, but we can say that we are *focusing on* them. Attention is the specific case of focusing on an object of current perceptual or introspective observation.

An indexical concept is linked to a presentation only if the subject is focusing on an object through it. I say in that case that the presentation is focused on the object. If ρ(x) is a veridical presentation focused on x, the extension of $℞^{\rho(x)}$ is x.

7 Self-concepts and *De Se* attitudes

Like Evans and Peacocke, I take 'I,' when used as the personal pronoun rather than the chemical name of iodine, to express a particular thought part: the generic mode of representation through which people think about themselves in the *de se* manner. Following my custom, I use '*c(I)*' instead of Peacocke's 'SELF' to refer to the concept 'I' expresses. As (15) illustrated, 'I' is like other indexicals in having anaphoric, demonstrative, and deictic uses. In (15)(c), 'I' is anaphoric with 'Sam' as its antecedent. So 'I' in this context expresses $c(I)^{c(Sam)}$, the generic self-concept linked indexically to the concept of Sam Sheppard. When 'I' is demonstrative, as in (15)(b), *c(I)* is linked to a determinant whose extension is the person in the picture pointed at (Simpson). What is the determinant when 'I' is used deictically, as in (15)(a)? Applying the theory sketched above, it must be a presentation. We can account for the distinctive properties of *de se* thoughts by taking the determinant to be *the subject's introspective awareness of himself*—S's "self-presentation" for short. If O. J. Simpson used 'I am guilty' deictically, he would use 'I' to express not only the generic self-concept *c(I)*, but also the specific self-concept $c(I)^{\alpha(OJ)}$, where α(OJ) is Simpson's introspective awareness of himself. $c(I)^{\alpha(OJ)}$ has the same extension as the concept expressed by the name 'O. J. (Simpson),' but is not *c(OJ)*. If '[SUB]PRED' designates a proposition in which SUB is the subject-concept and [ ]PRED the predicate-concept, Simpson might believe [*c(OJ)*]*c(is guilty)* without believing $[c(I)^{\alpha(OJ)}]$*c(is guilty)* if he has amnesia. That is, he might believe "O. J. is guilty" without believing "I am guilty." Peacocke's individual self-concept SELF_s can now be identified with $c(I)^{\alpha(S)}$, a sub-type rather than a token of *c(I)*.

Because the relevant determinant is the speaker's self-presentation, a sentence like *I am aware of myself* is true in any context in which the personal pronoun is used deictically. Recall that S's self-presentation is a form of *non-epistemic* awareness. Being aware of Mars in this sense, like attending to it, does not entail knowing or believing that the object is Mars nor even having the concept of Mars. The same is true of S's introspective awareness of S. Hence no circularity ensues from defining S's self-concept in terms of S's self-presentation.

On my view, then, we use 'I' to express *both* a common way of thinking *and* a special one. 'I' means "I" because we all use 'I' to express the common way of thinking of ourselves. And we each use 'I' deictically to express thoughts that no one else can express. In these thoughts, the subject concept is our own self-concept. My self-concept cannot occur to you because my introspective awareness of myself cannot occur to you. Your self-concept cannot occur to me for the same reason. Hence I cannot think of you the specific way I think of myself or the way you think of yourself. We can nonetheless think of, refer to and describe each other's self-concepts and recognize when they are expressed.

A complete statement of the linguistic conventions governing the use of personal pronouns must refer to both the generic self-concept and specific self-concepts. *It is conventional for all speakers of English to use 'I' to directly express c(I), and for each speaker S to use 'I' deictically to express* $c(I)^{\alpha(S)}$. Since no one else besides S uses 'I' to express S's self-concept, the use of 'I' to express $c(I)^{\alpha(S)}$ is not *itself* a convention for any given S even though it *accords with* the convention. Thus the rule giving the meaning of 'I' in English associates it with the generic self-concept and the class of its determinates but not with any specific speaker's self-concept.[14]

We still need to account for the difference between *de se* attitude reports and others. Recall the sentences in (2) and (3) above, renumbered and reordered here:

(20) (a) Reagan believes that Reagan was president.
(b) Reagan believes that he himself was president.
(c) Reagan believes "I was president."
(d) Reagan believes that I was president.
(e) Reagan believes that he was president.

If (20)(a) is given a fully opaque interpretation, it describes Reagan as believing a particular proposition, the one expressed on the occasion of use by the subordinate clause 'Reagan was president.' Thus (20)(a) says: *Reagan believes [c(Reagan)]c(was president)*. (20)(b) and (c) also describe Reagan as believing a particular proposition, equivalent to that identified in (20)(a), but having Reagan's self-concept as its subject concept. Thus (20)(b) says:

---

14 Cf. Husserl 1900: 316; Frege 1977: 12-3; D. W. Smith 1981; 1982a; 1982b; Böer 1995: 360-1; Künne 1997: §2.

Reagan believes [c(I)$^{\alpha(Reagan)}$]c(was president). The fact that the subject concept in the object of belief is the subject's self-concept is conveyed by the reflexive 'himself' in a that-clause or 'I' in a quoted clause. The fact that the self-concept in question is Reagan's is conveyed by the fact that 'Reagan' is the pronoun's antecedent.

Sentences (20)(d) and (e) do not have fully opaque interpretations, and do not describe Reagan as believing a particular proposition. In (20)(d), the 'I' is used deictically: it expresses the *speaker's* self-concept *c(I)*$^{\alpha(S)}$ and thus has the speaker S as its referent. (20)(d) describes Reagan not as believing a proposition containing the speaker's self-concept, but as believing some proposition whose subject concept has the same extension, namely S. So (20)(d) says: *Reagan believes some proposition [SUB]c(was president), where ex{SUB} = ex{c(I)$^{\alpha(S)}$} = the speaker.* So if I use (20)(d), it will be true if Reagan believes either "Wayne Davis was president" or "The author of *Meaning, Expression and Thought* was president." In (20)(e), let us suppose that 'he' is used anaphorically with 'Reagan' as its antecedent; then it says: *Reagan believes some proposition [SUB]c(was president), where ex{SUB} = ex{c(he)$^{c(Reagan)}$} = Reagan.* The interpretation is similar if 'he' is used deictically or demonstratively, or anaphorically with a different antecedent.

We can now account for the properties of the understood subject Higginbotham expressed using the surface element 'PRO' by identifying it as *c(I)*$^{\alpha(ex\{SUB\})}$, the self-concept of the referent of the subject concept of the propositional attitude proposition it occurs within. Thus (9)(a) 'John expects to win' says: *John expects [c(I)$^{\alpha(John)}$]c(will win)*, in contrast to (9)(b), which says: *John expects [c(he)$^{c(John)}$]c(will win).*

8 Individuating Primary Indexical Concepts

We can deepen our account of *de se* attitudes and indexicals if we can say more about the generic indexical concept expressed by 'I' and other pronouns. How does *c(I)* differ from *c(he)* and other primary indexical concepts? Are they atomic or do they have components? The problem of the essential indexical shows that a primary indexical concept ℞ cannot be completely analyzed into descriptive concepts. But that allows ℞ to have some descriptive components as long as it has others that make it non-descriptive. To account for all the similarities and differences in meaning among indexicals, I hypothesize that each primary indexical concept is composed of a very general *sortal* concept plus a nondescriptive *determiner*. I present evidence that the sortal component of *c(he)* is *c(male)*, whereas that of *c(I)* is the more general concept *c(animate)*. The sortal component of *c(this)*, expressed by 'this' as a pronoun, is *c(thing)*; that of a phrase of the form 'this N,' in which 'this' is a determiner, is *c(N)*. The sortal component places a condition on the derived reference rule (19): ex{℟$^{\delta}$} = ex{δ} *provided ex{δ} is in the extension of the sortal component of* ℟. Suppose Terry points at someone he mistakenly believes to be male, and says 'He is tall.' Even though Terry is referring to a woman, 'he' cannot refer to a woman because of its sortal component. His statement suffers from the same presupposition failure as 'This/The male is tall.' The sortal component of *c(I)* explains why we would interpret a note attached to a stone reading 'I am a stone' as either a joke or a piece of make-believe.

The determiner component of a primary indexical concept does a number of things. It combines with the sortal component to form an singular subject-concept that is indexical and therefore capable of linking to determinants. It furthermore determines the specific range of determinants the concept can link to. No two primary indexical concepts can occur with the same range of determinants. Each ℟ has a unique set of *determinant constraints*, which specify the determinants ℟ cannot link to. Some pronouns, such as 'this,' 'that,' and 'it,' differ only in their determinant constraints; there is no difference in their sortal components. Others, like 'he' and 'I,' have differences in determinant constraints that are independent of their sortal components. One such difference between 'I' and 'he' is illustrated by (20)(d) and (e). In this context, 'I' can refer to Reagan if, for example, Reagan used the sentence. But 'Reagan' cannot be the antecedent of 'I' as it must be in (20)(c). In marked contrast, the 'he' in (20)(e) can be interpreted anaphorically with 'Reagan' as its antecedent, but cannot be interpreted as referring deictically to the speaker the way 'I' must in (20)(d). 'He' can be used deictically there, and can even refer to the speaker, but *c(he)* must have a perceptual or memorial rather than introspective determinant. In the conceptual context expressed by 'Reagan believes that __ was president,' the determinant of *c(I)* can be the speaker's self-presentation α(S) but not *c(Reagan)*, π(Reagan) (a sense-impression focused on Reagan), or even π(S) (a sense-impression of the speaker himself); the determinant of *c(he)* can be *c(Reagan)*, π(Reagan), or π(S), but not α(S).

Another distinctive characteristic of English 'I' arising from determinant constraints is that its only possible anaphoric interpretation is the logophoric. Consider the sentences in (21):

(21) (a) Caesar met Vercingetorix and thought "I will be victorious."
(b) Caesar met Vercingetorix and thought "He will be victorious."

In (21)(a), the pronoun can only have 'Caesar' as its antecedent because that is the subject of the propositional attitude verb 'thought.' In (21)(b) the pronoun can be interpreted as referring back to Caesar (especially given Caesar's unusual practice of referring to himself in the third-person), but is most naturally interpreted as referring to Vercingetorix. It is easy to imagine languages in which the occurrence constraints characterizing the personal pronouns are different. Indeed, Amharic (Schlenker 2003: 31, 76) and Kannada (Bhat 2004: 58, 68) are languages from different families in which a pronoun expressing $R^{\alpha(S)}$ in main clauses may be logophoric in that-clauses. Gokana has a third-person pronoun occurring logophorically there (Bhat 2004: 62).

A satisfactory theory of *de se* attitudes must be part of a comprehensive theory of indexicals and indexical concepts. What I have tried to do here is sketch the theory I develop in *Indexical Meaning and Concepts*. Everything requires further defense, and many questions remain to be answered.

References

Bhat, D. N. S. 2004. *Pronouns*. Oxford: Oxford University Press

Boër, S. 1995. Propositional attitudes and compositional semantics. In *Philosophical Perspectives, 9: AI, Connectionism, and Philosophical Psychology*, ed. J. Tomberlin, pp. 341-79. Atascadero, CA: Ridgeview

Castañeda, H.-N. 1987. Self-consciousness, demonstrative reference, and the self-ascription view of believing. In *Philosophical Perspectives, I: Metaphysics*, ed. J. Tomberlin, pp. 406-54. Atascadero, CA: Ridgeview

Chierchia, G. 1989. Anaphora and attitudes *de se*. In *Semantics and Contextual Expression*, ed. R. Bartsch, J. van Benthem, and P. van Emde Boas, 1-31. Dordrecht: Foris Publications

Chisholm, R. M. 1981. *The First-person*. Minneapolis: University of Minnesota Press

Chomsky, N. 1981. *Lectures on Government and Binding*. Dordrecht: Foris Publications

Davis, W. A. 2003. *Meaning, Expression, and Thought*. New York: Cambridge University Press

Davis, W. A. 2005. *Nondescriptive Meaning and Reference*. Oxford: Oxford University Press

Dretske, F. 1969. *Seeing and Knowing*. Chicago: University of Chicago Press

Evans, G. 1985. Understanding demonstratives. In *Collected Papers*, pp. 291-321. Oxford: Oxford University Press.

Forbes, G. 1989. Indexicals. In *Handbook of Philosophical Logic, Vol. IV*, ed. D. M. Gabbay & F. Guenthner, pp. 463-90. Dordrecht: Kluwer

Frege, G. 1977. *Logical Investigations*, ed. P. T. Geach. New Haven: Yale University Press

Grice, H. P. 1989. *Studies in the Way of Words*. Cambridge, MA: Harvard University Press

Hagège, C. 1974. Les pronoms logophoriques. *Bulletin de l'Association de Paris*, **69**, 287-310

Higginbotham, J. 2009. *Tense, Aspect, and Indexicality*. Oxford: Oxford University Press

Higginbotham, J. 2010. On words and thoughts. In *Context-Dependence, Perspective, and Relativity*, ed. I. Stojanovich, F. Recanati & N. Villanueva, pp. 253-82. Berlin: Mouton de Gruyter

Huang, Y. 2006. Anaphora, Cataphora, Exophora, Logophoricity. In *Encyclopedia of Language and Linguistics, 2nd Ed.*, ed. K. Brown, pp. 231-40. Amsterdam: Elsevier

Hume, D. 1739. *A Treatise of Human Nature*, ed. L. A. Selby-Bigge. Oxford: Clarendon Press, 1888

Husserl, E. 1900. *Logical Investigations*, trans. J. N. Findlay. New York: Humanities Press, 1970

Kaplan, D. 1977. Demonstratives. In *Themes from Kaplan*, ed. J. Almog, J. Perry & H. Wettstein, pp. 481-563. Oxford: Oxford University Press 1989.

Künne, W. 1997. First-person propositions: A Fregean account. In *Direct Reference, Indexicality, and Propositional Attitudes*, ed. W. Künne, A. Newen & M. Anduschus, pp. 49-68. Stanford, CA: CSLI Publications

Levine, J. 1988. Demonstrating in mentalese. *Pacific Philosophical Quarterly*, **69**, 222-40

Lewis, D. 1969. *Convention*. Cambridge, MA: Harvard University Press

Lewis, D. 1975. Languages and language. In *Minnesota Studies in the Philosophy of Language*, ed. K. Gunderson, vol. 7, pp. 3-35. Minneapolis: University of Minnesota Press.

Lewis, D. 1979. Attitudes *de dicto* and *de se*. *Philosophical Review*, **88**, 513-43

Loar, B. 1976. The semantics of singular terms. *Philosophical Studies*, **30**, 353-77

Lyons, J. 1977. *Semantics*. Cambridge: Cambridge University Press

Newen, A. 1997. The logic of indexical thoughts and the metaphysics of the 'self'. In *Direct Reference, Indexicality, and Propositional Attitudes*, ed. W. Künne, A. Newen & M. Anduschus. Stanford, CA: CSLI Publications

Peacocke, C. 1981. Demonstrative thought and psychological explanation. *Synthese*, **49**, 187-217

Peacocke, C. 1983. *Sense and Content: Experience, Thought, and Their Relations*. Oxford: Oxford University Press

Perry, J. 1979. The problem of the essential indexical. *Noûs*, 13, 3-21

Perry, J. 1983. Castañeda on He and I. In *Agent, Language, and the Structure of the World*, ed. J. Tomberlin, pp. 15-39. Atascadero, CA: Ridgeview

Saxena, A. 2006. Pronouns. In *Encyclopedia of Language and Linguistics, 2nd Ed.*, ed. K. Brown, pp. 131-3. Amsterdam: Elsevier

Schiffer, S. 1972. *Meaning*. Oxford: Clarendon Press

Schiffer, S. 1978. The basis of reference. *Erkenntnis*, **13**, 171-206

Schlenker, P. 2003. A plea for monsters. *Linguistics and Philosophy*, **26**, 29-120

Smith, D. W. 1981. Indexical sense and reference. *Synthese*, **49**, 101-28

Smith, D. W. 1982a. Husserl on demonstrative reference and perception. In *Husserl, Intentionality, and Cognitive Science: Recent Studies in Phenomenology*, ed. H. Dreyfus, pp. 193-214. Cambridge, MA: MIT Press

Smith, D. W. 1982b. What's the meaning of "this"? *Noûs*, **16**, 181-208

Sosa, E. 1983. Propositions and indexical attitudes. In *On Believing: Epistemological and Semiotic Approaches*, ed. H. Parret, pp. 316-31. New York: Walter de Gruyter

Stalnaker, R. 1981. Indexical belief. *Synthese*, **49**, 129-52

Vendler, Z. 1972. *Res Cogitans: An Essay in Rational Psychology*. Ithaca, NY: Cornell University Press

Zemach, E. 1985. De se and Descartes. *Noûs*, **19**, 181-204

2

Speaking (and Some Thinking) of Oneself

JAMES HIGGINBOTHAM

The vexatious issue of the first person pronoun emerged early on in modal accounts of the semantics of embedded non-extensional clauses in natural languages, and was made notorious especially through the work of Hector-Neri Castañeda, who drafted a number of eminently plausible scenarios in which it was natural to say that NN said something, or had a belief (desire, item of knowledge, etc.) that was strongly about him/her self=x, but did not have a first-personal stance toward it, as I have, for instance, to the belief that I have at the present moment that I am writing a few lines in English. Since then there have been many significant contributions. A view that I myself proposed (Higginbotham (2003), based on a talk from 2000), was that we should take advantage of Donald Davidson's hypothetical event position (extending it to all predications, not just action sentences), and say that a speaker using the first person refers to him/her self *as* the speaker $s(u)$ of his/her very utterance u; similarly for states e of belief and desire, activities such as remembering or imagining perceptual experience, and the rest.

Speech is deliberate action, so that we can ask of a person's reference to anything, how was it secured? But our doxastic, or epistemic, or desiderative states do not involve action at all. It follows, then, that if we are to take the first person in thought along the lines that I adumbrated for speech, we must conclude that many ordinary thoughts we have about ourselves must involve the capacity for thinking of ourselves as the possessors of these thoughts. I will accept this consequence, but concede a possible, at least occasional, alternative toward the end.

Attitudes De Se: Linguistics, Epistemology, Metaphysics.
Neil Feit and Alessandro Capone (eds.).

The first person pronoun is an indexical expression, one among many. For the semantics of demonstrative and indexical expressions, I continue to assume a view first outlined in some detail by Tyler Burge (1974), according to which their contribution shows up in the speaker's *use* of these expressions to refer to this or that, constrained by what the speaker knows to be the rules governing such use, in the course of saying something *about* this or that. Thus the rule of use for, say, 'that dog' would be: it is to be used to refer to a single thing, which is in point of fact a dog. A statement 'That dog so-and-so', where (a) the rule is followed, and (b) what is referred to is indeed a dog, is true just in case the object x to which the speaker referred is indeed so-and-so.

Two consequences of this account are critical. First, the implication is that the truth conditions of utterances in ordinary human languages are *conditional*: so for (1) we would (ignoring tense) have (the universal closure, for English, of) (2):

(1) That dog runs fast.

(2) If u is an utterance of (the syntactic structure Σ for) 'that dog runs fast', and the speaker s of u refers with her utterance of the words 'that dog' therein to x and x alone, and x is a dog, then u is true if and only if x runs fast.

The antecedent of the conditional handles the demonstrative. If it is satisfied, then the truth conditions are fixed. Second, and correlatively, these truth conditions are sensitive only to predication of the *object* of reference, and not to how that reference was achieved. So in an account with modality, assuming a standard Kripkean picture, the consequent for (3) would be as in (4):

(3) That dog might have run fast.

(4) … then u is true if and only if $\Diamond$(x runs fast).

The theory thus rules out, *de jure*, the possibility of "monsters," in the sense of Kaplan (1977); that is, demonstratives or indexical expressions whose behavior shifts depending upon whether they are embedded.[1]

Following the above very general suggestion, the rule of use for the first person pronoun is obvious: it is to be used to refer to oneself. Naturally, this rule can be followed only by one who has a conception of reference in general, and of herself in particular: it can no more be used to impart such a conception than an explanation of the distinct roles of singular term and

[1]There is now a considerable literature on the question of monsters in natural language, which I will further consider only briefly here; but see Higginbotham (outline ms., 2012) for some details.

predicate could be given to someone who lacked the notion of an object, or predication.[2] Then for, say, (5) we might propose (6):

(5) I am sitting down.

(6) If u is an utterance of (the syntactic structure Σ for) 'I am sitting down', and the speaker s of u refers with her utterance of the word 'I' therein to $s(u)$, then u is true if and only if $s(u)$ is sitting down.

At just this point, however, Castañeda's examples make themselves felt. I see someone in a mirror, whom I fail to recognize to be myself. I say, "He looks funny," with demonstrative 'he', and the truth condition that the object of reference x looks funny. Realizing at last that I am looking at myself, I say, "I look funny." But the truth condition of *that* is just the same; for I am the thing x to which I referred by saying, "He looks funny." In what sense, then, did I acquire new knowledge when I realized, "That's me?" Well, doubtless the reference of 'he' was secured through a way in which the object was presented to me; and my reference (in thought) to myself is as the subject of the state that I am in with respect to that thought. As subject of the thinking I am, so to speak, the *center* of the thought.

The view that I sketched above may be contrasted with that of David Lewis (1979). His account of first-personal belief etc. is cast in terms of his conception of modality, according to which no individual can occupy more than one possible world. This feature of his views is, however, inessential, and I will therefore take the liberty of "translating" it into the framework of Intensional Logic (IL), itself a higher-order generalization of Kripke's model theory for modalities. Lewis urges two points: (i) belief about oneself is "self-ascription of a property;" and (ii) belief *de re* rests on belief "under a description."[3] In his framework, a property is just a set of possible individuals (because each individual determines a world). In IL, this will not suffice; but λ-abstraction can pull out properties, so that the property of being φ, for example, is just $\hat{}(\lambda x)\ \varphi(x)$, or the function that, for each world w, maps objects x that are φ in w to Truth, and others to Falsehood. To inhabit a world is to exist there, a notion captured by a logical constant E whose intension yields, for each w, Truth for those individuals in the domain $D(w)$ of w and Falsehood for all other possible individuals. So: to self-ascribe the property of inhabiting a possible world where one is φ is to self-ascribe (7):

(7) $\hat{}(\lambda x)\ (E(x)\ \&\ \varphi(x))$

---

2 On this theme, see also Kripke (200[illegible]).

3 Lewis (1979: 539 *passim*).

Belief in ordinary propositions goes along for the ride, as in Lewis: so one who believes that snow is white self-ascribes (8):

(8) $\hat{}(\lambda x)$ ($E(x)$ & snow is white)

Belief *de se* really is just "about a thing," namely oneself. Belief *de re*, however, is a manner of speaking: for a thing y to be such that one believes (self-ascribes) $\hat{}(\lambda x)$ $(E(x)$ & $\varphi(y))$ is for there to be an appropriate description δ such that one believes (self-ascribes) $\hat{}(\lambda x)$ $(E(x)$ & $\varphi(\delta))$. In my toy example above, the description would be "the person in the mirror," or something of the sort (that description itself contains indexicals, but we might hope for them to be eliminated, or else made to depend just upon the subject of belief).

Evidently, with this apparatus we can distinguish the belief that he looks funny (the man in the mirror, that is) from the belief about myself that I look funny, and characterize what I come to believe when I come to believe what I would express by saying, "That's me." The latter would amount to self-ascription of the property of being an x such that the so-and-so=x, where the description 'the so-and-so' recovers the conceptual content through which I refer to the subject as 'he'. The description is not eliminable, even if *de re* representation of thought is not a manner of speaking: where the person Higginbotham is the so-and-so, I would (insofar as sane) throughout the day have self-ascribed the property of being that person; that cannot be what I learned when I realized it was me in the mirror.

Lewis makes much of the sense in which those who believe they (themselves) are F believe "the same," in the strong sense of being numerically the same. He held that psychological states must be states "of the head" if they are to play their proper roles of causes and effects of other states and of actions. Similar reflections lead him to conclude that linguistic meaning and what a person understands by a sentence must come apart, as in the case of one who has imperfect knowledge of meaning (something that is not assumed here).

It would appear, however, that ordinary explanations of action often speak of distinct beliefs among those who believe, as we say, the same thing. Both John and Bill believe their children are wonderful. That's why John buys Mary, and Bill buys Susan, an ice cream. But these are different actions. Of course we can say that John and Bill both self-ascribe the property of having wonderful children, but that is hardly necessary for the explanation.

Finally, the distinction Lewis makes between *de re* belief about oneself and self-ascription of a property, a version of a case made notorious in Kaplan (1977), would survive even if talk of properties were abandoned. Lewis considers:

> ...watching is a relation of acquaintance. I watch myself in a reflecting

> glass, unaware that I am watching myself. I ascribe to myself, under the description "the one I am watching," the property of wearing pants that are on fire. I therefore believe *de re* of the one I am watching—that is, myself—that his pants are on fire. But I do not self-ascribe the property of wearing pants that are on fire. Very soon I will, but not yet. So self-ascription isn't quite the same thing as ascription, *de re*, to oneself (Lewis (1979: 543)).

But this argument presupposes that ascription *de re* to oneself *must* be seen as in other cases; that is, as resting upon a conceptual grip on the *res* in question. If that assumption were abandoned, then we would have a rather different outcome: belief *de re* that is primitively about oneself would be the only genuinely *de re* belief there is; and in all other cases the conceptual background would have to be supplied. So in Lewis's example one would first of all believe just that the pants of the man one is watching are on fire, and the transition to "My pants are on fire" would follow my realization that *x*'s pants are on fire, a *de re* belief that is directly about me=*x*.[4]

I have now canvassed three distinct accounts of the alleged peculiarity of first-person speech and thought: (i) the one I have defended elsewhere, according to which there is indeed a special way (namely, as self-conscious subject) that one is presented to oneself in using the first person; (ii) Lewis's account, which distinguishes property-belief (uniquely about oneself) from belief in propositions; and (iii) a hypothetical view that distinguishes the first person by making it truly bare of descriptive content. To these one may add the skeptical view; namely, that the *de se* is a kind of illusion, fostered by an attempt to recapture the indexical source of reference in a report of what is said or thought.[5] I will, however, not attempt to answer the skepticism here.[6]

We have seen that each of (i)-(iii) above can distinguish the cases that Castañeda made notorious. A point that is notable, however, and that it appears must be covered by any account of the first person, is what Shoemaker (1968) and elsewhere called *immunity to error through misidentification* (hereafter: IEM). In thinking a first-personal thought, or in making a first-personal statement, I often do not in any way *identify* myself in the

---

4 Similar considerations would apply to Lewis's case of the two gods, and others. They would also apply to Castañeda's original examples, e.g., where one fails to realize that the person one is reading about is oneself.

5 This view was suggested briefly by David Kaplan in lectures in Bielefeld, Germany in 1995, and later at the University of Oxford. As he remarked there, considerations that appear to make the first person special would also apply to other indexicals, 'now' and 'today' for instance. Below I will accept this observation, but I will not conclude, as he did, that such an extension of applications is implausible.

6 A strong answer to the skepticism comes from the existence of linguistic "monsters" in Schlenker's sense, as in a variety of languages. See Anand (2006) among others.

content of that thought or statement. In a photograph I see that the subject is smiling, and I take the subject to be myself (rightly or wrongly). I say, "I am smiling (in the photograph)." Here I have perhaps misidentified someone as myself, and could in principle be mistaken. As made notorious by Shoemaker, following in part Wittgenstein, in other cases there is no room for misidentification: if, gazing out the window, I think I see a robin, I cannot coherently wonder whether, given that I know that someone sees a robin, whether that someone is me (Shoemaker's example). Similarly, as observed in Morgan (1970) and Higginbotham (1978), and elaborated at length in Chierchia (1990), how does it happen that the contents of many "understood subjects," as the subject of the complements in (9) and (10), are necessarily first-personal?

(9) John wants [to eat a hamburger].

(10) John remembered/imagined [walking to school in the morning].

A Lewisian account of these examples would allow that, in (9), there is a kind of self-desideration of a property; likewise a kind of self-memorialization/imagining for the gerundive complements in (10). And the bargain-basement version, as in (iii) above for belief, would propose that these contexts are necessarily, and primitively *de re*. Furthermore, they must reckon with the fact that if (9) and (10) are true, then so are the results of making the subject explicit, as in (11) and (12):

(11) John wants [himself to eat a hamburger].

(12) John remembered/imagined [himself walking to school in the morning].[7]

Finally, the phenomenon of IEM arises for these cases as well. It cannot seem to John that he wants to eat a hamburger, or remembers or imagined walking to school in the morning, whilst in fact it's someone else that he wants to eat the hamburger, or someone else that is remembering or imagining (of course he can wonder whether he is remembering or perhaps only imagining, but not whether, given that he is remembering, whether the memory is his).[8] So he must know that the his desire, memory, or imaginative content concerns himself, without having identified himself as the object of concern. According to the view (i) for speech and thought, elaborated for these cases, this happens because he is given to himself just as *the subject s(e) of the higher state* of desire, memory, or imagination. The ex-

[7] The converses are not true, as observed in examples going back to Castañeda, and to Fodor (1975).

[8] I consider a couple of exceptional cases in Higginbotham (2010), but do not discuss them here.

tension of IEM from first-personal speech in response to a present perception to a variety of cases involving propositional attitudes and other states or activities of mind is then immediate.

There are, I believe, other advantages to the view (i). One is that (unlike Lewis) we can speak as needed of "ascription of a property to an object" for *any* object, not just oneself (or, correlatively, of genuine *de re* belief etc. that does not rest upon a conceptual content; or, to the extent that it does, need not be individuated by such content); I see no reason to deny that we have many such beliefs. A second point, to which I advert in closing, is that the account enables us to deal with the embedded *overt* first person, found in some languages, without resorting to anything more than an elaboration of anaphoric reference.

Schlenker (2003) partly concerns a well-known phenomenon in the language Amharic: the first-person pronoun, when embedded under the equivalent of 'say', refers not to the speaker, but to the subject whose speech is reported. I reproduce this phenomenon using a hypothetical word 'Ĭ'. An utterance u of the sentence 'Ĭ am F' by s means, as in English, that the speaker $s(u)$ is F. But an utterance of (13) means—and means *de se*—that John said that he himself was a hero:

(13) John said that Ĭ am a hero.

Schlenker, Anand and others have been at pains to show that these contexts are not quotational. In their preferred semantic exposition, according to which abstract contexts are parameters for assignments of reference and truth conditions, accommodating the "monster" 'Ĭ' calls for a shift in those parameters in the course of a single utterance. With the view that I am advocating, however, a very different course is open.

Suppose it is right to say that 'I' is to be used to refer to the speaker $s(u)$ of an utterance u. The utterance itself is the element bearing truth conditions; and utterances are actions. So when I utter a sentence as in (14) there is an existentially quantified event position in the main Verb 'say', as in (15) (ignoring Tense, and letting the complement clause stand as is):

(14) John said that p.

(15) $(\exists u)$ Say(John, that p, u).

If the complement 'p' should contain the first person, then utterance of (14), call it u' refers to me as speaker of u', exactly as if the first person were not embedded. But with 'Ĭ' things are different. Unlike the rule of use (16) for 'I', the rule of use of 'Ĭ' is as in (17):

(16) 'I' is to be used, for any u, to the speaker s of u.

(17) 'Ĭ' refers to the speaker s of the utterance of the clause with which it is in construction.

(13) now comes out as (18):

(18) ($\exists u$) Say(John, that $s(u)$ is a hero, u).

It follows that, even though the speaker of (13) is not quoting John, his speech must have been *de se*. Similarly for English (9), which is now as in (19):

(19) ($\exists e$) Want(John, that $s(e)$ eat a hamburger, e).

There are further applications of the view presented here, to embedded Tense amongst others, that space will not permit. However, I do wish to grant a concession that may well be appropriate, and which may vindicate part of Lewis's views, to which I have offered the above alternative.

The concession is this. Evidently an account of the first person in speech and thought in terms of higher-order subjects is appropriate only for self-conscious creatures, who are moreover keeping track of themselves as they go about their business: my desire for a hamburger causes me to go to the neighborhood joint and order a hamburger, all the while thinking, expressing distinct first-personal thoughts, and moving my body in various ways, that are nevertheless all of them coordinated toward my goal. I am the center of those thoughts and utterances, the assumption of the identity of the subjects of which gets things done. We can, however, consider the possibility of thoughts that have *no* center; i.e., of perceptions of scenes, or rumblings in the stomach, that are not referred to myself, or any other object. These would show IEM, but in a different way: there would be no subject to be identified at all. There could not, if I am right, be speech of this kind; for speech is deliberate action. But there could perhaps be thinking of this sort. For this reason, I have not claimed that all thought is self-conscious.

In the current state of the cognitive sciences it is an open question how far to attribute conceptual content to some of the processes that guide us and other animals, let alone how far to attribute consciousness of an enduring self in the planning and execution of prudential action. For this reason, I would not routinely describe all of our ordinary first-personal attributions of thought to any special way at all in which we or those animals are presented to ourselves.

References

Anand, P. 2006. *De De Se*. Unpublished doctoral dissertation, Massachusetts Institute of Technology, Cambridge, Massachusetts.

Burge, T. 1974. 'Demonstrative Constructions, Reference, and Truth'. *The Journal of Philosophy* **71**. pp. 205-223.

Castañeda, H-N. 1966. "'He': A Study in the Logic of Self-Consciousness." *Ratio* **8**. pp. 130-157.

Chierchia, G. 1990. 'Anaphora and Attitudes *De Se*', in R. Bartsch *et al.* (eds.), *Language in Action*. Dordrecht, Holland: Foris Publications. pp. 1-31.

Fodor, J. 1975. *The Language of Thought*. New York: Crowell.

Folescu, M. and Higginbotham, J. 2012. "Two Takes on the *de se*," in S. Prosser and F. Recanati (eds.), *Immunity to Error Through Misidentification*. Cambridge: Cambridge University Press. pp. 46-61.

Higginbotham, J. 1980. "Pronouns and Bound Variables." *Linguistic Inquiry* **11**, 4. pp. 679-708.

Higginbotham, J. 2003. "Remembering, Imagining, and the First Person." Alex Barber (ed.), *Epistemology of Language*. Oxford: Oxford University Press, 2003. pp. 496-533.

Higginbotham, J. 2010. "On Words and Thoughts About Oneself." Isidora Stojanovich, François Recanati, and Neftali Villanueva (eds.), *Context-Dependence, Perspective, and Relativity*. Berlin: Mouton de Gruyter. pp. 253-282.

Higginbotham, J. 2012. "Embedded Indexicality." Ms., University of Southern California.

Kaplan, D. 1977. *Demonstratives*. Published with afterthoughts in *Themes From Kaplan*, Joseph Almog, John Perry, and Howard Wettstein (eds.), 1989, pp. 481-614. Oxford: Oxford University Press.

Kripke, S. 2011. "The First Person." Kripke, S., *Philosophical Troubles*. New York: Oxford University Press. pp. 292-321.

Lewis, D. 1979. "Attitudes *de dicto* and *de se*." *The Philosophical Review* **88**. pp. 513-543.

Morgan, J. L. 1970. "On the Criterion of Identity for Noun Phrase Deletion." Papers from the Sixth Regional Meeting, Chicago Linguistic Society. Chicago Linguistic Society, 1970. pp. 380-389.

Schlenker, P. 2003. "A Plea for Monsters." *Linguistics and Philosophy* **26**. pp. 29-120.

Shoemaker, S. 1968. 'Self-Reference and Self-Awareness'. *The Journal of Philosophy* 65. pp. 555-567.

3

Contextualism and Minimalism on *De Se* Belief Ascription

KASIA M. JASZCZOLT

'The indexical fact may have to be taken as primitive.'
Chalmers (1996: 85)

1 Introduction

Early discussions of *de se* belief ascription focused on the status of the objects of attitudes and stemmed out of consolidated attempts to exorcise propositions and introduce properties and 'relations to oneself' instead (Lewis 1979; Perry 1979). Propositions were revindicated via various rescue plans (Cresswell 1985; Kaplan 1989a; Crimmins and Perry 1989; Schiffer 1992; Perry 2001) but the problem of compositional semantics of belief reports, including *de se* attributions, has remained a testing ground for semantic theories to this day. In this paper I propose to look at *de se* belief reports in the light of the current debate between minimalism and contextualism in semantics. I argue that the differences in the reference-securing functions between *de re* and *de se* occur on the level of semantic content itself where the latter has to be understood as on contextualist accounts. The contextualist orientation is required for the essential ingredient of self-awareness to be included in the semantic representation. This representation is regarded as compositional in the contextualist sense of compositionality of meaning. In the course of the discussion I propose some amendments to Chierchia's (1989) claim of the systematicity of retrieval of the cognitive access to oneself from the types of grammatical expressions, and discuss the

Attitudes De Se: Linguistics, Epistemology, Metaphysics.
Neil Feit and Alessandro Capone (eds.).

different roles that the concepts of self-ascription, self-attribution, and self-awareness play in a contextualist semantic theory of *de se* belief reports. I conclude that expression of self-awareness does not require a specific type of grammatical marker in English such as 'I' in *oratio recta* or (coreferential) '(s)he' in *oratio obliqua*, neither do such expressions come with guaranteed expression of self-awareness. There doesn't seem to be lexical or grammatical 'peg' to hang the property of expressing self-awareness on. Sometimes the property is externalized through the grammar, at other times by default interpretations of this grammatical form, and at yet others by pragmatic resolution of the truly underspecified representation. Contextualist framework and pragmatic compositionality embraced by Default Semantics (Jaszczolt 2005, 1010) allow us to provide for this diversity.

2 Semantics vis-à-vis Intuitions on *De Se*

Noticing that guests are arriving at a faculty drinks reception and neither the glasses nor the drinks are in sight, I utter (1).

(1) The person who agreed to organize the drinks is to blame.

A few minutes later, I realize that at a faculty meeting a couple of months ago I agreed to organize the drinks reception. Now I correct myself, utter (2) with considerable embarrassment, and rush to remedy the situation.

(2) I am to blame. I completely forgot I was put in charge.

A semanticist of a referentialist orientation would let his/her theory pass unscathed when faced with such a social fiasco. The use of language, the things we do by employing language for acts of communication, are the business for pragmatics and sociolinguistics, possibly also for cognitive science. A semanticist is responsible for what Perry (2001) calls the referential, or 'official', content.

There are good arguments in favor of referentialism. Natural languages are systems with an accountable structure and a fairly stable lexicon. The main task of a theory of meaning should be to employ information available in the system, such as rules of functional application and lexical content, to explain how meaning is composed, using in the process the idea of reference to explain the meanings of the parts by means of applicable extensions (such as 'Stalnaker-restricted' sets of possible worlds). This approach works for a considerable number of situations where the meaning of the sentence and the intended meaning of the utterance of it do not diverge. Perry (2001: 121) surmises that referential content could be the 'default' kind of content, allowing for it to be overridden sometimes. This can happen in a case where a speaker uses a 'shortcut' in the form of an indexical expression; the shortcut has to be unravelled and the referential link established.

Or does it have to be? There are two possible ways to argue that it does not. One comes from within the kind of semantics envisaged above, namely the semantics that pertains to the language system (as contrasted with the use of this system in communication). When the sentence contains an indexical expression, for example 'I' in (2) above, it is arguably the linguistic meaning of the indexical that such a semantics should be concerned with. If so, the referential link remains unresolved and the semantics relies on the linguistic meaning of 'I' (Kaplan's (1989a) character), namely 'the person who is uttering this sentence'. This stance comes close to the most radical form of minimalism advocated by Bach (2004, 2006) as far as the content is concerned.[1] The other comes from a cognitive take on semantics. Addressees can assign different kinds of referent, and also different kinds of information, to the first-person singular pronoun. Some examples are listed in (3).

(3) a. the person who is just talking to me whoever she may be
b. Kasia Jaszczolt (i.e. the correct referent)
c. the person who agreed to organize the drinks reception (whatever her name is)
d. Aly Pitts (in the case of a referential mistake)

Analogously, albeit somewhat less commonly, the speaker may think of oneself with various deficits and falsehoods incorporated in the concept of the self as in (4).

(4) a. the person who agreed to organize the drinks reception
b. the person who agreed at the meeting of the Faculty Board that Professor Brown should organize the drinks reception
c. Kasia Jaszczolt
d. Aly Pitts (in the cases of mistaken reference)

There have been various types of content proposed that semantics, with the help of pragmatics, can choose from (see e.g. Perry 2001; 2009), all of them with labels that have now been well established in pertinent discussions. At this point I am concerned with an issue that is orthogonal to this elaborate taxonomy of contents, namely with the fact that even one type of content can yield different interpretations on different occasions, as evidenced by referential mistakes of the type (3d). A cognitively accountable semantics not only has to distinguish between the information conveyed by, say, the definite description in (1) and the pronoun in (2), but it also has to distinguish among the varieties of informational content that can be carried

[1] Unlike Bach's account, however, it insists that the output of grammar be propositional. This can be achieved by dissociating truth conditions from conditions of verification (see Borg, e.g. 2004, 2007. For criticism see e.g. Recanati 2005b; Jaszczolt 2005b; Atlas 2006).

by the latter. So, when we go beyond the minimalist account invoked above, there are still various options open as to how this cognitive significance of the expression used can be captured in semantics. Substituting the referent is the least attractive option as it would, of course, conflate (1) with (2) into (5).

(5) λx [to-blame(x)] (kasia jaszczolt)

In short, when we opt for a 'pure' semantics whose aim is to explain meaning construction in a system of natural language, Kaplanesque characters may arguably suffice. When we opt for a 'cognitively real' semantics and intuitive truth conditions, the referent (correct or incorrect) is just one component of the meaning of the first-person pronoun. Even recognizing the indexicality and thereby the special status of first-person reference, it appears that reference *de se* opens up problems for a meaning theory that go far beyond the identity of reference, both for first-person expressions of belief as discussed above and for *de se* belief attributions addressed in what follows.

Kaplan's content-character distinction is therefore best regarded not as affording a choice between minimal linguistic meaning of 'I' and the referent. Instead, it is best regarded as availing the dual perspective on content itself: the referent is fixed for the context, understood as an index consisting of various pertinent parameters, but it can also be fixed otherwise for a different index and different values for the parameters. The indexical expression brings with it two kinds of cognitive significance: availability of the referent and the potential availability of other referents for different indices. Both are equally important for semantic representation. This idea is further exploited in two-dimensional semantics and in particular Stalnaker's (e.g. 1978, 2011) propositional concept: the proposition that is true at a world and context if and only if what is expressed in this context and world is true there. In addition, it acquires there an intentional perspective. While Kaplan's context (index), at least as presented in *Demonstratives* (1989a), is a metaphysical concept, Stalnaker's context is founded on presuppositions that underlie intentional communication; context is understood as common background, the so-called context-set, that is a set of those possible worlds which are compatible with what is *presupposed by the speaker* in a situation of discourse. Normally the presuppositions in the speaker's context-set coincide with those in the addressee's context-set, the context is nondefective and discourse proceeds on the justified understanding of shared mutual assumptions.[2] In what follows I attempt to give due credit to both of these aspects of meaning of indexicals, the constant and the variable, the linguis-

[2] NB, in *Afterthoughts*, Kaplan's (1989b) idea of context undergoes a transformation in view of the introduction of the directing intention. See Perry 2009 and Jaszczolt 2012b, 2012c.

tic and the referential. I provide some arguments in support of the view that the concept of *de se*, pertaining to belief expressions and attributions alike, is ineliminable from any kind of approach to meaning, be it minimalist or contextualist. In Section 3 I present a contextualist approach to *de se* ascription that is compatible with deriving the default assumption that self-awareness has been expressed from the grammar of the relevant expression, and make a case for a contextualist analysis of a Default-Semantics type. Section 4 assesses the utility of minimalist accounts of *de se* and concludes with pointing out that *de se* is entrenched in both minimalist and contextualist enterprises, irrespective of the status of their represented objects and their aims. Section 5 offers an example of a representation of *de se* reports as well as *de se* self-attributions in the radically contextualist framework of Default Semantics and makes a case for a 'post-contextual' grammar and thereby for contextualist compositionality. I conclude with observations on the persistence of self-awareness and the plausibility of a semantically ineradicable *de se*.

3 Contextualist Perspectives on *De Se*

3.1 Rich Semantic Content: A Grammar-Fuelled Contextualism?

Firstly, by contextualism I shall mean the broadly understood idea that a semantic representation, or at least the truth-conditionally evaluable representation if the controversial label 'semantic' is to be avoided, comprises diverse aspects of utterance meaning. It is in this light that the title of this section has to be read to avoid a seeming oxymoron. For the purpose of this paper, let us focus on two orientations in contextualism: free, top-down modulation, allowing for unarticulated constituents (e.g. Recanati 2004, 2005b, 2010; henceforth FM for 'free modulation') and the hidden-indexical theory according to which the additions to the sentence meaning are traceable to the logical form (e.g. Schiffer 1977, 1992, 1996, henceforth HIT; also e.g. Crimmins and Perry's 1989 'notion'). The latter has clear affinities with Jason Stanley's (e.g. 2002; Stanley and Szabó 2000) more radical view that all truth-conditional effects of context can be traced to logical form, and what Recanati calls unarticulated constituents can in fact obtain an explanation through binding on the level of logical form. Belief ascription triggered by sentence (6) and represented in (7) obtains the representations in (7a) and (7b) respectively on these contextualist accounts.[3]

(6) John Perry: I am making a mess.

(7) John Perry believes that he is making a mess.

---

[3] It has to be pointed out that my definition of contextualism is more inclusive than Recanati's (e.g. 2004, 2005b) who excludes all accounts that trace pragmatic aspects of meaning to the logical form.

(7a) FM: John Perry believes of himself that he is making a mess.

(7b) HIT: There is a contextually salient mode of presentation *m* of a type Φ* and John Perry believes of John Perry that he is making a mess, under *m*.

→ John Perry believes of himself that he is making a mess.[4]

It is evident from the above that as far as the truth-conditional *content* is concerned, (7b), after filling in the *m* argument, collapses to (7a). But what is it exactly that makes *m* adopt the value of a self-referring type? It seems that the simplest solution is to rely on the semantic properties of the first-person pronoun and instead of, as it is common practice in a variety of referential semantics, granting it a role of a slot-holder for a referent, endow it with the special self-referring semantic function. If we do so and thereby endow the pronoun with this particular ego-centered function, we find that we can represent the meaning as it is normally ascribed to utterances of this type by speakers and addressees. Attempts at cancelling this self-attribution for situations where (6) does not apply are indeed rare and cumbersome as exemplified in (8).

(8) John Perry believes that he is making a mess but he doesn't realize it is him.

In other words, 'he' functions here by default as what Castañeda (1966, 1967) called a 'quasi-indicator' and what became to be known as a 'quasi-indexical' or 'indirect reflexive pronoun'. Analogously, on Jason Stanley's (e.g. 2002) account, logical form will be indexed with this ego-centered function. We obtain in this way context-dependent propositions and at the same time a compositional semantic structure.[5]

To sum up the argument so far, FM and HIT give the same overall rich result for the truth-conditional content whereby self-ascription is its part and parcel. But these are not the only ways to arrive at the rich content that incorporates information about self-awareness. We could attempt to ascribe the self-reference in (6), as well as, arguably, expression of self-awareness in *de se* ascription in (7) to the grammar, and acknowledge that it is the grammar that produces the self-referring function. However, there is a difficulty with this option that was already pointed out by Kratzer (2009), namely that pronouns can be ambiguous between a referential and a bound-variable interpretation as in (9) or, even more conspicuously, in (10).

(9) *I*'m the only one around here who can take care of *my* children.

---

[4] See fn 18 for a summary of the relevant scenario from Perry (1979).

[5] See also King 2007 on the defense of context-dependent propositions as values of sentences.

(from Kratzer 2009: 188).

(10) Only *I* admitted what *I* did wrong.[6]

This difficulty, however, is not widespread in that bound-variable uses are rare, restricted, and differ substantially from language to language. For example, in Polish, the bound-variable 'I' ('ja') would normally be signalled by adding 'sole' ('jeden') as in (11).

(11) Tylko ja jeden przyznałem się do
only *1Sg* sole*SgMNom* admit*1SgPastM* *Refl* to
błędu.
mistake*SgMGen*

Similarly, in (9), 'my children' becomes translated by a reflexive 'own children' ('swoje dzieci') as in (12).

(12) Tylko ja jedna tutaj potrafię
Only *1Sg* sole*SgFNom* here can*1SgPres*
zajmować się swoimi dziećmi.
care*Inf* *Refl* *ReflPronPlInstr* child*PlInstr*

Kratzer tentatively suggests that bound-variable pronouns may underlyingly be referential pronouns whose meaning can be accounted for through context-shifting. Alternatively, they are unspecified and obtain the meaning through feature transmission from their binders in functional heads. So the theory of the grammatical foundation of self-reference can still be defended, at least as the default meaning assignment. An even stronger line of defense would be to point out that it may not be *self-reference* but rather information about *self-awareness* that grammar conveys. In Kratzer's examples (viz. 9), self-awareness is conveyed by a relation between a parent (whoever this may be) and his/her own offspring. Any attempts to cancel this relation in a discourse would be cumbersome. Similarly, although more contentiously, (7) reports on self-awareness in view of the anaphoric link between 'he' and 'John Perry' that can be defended as a universal tendency realized by using different devices and with various degrees of predictability in various languages, to witness only logophoric pronouns and what is analyzed in

---

[6] NB the bound-variable use is more pronounced in the following example with the second-person pronoun, in that the first instance of 'you' is normally interpreted as 'one' or 'a person':

'Only *you* can eat what *you* cook.'

meaning that when one cooks food, only the person who cooked it can eat it (from Kratzer 2009: 188).

generative grammar as an empty category PRO. This argument gained a lot of support in the literature. I come back to it in Section 3.2.

The main argument of this section is this. Truth-conditional content can be construed generously or sparingly; it can be contextualist or minimalist. But it is a mistake to conflate contextualism with free contextual modulation and minimalism with the output of grammar that is indifferent to the *de se/de re about oneself* alternation. Both contextualism and minimalism may allow for construals on which grammar provides information about self-awareness as a component of the semantic content. The discussion between the defenders of free modulation unconstrained by grammar and the indexicalists of various orientations is of no particular interest to the semantics of *de se* belief expressions and *de se* belief reports; it is the absence or presence of the component of meaning that signals self-awareness that is of interest. Its allocation to grammar is a matter of an agreement as to what we want the grammar to do: capture strong tendencies or capture patterns that underdetermine meaning. Arguably, grammar is post-contextual, just as concepts are post-contextual. There is increasing experimental evidence to the effect that the concepts are constructed for the purpose of a particular exchange, in what late Wittgenstein (1953) would call a language game. Larson *et al.* (2009), for example, demonstrated that what subjects consider to be literal meaning has no clear reflection in the categories of sentence meaning or generalized conversational implicatures but is instead a matter of gradation that cuts across Gricean components of meaning$_{NN}$. What it means is that the lexicon gives rise to a variety of context-dependent concepts and it is plausible to hypothesize that these concepts already contain the pragmatic elements that would otherwise have to be ascribed to free modulation or to hidden indices of the logical form. If word meaning is indeed as free as late Wittgenstein has it, then the onus is on grammar to generate the default anaphoric links and default 'characters' for contents. *De se* ends up as a default interpretation that is horrendously difficult to override in conversation, both in self-ascriptions (6) and in third-person ascriptions (7): 'but I didn't know that it was me' and 'but he didn't know it was him' for (6) and (7) respectively are notoriously marked and best regarded as repair strategies.

Naturally, one has to account first for the possibility of non-coreferential readings. But there is a strong tendency for coreference and this can be explained via van der Sandt's (1992) heuristics for local accommodation that lay down strict principles for the search for an antecedent along the projection line, whereby 'she' in (13) repeated below picks up the closest suitable antecedent.

(13) Kasia believes that she is to blame.

Such 'contextual binding' is of course cancellable, but again, it is cancellable with some difficulty, not unlike the cancellation of the presumed conveyance of self-awareness in the case of first-person singular pronoun. Non-self-awareness 'he' in (7) is, on the other hand, natural but marked and always triggered by context. While extending the concept of grammar to cater for such strong tendencies, and for detaching binding from c-commanding, is perfectly legitimate, there do not seem to be good arguments for such an extension. I shall therefore proceed having given this observation the status of a theoretical assumption. In short, on the hypothesis entertained and defended here, grammar delivers contextualist default contents.

3.2 Reports *De Se*: A Contextualist Syntax-Pragmatics Mix

Under the umbrella problem of the semantics of self-referring there is a more specific issue of the relationship between *de se* and *de re* belief reports. The most radical and at the same time the most counterintuitive view comes from what we can call the syntactic ambiguity faction. According to this orientation, sentence (13) can have different logical forms, depending on whether the holder of the belief holds a belief *de se*, as in (2) above, or merely *de re* about oneself, as in (1) above.

(13) Kasia believes that she is to blame.

According to Percus and Sauerland (2003: 238), the logical form contains the so-called 'variables over concept-generators'. On the *de re* reading, the complement of 'believes' in (13) denotes a function from such concept-generators to a proposition. On the *de se* reading, following Chierchia (1989), they propose that the complement of 'believes' denotes a function from concept-generators to properties, achieved via type-shifting. This brings the proposal in line with Lewis's (1979) and Perry's (1979) seminal concept of belief *de se* as self-ascription of properties.[7] Or, as Abbott (2010: 189) puts it, the meaning of 'believe' subsumes the indexicality of these cases and we can represent (13) simply as (14).

(14) Bel (k, $^\wedge\lambda x$ [to-blame (x)])

The main reason for proposing this rather complicated move involving type-shifting is to bring the *de se* interpretation of pronouns like 'she' in (13) in line with the behavior of other referring expressions.[8] Chierchia (1989: 28) points out that the cognitive access to oneself is

[7] Where a property is understood as a class of centered worlds – the idea also used in DRT accounts discussed below.

[8] See also Schlenker (2011), who addresses the question as to whether 'she' can have a *de se* reading.

> systematically excluded from the interpretation of (non-pronominal) referential expressions. It is systematically present in the interpretation of overt pronouns. It is systematically and unambiguously associated with the interpretation of PRO the null subject of infinitives and gerunds. It is associated with the interpretation of long-distance reflexives[9] (at least in some languages).

This evidence leads him to the hypothesis that the cognitive access to the self is present in the semantics of English. But in order to endorse the irreducibility of *de se*, one has to win some other arguments as well. First, there is the methodological principle of Modified Occam's Razor (Grice 1978) which provides a good reason for searching for unary accounts and resorting to ambiguities as the last resort. Next, cognitive access to oneself is not, contrary to what Chierchia says, so 'systematically' excluded from the interpretation of non-pronominal expressions. Referring to oneself by means of a description or a name is not uncommon, and is attested as a natural stage of language development in children, utilized in parent-child speech, as exemplified in (15)-(16).

(15) Sammy wants a biscuit.

(16) Mummy will be with you in a moment.

Moreover, the boundary between pronominal and non-pronominal expressions is blurred in languages with honorifics where a common noun (e.g. Thai 'mouse') may evolve into a grammatical function of the first-person pronoun, but retaining the sense of self-denigration which clearly comes from some of the features associated with the concept of that small, insignificant rodent.[10] Further, the 'systematic presence' of the access to the self in the interpretation of pronouns also yields to fuzzy intuitions and fuzzy boundaries in that it is not, to use Chierchia's words, 'systematic *and* unambiguous'. It is possible to come up with scenarios on which one can report on one's beliefs *de re* about oneself using first-person pronoun, and thereby use it without the cognitive access at the base level of beliefs, but only with cognitive access at the higher level of reflecting on the belief in the report. This is exemplified in (17) and, indeed, is often exploited in sitcoms that commonly use the model of *quid-pro-quo*. The subscripts t_1 and t_2

[9] Long-distance reflexives, such as Chinese *ziji*, Japanese *zibun*, or Korean *caki*, are not specified for person, number of gender (have no φ-features) and can have many functions such as subject, object, indirect object, or possessor. For example,

Takasi-ga	*zibun*-ga	tensai	da	to	omotteiru.
Takasi-SUBJ	self-SUBJ	genius	is	COMP	think

Takasi$_1$ thinks that he$_1$ is a genius.

(adapted from Huang 2000: 191).

[10] This honorific is used by women, the, alas, still underprivileged part of society.

stand for the time of the speaker noticing that there were no drinks prepared and the time of realization by the speaker that she herself should have prepared them, respectively. Normally, first-person pronoun does not relativize to times, as predicted by Kaplan's account. On some heavily marked occasions, however, this relativization seems possible and t_n becomes dissociated from other temporal indices as in the case of t_1 below.

(17) I_{t1+t2} believe I_{t1+t2} should have prepared the drinks party. In a way I_{t1} also believed that I_{t1+t2} should have done it when I_{t1} walked into the room. The fact is, the person appointed by the Faculty Board should have done it and as I_{t1} later realized I_{t1+t2} was this person.

So, juxtaposing two temporal perspectives suffices to blur the intuitions on the access to the self that is arguably encoded in 'I'. This access has been assumed without questioning by direct reference theorists with Kaplan at the forefront. But although Kaplan (1989a: 491) is right in pointing out that uttering 'I' and pointing at someone else is 'irrelevance or madness or what?', he does not allow for the uses in (17) which superimpose the brain state of the ego as the reporter onto the brain state of the ego as the holder of the belief. This is quite a different kind of a 'monster' context.[11,12]

Example (17) demonstrates that the distinctions we have been operating with so far are insufficiently finely-grained. The concept of the self enters the debate in several different guises; there is *self-reference* (reference to oneself), *self-attribution* (of mental states, used here interchangeably with

---

[11] NB, the Polish equivalent of (17), adjusted for sociopragmatic adequacy (i.e. made to sound natural in a Polish conversation), is also feasible albeit strongly marked:

Wiem$_{t1+t2}$,	że	to	ja$_{t1+t2}$	powinnam była$_{t1+t2}$
know*1SgPres*	that	*Dem*	I	should*1SgFPast*

przygotować	te	drinki.	W	pewnym
prepare*Inf*	this*AccPl*	drink*PlMAcc*	In	certain*SgMInstr*

sensie,	wtedy	też	wiedziałam$_{t1}$,	ponieważ
sense*SgMInstr*	then	also	know*1SgFemPast*	because

miała	je	przygotować	osoba
be-to*SgFPast*	*theyNMAcc*	prepare*Inf*	person*SgFNom*

wybrana	przez	Radę	Wydziału,	a	to
selected	by	Board*SgFAcc*	Faculty*SgMGen*	and	*Dem*

ja$_{t1+t2}$	byłam	tą	osobą.
I*Nom*	be*SgFPast*	Dem*SgFInstr*	person*SgFInstr*

See also example (26a) and fn 20.

[12] See also Schlenker 2003 for 'monster contexts'.

self-ascription[13]), and *self-awareness* (the mental state of first-person awareness). The concept of self-reference is of limited use in the current considerations in that it is so malleable that it will not serve the necessary explanatory function; one can refer to oneself without consciously ascribing properties to oneself, or, alternatively, we can construe a theoretical term of self-reference as necessitating self-awareness. All depends here on our theoretical assumptions. But self-attribution and self-awareness are crucial in the discussion, and so is a differentiation between them. (17) exemplifies the latter distinction perfectly: self-ascription can go ahead with the index limited to t_1, whereas self-awareness cannot; 'I didn't realize that I was that person' shows how we can attribute certain states to oneself without attributing self-awareness at the time. The question that remains is, which one of these concepts does grammar help us reach as the default scenario: the 'self-awareness I' or the 'self-ascription I'?[14] Further discussion of Chierchia will suggest that it is likely to be the first alternative.

Chierchia also uses an argument from PRO with gerundive and infinitival constructions. From the perspective of a pragmatics-rich, contextualist semantics, his claims deserve a closer scrutiny. In (18), the father can report that 11-year old Lidia wants to be a scientist because he observed her on various occasions playing with her 'crazy science' kit or attending events for kids at the Cambridge Science Festival.

(18) Lidia wants to be a scientist.

The fact that the child herself has never considered the question of her future profession does not seem to invalidate the utterance and thereby, on the contextualist construal, does not seem to make (18) false. In other words, there is no (19) in the context, either as an utterance or as a propositional thought, and therefore no 'I'-reference, that underlies (18) on this scenario.

$_x$(19) Lidia: I want to be a scientist.

Equally, the most natural interpretation of (21) is that Lidia's mother wants her daughter (rather than, implausibly, herself) to be the smartest kid. Analogous to (18)-(19), the self-reference and self-ascription of the kind 'I want to be the smartest kid' do not necessarily figure behind (20). Neither do they carry through to (21), while the assigned referent does.

(20) Lidia wants to be the smartest kid in the class.

---

13 Strictly speaking, it seems that an even more finely-grained classification is possible whereby self-attribution refers to attributing mental states to oneself, while self-ascription refers to the property of linguistic expressions of ascribing such properties.

14 Small capital 'I' stands for a concept (*ego*).

(21) Lidia's mother wants what Lidia wants and that's why she is buying her lots of academic books.

At the first glance examples of this kind make a fairly strong case against Chierchia's and Percus and Sauerland's claims that the special status of *de se* is encoded in the semantics. If that were the case, the above examples would have to rely on some mechanism that makes *de se* attribution independent of self-ascription associated with the standard use of first-person singular pronoun. This would not, however, carry through to the possibility of dissociating *de se* from *self-awareness*: while Lidia may not have formulated a propositional thought to the effect of her being a scientist, there is no ambiguity in the 'want PRO' case analogous to that between *de re* and *de se* cases of Perry's spilt sugar scenario, or of my forgotten drinks scenario of (1)-(2). In other words, there is no 'that person wants to be a scientist' vs. 'I want to be a scientist' alternative; there is merely a strongly or weakly articulated awareness of one's own wants. Self-awareness thus seems to be the concept that we should pursue as semantically relevant, in preference to self-ascription/self-attribution.

There are ample possibilities of construing an adequate contextualist representation of the self-awareness reading of first-person belief statements and, of the FM type, corresponding *de se* reports. A *de se* belief is then construed as a *de re* belief about oneself that includes conscious awareness of the self's identity with the *res*. The standard underdetermination view holds that syntax generates logical forms that are underspecified as to the *de re* or *de se* sense, while pragmatics provides the missing aspects of intended/recovered[15] meaning. A version of this idea is for example used in Discourse Representation Theory by Maier (2009) who makes use of van der Sandt's (1992) presupposition as anaphora to derive the *de se* reading. Preliminary DRSs are underspecified as to *de re*, *de dicto* or *de se* reading and pragmatics completes the representation.

But here is where the proponents of the syntactic *de se* can rejoin. *De se* readings of (13) are common and taken for granted. *De re* that lacks self-awareness is cumbersome and heavily marked in that it normally requires a disclaimer, hedging, or a repair mechanism as in (17). Would it not be methodologically more judicious to assume that grammar produces standard readings? The supporting evidence comes from the conceptual universal of self-reference. The omission of the pronoun in pro-drop languages without introducing ambiguity as in Polish (22) supports this argument.

(22) Kasia	wie,	że	jest	winna.
Kasia*Nom*	know*3SgPres*	that	be*3SgPres*	guilty*SgFNom*

---

15 Intended by the speaker or inferred by the addressee, depending on the post-Gricean orientation. See e.g. Saul 2002 and Jaszczolt 2005a.

On the other hand, the insertion of the pronoun points to the lack of coreference as in (23). Resuming the anaphoric link can then be achieved pragmatically by the addition of an emphatic demonstrative as in (24), thereby showing that coreference is not the default reading of (23).

(23) Kasia wie, że ona jest winna.
KasiaNom know3SgPres that she be3SgPres guiltySgFNom

(24) Kasia wie, że to ona
KasiaNom know3SgPres that Dem she
jest winna.
be3SgPres guiltySgFNom

Further, the unequivocal assessment of PRO as *syntactically de se*[16], along with logophors, which Maier (2009) is happy to accept, also points in the direction of the strong syntactic foundation of the semantic representation of *de se* at large, as a universal conceptual category[17].

Let us sum up the facts so far.

1. The essence of *de se* is self-awareness, the epistemic concept of one's conscious access to oneself.
2. *De se* is either the only interpretation or the strongly preferred, unmarked interpretation of the sentences that attribute it, depending on the language, expression, and structure (cf. anaphoric pronouns, PRO, logophors).
3. Cancelling this preferred reading is a cumbersome conversational strategy.

These are to be juxtaposed with more tentative proposals argued for above:

4. Grammar plays a significant role in conveying information about self-awareness in *de se* belief expressions and belief reports.
5. Contextualist approaches to truth-conditional content are compatible with deriving some of the optional aspects of meaning, such as *de se* reading of third-person pronouns in belief reports (their 'quasi-indicators' meaning), from the grammar.
6. FM, hidden-indexicality and other forms of annotating the logical form render the same (enriched) output as far as the truth-conditional content is concerned.

---

16 See Chierchia (1989: 15) on PRO as a λ-abstractor, to handle examples such as 'The cat wanted to eat the cheese' & 'The mouse got what the cat wanted' → 'The mouse got to eat the cheese'.

17 For an introduction to logophors see Huang 2000. For a discussion on logophors and 'monster' contexts see Schlenker 2003.

It appears that if the grammar can be argued to throw up the *de se* readings, the onus of proof is on those contextualists of the FM orientation who consider self-awareness to be a free, structure-independent enrichment. Such enrichment would by the logic of the argument have to be optional. Therefore, its default status would remain conspicuously unexplained. And so would the cross-linguistic and cross-structural discrepancies in attributing *de se* thoughts.

Further, it seems to be the case that self-awareness persists across self-attribution and third-person attribution, namely reports on someone's beliefs about themselves. In situations exemplified in (2), there is only the self-awareness reading. But when uttered with past- or future-time reference, shifted from the epistemic certainty of the 'here and now', self-awareness weakens to a mere strong preference. Third-person reports share this property of a strong tendency for expressing self-awareness. It seems that this pattern pertaining to strong preferences has to be captured in the semantics of expressions of self-awareness.

What remains to be explored is this. Firstly, the contextualist outlook that has been assumed so far has to be confronted with the options available in minimalist semantics so as to assess whether the combination of syntactic foundations of *de se* with contextualism is the right way forward. This is attended to in Section 4. Next, in Section 5, I return to the favored view that *de se* is part of the semantic content, being at the same time (i) grammar-driven and (ii) optional and thereby pragmatic, along the lines proposed for a sub-set of generalized conversational implicatures by Chierchia (2004). I resume the discussion on the default status of *de se* and propose how it can be represented in a contextualist approach of Default Semantics. I also comment on the implications for compositionality of adopting this perspective.

4 Minimalist Standpoints and *De Se*

Minimalism comprises three related but distinct views: Borg's (e.g. 2004, 2007, 2012) version with the so-called 'liberal truth conditions' (henceforth MS for 'minimal semantics'); Cappelen and Lepore's (e.g. 2005) view founded on the recognition of a 'basic set' of context-sensitive expressions (henceforth IS for 'insensitive semantics'); and Bach's (e.g. 2004, 2006, 2007) radical semantic minimalism (henceforth RSM) which entails the rejection of propositionalism from semantics. Merging RSM and MS allows for a version of minimal semantics that allows for the truth conditions to be fuelled by logical forms that are unresolved as to the referents or lexical concepts, for example in the case of the use of indexicals and imprecise predicates as in (25).

(25) He cut the sun.

'Liberating' truth conditions from the status of conditions of verification allows for this move. Minimal semantics so construed accounts for the meaning possibilities offered by a language system but at the same time is perfectly compatible with a rich, contextualist semantics in view of their differing objectives. The objective of the latter is to represent the primary message intended by the speaker and/or inferred by the addressee – depending on which contextualist camp we adhere to.[18] Cappelen and Lepore are much less 'minimalist' in their construal in that they identify a list of expressions that require attention from pragmatics before the minimal proposition is recovered. This minimal proposition can then give rise to a plurality of speech acts performed with its help. Borg follows the same line on content, restricting, however, pragmatic 'filling in' to overt indexicals in her earlier arguments (2004, 2007, as contrasted with 2012). Finally, Bach advocates a strict syntax/semantics parallelism, denying the need for propositions or truth conditions alike, placing them strictly outside *what is said.*

In the case of the first-person indexical, the phenomenon of *de se* reference is present in the semantic representation on all three accounts as it is generated by the default prediction of the grammar itself through the phenomenon of sentential anaphora specific for the first-person singular pronoun. The character of the first-person indexical is sensitive not only to context (in the sense of Kaplan 1989a) but also to the grammar itself and 'survives', so to speak, through the second stage of processing recognized in two-dimensional semantics, namely through the route from circumstances of evaluation to extensions. Sentence (26), pertaining to the well-quoted situation discussed in the opening passage of Perry (1979: 3)[19], secures the self-attributive reading via the default output of grammar in the sense of Chierchia (2004). It also secures by default the self-awareness reading. To repeat, cancellation of the default conscious self-attribution is a heavily marked conversational strategy. One can envisage for example a scenario on which the speaker watches a film of him/herself and utters (26) with a shift of temporal reference to that of the action in the film, adding a disclaimer as in (26a). But such cases are marked and uncommon. From the semantic perspective, they can also be analyzed as a form of a grammar-semantics mismatch, with the *first-person pronoun used for a third-person concept.* The temporal reference is represented by subscripts t_1 and t_2, where t_1 is the time on the film and t_2 is the time of speaking. The subscript t_1+t_2 reflects the identity of the referent arrived at through the accepted perma-

---

[18] See Perry 2009 and Jaszczolt 2012b, 2012c on the need for both perspectives.

[19] 'I once followed a trail of sugar on a supermarket floor, pushing my cart down the aisle on one side of a tall counter and back the aisle on the other, seeking the shopper with the torn sack to tell him he was making a mess. With each trip around the counter, the trail became thicker. But I seemed unable to catch up. Finally it dawned on me. I was the shopper I was trying to catch.' Perry (1979: 3)

nence of first-person reference. The subscripts t_1 and t_2 reflect the possibility, albeit heavily marked (as reflected in the disclaimer 'in a sense'), for dissociating the first-person indexical from self-awareness. The oddity of 'I_{t1} don't know it is me_{t1+t2}', reflected in the lack of co-indexing and denial of the epistemic state normally associated with it, signals this markedness.

(26) I_{t1} believe there, in a sense, that I_{t1+t2} am making a mess.

(26a) Look, I_{t1} believe in this scene, in a sense, that I_{t1+t2} am making a mess but I_{t1} don't know it is me_{t1+t2}.[20]

Now, on this reasoning, acknowledging the marked, marginally acceptable status of differential indexing scenarios, (26b) normally acquires the content in (26c)-(26e) in the respective versions of minimalism. In other words, 'he' and 'she' are normally quasi-indicators.

(26b) I believe that I am making a mess.

(26c) RSM+MS: The contextually salient speaker believes of himself /herself that he/she is making a mess.

(26d) IS, MS: John Perry believes of himself that he is making a mess.

(26e) RSM: The $speaker_x$ believes that he/she_x is making a mess.[21]

Leaving the issue of self-awareness aside for a moment, (26c)-(26e) reflect what we want a minimalist account to reflect, namely self-attribution. On the other hand, the sentences (27) and (28) can only receive the self-attributive interpretation contextually and hence this interpretation is absent on the minimalist accounts which don't allow for this contextual enrichment to be present in the semantic content.

(27) I believe the person spilling the sugar is making a mess.

(28) I believe that (non-demonstrative) man is making a mess.

It seems that (27) and (28) demonstrate that IS lands half-way between what semantics aims to achieve. (27) ends up having the semantics of the attributive reading and pragmatics of either attributive or referential, while (28) necessitates reference assignment but does not express self-reference. These examples clearly act in favor of RSM+MS and against MS and IS in that they demonstrate that the latter go part of the way towards enrichment

---

[20] One could also propose a different method of differentiation in indexing, such as a three-way distinction between t_1, t_2, and t_1+t_2. Nothing depends on the choice of the vantage point.

[21] My intuitions on Bach's RSM are unclear: for him semantic content is not propositional and so his idea of how semantics is a by-product of syntax seems to be equally murky as that of Chomsky. See Ludlow 2003 and Chomsky's response (Chomsky 2003).

but can never go the whole way. Methodological grounds for such a construal of semantics are very dubious indeed.

What is required of an adequate minimalist account of meaning is delivering the principles of meaning construction that are based on the language system alone. What is required of a contextualist account of meaning is delivering the principles of meaning construction that capture the primary message intended by the speaker, and normally, if all goes well, recovered by the addressee. Any account that falls short of either objective is by definition defunct. Contextualism that embraces *de se* awareness passes the test. The question as to how much this contextualist construal attributes to grammar is an independent object of inquiry. Next, minimalism that remains within the confines of the language system, and therefore does not make predictions about the reference of the third person pronoun in (7) repeated below, also passes the test.

(7) John Perry believes that he is making a mess.

Only RSM+MS, and possibly RSM,[22] pass the test.

The follow-up question is this: having established that some versions of minimalism are true to the objective of a kind of semantics that is to be geared to the language system, how does such a minimalist outlook fare with what grammar can actually accomplish? In other words, we seem to have arrived at a mismatch. There are two ways in which semantics can be construed, listed as (A) and (B) below.

A. Semantic theory accounts for the intended meaning and takes the intended meaning as the truth-conditional content of the utterance

or

B. Semantic theory accounts for the array of meanings that the lexicon and syntax of a language are capable of providing.

At the same time, we have suggested that the *de se* awareness that is either explicitly present in PRO or logophors, or strongly present in anaphoric pronouns as the well-entrenched default reading, is best ascribed to the output of grammar. In order to reconcile this line of argument with the A/B alternative, it seems that the strongly preferred option is a kind of semantics that does not 'split' the power of grammar into that pertaining to the system and that pertaining to how grammar functions *in situ*. In other words, *de se* belief ascription appears to provide strong support for a contextualist construal; grammar can trigger default interpretations but if it is so, then confining semantics to the output of, so to speak, 'less than the grammar can do' would go against the requirement of psychological reality. If *de se* is the

22 See fn 21.

norm, then semantics should acknowledge it *tout court*. To repeat, our definition of contextualism emphasizes the availability of extra-sentential information in the truth-conditional content without making commitments concerning its exact provenance.

To sum up, it is evident from this analysis that in the example of *de se* attributions minimalism on the IS, and to a lesser extent also MS, version collapses to a rather poor version of contextualism in virtue of sitting midway between contextualism and minimalism and hence, for the kinds of examples confined to the filling in of expressions from the basic set such as personal pronouns, becomes indistinguishable from contextualism.[23] The RSM+MS and (possibly) RSM versions of minimalism, on the other hand, fulfill their raison d'être with respect to the language system but at the expense of misrepresenting the power of grammar in that they do not lead to the default *de se* interpretation, stopping at self-ascription but short of guaranteeing the expression of self-awareness. The grammar-pragmatics interface does not allow for a theoretical divide in that when we attribute strong tendencies to grammar, there has to be an option for them not to be realized in a particular situation of discourse. It is on the basis of this argument that we pursue a contextualist construal of *de se* in what follows, but a contextual construal that acknowledges grammar as a possible source of pragmatic information in preference to generalizing the role of free, top-down enrichment.

5 Default *De Se*

Although a non-*de se* interpretation of reports such as (13), repeated below, is possible, there is no need to add that it is rather uncommon, marked, and often in need of further elaboration as for example in (29).

(13) Kasia believes that she is to blame.

(29) Kasia believes that she is to blame although she doesn't realize that the person to whom she refers as the organizer of the drinks party is she herself.

Maier's (2009) analysis has no problem with this special status of *de re* about oneself. Syntactic processing results in a straightforward *de dicto* reading: a discourse referent *x* is in need of a resolution of a presupposition to result in Kasia (x), and Bel_x takes a DRS with the condition to-blame (y), where 'she' (y) is to be presuppositionally resolved. Then, following a specially proposed principle ('equality first'), coreference between 'Kasia' and 'she' is established as a default link. Had there been an additional condition added that stipulates that Kasia does not realise that she is blaming herself

[23] Cf. remarks in Borg 2007 to the effect that IS is not sufficiently minimal.

(say, to follow Maier, ¬ recognize (x,x)), then coreference, understood as coreference with respect to discourse referents, would not have been possible and the search for the correct representation would continue.

Now, when we adopt radical contextualism, there is scope for some improvement on this solution, although the spirit will be preserved. In my 2005a and 2007, I proposed a contextualist analysis of belief reports according to which 'believe' takes a variable number of arguments depending on its reading and on the sensitivity to the possibility of substitution of various coreferential expressions. I employed Recanati's (2002, 2005a) device of variadic function to explain how substitutivity *salva veritate* goes through unconditionally in some readings (*de re*), and with more difficulty or not at all in others (for this purpose I distinguished two sub-types of *de dicto*).[24] The following analysis is conducted in the framework of the revised version of Default Semantics (Jaszczolt 2010, henceforth DS) where contextualist semantic representations, called merger representations and symbolized as Σ, merge information coming from different identified sources and the output of each source can not only interact with, but also override the output of other sources, including grammar and lexicon.[25] The semantic contribution from the mode of presentation is present when substitutivity requires it and absent when it can go through without specifying *m*. Further, *m* allows for different degrees of granularity: 'coarser', so to speak, for the cases of referential mistakes (*de dicto*$_2$) and more finely-grained for the cases where psychological mode of presentation is required (*de dicto*$_1$). In this final rejoinder, I replace the variable-adicity merger representation of DS proposed in Jaszczolt 2005 with an analysis that derives *m* directly from the kinds of processes that operate on the units of the utterance. The analysis accommodates the self-attribution in (1) as well as the lack of substitutivity *salva veritate* between (1) and (2) above.

5.1 Sources of *De Se* Knowledge and Contextualist Compositionality

Default Semantics belongs to the contextualist orientation but at the same time challenges some of its assumptions. Following Grice and neo-Griceans, its aim is to model utterance meaning intended by the Model Speaker and recovered by the Model Addressee. Its radical flavor in the contextualist camp is dictated by the rejection of what is called the syntactic constraint. DS does not recognize a level of meaning at which the logical

[24] See also Jaszczolt 2012a on the pragmatics of propositional attitude reports.

[25] In other words, while in other versions of contextualism pragmatic inference and sometimes default interpretation develop/enrich the logical form of the sentence (the output of grammar), in DS this syntactic constraint is rejected. What is modeled in merger representation is the primary, main, intended meaning, irrespective of its relation to the output of grammar. Compositionality is understood as *pragmatic compositionality* – a methodological requirement that operates on the level of the merger. See Jaszczolt 2005 and Section 5.1 below.

form undergoes pragmatic modulation. In other words, what is variously known as the explicit/implicit distinction or what is said/what is implicated distinction in post-Gricean literature is construed differently in DS. The role of pragmatic sources of information about meaning is not restricted to additions to the logical form arrived at through syntactic processing. In some instances pragmatic processing may extend the logical form but in others it may also override it.

DS follows only one criterion for what the semantic representation has to be: it has to represent the main intended meaning of an utterance, be it implicit, explicit, minimal, or enriched. The syntactic restriction imposed on other contextualist accounts by the structure of the uttered sentence on the representation of the main modeled meaning is lifted, which allows DS to account for the cases of communicating the main content indirectly and revindicating this main content to the status of the object of the representation of the truth-conditional account of meaning.

Such main intended meanings are modeled in DS as so-called *merger representations*, in that they reflect the merger of the information about meaning that comes from a variety of linguistic and non-linguistic sources. The revised version of DS (Jaszczolt 2010) identifies five sources of such information:[26]

i. world knowledge (WK);
ii. world meaning and sentence structure (WS)
iii. situation of discourse (SD)
iv. properties of the human inferential system (IS)
v. stereotypes and presumptions about society and culture (SC).[27]

WK supplies information pertaining to the physical laws, such as for example allowing for the resultative interpretation of 'and' in (30b).

(30a) The temperature rose above 100 degrees Celsius and water evaporated.

(30b) The temperature rose above 100 degrees Celsius and as a result water evaporated.

Next, WS is responsible for the syntactic processing of the sentence and for lexical access. It is WS that generates what is standardly understood as the logical form. SD contributes situational context. IS is responsible for standard, salient meanings that arise due to the particular structure and operations of the human brain and therefore the properties of mental states, such as the property of intentionality. For example, it is IS that secures the

[26] This, however, does not preclude the possibility that the sources can be construed somewhat differently, leading to the same overall resulting merger representation.
[27] Adapted from Jaszczolt 2010.

default referential reading of definite descriptions, or a default *de re*, rather than *de dicto*, reading of attitude reports – unless one of the other sources prevents the default from arising.[28]

The final source, SC, triggers interpretations that are salient for members of a particular culture and society, such as for example (31b).

(31a) When we arrived in Florence, we first went to see David.

(31b) When we arrived in Florence, we first went to see the sculpture of David by Michelangelo.

In agreement with the rejection of the syntactic constraint mentioned above, the outputs of these sources are all treated on an equal footing, which means that the logical form of the uttered sentence provided by WS is not given priority over any other information. Since all sources of information are treated on a par in DS, the defaults of the IS or SC type only arise when they are not contradicted by information coming from any of the other sources. For example, in (31a), it may be contextually salient that the speaker went to see her brother David who lives in Florence. In this sense, defaults of DS are simply interpretations that are automatically attained in the particular situation of discourse and as such have little in common with strong, language-system-based defaults (presumptive meanings) of Levinson 2000.[29]

Next, DS identifies five types of processes that interact in producing the merger representation:

i. processing of word meaning and sentence structure (WS)
ii. pragmatic inference (from situation of discourse, social and cultural assumptions, and world knowledge) (CPI)
iii. automatic production of cognitive defaults (CD)
iv. automatic production of social, cultural and world-knowledge defaults (SCWD)

These processes can be mapped, albeit not always bi-uniquely, onto the sources of information. WK and SC can result in automatic, default interpretations of the SCWD kind, but also in inferentially reached ones (CPI). SD will always trigger CPI. Next, there is a one-to-one correspondence between IS and a process that produces CD, since CDs are precisely the salient interpretations that arise out of the properties of IS.

This contextualist DS-theoretic proposal is more radical than other extant versions of contextualism in that in its modeling of utterance meaning it allows for a common-sense, unconstrained interaction of the outputs of the

---

[28] See Jaszczolt 2005a, 2007 for examples and the argument.

[29] This remark is important in that semantic defaults are too often identified with Levinson's system-based defaults where the latter is called '*the* (sic) default account'. But see e.g. Katsos 2012 for a disclaimer.

identified sources; when the syntactic structure of the uttered sentence pertains to the structure of the propositional thought that constitutes the main intended message, the syntactic structure is preserved in the merger representation. But when the main message is indirect, DS allows for this structure to be suitably replaced with the correct one, the one that reflects that main thought. As such, the DS-theoretic distinction into the main meaning and secondary meanings cuts across the traditional explicit/implicit divide: what is primary may be either explicit or implicit, and likewise for secondary meanings. DS is also more cognitively adequate in that there is no need for levels of preliminary representations; syntax, pragmatic inference, and contextual and cultural assumptions interact to produce a single merger representation. The issue of the compositionality of such a representation, which, arguably, would have to be a necessary requirement if merger representations were to aspire to a semantic status, is taken up in the following section.

Now, in representing *de se* self-attribution and *de se* belief reports, various processes identified in DS, as well as various sources of information, will play a role. When we suggested above the possibility of the grammatical source of *de se*, in DS-terms we can represent it as *de se* arising via WS. In (26b) repeated below, the self-reference is available from WS. The lack of self-awareness, for example as expressed in (32), can be arrived at through WS+CPI.

(26b) I believe I am making a mess.

(32) When I first noticed the trail of sugar, I also believed, in a sense, that I was making a mess.

De se belief ascription in sentence (7) repeated below, could, on the strength of the lack of good arguments to the contrary, as well as the supporting argument from the superiority of the contextualist analysis,[30] be represented by ascribing it to WS.

(7) John Perry believes that he is making a mess.

But first, of course, the coreference has to be represented as arrived at via CD through a process analogous to the one that produces salient, preferred referential and salient, preferred *de re* interpretations: the default intentionality of the corresponding mental state, summarized as a heuristic for example in van der Sandt's (1992) presupposition as anaphora theory, predicts coreference. CD and WS together are thus responsible for the ordinary *de se* representation for (7) and this account carries more strength than the ascription of *de se* to WS alone.

---

[30] In Section 4.

5.2 Merger Representations for *De Se*

Merger representations constructed through the interaction of the outputs of these sources have the status of mental representations. They are proposition-like structures, in the sense of representing propositional thoughts. As such, they conform to the methodological requirement of compositionality. Compositionality is a malleable property; it has to be present in the construction and recovery of meaning but it can be allocated to different levels of language or communication in language. It can be assumed as a property of language itself and as such can inform the formal semantic theory, as was attempted by Richard Montague and his followers.[31] Along these lines, one can assume compositionality as a methodological principle and adjust the syntax or semantics in such a way that a compositional theory ensues.[32] Or, one can assign to compositionality the status of an empirical assumption about possible human languages whereby meaning supervenes on the structure and it is the correct account of the structure that has to be uncovered.[33] Alternatively, one can take intensional contexts such as belief reports seriously and question the possibility of compositional semantics for natural languages. This negative stance can lead to proposing a supervenience relation between linguistic expressions and some kind of metaphysical (compositional) foundation[34] or, less radically but in a compatible spirit, a shift of compositionality requirement to the level of interaction of semantic and pragmatic properties.[35] DS adopts the latter stance on compositionality and construes it as a methodological requirement on merger representations, as well as the empirical assumption about meaning so construed. The theory is still in its early stages and it remains to be seen how far the proposed structures reflect the output of the actual processes of utterance interpretation. The proof will lie in neuroscientific evidence on the one hand, and in the availability of algorithms for the interaction of processes on the other. At the current stage, we can only make informed conjectures about the processes, their interaction, and their output.

In what follows I present merger representations (Σs) for sentences expressing beliefs *de se*/reporting on one's own beliefs *de se*[36] such as (26b) and sentences reporting on other party's beliefs *de se* such as (7). This juxtaposition will allow us an adequate insight into the question of representing self-awareness via the grammatical devices used by the speaker, and there-

[31] The literature on this subject is vast. See e.g. Partee 2004.

[32] See Groenendijk and Stokhof 1991 and Jaszczolt 2005a, 2010.

[33] See Szabó 2000 and the implementation in e.g. Stanley and Szabó 2000.

[34] See Schiffer, e.g. 1992, 1996, 2003.

[35] See Recanati 2004, 2010; Jaszczolt 2005a, 2010.

[36] Note that shifting the temporal reference brings about this shift.

by also into the category of quasi-indicators. Let us first consider self-attribution in (26b).

(26b) I believe I am making a mess.

In Σ, a belief report is represented as Bel (x Σ′) standing for '*x* believes that Σ″, meaning that on a particular interprettion the individual *x* has the cognitive state represented as an embedded representation Σ′. Σs are modeled on discourse representation structures of DRT (Kamp and Reyle 1993), using an extended language of DRT but they use a radically pragmaticized concept of compositionality as summarized above. The reference assignment to the discourse referents *x* and *y* is accomplished via the process resulting in CD, in that intentionality and, on the level of intentions, the referential intention that standardly accompanies the use of pronouns, results in reference assignment. The belief predicate is also indexed as CD to reflect the default status of the *de re*, as opposed to the *de dicto*, interpretation. This part of the representation is applicable to all belief reports and carries through to the *de se* cases. Combined with information from coreference x=y, default *de re* surfaces here as *de se* and obtains the combined index 'CD, WS' as in Fig. 1. The types of processes responsible for various parts of the output are represented by indexing the relevant components of Σ with a subscript standing for the type of process.

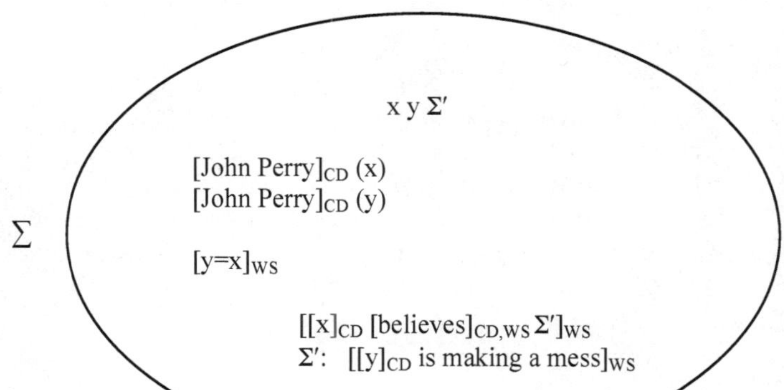

Fig. 1: Σ for sentence (26b)

In this way we can represent the *de se* interpretation by resorting to coreference alone, without making use of the first-person pronoun. Indeed, this is what we wanted to obtain in view of the earlier arguments to the effect that *de se* self-ascription and *de se* reports are to be treated analogously, as grammar-based default *de se*. The analysis can be extended to third-person reference in (7) which turns out to be almost identical as Fig. 1, save for the addition of the indication that this is the default reading of (7) on which 'he' functions as a quasi-indicator . The condition $[y=x]_{WS,CD}$ signals coreference that comes with self-awareness.

(7) John Perry believes that he is making a mess.

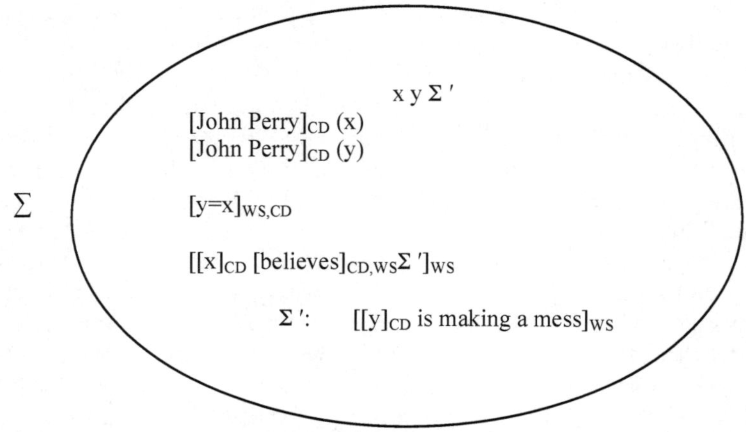

Fig. 2: Σ for the default reading of (7)

The similarity of Fig. 1 for the (only) reading of (26b) on this assignment and Fig. 2 for the default reading of (7) is precisely what the account predicts.[37] In non-default readings of (7), the discourse referents *x* and *y* come with varying referents (x≠y) or with varying information about the referent (x=y but no self-awareness) and via varying processes (WS as opposed to WS+CD). On the latter reading, the pronoun 'he', while retaining coreference through $[y=x]_{WS}$, is processed with the use of contextual information that allows for the situation where there is a lack of information about coreference on the part of the holder of the belief. As a result, *y* is associated with the discourse condition $[\text{John Perry}]_{CPI}$ (y). In addition, the index on the belief predicate would change accordingly to $[\text{believes}]_{CPI}$ as in Fig. 3.

[37] Note that the identity can be attained when coreference x=y is ascribed to the WS source and this is justified when we extend the concept of binding as discussed earlier in this section. Alternatively, coreference for the third person pronoun 'he' in (7) can be modeled as attained through CD in that the strongest intentionality and thereby the strongest referential intention pertain to the coreferential reading.

Σ

x y Σ'

[John Perry]$_{CD}$ (x)
[John Perry]$_{CPI}$ (y)

[y=x]$_{WS}$

[[x]$_{CD}$ [believes]$_{CPI}$ Σ']$_{WS}$
Σ': [[y]$_{CPI}$ is making a mess]$_{WS}$

Fig. 3: Σ for the coreferential non-default reading of (7)

Needless to say, the markedness of this interpretation is diaphanous in that normally a disclaimer phrase would be added by the speaker, as in (26). Alternatively, the coreferential pronoun would be avoided and a description would be substituted. The absence of *de se* would then be accounted for by the same mechanism of indexing with CPI. The presence or absence of coreference with a definite description (from the perspective of the reporter) can also be manipulated, but the normal case will of course be the one with no coreference being expressed. An utterance with a substituted demonstrative phrase or a description can on this account be represented as in Fig. 4 for example (33).

(33) John Perry believes that that man/the man with a split bag of sugar[38] is making a mess.

[38] DRT-style accounts assume discourse referents for directly referential and contextually referential expressions alike. Examples such as (33) testify to the plausibility of making the distinction between direct referentiality and contextual referentiality more malleable and discourse-dependent.

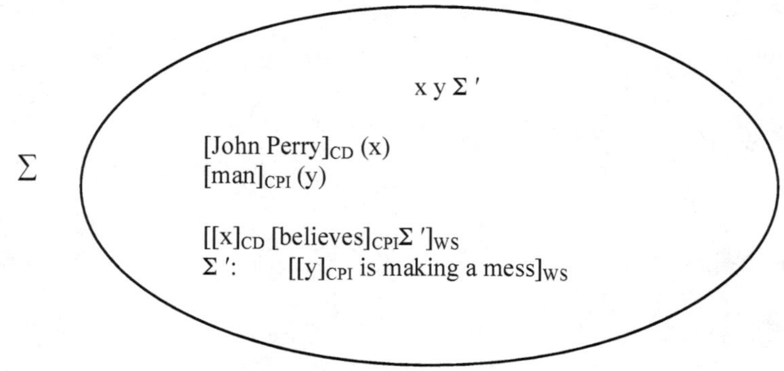

Fig. 4: Σ for sentence (33)

Coreference would have to be expressed via a clarification as for example in (34). Note that there is no non-default, coreferential reading of (33) as this is not what any of its possible utterances expresses.

(34) John Perry believes that that man/the man with a split bag of sugar is making a mess and he doesn't realize that he is that man.

Finally, the fact that the representation of *de se* was produced without resort to the first person has the advantage that we can also represent the dissociation of the first person from self-awareness as in the past-tense variant of (26b) in (35) which is acceptable when accompanied by disclaimers as in (35a).The analogy between (35a) and (26a) is diaphanous and stems out of the fact that the only semantic difference between them is the presence of historic present tense that corresponds to the semantic temporal category of the so-called past of narration (see e.g. Jaszczolt 2009; Jaszczolt and Srioutai 2011). In both utterances, when enriched with disclaimers as in the (26a) and (35a) variants, it is the identity of the indices in the final clause juxtaposed with the negation of the corresponding default mental state of self-awareness that testifies to the markedness of the reading.

(26b) I_{t1} believe there I_{t1+t2} am making a mess.

(26a) Look, I_{t1} believe in this scene that I_{t1+t2} am making a mess but I_{t1} don't know it is me_{t1+t2}.

(35) I_{t1} believed I_{t1+t2} was making a mess.

(35a) In a sense, I_{t1} believed I_{t1+2} was making a mess. I_{t1} just didn't know that the person I_{t1} referred to was I_{t1+t2}.[39]

Past-time reference in DS is represented by means of a modal operator on an embedded representation but for the purpose of this argument the intri-

[39] See fn 20.

cate DS-theoretic analysis of temporality can be put aside.[40] In Fig. 5, co-reference is represented by the condition [y=x]$_{WS}$, while the lack of self-awareness by the differentiation of indexing on *x* and *y* (CD vs CPI) and by the non-default use of the belief operator (CPI).

Σ

x y Σ'

[John Perry]$_{CD}$ (x)

[John Perry]$_{CPI}$ (y)

[y=x]$_{WS}$

[[x]$_{CD}$ [believe]$_{CPI}$$\Sigma'$]$_{WS}$

Σ': [[y]$_{CPI}$ is making a mess]$_{WS}$

Fig. 5: Σ for the non-standard reading of sentence (35), normally with disclaimers ('in a sense')

To sum up, in virtue of its recognition of default interpretations, the contextualist DS-theoretic account sits mid-way between Chierchia's semantic and Maier's pragmatic solutions to *de se*. While the default assumption in discourse interpretation seems to be that the anaphoric use of a pronoun in attitude reports comes with conscious self-reference, this cognitive default may not be present on some scenarios, or can be overridden by clarifications and disclaimers. Similarly, although less intuitively, 'I' normally comes with conscious self-reference, dubbed here self-awareness (as distinct from (not necessarily conscious) self-ascription and (linguistic) self-attribution) and this self-reference is carried by the lexical item and thereby by the grammar, on the understanding of the role of grammar discussed at the end of Section 4. But when we consider the phenomenon in the wider perspective, taking into consideration examples invoked by Kratzer, Chierchia, and above all the Castañeda tradition of quasi-indexicality, we have to recognize, and thereby account for the fact that there are expressions reporting self-awareness that do not involve first-person reference, and likewise, there are expressions using first-person pronoun that don't come with self-awareness. In the framework of DS that adopts the Σ-compositionality view, the lexicon and grammar (WS) are regarded as only

[40] For a detailed account of the representation of time in DS see Jaszczolt 2009.

one of several sources of meaning that contribute to Σ; what syntax would have generated may not in fact arise if CD or CPI override its output. The important corollary of this construal of sources and processes in meaning (re)construction is this: once we have shifted compositionality to the level of the merger of information (Σ), the differences between syntactic and pragmatic solutions are significantly reduced. Rather than argue whether conscious self-reference (self-awareness) comes from the logical form or from pragmatic enrichment, we simply acknowledge its default status triggered by the grammar and aided by the IS source and the CD process that produces an interpretation pertaining to the strongest intentionality of the speaker's mental state. We also embrace the experimentalists' finding that pragmatic manipulation of content is performed online, locally, and therefore even what syntax and lexicon throw up (or would have thrown up) can be locally altered. The *de se/de re about oneself* alternation fits well with this localist contextualist picture.

To compare, neither Meier's DRS-theoretic nor the DS-theoretic account is compositional in the Montagovian sense, but once compositionality is assumed to hold on the level of the contextualist semantic representation, both are equally so, and the latter gains an advantage by offering just one single level of such representation, with pragmatic enrichments identified by the source of information and type of cognitive process, at various stages of interpretation.

6 Concluding Remarks

The cognitive significance of 'I' comes from its being an inherently perspectival concept: the referent is presented from a certain privileged point of view. This privileged point of view permeates human thoughts and activities; whatever we think, do, or experience, we are conscious of being the thinker, agent, or experiencer. Any reductive explanation of this self-consciousness is a challenge, as is evident from the discussions of *de se* beliefs and from theoretical attempts at such a reduction.[41] Likewise, any reductive explanation of the expression of this self-consciousness poses a challenge as is evident from the comparison of the properties of first-person pronoun with those of other directly referring expressions.

The ascription of this privileged point of view poses yet another challenge in that this privileged point of view need not be part of the essence of the intentional content of the expression.[42] On the other hand, this privileged point of view normally seems to be part of this essence, both for indexicals and for quasi-indexicals. Cancelling self-awareness by adding dis-

[41] See Chalmers, e.g. 1996, 2006.

[42] For an extensive discussion and the pertinent semantic concept of quasi-indicators ('he himself') see Corazza 2004, esp. Chapter 9.

claimers of the kind '...but she does not realize that she is that person' is notoriously cumbersome and rarely practiced, although an empirical study of the relative frequency of relevant disclaimers would be pertinent here. In short, expression of self-awareness does not require a specific grammatical marker in English such as 'I' in *oratio recta* or (coreferential) '(s)he' in *oratio obliqua*, neither do such expressions come with guaranteed expression of self-awareness.

We don't seem to have a lexical or grammatical 'peg' to hang the property of expressing self-awareness on. Sometimes the property is externalized through the grammar, at other times by default interpretations of this grammatical form, and at yet others by pragmatic resolution of the truly underspecified representation. Contextualist framework and pragmatic compositionality embraced by DS allow us to provide for this diversity. As a result, various extant plausible hypotheses of the syntactic underpinning of this self-consciousness can be incorporated as one possible source, and one possible process, that lead to the semantic category of *de se* –semantic in the contextualist sense. The possibility of acknowledging this diversity in the provenance of *de se* makes the DS much more compelling than any of the extant semantic or pragmatic construals.

On the latter issue, I have argued here that contextualism on the DS version is compatible with the two versions of minimalism defended above, namely RSM+MS, in yielding consistent predictions *pace* the difference in respectively modeling or not modeling sources of meaning that lie outside grammar as part of the semantic content. On the strength of various suggestions and observations put forward above, it seems to be at least arguable that grammar plays a major role in expressing conscious self-attribution, 'the triumph of the self', but it is the above contextualist construal of the role of grammar that allows for adequate representation of the relevant processes and their outputs on the default and non-default interpretations. The derivation of the salient *de se* reading of belief reports from the processes WS and CD and the availability of a DS-theoretic representation on which they seem to be processed analogously to the cases of first-person self-ascription constitute sound arguments in favor of his stance.

Returning to the quotation from Chalmers (1996: 85) used as a motto for this article, although the 'indexical fact' may have to be regarded as primitive due to the non-reducibility of consciousness, *indexical fact* is not the *indexical expression per se*. Instead, the indexical/quasi-indexical expressions used to express self-awareness may have to be approached with the assumption of some version of the contextualist outlook in order to obtain a plausible account of the grammar/pragmatics division of labor in producing *de se* readings of belief reports, and also, more contentiously, belief expressions. But we are still some way away from the final word on the semantics of *de se*.

References

Abbott, B. 2010. *Reference*. Oxford: Oxford University Press.

Atlas, J. D. 2006. Remarks on Emma Borg's *Minimal Semantics*. Unpublished paper.

Bach, K. 2004. 'Minding the gap'. In: C. Bianchi (ed.). *The Semantics/Pragmatics Distinction*. Stanford: CSLI Publications. 27-43.

Bach, K. 2006. 'The excluded middle: Semantic minimalism without minimal propositions'. *Philosophy and Phenomenological Research* 73. 435-42.

Bach, K. 2007. 'Regressions in pragmatics (and semantics)'. In: N. Burton-Roberts (ed.). *Pragmatics*. Basingstoke: Palgrave Macmillan. 24-44.

Borg, E. 2004. *Minimal Semantics*. Oxford: Clarendon Press.

Borg, E. 2007. 'Minimalism versus contextualism in semantics'. In: G. Preyer and G. Peter (eds). *Context-Sensitivity and Semantic Minimalism*. Oxford: Oxford University Press. 339-59.

Borg, E. 2012. *Pursuing Meaning*. Oxford: Oxford University Press.

Cappelen, H. and E. Lepore. 2005. *Insensitive Semantics: A Defense of Semantic Minimalism and Speech Act Pluralism*. Oxford: Blackwell.

Castañeda, H.-N. 1966. ' "He": A study in the logic of self-consciousness'. *Ratio* 7. 130-157.

Castañeda, H.-N. 1967. ''Indicators and quasi-indicators'. *American Philosophical Quarterly* 4. 85-100.

Chalmers, D. J. 1996. *The Conscious Mind: In Search of a Fundamental Theory*. New York: Oxford University Press.

Chalmers, D. J. 2006. 'Foundations of two-dimensional semantics'. In: M. García-Carpintero and J. Macià (eds). *Two-Dimensional Semantics*. Oxford: Clarendon Press. 55-140.

Chierchia, G. 1989. 'Anaphora and attitudes *de se*'. In: R. Bartsch, J. van Benthem and B. van Emde Boas (eds). *Semantics and Contextual Expression*. Dordrecht: Foris. 1-31.

Chierchia, G. 2004. 'Scalar implicatures, polarity phenomena, and the syntax/pragmatics interface'. In: A. Belletti (ed.). *Structures and Beyond: The Cartography of Syntactic Structures*, vol. 3. Oxford: Oxford University Press. 39-103.

Chomsky, N. 2003. 'Reply to Ludlow'. In: L. M. Antony and N. Hornstein (eds). *Chomsky and His Critics*. Oxford: Blackwell. 287-295.

Corazza, E. 2004. *Reflecting the Mind: Indexicality and Quasi-Indexicality*. Oxford: Clarendon Press.

Cresswell, M. J. 1985. *Structured Meanings: The Semantics of Propositional Attitudes*. Cambridge, Mass.: MIT Press.

Crimmins, M. and J. Perry. 1989. 'The prince and the phone booth: Reporting puzzling beliefs'. *Journal of Philosophy* 86. 685-711.

Grice, H. P. 1978. 'Further notes on logic and conversation'. In: P. Cole (ed.). *Syntax and Semantics*. Vol. 9. New York: Academic Press. Reprinted in: H. P. Grice. 1989. *Studies in the Way of Words*. Cambridge, Mass.: Harvard University Press. 41-57.

Groenendijk, J. and M. Stokhof. 1991. 'Dynamic Predicate Logic'. *Linguistics and Philosophy* 14. 39-100.

Huang, Y. 2000. *Anaphora: A Cross-Linguistic Approach*. Oxford: Oxford University Press.

Jaszczolt, K. M. 2005a. *Default Semantics: Foundations of a Compositional Theory of Acts of Communication*. Oxford: Oxford University Press.

Jaszczolt, K. M. 2005b. Review of E. Borg, 2004, *Minimal Semantics*. *Journal of Linguistics* 41. 637-642.

Jaszczolt, K. M. 2007. 'Variadic function and pragmatics-rich representations of belief reports'. *Journal of Pragmatics* 39. 934-959.

Jaszczolt, K. M. 2009. *Representing Time: An Essay on Temporality as Modality*. Oxford: Oxford University Press.

Jaszczolt, K. M. 2010. 'Default Semantics'. In: B. Heine and H. Narrog (eds). *The Oxford Handbook of Linguistic Analysis*. 193-221.

Jaszczolt, K. M. 2012a. 'Propositional attitude reports: Pragmatic aspects'. In: K. Alan and K. M. Jaszczolt (eds). *The Cambridge Handbook of Pragmatics*. Cambridge: Cambridge University Press. 305-327.

Jaszczolt, K. M. 2012b. 'Context: Gricean intentions vs. two-dimensional semantics'. In: R. Finkbeiner, J. Meibauer & P. Schumacher (eds). *What is Context? Linguistic Approaches and Challenges*. Amsterdam: J. Benjamins. 81-103.

Jaszczolt, K. M. 2012c. ' 'Pragmaticising' Kaplan: Flexible inferential bases and fluid characters'. *Australian Journal of Linguistics* 32. 209-237.

Jaszczolt, K. M. and J. Srioutai. 2011. 'Communicating about the past through modality in English and Thai'. In: A. Patard and F. Brisard (eds). *Cognitive Approaches to Tense, Aspect, and Epistemic Modality*. Amsterdam: J. Benjamins. 249-278.

Kaplan, D. 1989a. 'Demonstratives'. In: J. Almog, J. Perry, and H. Wettstein (eds). *Themes from Kaplan*. New York: Oxford University Press, 481-563.

Kaplan, D. 1989b. 'Afterthoughts'. In: J. Almog, J. Perry, and H. Wettstein (eds). *Themes from Kaplan*. New York: Oxford University Press, 565-614.

Katsos, N. 2012. 'Experimental investigations and pragmatic theorising'. In: K. Allan and K. Jaszczolt (eds). *The Cambridge Handbook of Pragmatics*. Cambridge: Cambridge University Press. 275-290.

King, J. C. 2007. *The Nature and Structure of Content*. Oxford: Oxford University Press.

Kratzer, A. 2009. 'Making a pronoun: Fake indexicals and windows into the properties of pronouns'. *Linguistic Inquiry* 40. 187-237.

Larson, M. *et al.* 2009. 'Distinguishing the *Said* from the *Implicated* using a novel experimental paradigm'. In: U. Sauerland and K. Yatsushiro (eds). *Semantics and Pragmatics: From Experiment to Theory*. Basingstoke: Palgrave Macmillan.74-93.

Levinson, S. C. 2000. *Presumptive Meanings: The Theory of Generalized Conversational Implicature*. Cambridge, Mass.: MIT Press.

Lewis, D. 1979. 'Attitudes *de dicto* and *de se*'. *Philosophical Review* 88. 513-543.

Ludlow, P. 2003. 'Referential semantics for I-languages?'. In: L. M. Antony and N. Hornstein (eds). *Chomsky and His Critics*. Oxford: Blackwell. 40-161.

Maier, E. 2009. 'Presupposing acquaintance: A unified semantics for *de dicto*, *de re* and *de se* belief reports'. *Linguistics and Philosophy* 32. 429-474.

Partee, B. H. 2004. *Compositionality in Formal Semantics*. Oxford; Blackwell.

Percus, O. and U. Sauerland. 2003. 'On the LFs of attitude reports'. In: M. Weisgerber (ed.). *Proceedings of Sinn und Bedeutung* 7. Konstanz: Universität Konstanz. 228-242.

Perry, J. 1979. 'The problem of the essential indexical'. *Noûs* 13. 3-21.

Perry, J. 2001. *Reference and Reflexivity*. Stanford: CSLI Publications.

Perry, J. 2009. 'Directing intentions'. In: J. Almog andP. Leonardi (eds). *The Philosophy of David Kaplan*. Oxford: Oxford University Press. 187-201.

Recanati, F. 2002. 'Unarticulated constituents'. *Linguistics and Philosophy* 25. 299-345.

Recanati, F. 2004. *Literal Meaning*. Cambridge: Cambridge University Press.

Recanati, F. 2005a. 'It is raining (somewhere).' Manuscript at http://jeannicod.ccsd.cnrs.fr/documents.

Recanati, F. 2005b. 'Literalism and contextualism: Some varieties'. In: G. Preyer and G. Peter (eds). *Contextualism in Philosophy: Knowledge, Meaning, and Truth*. Oxford: Clarendon Press. 171-96.

Recanati, F. 2010. *Truth-Conditional Pragmatics*. Oxford: Oxford University Press.

van der Sandt, R. A. 1992. 'Presupposition projection as anaphora resolution'. *Journal of Semantics* 9. 333-377.

Saul, J. M. 2002. 'What is said and psychological reality: Grice's project and relevance theorists' criticisms'. *Linguistics and Philosophy* 25. 347-72.

Schiffer, S. 1977. 'Naming and knowing'. *Midwest Studies in Philosophy* 2. Reprinted in: A. French, P. Uehling, T. E., and Wettstein, H. K. (ds), 1979, *Contemporary Perspectives in the Philosophy of Language*. Minneapolis: University of Minnesota Press. 61-74.

Schiffer, S. 1992. 'Belief ascription'. *Journal of Philosophy* 89. 499-521.

Schiffer, S. 1996. The Hidden-Indexical Theory's logical-form problem: A rejoinder. *Analysis* 56. 92-97.

Schiffer, S. 2003. *The Things We Mean*. Oxford: Oxford University Press.

Schlenker, P. 2003. 'A plea for monsters'. *Linguistics and Philosophy* 26. 29-120.

Schlenker, P. 2011. 'Indexicality and *de se* reports'. In: K. von Heusinger, P. Portner and C. Maienborn (eds). *Semantics: An International Handbook of Natural Language Meaning, Volume 2*. Berlin: Mouton de Gruyter. 1561-1604.

Stalnaker, R. 1978. 'Assertion'. *Syntax and Semantics* 9. New York: Academic Press. Reprinted in R. Stalnaker, 1999, *Context and Content*, Oxford: Oxford University Press. 78-95.

Stalnaker, R. 2011. 'The essential contextual'. In: Brown, J. and H. Cappelen (eds). *Assertion: New Philosophical Essays*. Oxford: Oxford University Press. 137-150.

Stanley, J. 2002. 'Making it articulated'. *Mind and Language* 17. 149-168.

Stanley, J. and Z. G. Szabó 2000. On quantifier domain restriction. *Mind and Language* 15. 219-261.

Szabó, Z. G. 2000. 'Compositionality as supervenience'. *Linguistics and Philosophy* 23. 475-505.

Wittgenstein, L. 1953. *Philosophical Investigations*. Oxford: Blackwell.

4

Belief Reports and the Property Theory of Content

NEIL FEIT

The property theory of content is a view about the metaphysics of mental content, which is motivated chiefly by standard examples of *de se* attitudes. According to the property theory, the contents of beliefs and other cognitive attitudes are not propositions. Instead they are properties, that is, entities without truth values that are constant across persons and other objects, places, and times (although properties can be said to be *true of* persons and other objects). In this essay, I develop an account of truth conditions for cognitive attitude reports – belief reports in particular – which appeals to the property theory of content. The theory of belief and the theory of belief reports are different things, but it seems clear that facts about what we believe must be what make our true belief reports true. Along the way I consider some competing semantic accounts that appeal to the doctrine of propositions, that is, the view that belief contents are propositions, conceived somewhat neutrally as entities with possible-worlds truth conditions. This essay is divided into four sections. The first has to do with the property theory of content and reports of *de se* belief, the second with belief reports in which *that*-clauses contain proper names or natural kind terms, and the third with what we might roughly describe as reports of purely *de dicto* belief. The result of the first three sections will be a few apparently disparate accounts of truth conditions for belief reports, offered without any claim to comprehensiveness. The fourth section contains some ideas about unifying the accounts offered in the first three sections, as well as a discussion of the logical form of belief reports and the sort of proposition they express.

Attitudes De Se: Linguistics, Epistemology, Metaphysics.
Neil Feit and Alessandro Capone (eds.).

1 *De Se* Belief Reports

The problem of *de se* belief is one of several great puzzles in contemporary philosophy of mind. The problem is best set against a background framework that includes the doctrine of propositions. Suppose, for example, that Valerie has the *de se* belief that she herself is a spy, that is, she believes herself to be a spy. Joe, on the other hand, has a belief that he would express by saying 'Valerie is a spy' or perhaps 'She [pointing to Valerie] is a spy'. For concreteness, let's suppose that Joe has read in the newspaper that Valerie is a spy, and that he sees Valerie wearing a trench coat, and thinks that everyone who wears a trench coat is a spy. For comfort, we might even wish to assume that Joe knows Valerie by name. In this case, the following claims are true:

(1) Joe believes that Valerie is a spy.

(2) Valerie believes that she herself is a spy.

The problem is to identify a proposition such that Valerie believes it, and such that her believing it makes (2) true. This is the belief she would express by uttering the words 'I am a spy'. However, it seems that Valerie could believe the proposition *that Valerie is a spy* without believing that she herself is a spy, since she might somehow fail to realize that she is Valerie. It seems too that for any property *F*, she could believe the proposition *that the F is a spy* without believing that she herself is a spy, since she might not think that she is the *F*. So, it seems that there is more to Valerie's *de* se belief that she herself is a spy than her belief in any proposition. How, then, is this kind of belief to be understood?

To get a bit clearer on this presentation of the problem, consider claim (1) above. What makes this true? Which proposition might Joe believe, and thereby believe that Valerie is a spy? Suppose we identify such a proposition and call it '*P*'. Joe believes *P* in virtue of some *third-person perspective* on Valerie. So, it seems possible for Valerie to believe *P* in virtue of a third-person perspective on herself, and as a result without the *de se* belief and first-person perspective associated with it. Whichever proposition Joe believes, then, it seems to be such that Valerie could believe it without believing herself to be a spy. Unless the doctrine of propositions is bolstered by other claims about the nature of belief, we seem to have the following result. The elusive proposition, which makes (2) true when Valerie believes it, cannot be the proposition *that Valerie is a spy*, cannot be the proposition *that the F is a spy*, and cannot be a proposition that anybody other than Valerie could believe.

The property theory of content solves the problem of *de se* belief by maintaining that the elusive content is not a proposition at all. The content of Valerie's belief is the property *being a spy*, which Valerie takes herself to have. The contents of such beliefs are properties that their subjects believe themselves to have, not propositions that they believe to be true. Following Lewis (1979), I shall use the term 'self-ascription' for the relation between conscious subjects and properties that they believe themselves to have. Valerie, then, self-ascribes the property *being a spy*. The self-ascription relation is in an important way necessarily reflexive. To self-ascribe a property is to ascribe it *to yourself* and not to any other thing. One person simply cannot self-ascribe a property to another.

The version of the property theory that I will defend maintains that *in general*, belief can be understood as the self-ascription of properties. There is no good reason to restrict self-ascription to special beliefs like Valerie's. For example, when you believe that the smallest mountain is bigger than the largest bicycle, you self-ascribe a property, and when Joe believes that Valerie is a spy, he self-ascribes a property.[1] So, on the view I am defending, all belief turns out to be *de se* belief. Properties serve generally and uniformly as the contents of our beliefs.

Some property theorists, especially those inclined toward unstructured conceptions of propositions and properties, might wish to say that *de se* contents are centered propositions. A centered proposition is a set of centered worlds, and a centered world is a pair consisting of a possible world and an inhabitant of that world – the world is "centered on" the inhabitant. (This is one of several different but related conceptions of centered worlds.) On this account, the content of Valerie's *de se* belief that she is a spy is the set of centered worlds in which the center is a spy. This centered proposition corresponds in a strong way to the property *being a spy*. The content of the belief that the smallest mountain is bigger than the largest bicycle is also a set of centered worlds, but one that does not discriminate between worldmates (that is, for any world w and for any individuals x and y that inhabit w, <w,x> is in the set if and only if <w,y> is).[2] I shall continue to use properties rather than centered propositions, but the property theory can incorporate either approach. Since centered worlds are in a way isomorphic to properties, the different approaches might be (quite close to) mere terminological variants.

Even more generally, properties serve as contents not just for belief but for all of the so-called propositional attitudes. For example, Valerie's desire to be anonymous is understood in terms of her bearing the appropriate cog-

---

[1] This view has been defended by Chisholm (1979, 1981), Lewis (1979, 1986: 27-40), and Feit (2008). Loar (1976) proposes a more restricted version of the view, according to which certain beliefs, but not all of them, are to be understood in terms of a self-ascription relation between believers and propositional functions.

[2] Egan (2006) calls this a *boring* centered proposition. The set of centered worlds in which the center is a spy, on the other hand, is *interesting* – it contains the pair of a world with one of its inhabitants but not the pair of that world and another of its inhabitants.

nitive relation – the analogue of self-ascription for desire – to the property *anonymity*. She wants to have this property. Having said that, I will restrict our official version of the property theory herein to the case of belief. The view is as follows:

> *Property Theory of Content*: Necessarily, a subject S believes something if and only if there is a property *F* such that S self-ascribes *F*. Belief is a dyadic relation – viz., *self-ascription* – between a subject and a property. The content of a belief is the property that the subject self-ascribes.

The property theory is built for *de se* belief. As such, an account of the truth conditions for *de se* belief reports flows naturally from it. (Throughout this essay, I will take a belief report to be an assertive utterance of a belief sentence.) According to this semantic account, (2) above does not have Valerie believing a proposition; instead it has her self-ascribing the property *being a spy*. The general account can be given as follows (to make things simple here, let S be a name for the subject of the belief and let F be a predicate that contains no demonstratives, indexicals, proper names, or kind terms):

> *Semantics for De Se Reports*: A belief report of the form ⌈S believes that she herself (or he himself) is F⌉ is true iff the bearer of S self-ascribes the property expressed by F.

The same account also provides truth conditions for attributions that contain infinitives, in particular those of the form ⌈S believes herself (or himself) to be F⌉, but for simplicity I shall focus on the other form here.

As I see it, the metaphysics of cognitive content is conceptually prior to the semantics of attitude reports, that is, before we undertake the task of giving an account of truth conditions for belief reports, we need to have a theory about the nature and content of belief. The case for the property theory of content, again as I see it, is overwhelming.[3] If this is correct, then any adequate semantic account must appeal to the property theory at the level of truth conditions; other accounts would be non-starters. Nevertheless, it will be useful here to compare the property-theoretic semantic account with a couple of its main rivals.

According to many neo-Fregeans, the Fregean conception of thoughts can accommodate the issues concerning *de se* attitudes.[4] These philosophers follow Frege in saying that each of us can employ a first-person mode of presentation that is inaccessible to others and is necessary and sufficient

[3] See the works cited in footnote #1.

[4] For example, Peacocke (1981) and Forbes (1987) explicitly address *de se* belief and offer analyses along Fregean lines. See also Evans (1982), McDowell (1984).

for *de se* belief. Consider an utterance of 'Ralph believes that he (himself) is making a mess'. Forbes (1987: 23) offers the following analysis:

B(Ralph, $[\text{self}]_{\text{Ralph}}$ ^ ⌈making a mess⌉)

The analysis is Fregean in that the pronoun 'he' and the predicate 'is making a mess' do not have their customary references. In the regimentation, corner quotes are used to form a name of the sense of the expression within them, '^' stands for the way in which senses are combined together to form a single complex sense, and '$[\text{self}]_{\text{Ralph}}$' designates the mode of presentation of Ralph that only Ralph can employ in thought.[5] The idea is that there is a *type* of mode of presentation, namely [self], tokens of which are employed in thought on specific occasions. For example, when I believe myself to be making a mess, I grasp a *different* token of the same first-person type, which accounts for the way in which Ralph and I believe alike. Token senses – rather than types – must make up the contents of these beliefs, since different tokens of [self] determine different objects, and so this is the only way in which the beliefs could bear truth values.

The modes of presentation or senses at issue here – we might call them '*de se* senses' – are allegedly entities that can exist without being grasped or entertained, but that depend for their existence on a given individual (for example, $[\text{self}]_{\text{Ralph}}$ would not exist if Ralph did not exist). This is a departure from Frege's thought and part of what makes the present view *neo*-Fregean. *De se* senses belong to a class of neo-Fregean entities that are supposed to present or determine individuals, but not descriptively, that is, not purely in virtue of properties that the individuals uniquely possess. The entities in this broader class have been labeled '*de re*', 'demonstrative', 'indexical', and 'non-descriptive', and have been understood differently by different thinkers. Their exact nature is somewhat mysterious, insofar as *how* they pick out or determine particular individuals is not fully clear (at least not to me). In any case, the neo-Fregean semantic account will look something like this:

> *Neo-Fregean De Se Semantics*: A belief report of the form ⌈S believes that she herself (or he himself) is F⌉ is true iff the bearer of S believes the proposition: *$[\text{self}]_S$ ^ ⌈is F⌉*. (The corner quotes around 'is F' are sense-quotes.)

What shall we make of this attempt to solve the problem of *de se* belief while holding onto the doctrine of propositions? I shall briefly enumerate several problems, which seem to me quite serious when taken as a group. First, on the neo-Fregean view, the content of one's *de se* belief is a thought that nobody else can even grasp, let alone believe. This commitment to

---

[5] Peacocke offers the same sort of analysis. For example, see Peacocke (1981: 191).

content that is in principle unshareable, I would argue, should be a last resort.

Second, the distinction between the various *token* senses – for example, $[\text{self}]_{\text{Ralph}}$ – and the *type* to which they belong adds an additional layer of complexity to the theory (especially since on many accounts token neo-Fregean senses are repeatable, which makes type/token terminology a bit misleading; determinable/determinate terminology would be better.) This worry would not amount to much if the content of a token of [self] were, as is sometimes suggested, a mixed descriptive-demonstrative sense expressible in such terms as 'the subject of *this* experience'. However, the claim that *de se* thoughts have the form 'the subject of this experience is F' is not plausible. For example, it is possible for somebody to believe (correctly or mistakenly, it does not matter) that he is not the only thinker of a certain thought, for example she might believe that God is thinking it too. More generally, she might think that she is not the only subject of any of her experiences, but it seems that she could still have plenty of *de se* beliefs. If this is the case, however, then the contents of those beliefs cannot have the form 'the subject of this experience is F', since she does not think there is a unique subject, *the* subject, of her experiences. Moreover, if somebody else (God perhaps, or a Siamese twin who shares some brain tissue) really were having the same token experiences, then all these neo-Fregean beliefs would be false. But surely she could have some true *de se* beliefs. I conclude that [self] cannot have a sense expressible in such terms as 'the subject of this experience'. The upshot is that the nature of *de se* senses, and the way they function, is a matter of controversy and mystery. If a *de se* sense does not determine an individual by means of a property or cluster of properties that the individual has, or by means of a mental state that she herself is experiencing, how then *does* it determine an individual?

Finally, any neo-Fregean semantics will inherit problems that confront the Fregean account of meaning in general and attitude reports in particular. There are familiar and powerful reasons to reject Frege's thesis that all singular terms express (descriptive) senses. In addition to conflicting with the thesis of direct reference for singular terms, the Fregean account also violates the plausible principle of semantic innocence, according to which the semantic value of a term does not change when it is embedded in a 'that'-clause. There are several other lines of criticism that make for a compelling case against the Fregean account, but I shall not review them here.

The Fregean account preserves the traditional conception of belief as a dyadic relation between the subject and the content of her belief. Another popular account of belief holds that (even if belief itself is a dyadic relation between subject and proposition, and even if 'believes' expresses this relation) there is always more to having a belief than simply being related in a suitable way to a proposition. On this account, which I call the triadic view of belief, the relation between a subject and a believed-true proposition is mediated by the *way* in which the subject takes the proposition, or the *guise* under which she is familiar with it.[6] On the triadic view, subject S believes proposition P when there exists some third entity – a proposition guise or way of taking a proposition – such that S assents to P when S takes P in this way. Following Salmon (1986, 1989), I shall use the name 'BEL' for this triadic relation. So, S believes P if and only if there exists an X such that BEL (S, P, X).

The triadic view can provide a solution to the problem of *de se* belief. The triadic theorist can say that sentences (1) and (2) above have Joe and Valerie believing the same proposition after all. For the moment, let's suppose that guises are natural language sentences. When Joe believes that Valerie is a spy, then, he is related by BEL to the proposition *that Valerie is a spy* and the guise 'Valerie is a spy' (or perhaps 'That woman is a spy'). When Valerie believes that she herself is a spy, she is related by BEL to the same proposition but a different guise, 'I am a spy'. For many reasons, sentences will not adequately play the role that guises need to play: people who speak different languages can be related to the same proposition in the same way, creatures without language can have beliefs, etc. Sentence *meanings* are far better suited to such a role (though perhaps they do not play it perfectly). For example, when Valerie believes that she herself is a spy, the relevant guise is the linguistic meaning (the character) of 'I am a spy', that is, a function from contexts to propositions that maps each context to a proposition about the speaker of the context, to the effect that she is a spy. (It is interesting to note that this propositional function is importantly similar to the property *being a spy*.)

One advantage of the triadic view, at least *prima facie*, is that it seems able to provide a single, general semantic theory that applies to all belief reports, not just *de se* reports. The account of truth conditions goes like this:[7]

> *Triadic Semantics*: A belief report of the form ⌈S believes that P⌉ is true iff the bearer of S believes the proposition expressed by P, that is, iff (∃x) BEL (S, P, x).

[6] This general view of belief is shared by a wide variety of theorists who defend several different accounts of belief reports. The account of truth conditions to be considered in the text goes by many names, including *neo-Russellianism*, *Millianism*, *Guise Millianism*, *Ways Millianism*, and more.

[7] This account does make use of the metaphysics of content given by the triadic view of belief, but the name 'Triadic Semantics' might be misleading. Unlike, say, the hidden indexical theory, this account does not require or imply that 'believes' and other attitude verbs express three-place relations between subjects, propositions, and guises.

However, there are well known problems with this general account. For example – if we treat the Superman stories as fact – the sentence 'Lois believes that Clark Kent can fly' seems false, but there is a guise x such that BEL (Lois, *that Clark Kent can fly*, x). This is because the proposition *that Clark Kent can fly* is the proposition *that Superman can fly*, and Lois accepts this proposition when she takes it in some way. So, proponents of the triadic semantics must reject or explain away the intuition that Lois does not believe that Clark Kent can fly. Moreover, consider the famous example from Kaplan (1989) of the man with his pants on fire. He does not believe that he himself is wearing pants that are on fire (he will very soon!), but he is looking into a mirror, pointing to himself, and sincerely uttering 'His pants are on fire'. The sentence 'He believes that he is wearing pants that are on fire' seems to have a false reading, but (in the context) the *that*-clause expresses a proposition about this man to the effect that his pants are on fire – and he does accept this when he takes it in some way. So, the triadic semantics seems to give counter-intuitive truth conditions in these cases.

Triadic theorists have offered substantial explanations of the apparent difference in truth value between utterances of, say, 'Lois believes that Superman can fly' and 'Lois believes that Clark Kent can fly'. Most of them say that when we take an utterance of 'Lois believes that Clark Kent can fly' to be false, we are confusing the (true) semantic content of the report with what is really false, which is something that is pragmatically implicated or communicated in some way by the utterance.[8] For example, an utterance of 'Lois believes that Clark Kent can fly', might pragmatically implicate the falsehood that Lois believes *that Clark Kent can fly* under the mild-mannered reporter guise, or that she would assent to the sentence 'Clark Kent can fly'. Since I reject the metaphysics of belief associated with the triadic view, I shall have little to say about the plausibility of this or other explanations of apparent truth-value differences like those above. Instead, I would like to consider briefly whether the triadic view of belief might be able to accommodate our intuitions about *de se* belief reports.

What follows is a plausible triadic semantics for *de se* reports, although it might be more attractive to defenders of hidden indexical (or related) theories than to typical neo-Russellians. Let's use the term 'I-guise' for the character of a sentence with the form 'I am F'.[9] Neglecting some conven-

---

[8] For examples, see McKay (1981), Salmon (1986, 1989), and Soames (1987, 1995). Braun (1998) offers a different sort of explanation, one that appeals to differences in *ways* of believing a single proposition but does not invoke pragmatic implications.

[9] This assumes that guises are sentence meanings or characters. In Feit (2008: 69), I give a more general account of an I-guise. The account to be given in the text is not unlike the semantics of *de se* belief reports given by Richard (1983).

tions for corner quotes to facilitate exposition, we can give the view as follows:

> *Triadic De Se Semantics*: A belief report of the form ⌈S believes that she herself (or he himself) is F⌉ is true iff there exists an x such that (i) x is an I-guise, and (ii) BEL (S, *that S is F*, x).

This semantic account, I think, adequately handles *de se* belief reports. The role that I-guises play here mirrors the role properties play in the property-theoretic semantics for *de se* attributions. Issues having to do with the metaphysics of content, however, tip the scale in favor of the property-theoretic account. I have argued elsewhere, particularly in Feit (2008), that the total evidence favors the property theory over the triadic view. What follows is a short review of the reasons that weigh in favor of the property theory.

First, the triadic view is a more complicated account of the metaphysics of cognitive content than the property theory is. Instead of a dyadic relation to properties, it analyzes belief in terms of a triadic relation to propositions and guises. The added complexity brings no theoretical advantages, as we shall see in the next section. Second, and related, the triadic view is less clear than the property theory insofar as the precise nature of guises is controversial. We have assumed that guises can be taken to be characters in Kaplan's sense, but it is unclear that such entities are adequate. Third, the triadic view has some controversial metaphysical commitments that the property theory does not have. For example, the triadic view entails that externalism – that is, anti-individualism about mental content – is correct, and so it begs an important question in the philosophy of mind. Any version of the doctrine of propositions must make this commitment, since it implies that intrinsic duplicates who believe themselves to have the same property will believe *different* propositions – one that contains or otherwise tracks one of the duplicates, and one that contains or tracks the other – and hence have different belief contents. The triadic view also implies that a plausible version of physicalism is false, since physically indiscernible worlds will differ mentally when intrinsic duplicates have different belief contents.[10]

2 Names and Natural Kind Terms

At the beginning of the first section, we used two sentences to illuminate the problem of *de se* belief. We have already dealt with sentences like (2) above, that is, *de se* reports. What about those like (1), according to which

---

[10] See Feit (2006, 2008: 42-52) for arguments along these lines. Although I am now less confident in the argument from physicalism than I once was, I still think that it causes trouble for the triadic view that it does not cause for the property theory.

Joe believes that Valerie is a spy? In order to build up to an adequate account of the desired sort, let's start by considering Lewis's analysis of *de re* belief. (I am not claiming that (1) is a *de re* attribution of belief, which will become clearer soon.) Let's suppose for now that what makes (1) true is that Joe has a belief, about Valerie, to the effect that she is a spy. On Lewis's property-theoretic view, this amounts to two things. First, there must be a *relation of acquaintance* that Joe bears uniquely to Valerie, that is, to Valerie and only to Valerie. Perceptual relations like *looking at*, *listening to*, and the like are paradigm cases of relations of acquaintance, but any causal relation that enables a *de re* belief about a particular object will suffice. Second, Joe must take himself to bear this relation to somebody who is a spy. This consists in Joe self-ascribing a property of a certain sort. If we let 'R' name the relation of acquaintance that Joe bears to Valerie, then Joe must self-ascribe the property *bearing R uniquely to a spy* (for example, Joe might see Valerie in her trench coat, and he might self-ascribe *looking at one and only one person, who is a spy*). When these two conditions are met, Lewis says that Joe *ascribes* the property *being a spy* to Valerie.[11]

This sort of ascription is other-ascription, not self-ascription (though it is possible to ascribe properties to oneself in this way, as in the case of the man whose pants are on fire). Let's consider an account of belief reports with names that makes use of it. What follows is a preliminary account of truth conditions for belief reports in which the complement sentences contain proper names (here N is a proper name for individual *N*, and F is a predicate that expresses the property *F*):

> *Preliminary Semantics for Belief Reports with Names*: A belief report of the form ⌈S believes that N is F⌉ is true iff there exists a relation of acquaintance R such that (i) the bearer of S bears R uniquely to *N*, and (ii) the bearer of S self-ascribes the property *bearing R uniquely to something that has F*.

Notice a couple of things about this preliminary account. First, a proper name embedded in a *that*-clause introduces (at least at the level of truth conditions) an existential quantifier over relations of acquaintance. Second, relations of acquaintance play the same kind of role that guises, modes of presentation, or descriptions play for other theories. Third, on this account, the thing that bears the name N does not enter into the content of a belief that would make a belief report of this form true (the content is given by the italicized property in clause (ii) of the account above). So, the *that*-clause does not specify the content of a belief that would make the report true; if it

[11] In Feit (2000), I argue that Lewis's two conditions are not jointly sufficient for *de re* belief, but this need not concern us right now.

did, then the content would have to be a singular proposition about the bearer of N.

It seems to me that these consequences are correct and that they are advantages of this account, and I will argue for this below. However, there seem to be two problems, at least *prima facie*, with the preliminary account. First, it implies that co-referential names are substitutable in belief contexts, and thus falls prey to Frege's puzzle (this is a result of incorporating a view of *de re* belief into the semantics for belief reports containing proper names within the scope of 'believes', that is, *de dicto* attributions of belief). So this account violates the intuition that substitution can make a difference to the truth value of a belief report. Second, the account implies that a belief report with a name in its *that*-clause cannot be true unless the name refers to something, and thus falls prey to the problem of empty names. In the rest of this section, I will briefly discuss these problems and tentatively construct a semantics that avoids them.

Let's consider the substitutivity issue first. Suppose that Ed has heard of a certain author under the name 'Mark Twain' and has even read one of his books. He sincerely utters 'Mark Twain was a novelist'. However, Ed is unfamiliar with the proper name 'Samuel Clemens' and would not assent to 'Samuel Clemens was a novelist'. It seems, then, that an utterance of (3) below would be true but an utterance of (4) would be false:

(3) Ed believes that Mark Twain is a novelist.

(4) Ed believes that Samuel Clemens is a novelist.

This causes trouble for the preliminary property-theoretic semantics, since the account – given that Clemens = Twain – does not allow such utterances to diverge in truth value.

According to the preliminary account, what makes (3) true, at least in part, is that Ed bears a relation of acquaintance uniquely to Mark Twain. (Since Clemens = Twain, he also bears this relation to Clemens, which causes the trouble here.) The relation is something like this one: *having heard of someone under the name 'Mark Twain'*. Let's call a relation like this a 'Twainish' relation. Such a relation need not be metalinguistic, for example there might be a Twainish relation that involves looking at a photograph of a man with such-and-such features. In any case, we can modify the preliminary account, with an eye toward making an utterance of (4) false, if we somehow exclude or disallow Twainish relations of acquaintance from entering into the evaluation of (4). We will do this in the final version of the account by maintaining that a relation of acquaintance must be *appropriate*. The idea is that there are contextually-supplied restrictions on which relations are appropriate, and so, for example, in a typical context of utterance for (4), no Twainish relations are appropriate.

Whether or not a relation of acquaintance is appropriate varies from context to context and is not determined by the semantic value of an embedded name. For example, an utterance of 'Lois believes that Superman is a reporter' would seem false relative to a context in which Supermanish relations of acquaintance (for example, ones incorporating the property *being a caped superhero*) are appropriate but where Clark-Kentish ones are not. However, there are contexts in which 'Superman' is embedded in a *that*-clause but Clark-Kentish relations are appropriate. Consider this example from Berg (1988):

> A viewer marveling at Superman's ability to conceal his identity might remark to another viewer, "Look, there's Superman in his Clark Kent outfit; he's incredibly convincing! *Everyone* thinks he's a reporter – Jimmy Olson, Mr. White – why even that clever *Lois Lane believes that Superman is a reporter*." (1988: 355)

The second problem concerned empty names, that is, names without bearers. By requiring a true belief report to be such that its subject is acquainted with the bearer of the relevant name, the preliminary account above has the intuitively implausible implication that utterances of the following could not be true:

(5) Virginia believes that Santa Claus will bring her presents.

(6) Le Verrier believed that Vulcan is the closest planet to the sun.

It has become fashionable, especially among direct reference theorists, to maintain that names like 'Santa' and 'Vulcan' do in fact refer, for example to abstract artifacts that are somehow brought into existence by human activity. I think this is unfortunate, especially since there are several plausible accounts of (genuinely) empty names that are consistent with the theory of direct reference.[12] We can, I think, achieve an adequate semantic account of utterances of (5) and (6) by making use of some theoretical machinery common to the theory of direct reference and the causal theory of names.

According to the picture developed in Kripke (1980), a name is first used in an initial baptism, whereby its bearer is identified by ostension or its reference is fixed by a description. The name is then passed from person to person, and an elaborate chain of communication involving uses of the name develops. Following Everett (2000), let's use the term 'referential framework' for this network of related utterances, mental states, and reference-fixing events. Consider, for example, uses of 'Plato' or 'Platon'. Nora's use of 'Plato' in New York in 2011, Terry's use in Toronto in 1995, and Pierre's use of 'Platon' in Paris in 1979 all belong to the same referen-

[12] See Feit (2009) and the relevant works cited therein, including Braun (1993).

tial framework since all of them can be traced back to the same reference-fixing event around the time of Plato's birth.

There are also referential frameworks for empty names. These begin not with reference-fixing events, but with acts of misperception, misdescription, make-believe, and the like. For example, different uses of 'Vulcan' can belong to the same referential framework since they can be traced back to a common source, perhaps a single initial act of misdescription (along the lines of 'the planet causing the irregularities in Mercury's orbit'). Likewise, different uses of 'Sherlock Holmes' belong to the same referential framework since they can be traced to a single act of storytelling. In general, then, whether a name is empty or not, uses of it will belong to the same referential framework provided that they can be traced back to a common source. For co-referential non-empty names, this common source will be their referent, the bearer of the names. For empty names, the common source might be an act of misdescription, misperception, make-believe, or the like.[13]

I said above that a referential framework contains utterances and (token) mental states; overt utterances of names are not the only things that may belong to a referential framework. Such a framework, then, can contain token belief states (particular events of a subject believing something at a time) and the like. Such a belief state need not even involve a "mental tokening" of a proper name at all, so long as it is appropriately related to other events in a causal chain that began with a reference-fixing event or an act of misperception, misdescription, or make-believe. For example, a believer might employ in thought a description that she somehow associates with the relevant name. What goes for names also goes for these other items that might belong to a referential framework – two such items belong two the same referential framework just in case they can be traced back to a common source.

The following account, I think, adequately handles the problem of substitutivity and the problem of empty names, and thereby improves on the preliminary property-theoretic semantics given above (here N is a possibly empty proper name, and F is a predicate that expresses the property *F*):

> *Semantics for Belief Reports with Names*: A belief report of the form ⌜S believes that N is F⌝ is true iff (i) there is an appropriate relation of acquaintance R such that the bearer of S self-ascribes *bearing R uniquely to something that has F*; and (ii) the token self-ascription in (i), and the use of N in the utterance of the report, belong to the same referential framework.

[13] This is overly simplistic, but will serve my purposes here. See Everett (2000) for more discussion, including discussion of how names like 'Santa' and 'Father Christmas' can belong to the same referential framework.

This account accommodates the intuition that an utterance of (3) above might be true while an utterance of (4) is false, that is, the intuition that co-referential names are not always substitutable *salva veritate*. As discussed above, there can be contexts where a given relation of acquaintance is not appropriate – in virtue of contextually determined restrictions that rule it out – even though the believer stands in that relation to the bearer of the relevant name. For example there are natural contexts of utterance for sentence (4) in which Twainish relations are not appropriate. The relation *having heard of an author under the name 'Mark Twain'*, even though Ed bears it to Samuel Clemens, would not be appropriate in such a context and so could not help to make true an utterance of (4).

The account also accommodates the intuition that true belief reports can contain empty names in their *that*-clauses. Unlike the preliminary account, the present view does not require the alleged believer to stand in any relation of acquaintance to the bearer of the relevant proper name. Instead, all that is required is that the believer's act of self-ascription belong to the same referential framework as the speaker's use of the name in the belief report. This can be the case even if the name lacks a bearer. So utterances of sentences such as (5) and (6) can be true on the proposed semantics. For example, if I utter (5) – 'Virginia believes that Santa Claus will bring her presents' – then I use the name 'Santa Claus', and this token belongs to a certain referential framework. Virginia might self-ascribe the property *having heard of a jolly man named 'Santa' who will bring me presents* (or, somewhat more formally, λx*[x has heard of some y such that y is a jolly man named 'Santa', and y will bring x presents]*). If Virginia's token self-ascription of this (relational) property belongs to the same referential framework as my utterance of 'Santa Claus', as it very well might, then my utterance is true.

I should note that with respect to belief reports containing embedded non-empty names, this account gives the same results as the preliminary account (putting aside the issues about "appropriate" relations). Suppose that I utter 'Ben believes that Obama is president'. Suppose also that for some (appropriate) relation of acquaintance *R*, Ben self-ascribes *bearing R uniquely to somebody who is president*. Now, if Ben's act of self-ascription and my use of the name 'Obama' belong to the same referential framework, they must share a common source, which in this case is Obama himself. But this means that Ben must bear *R* to Obama, as the preliminary account required.

The account of truth conditions given above seems a bit clumsy and complex. There is a way to simplify it, or at least to make it appear simpler. This is a matter of what makes a relation of acquaintance *appropriate* in a given context. Up until now, I have been thinking of this in descriptive terms. For example, imagine a context in which I am reporting the beliefs of Lois Lane, and in which it would seem false for me to say 'Lois believes that Clark Kent can fly'. (Treat the Superman stories as actual fact – empty names are not the issue here.) Lois bears several relations of acquaintance to Superman/Clark Kent. Here are four: (a) *looking at a superhero in a blue and red suit*, (b) *having heard of somebody under the name 'Superman'*, (c) *having heard of somebody under the name 'Clark Kent'*, and (d) *remembering a mild-mannered reporter who wears black-rimmed glasses*. On the basis of descriptive information contained in the relations (which happens to be metalinguistic in two cases), I want to call the first two relations 'Supermanish' and the second two 'Clark Kentish'. I also want to say that this is a context in which Supermanish relations are not appropriate. And I have been supposing that what makes this the case is somehow a matter of the descriptive information, that is, of the way in which Lois thinks of Superman/Clark Kent. (An adaptation of the hidden indexical theory might explain why Supermanish relations are not appropriate in this context by maintaining that my utterance involves implicit reference to a Clark Kentish type of relation. More on this in section 4 below.)

So, descriptive information is relevant to what makes a relation of acquaintance appropriate in a given context of utterance. But if we count the information concerning referential frameworks as part of what makes a relation appropriate, we can simplify the account. That is, we can say that a relation of acquaintance *R* is appropriate only if its self-ascription by the subject belongs to the same referential framework as the speaker's use of the relevant embedded name in the belief report. For example, suppose I utter 'Lois believes that Clark Kent can fly', and suppose Lois self-ascribes a property of the form *bearing R uniquely to somebody who can fly*. Then, *R* is appropriate only if Lois' act of self-ascription belongs to the same referential framework as my use of 'Clark Kent' in the belief report. This just packs the content of condition (ii) from the *Semantics for Belief Reports with Names*, as well as the contextually supplied restrictions on descriptive information, into the concept of an appropriate relation of acquaintance. The simpler account looks like this:

> *Simplified Semantics for Belief Reports with Names*: A belief report of the form ⌜S believes that N is F⌝ is true iff there is an appropriate relation of acquaintance R such that the bearer of S self-ascribes *bearing R uniquely to something that has F*.

Again, an appropriate relation of acquaintance must conform to contextually supplied restrictions on descriptive information, and must be such that its self-ascription by the subject of belief belongs to the same referential framework as the speaker's use of N.

I would like to conclude this discussion by applying the foregoing semantics for proper names to Kripke's puzzle about belief. In Kripke's

(1979) example, utterances of 'Pierre believes that London is pretty' and 'Pierre believes that London is not pretty' are true, but Pierre himself is perfectly consistent and does not hold contradictory beliefs. My account is consistent with this natural description and provides a satisfying account of the example. Pierre bears two different relations of acquaintance (R1 and R2, let's say) to London, and he self-ascribes these two properties: *bearing R1 to a city that is pretty*, and *bearing R2 to a city that is not pretty*. These self-ascribed properties are perfectly consistent in the sense that it is possible to have both of them, and so Pierre is consistent. In the imagined contexts of utterance, R1 and R2 are appropriate relations and so the two belief reports about Pierre are both true. Again, the *that*-clauses in the reports do not specify the contents of Pierre's beliefs, that is, the properties that he self-ascribes. Pierre *ascribes* (in Lewis's sense) inconsistent properties to London, namely *being pretty* and *not being pretty*, but he does this in virtue of self-ascribing properties that are themselves consistent. So the property theory accounts for Pierre's consistency, and also provides some sense in which he might be said to have contradictory beliefs.[14]

I will conclude this section with a short discussion of natural kind terms and other general terms that can give rise to puzzles like Frege's and Kripke's. It is well known that such terms behave much like proper names, and (like the account of belief reports containing names) my account will respect the Kripke-Putnam semantics for such terms. In particular I will assume that there are referential frameworks for kind terms as well as for names. I will first present the semantics for belief reports with kind terms, which is analogous to the account of names, and then briefly make some remarks to clarify it. I make no claim to exhaustiveness here – the account of truth conditions applies to only one sort of belief report. Here is the account (let 'K' be a kind term, and let "appropriate" be understood as in the *Simplified Semantics for Belief Reports with Names*):

> *Semantics for Belief Reports with Kind Terms*: A belief report of the form ⌈S believes that K is F⌉ is true iff there is an appropriate relation of acquaintance R such that the bearer of S self-ascribes *bearing R uniquely to a kind of thing that has F*.

I take it that a subject bears a relation of acquaintance to a *kind* of thing provided she bears one to an instance of the kind. But to have a belief about the kind rather than about the instance, she must self-ascribe a property of the sort italicized above, that is, she must take herself to be related to a kind and not just to an instance. (This condition makes use of the notion of a kind having a property, but this might be construed as its instances having the property as context requires.) To illustrate the account, consider an ut-

[14] See Feit (2001) and (2008: Chapter 6) for more discussion.

terance of 'Tom believes that gorse is spiny'. Suppose that Tom has heard of gorse under the term 'gorse' and that in the relevant context this relation of acquaintance is not ruled out on the basis of descriptive information. Then, if Tom self-ascribes a property such as *having heard of a spiny kind of shrub under the term 'gorse'*, and if Tom's self-ascription belongs to the same referential framework as the occurrence of 'gorse' in the utterance, this would make the report true.

By requiring a relation of acquaintance to be appropriate (in the relevant context of utterance) this account is consistent with intuitions about substitutivity. For example, it seems 'Tom believes that furze is spiny' might not be true in some context of utterance (even though furze is gorse). This is because contextually supplied restrictions might render inappropriate such relations as *having heard of a spiny kind of shrub under the name 'gorse'*. By not requiring the believer to bear some relation of acquaintance to the kind of thing picked out by the relevant general term, this account has no problem with empty kind terms. For example, an utterance of 'Joseph believes that phlogiston is released in combustion' might be true despite the fact that there is no phlogiston. As long as Joseph *takes himself* to be acquainted with a certain fiery element under an appropriate relation R, and self-ascribes a property of the form *bearing R to a kind of thing released in combustion*, the utterance is true. (Remember that part of what makes R appropriate is that Joseph's self-ascription involving it, and the occurrence of the term 'phlogiston' in the utterance, belong to the same referential framework).

In this section, I have defended an approach to the truth conditions of certain belief reports that respects a Kripke/Putnam/direct reference view of proper names and certain general terms. This sort of semantic externalism is compatible with the type of psychological internalism that I favor, according to which molecule-for-molecule intrinsic duplicates have the same cognitive contents – they self-ascribe all the same properties. (The property of self-ascribing a relational property can itself be an intrinsic property. I can be alone in my world, for example, but have the property *self-ascribing the property of looking at somebody who is a spy*.) Intuitions about substitutivity are handled with the notion of appropriate relations of acquaintance – any non-Fregean view will have to employ something of this sort, I think, either at the level of semantics or pragmatics. Embedded empty names and general terms in belief reports are handled by not requiring the (alleged) believer to stand in a relation of acquaintance to the name's bearer, but instead to have a mental token that belongs to the same referential framework as the speaker's use of the name. In the case of an embedded non-empty name, this has the effect that the believer must be acquainted with the name's bearer in order for the belief report to be true.

3 Purely *De Dicto* Belief Reports

In this section, I shall outline very briefly a semantics for belief reports that the previous two sections do not address. Reports like those given in (3)-(6) above are appropriately labeled *de dicto* in order to contrast them with *de re* attributions, but here I shall address reports that do not contain any of the following items: emphatic reflexives, pronouns, demonstratives, indexicals, proper names, and general terms for which Frege/Kripke puzzle cases might arise. So, I will briefly outline and defend an account of attributions of *purely de dicto* belief (if such there be). The following might be an example:

(7) Fred believes that everyone who is good is happy.

The beliefs that we attribute to one another with utterances of (7) and the like are uncommon. *Purely de dicto* belief (belief that is expressible without kind terms, names, pronouns, etc.) is quite rare, much more so perhaps than is typically assumed. For belief of this sort, I adopt the property-theoretic account advanced by Chisholm and Lewis. Every proposition P has a corresponding property, *being such that P*, and an individual has this property just in case P is true. That is, necessarily, for every individual X and proposition P, X has *being such that P* if and only if P. To believe a purely *de dicto* proposition (that is, one expressible without pronouns, names, etc.) is to self-ascribe the corresponding property. This results in a welcome theoretical uniformity of belief contents – they are always properties. Given this, we can state the following semantic account of purely *de dicto* belief attributions (here, let the complement sentence 'P' contain no names, kind terms, pronouns, etc., and let '*P*' designate the proposition it expresses in the context of utterance):

> *Semantics for Purely De Dicto Belief Reports*: A belief report of the form ⌈S believes that P⌉ is true iff the bearer of S self-ascribes *being such that P*.

This semantic account makes use of the reduction of the *de dicto* to the *de se* discussed above. I have defended this view against several sorts of objection.[15] Here I will briefly discuss just one worry, which has to do with the cognitive abilities needed to self-ascribe a property. Some have claimed that since a certain amount of self-awareness is necessary to self-ascribe a property, the property theory entails that many children and non-human animals fail to have any beliefs (see Markie (1988) for example). It seems to me, however, that the property theory has no such implication about the mental states of children and non-human animals. One need not have a

[15] See Feit (2010, 2008: chapter 4 especially).

robust sort of self-awareness in order to self-ascribe a property. There is no reason to think that the beliefs that require such self-awareness exhaust all of our beliefs; they might just make up a special subclass of *de se* beliefs. Non-human animals cannot self-ascribe many of the properties that we can self-ascribe (e.g., *being a philosopher*, *wanting the telephone to ring*), but this is a matter only of the peculiar contents of these beliefs. The property theory allows for the possibility that a subject might be capable of self-ascribing properties that correspond to propositions, while lacking the sort of rich psychology or self-awareness that is required to self-ascribe certain other properties. There is no good reason to deny that if one can believe the proposition *P*, then one can self-ascribe the property *being such that P*.

So, it seems that the present objection has no more force than, for example, the charge that the doctrine of propositions denies beliefs to children and animals because they lack the cognitive resources required to assent to propositions. One who wishes to press this objection must show that there is a need to distinguish believing a proposition from self-ascribing the corresponding property, and hence that *de dicto* belief cannot be subsumed under *de se* belief. The way to do this would be to show that believing a given proposition and self-ascribing the corresponding property must play different roles in the explanation of behavior. But I cannot think of any way to show this, and so I do not see any such need.

4 Truth Conditions, Logical Form, and Propositions Expressed

So far, I have proposed a few accounts of truth conditions for various types of belief report. In this final section, I will briefly consider how we might subsume these accounts under a more general approach to the truth conditions of belief reports. I will then briefly sketch my view on the implications of this for the project of providing interpretations of the logical forms of belief reports and identifying the propositions expressed by such reports (and attitude reports more generally).

I have proposed different accounts of truth conditions for different types of belief report: one account for *that*-clauses containing emphatic reflexives, such as 'she herself', another for *that*-clauses containing proper names, and so on. Might there be a more general account that applies to all types of belief report, regardless of the peculiarities of their *that*-clauses? The answer, I think, is yes and no. Yes in the sense that a general account can be provided, and no in the sense that the various specific accounts are still needed to make the general account precise.

The general account that I have in mind has been defended by Bach (1997). On this sort of account, a *that*-clause in a belief report does not function to specify, or refer to, something that someone believes. Bach puts the point this way:

> The Specification Assumption is false: even though their 'that'-clauses express propositions, belief reports do not in general specify things that people believe (or disbelieve) – they merely describe or characterize them... A belief report can be true even if what the believer believes is more specific than the proposition expressed by the 'that'-clause used to characterize what he believes. (1997: 225)[16]

On the view I wish to defend, a *that*-clause of a belief report might very well express a proposition, but the belief report (the uttered belief sentence) can be true even if its subject does not believe this proposition. In fact, the proposition expressed by the *that*-clause might be a part of the report's logical form, and the belief report itself might express a proposition relating the believer to the proposition expressed by the *that*-clause. All of this, however, is consistent with the possibility that the belief report is true even though the proposition expressed by the *that*-clause is not the content of any of the subject's beliefs.

So, property theorists (and others who reject the Specification Assumption) might just make use of Bach's terminology and help themselves to something like the following general account of truth conditions for belief reports with *that*-clauses:

> *Semantics for Belief Reports*: A belief report of the form ⌈S believes that P⌉ is true in context c iff in c, the semantic content of P characterizes something that the bearer of S believes (that is, the psychological content of one of her beliefs).

In the absence of an account of what it is for something to *characterize* a belief, this view is not precise enough to do much work. However, we can take the accounts of truth conditions given in the previous sections to provide the desired precision. For example, if P contains an emphatic reflexive, as in 'Valerie believes that she herself is a spy', then the content of P characterizes one of Valerie's belief contents if and only if this belief content is the property *being a spy*. And if P contains a proper name, as in 'Ed believes that Mark Twain is a novelist', then the content of P characterizes one of Ed's belief contents if and only if it is the property *bearing R uniquely to a novelist*, where *R* is a contextually appropriate relation of acquaint-

[16] Bach (1997) argues against the Specification Assumption, the view that *that*-clauses of true belief reports specify the contents of their subjects' beliefs. Here I agree with Bach. However, because of differences in our views about singular thought, I do not accept the view of truth conditions that Bach proposes (1997: 238). On Bach's view, moreover, although uttered belief sentences can communicate truths, they lack truth values (belief reports are not simply uttered belief sentences); this is something I would prefer to avoid.

ance. And so on. The specific accounts are doing the work, but the general semantics does seem to be a helpful way to unify them.

The general account above allows for a kind of context dependence of belief attributions. An utterance of a belief sentence might be true in one context while another utterance of the very same sentence is false in some other context. On the same note, the substitution of coreferential singular terms might change the truth value of a given belief sentence. As we have seen, the account offered in this paper posits contextually supplied restrictions on which relations of acquaintance are appropriate in order to allow this kind of context dependence. The impact this has on the logical form of, and the proposition expressed by, a belief report will be considered shortly.

Before turning to the issues concerning logical form, I would like to say one more thing about the general account of truth conditions just sketched. On this account, for a belief report to be true, the *semantic content* of the embedded sentence must characterize something that the subject believes. Why not just say that the *proposition expressed* by the embedded sentence must do this? There are, I think, a couple of reasons. One of them has to do with empty names. It is plausible to think that sentences with empty names (even when embedded) do not express propositions, and so – if we want true belief reports with embedded empty names – we cannot make use of propositions generally.[17] The other reason has to do with reports of *de se* belief. Chierchia (1989) argues persuasively, at least to my mind, that in cases of *de se* belief reports, *that*-clauses denote properties rather than propositions. Chierchia's main idea is that embedded sentences that contain pronominal elements can behave as open formulae, or properties. (This is similar to, and derives some support from, the way in which infinitives – as in, for example, 'Valerie wants to wear a trench coat' – plausibly denote or express properties.) So, if the semantic content of a *that*-clause containing a pronoun or emphatic reflexive is a property rather than a proposition, we have another reason not to make general use of the proposition expressed by an embedded sentence.

I would like finally to turn to the issue of the logical form of belief reports. If Chierchia is right, and I think he is, then at the level of form, belief reports sometimes report relations to properties and sometimes to propositions. More precisely, belief reports with embedded emphatic reflexives will report relations to properties, those with other pronominal elements (for example, 'Valerie believes that she is a spy') will have a reading on which they report relations to properties, and the others will report relations to

[17] I assume that an embedded sentence with an empty name has some semantic content, which, although it is not a proposition, can play the role of characterizing a belief in a given context. For more discussion, see Feit (2009).

propositions. But I also think that a certain sort of contextualism makes the best sense of our total evidence having to do with attitude reports generally. That is, I am inclined to think that belief reports do not *just* report relations to properties or propositions, but to something else as well. This something else is most commonly taken to be a type of mode of presentation by means of which the subject is said to grasp the proposition in question (or perhaps one or more of its constituents). On my view, the something else will be a type of relation of acquaintance that the subject is said to bear to one of the proposition's constituents. So, I am inclined to accept a kind of hidden indexical or contextualist account of belief reports.[18]

Consider an utterance of 'Joe believes that Valerie is a spy', which is (1) above. The view that I favor assigns to this utterance something like the following form:

(1f) ∃m[Φm and Believes (Joe, <Valerie, being a spy>, m)][19]

This form has Joe standing in a relation to a certain proposition and a certain type of something else, m. We can think of m as a mode of presentation of, or a way of grasping, the relevant proposition. On the property-theoretic approach, m will either be, or consist of, relations of acquaintance between the subject and one or more constituents of the proposition. For example, if (the speaker thinks that) Joe is looking at Valerie, then m might be composed of the *looking at* relation.[20]

A contextualist account of this sort has many virtues. First, it respects Direct Reference, the view that the meaning of a proper name is simply its referent. Second, it respects Semantic Innocence, the view that the semantic content of a linguistic expression does not change when the expression is embedded in a *that*-clause. Third, it makes sense of the intuition that the substitution of co-referring terms can change the truth value of an attitude report. However, it does this in a way that is consistent with a standard, plausible principle of Substitutability, namely the view that if two terms are co-referring in a given context, then they are intersubstitutable *salva veritate* in that context. Belief reports like 'Ed believes that Mark Twain is a novelist' and 'Ed believes that Samuel Clemens is a novelist' can have different truth values relative to different modes of presentation or relations of acquaintance, but context supplies the modes or relations. So, in the same

[18] This sort of account was put forward by Schiffer (1977, 1992), although he does not actually endorse it. Versions of the general view, with important differences between them, have been defended by Crimmins and Perry (1989), Richard (1990), Crimmins (1992), Recanati (1993), Jaszczolt (1999, 2000), and others.

[19] See Schiffer (1992). On the view put forward by Schiffer, Φ is an "implicitly referred to and contextually determined type of mode of presentation" (1992: 503).

[20] In this case, m might also be composed of a type of way in which Joe is related to the kind *spy*, or to the plurality of spies. See Feit (2001, 2008: Ch. 6-7) for more discussion.

context the reports will have the same truth value, as Substitutability implies.

I will conclude by considering a few objections to the account just sketched, and by offering some replies. On my account, as it turns out, belief reports do report relations between believers and propositions (and something else, but the concern here has to do with propositions). One might worry that this is not consistent with the property theory of belief content presented at the beginning of this paper, or with the subsequent accounts of truth conditions. If the *that*-clause of a true belief report expresses a proposition, it seems, the subject must bear *some* relation to that proposition. Bach considers a similar sort of concern with his own account, and gives what I take to be the right response:[21]

> The trouble with this objection, however, is that the relation in question is not the belief relation. If it were, then Peter would bear the belief relation both to the proposition that Paderewski had musical talent and to the proposition that Paderewski did not have musical talent, in which case he would believe contradictory propositions. (1997: 232)

Bach's response has to do with rejecting the Specification Assumption. The proposition expressed by the *that*-clause does not specify the content of the subject's belief, it merely characterizes it. So, the relation between the subject and the proposition is not the belief relation itself; instead it is part of the characterization-of-belief relation. (Kripke's puzzles, as we saw briefly in section 2 above, give us strong independent grounds to reject the Specification Assumption.) The form of a belief report has the believer standing in a relation to a proposition and relations of acquaintance, and the report expresses the proposition that the believer is so related, but *this* proposition (the one expressed by the belief report) is not one that is true if and only if the believer believes the proposition to which she stands in the given relation. This is an important difference between my account and other hidden indexical theories.

Another objection to contextualist accounts has to do with compositionality. Since implicitly referred to, indexical entities (whether they be modes of presentation or relations of acquaintance) have no correlates in the grammar of belief sentences, the semantic value of a belief report is not merely a function of the structure of the uttered belief sentence and its constituents.[22] This is fair enough, a contextualist account of the sort I favor does violate this kind of compositionality, which might be taken to weigh against the account. But there are arguably many sorts of counterexample

---

[21] Here Bach alludes to Kripke's case of Peter, who has heard of Paderewski in two different circles. Peter assents to both 'Paderewski had musical talent' and 'Paderewski did not have musical talent', mistakenly thinking that he has heard of two different men.

[22] For some discussion of this issue, see Bach (1997) and Brogaard (2008).

to this kind of compositionality, some of which are discussed by Crimmins (1992).[23] So, there is good reason to think that this kind of compositionality does not hold in general. Contextualist accounts are consistent with other plausible principles – which also deserve to be called principles of compositionality and allow for "unarticulated constituents" in the sense of Perry (1986) – and so we should not be too quick to reject them.

The concern having to do with compositionality is closely related to a concern about the "adicity" of the relation expressed by the verb 'believes'.[24] If we look at form (1f) above, we see that 'believes' is taken to express a triadic relation. Many people find this to be unreasonable since, on the face of it at least, 'believes' appears to express a dyadic relation (and the same goes for other attitude verbs). It seems to me, however, that the present concern is nothing over and above the concern about compositionality. Moreover, the linguistic evidence that 'believes' expresses a dyadic relation is far from conclusive.[25] And finally, Ludlow (1996) argues that the hidden indexical theory can accommodate the view that 'believes' does indeed express a dyadic relation. Ludlow's account would replace (1f) with a form that treats 'believes' as expressing a dyadic relation and has the hidden indexical in adjunct position.

It is important to remember that, even if 'believes' does express a triadic relation between subjects, propositions, and something else, the triadic relation is not the belief relation. The belief relation relates the subject and the content of her belief (on my view, this is a dyadic relation between subjects and properties). The triadic relation, on the other hand, holds between a subject and that which *characterizes* her belief (a proposition, along with contextually supplied relations of acquaintance that the subject bears to its constituents). The proposition expressed by a belief report, then, is one that relates the subject to that which characterizes her belief. Much of this paper has been focused on exploring truth conditions for such propositions.

I would like to conclude with a brief comparison of my view and a couple of related accounts. On Bach's (1997) account, *that*-clauses in belief sentences do not serve to specify the exact content of the attributed belief. However, on Bach's view, belief sentences do not have truth values. An uttered belief sentence is taken to be semantically underdetermined or incomplete. So it fails to express a complete proposition, although it can be

---

[23] Crimmins calls this version of compositionality "full articulation," since it demands that everything that goes into the semantic value of an utterance be the content of some expression in the sentence uttered (see 1992: 9-21 for discussion). Utterances of 'It's raining' and 'I loved John's book' are plausibly taken to be counterexamples to full articulation since the first might involve implicit reference to a place that need not be the place of utterance, and the second might involve implicit reference to the relation John bears to the book, for example authorship or ownership.

[24] See especially Schiffer (1992, 1996).

[25] See Ludlow (1995, 1996) and Jaszczolt (2000) for discussion of the adicity problem.

used to *communicate* something with a truth value (Bach reserves the term 'belief report' for this).[26] What is communicated is partly a function of pragmatic information, but this does not contribute to the proposition expressed. On a second view – a pragmatic enrichment view – pragmatic information does contribute to the proposition expressed. Pragmatic processes enrich the logical form of a belief report to generate the complete proposition, which can include information about modes of presentation. On both of these views, the form of a belief report is simpler than it is on a hidden indexical account (these views agree with neo-Russellian views about form). I think the advantages of the hidden indexical view make up for this, but I see the second view just sketched as an attractive option if insuperable difficulties for hidden indexical theories arise.

The property theory of content provides the best treatment of *de se* belief and other *de se* attitudes. (I would also make the stronger claim that the property theory, or some variant of it, provides the only adequate treatment of *de se* attitudes.) Since *de se* attitudes and *de se* attitude reports are ubiquitous, and since the property theory provides an attractive account of the cognitive attitudes in general, our account of attitude reports should accommodate it. In this paper, I have appealed to the property theory to give an account of the truth conditions of a wide range of belief reports, and I have tried to show that a plausible and widely accepted (but not uncontroversial) account of logical form can yield these truth conditions.

References

Bach, K. 1997. 'Do Belief Reports Report Beliefs?', *Pacific Philosophical Quarterly*, 78: 215-241.

Berg, J. 1988. 'The Pragmatics of Substitutivity', *Linguistics and Philosophy*, 11: 355-370.

Braun, D. 1993. 'Empty Names', *Noûs*, 27: 449-69.

Braun, D. 1998. 'Understanding Belief Reports', *Philosophical Review*, 107: 555-595.

Brogaard, B. 2008. 'Attitude Reports: Do You Mind the Gap?', *Philosophy Compass*, 3: 93-118.

Chierchia, G. 1989. 'Anaphora and Attitudes *De Se*', in R. Bartsch et al., eds., *Language in Context* (Dordrecht: Foris), 1-31.

Chisholm, R. 1979. 'The Indirect Reflexive', in C. Diamond and J. Teichman, eds., *Intention and Intentionality: Essays in Honour of G. E. M. Anscombe* (Brighton: The Harvester Press), 39-53.

Chisholm, R. 1981. *The First Person* (Minneapolis: University of Minnesota Press).

Crimmins, M. 1992. *Talk about Beliefs* (Cambridge, Mass: MIT Press).

[26] See Brogaard (2008) for more discussion of Bach's descriptivist account.

Crimmins, M. and J. Perry. 1989. 'The Prince and the Phone Booth: Reporting Puzzling Beliefs', *Journal of Philosophy*, 86: 685-711.

Egan, A. 2006. 'Secondary Qualities and Self-Location', *Philosophy and Phenomenological Research*, 72: 97-119.

Evans, G. 1982. *The Varieties of Reference* (Oxford: Oxford University Press).

Everett, A. 2000. 'Referentialism and Empty Names', in A. Everett and T. Hofweber, eds., *Empty Names, Fiction, and the Puzzles of Non-Existence* (Stanford: CSLI Press), 37-60.

Feit, N. 2000. 'Self-Ascription and Belief *De Re*', *Philosophical Studies*, 98: 37-51.

Feit, N. 2001. 'Rationality and Puzzling Beliefs', *Philosophy and Phenomenological Research*, 63: 29-55.

Feit, N. 2006. 'The Doctrine of Propositions, Internalism, and Global Supervenience', *Philosophical Studies*, 131: 447-457.

Feit, N. 2008. *Belief about the Self: A Defense of the Property Theory of Content* (New York: Oxford University Press).

Feit, N. 2009. 'Naming and Nonexistence', *Southern Journal of Philosophy*, 47: 239-262.

Feit, N. 2010. 'Selfless Desires and the Property Theory of Content', *Australasian Journal of Philosophy*, 88: 489-503.

Forbes, G. 1987. 'Indexicals and Intensionality: A Fregean Perspective', *Philosophical Review*, 96: 3-31.

Jaszczolt, K. M. 1999. *Discourse, Beliefs, and Intentions: Semantic Defaults and Propositional Attitude Ascription* (Oxford: Elsevier Science).

Jaszczolt, K. M. 2000. 'The Default-Based Context-Dependence of Belief Reports', in K. M. Jaszczolt, ed., *The Pragmatics of Propositional Attitude Reports* (Oxford: Elsevier Science), 169-185.

Kaplan, D. 1989. 'Demonstratives', in J. Almog, J. Perry, and H. Wettstein, eds., *Themes from Kaplan* (Oxford: Oxford University Press), 481-564.

Kripke, S. 1979. 'A Puzzle about Belief', in A. Margalit, ed., *Meaning and Use* (Dordrecht: D. Reidel), 239-283.

Kripke, S. 1980. *Naming and Necessity* (Cambridge, Mass.: Harvard University Press).

Lewis, D. 1979. 'Attitudes *De Dicto* and *De Se*', *Philosophical Review*, 87: 513-545.

Lewis, D. 1986. *On the Plurality of Worlds* (Oxford: Blackwell).

Loar, B. 1976. 'The Semantics of Singular Terms', *Philosophical Studies*, 30: 353-377.

Ludlow, P. 1995. 'Logical Form and the Hidden-Indexical Theory: A Reply to Schiffer', *Journal of Philosophy*, 92: 102-107.

Ludlow, P. 1996. 'The Adicity of "Believes" and the Hidden Indexical Theory', *Analysis*, 56: 97-101.

Markie, P. 1988. 'Multiple Propositions and "*De Se*" Attitudes', *Philosophy and Phenomenological Research*, 48: 573-600.

McDowell, J. 1984. '*De Re* Senses', *Philosophical Quarterly*, 34: 283-294.

McKay, T. 1981. 'On Proper Names in Belief Ascriptions', *Philosophical Studies*, 39: 287-303.

Peacocke, C. 1981. 'Demonstrative Thought and Psychological Explanation', *Synthese*, 49: 187-217.

Perry, J. 1986. 'Thought without Representation', *Proceedings of the Aristotelian Society Supplementary Volume*, 60: 263-283.

Recanati, F. 1993. *Direct Reference: From Language to Thought* (Oxford: Blackwell).

Richard, M. 1983. 'Direct Reference and Ascriptions of Belief', *Journal of Philosophical Logic*, 12: 425-452.

Richard, M. 1990. *Propositional Attitudes* (New York: Cambridge University Press).

Salmon, N. 1986. *Frege's Puzzle* (Cambridge, MA: MIT Press).

Salmon, N. 1989. 'Illogical Belief', *Philosophical Perspectives*, 3: 243-285.

Schiffer, S. 1977. 'Naming and Knowing', *Midwest Studies in Philosophy*, 2: 28-41.

Schiffer, S. 1992. 'Belief Ascription', *Journal of Philosophy*, 89: 499-521.

Schiffer, S. 1996. 'The Hidden-Indexical Theory's Logical-Form Problem: A Rejoinder', *Analysis*, 56: 92-97.

Soames, S. 1987. 'Direct Reference, Propositional Attitudes, and Semantic Content', *Philosophical Topics*, 15: 47-87.

Soames, S. 1995. 'Beyond Singular Propositions', *Canadian Journal of Philosophy*, 25: 515-549.

5

The Myth of the Problematic *De Se*

MICHAEL DEVITT

1 Introduction

There is a lot that we don't know about the metaphysics of thoughts (propositional attitudes) and about the semantics of their ascriptions. But the received view is that there is something *particularly* problematic about first person thoughts, commonly known as '*de se*'. These are thoughts we express in a special way, using first-person pronouns; thus, I now have a *de se* thought that I might express, 'I am in New York'. Furthermore, the received view is that there is something *particularly* problematic about the ascription of *de se* thoughts. These are ascriptions we often make in a special way, using a reflexive pronoun; thus, someone might ascribe that *de se* thought to me, 'You believe that you yourself are in New York'. I think that the received view is a myth, an artifact of misguided philosophical approaches to the mind and semantics. I have implied this before (1981a, 1984, 1990, 1996), to sadly little effect. The myth lives on, as many papers in this volume, indeed the very conception of this volume, attest. I shall take this opportunity to deflate the myth a bit differently and more pointedly.

My main aim is to offer an approach that shows that the *de se is not* especially problematic (particularly in secs. 6, 9). Still, along the way, I will look critically at some aspects of other approaches that have helped create the myth that the *de se is* especially problematic. (i) It is common to think that the alleged problem of the *de se* has its roots in the talk of propositions that dominates theories of thoughts and their ascriptions (sec. 2). Yet that talk is unnecessary and mistaken. I shall harp on this often (but particularly in secs. 5, 8). (ii) I think that this mistake is encouraged by a failure to give appropriate priority to the theory of thought over the semantics of thought

Attitudes De Se: Linguistics, Epistemology, Metaphysics.
Neil Feit and Alessandro Capone (eds.).

ascriptions (sec. 3). For, it is wrongly taken for granted that we need to posit propositions to explain the semantics of ascriptions (sec. 8). (iii) Worse, there is a tendency to confuse thoughts with their ascriptions. This is most notable in the application of the unclear terms '*de dicto*' and '*de re*' to both. In my view (Appendix), these two terms have brought a great deal of confusion into the debate and are best avoided altogether.

I emphasize throughout that minds and their languages are parts of the natural world, interacting causally with other parts of that world. So the study of them should be an empirical enterprise (secs. 4, 7). (This does not mean that much of it cannot be done from an armchair.) This 'naturalizing' is central to my approach. I think, but will not argue, that the approaches that have led to the myth of the problematic *de se* have been far too influenced by formal semantics.

2 The Alleged Problem of the *De Se*

The myth is that the *de se* poses a serious problem. Indeed, Neil Feit (2013) describes it as 'one of several great puzzles in contemporary philosophy of mind'. So, what is the problem? The problem is so well-accepted that I shall be brief in describing it. I shall follow the custom and mostly use beliefs as examples of thoughts. And I shall use John Perry's delightful supermarket story to illustrate the alleged problem:

> I once followed a trail of sugar on a supermarket floor, pushing my cart down the aisle on one side of a tall counter and back the aisle on the other, seeking the shopper with the torn sack to tell him he was making a mess. With each trip around the counter, the trail became thicker. But I seemed unable to catch up. Finally it dawned on me. I was the shopper I was trying to catch.
>
> I believed at the outset that the shopper with a torn sack was making a mess. And I was right. But I did not believe that I was making a mess. That seems to be something I came to believe. And when I came to believe that, I stopped following the trail around the counter and rearranged the torn sack in my cart. My change in beliefs seems to explain my change in behavior. (1993: 33)

1. The first difficulty that this allegedly raises is that of identifying/expressing the belief that makes the difference in Perry's behavior. Perry puts the worry like this:

> all we have to identify the belief is the sentence 'I am making a mess'. But that sentence by itself does not seem to identify the crucial belief, for if [p.34] someone else had said it, they would have expressed a different belief, a false one. (33–4)

William Lycan makes a similar point, claiming that there 'seems to be no way for us to express the content' of a belief like Perry's 'outside a belief operator' (1988: 84–5). *We* can't express it by saying, as Perry did, 'I am making a mess'; we can only identify it by saying that Perry believed that *he himself* was making a mess. Now it is far from obvious where the problem is here. Why, for example, is Perry's belief not adequately identified/expressed by *Perry* saying 'I am making a mess', irrespective of what any other person would identify/express by uttering that sentence?

2. The real difficulties seem to start with talk of propositions. The standard view is that 'the objects' of beliefs are 'propositions', thought of as 'abstract mind- and language-independent objects' (Schiffer 1992: 506–7). And these Platonic entities are commonly identified with the sets of possible worlds in which they are true. So the propositional object of the belief Perry expresses, 'I am making a mess', is the set of all the possible worlds in which Perry is making a mess. But if we return to the supermarket, we can immediately see a problem. Suppose that Perry sees himself in a mirror without realizing that he is seeing himself. He comes to believe a proposition he would express, 'That man is making a mess'. And the problem is that this proposition is *also* the set of all the possible worlds in which Perry is making a mess. So this account of propositions fails to capture the dramatic *change* in Perry's beliefs when he realizes, 'I am making a mess', a realization that leads him to stop following the trail and rearrange the torn sack. Lycan discusses a similar example in which Smith changes from believing a singular proposition he would express using a demonstrative to believing one he would express using the first person:

> Yet what he does come to believe … has exactly the same truth conditions as that singular proposition and is true in just the same possible worlds … there is no clear sense in which the new belief differs in content from what Smith believed all along. (p. 85)

3. Lycan's talk of 'truth conditions' brings out that the problem goes beyond the possible-worlds view of Platonic propositions. A 'singular proposition' is often identified with a set of objects like Perry and properties like *making a mess*. But then, once again, the proposition that Perry believed when looking in the mirror would have to be the same one that he came to believe when he changed his behavior. But it clearly isn't.

Perry sums up the problem: '"I am making a mess" does not identify a proposition … something is badly wrong with the traditional doctrine of propositions' (1993: 37–8), a doctrine that he finds 'otherwise plausible' (p. 34). His solution is to 'make a sharp distinction between objects of belief and belief states' (p. 34). David Lewis' solution in his classic 1979 paper, 'Attitudes *De Dicto* and *De Se*' (in Lewis 1983), is to abandon propositions in favor of properties as the objects of beliefs. This is characteristically ingenious but nonetheless implausible, as Wayne Davis nicely shows (2013; see also

Recanati 2009: 262–6). My solution is very different. We don't need a sharp distinction between belief states and the traditional propositional objects of beliefs because we don't need those objects at all: We should get by, in effect, with just belief states. The apparent problem is an artifact of traditional doctrines of propositions.

To see what has gone wrong, we need to consider how we should approach theorizing about thoughts and their ascriptions. In the next section I shall argue that we should give priority to the theory of thoughts. In Sections 4–6, I shall make some suggestions for the theory of thoughts that seem sufficient to show that various 'puzzle' cases, including the *de se*, are not puzzling at the level of thoughts. These suggestions eschew all talk of propositions. In Sections 7–9, I shall do likewise for the theory of thought ascriptions.

3 'Put Metaphysics First'

A theory of thoughts (propositional attitudes) and a theory of their ascriptions are different, but they are clearly related. On the one hand, thoughts have semantic properties, 'contents', as they are usually called. So we cannot give a theory of thoughts without commitment to a semantic theory, which will have implications for a theory of thought ascriptions. On the other hand, we cannot give a theory of thought ascriptions without implying some view of the thoughts ascribed.

Some time back, Lycan pointed out that

> until recently, semanticists investigating belief sentences, particularly those semanticists working within the possible-worlds format, have paid no attention to the question of what psychological reality it is that makes such sentences true (1988: 8).

He rightly thinks that such attention is necessary for our theory of belief ascriptions. I took a similar line in 'Thoughts and Their Ascriptions' (1984) but went further in criticizing the traditional approach to the semantics of thought ascriptions. After emphasizing the distinction between a theory of thought ascriptions and a theory of thoughts, I continued:

> The question arises: Which theory should one start with? It is common for philosophers to start with the theory of thought ascription, leaving the theory of thought pretty much to look after itself. I think this is a mistake. (p. 385)

Now, my impression is that things have improved since Lycan and I made these criticisms (see, for example, Feit 2013). But I don't think that they have improved enough. In the rest of this section, I shall summarize an argument for the importance of giving priority to the theory of thought.

The case for the priority of a theory of thought rests on an argument for the *general* view that our semantic theories should be guided by our theories of the world rather than vice versa. In doing semantics, we should follow the slogan 'Put metaphysics first'.

Why? First, *because we know much more about the way the world is than we do about the semantics of our thought and talk about that world.* I have argued for this, and the methodology it supports, in the course of arguing against the linguistic turn in contemporary philosophy. Similarly, I have argued that we should reject the epistemological turn in modern philosophy, that so threatened 'realism about the external world', because we know much more about the way the world is than we do about how we know about that world. We should approach semantics and epistemology from a metaphysical perspective rather than vice versa because experience has taught us a great deal about the world but rather little about how we refer to and know about this world. We know much more about physics than about the language of physics, much more about biology than about the language of biology, much more about morals than about the language of morals, and, to take a recent issue, much more about knowing how than about the ascription of knowing how.[1] My argument for this position reflects a somewhat Moorean approach. More importantly, it reflects Quinean naturalism: The metaphysics that we should put first is a naturalized one (1996, 1997a, 2010).

Second, in semantics, as in any science, *we should be guided by Occam*, positing objects only when they do explanatory work. Now, in doing semantics we obviously need to posit the mental and linguistic objects that *have* the semantic properties that interested us in the first place (secs. 4, 7). The mental objects, thoughts, are concrete physical states. The linguistic objects are concrete physical sounds, inscriptions, and the like. But we should doubt that there could be any explanatory need in semantics to posit any *other* 'new' objects. Rather, we should expect to be able to explain the semantic properties of thoughts and the language that expresses them in terms of their relations to 'old' objects, objects we already suppose to exist for reasons quite independent of semantics. Thus, we should expect to explain the semantic properties of biological thoughts and language in terms of their relations to the objects that constitute *biological reality*. Thus, Occamist considerations count against other 'new' objects. Why? Because it is hard to see how any other specially semantic entity can help explain what needs to be explained: the roles that thoughts and language play in people's dealings with nonsemantic reality, for example, with biological reality (roles to be discussed in sections 4 and 7, respectively). These expectations might be wrong, of course. Still, before doing the semantics of thought and language that concerns a certain area of reality we should determine, as best we can, what makes up that reality, determine what are the

[1] See Devitt 2011, a response to Stanley and Williamson 2001.

relevant 'old' objects: we should do the metaphysics first. For, if the thought and language seems to be yielding a more or less successful account of that reality, its relations to those 'old' objects are likely to constitute its meanings.[2]

Putting metaphysics first has the claimed immediate consequence that we should tackle the theory of thoughts before the theory of thought ascriptions. For, before doing the semantics of thought ascriptions we need to get as clear as we can about the area of reality that concerns those ascriptions. And that reality is, of course, thoughts.

Putting metaphysics first also provides the first step in the case against propositions. For, as we shall see, propositions are not among the 'old' objects for either the theory of thoughts or the theory of their ascriptions.

It is time to turn to the theory of thoughts.

4 Thoughts in General

The first thing to ask is why we should go along with the folk in believing that there are thoughts (propositional attitudes) in the first place. Why be 'intentional realists'? Now if there are thoughts, they are parts of the natural world that we posit because they play some causal role. From that naturalistic perspective, the case for intentional realism is very strong (2006a: 125–7). We need to posit thoughts to people for at least two reasons: to explain people's behaviors; and to explain the way people use others as a guide to a largely external reality. Thus, ascribing to Mark a belief that he would express, 'It is raining', explains both Mark's picking up an umbrella and how those present gain information about the weather (by assuming that he is reliable about such matters). We clearly have a great theoretical interest in the details of this process of explaining behavior and learning from each other.

So, what is a thought? Lewis begins his article by noting that despite the apparent 'diversity of objects' that beliefs concern—'a particular cat, … no particular cat, … a season, a phenomenon, an activity, a state, … a state of affairs'—, there has been an interest in finding uniformity: The consensus is that 'the objects of belief are uniform in category …. We mostly think that the attitudes uniformly have propositions as their objects' (1983: 133). Lewis is surely right: People do mostly think that. Yet if we turn to the theory of the mind, often neglected by semanticists as Lycan pointed out, we find an appealing alternative: The uniform category is not that of propositions but that of *mental representations*. We should embrace the popular 'Representational Theory of the Mind' ('RTM'), according to which any thought involves standing in a certain functional relation to a mental representation. So,

---

[2] Even if there is no reality that the language purports to concern – for example, there are no gods or witches—so the language does not seem to yield a successful account, our semantics should start from the fact of that nonreality.

propositional attitudes can be seen as uniformly having mental representations as 'their objects'.[3] Believing is distinguished from other propositional attitudes like desiring by the distinctive functional role of its representations. And one belief is distinguished from another by its representation. A thought has its role of causing behavior and providing information about the world in virtue of both its functional relation and the semantic properties of its mental representation.

We are committed to belief states. According to RTM, these include mental representations. These representations serve as 'objects' of belief and we need no others (except, perhaps, any objects *referred to by* those representations). Hence there is no need for Perry's sharp distinction between such objects and belief states.

RTM is the only robust assumption about the mind that I shall make. However, it is worth mentioning another more controversial assumption: the 'Language of Thought Hypothesis' ('LOTH'). RTM raises a question about the nature of the representations that partly constitute thoughts. According to LOTH, these representations have syntactic structures like a natural language: They are language-like rather than, say, map-like. So, a thought's representation is a mental *sentence* made up of mental *words*. It follows that expressing a thought is a translation process from a mental sentence to a linguistic sentence; and understanding a sentence is translation from the linguistic to the mental. I favor this view (1981a: 75–80; –1996: 154–8; 2006a: 145–7) and it is a helpful one to keep in mind in discussing mental representations. Still, my argument does not depend on LOTH.

We need a way of identifying thoughts. Consider an example, adapted from one of Quine's. Ralph has observed a man in questionable circumstances whom he recognizes as Bernard J. Ortcutt. He is led to a belief which he expresses, 'Ortcutt is a spy'. We would ordinarily describe this belief by saying, 'Ralph believes that Ortcutt is a spy'. But describing it this way has implications about the meanings of such ordinary belief ascriptions. I want to avoid any such implications until we start discussing those ascriptions in Section 8. So I shall not use those ascriptions until then. Instead, I shall simply identify a person's belief with the help of the sentence that she would use to explicitly express it (if an English speaker). So, I identify Ralph's belief as one *he would explicitly express by the sentence, 'Ortcutt is a spy'.* We can abbreviate. According to RTM, that belief contains a certain mental representation. Let us use '*Ortcutt is a spy*' to refer to that representation and

---

[3] This view is not strictly right because people have 'tacit' thoughts, ones that they would readily admit to but have never entertained. This requires a modification that can be ignored for the purposes of this paper. There is also an interesting problem with what RTM tells us about believing (2006a: 142-4).

then 'B*Orcutt is a spy*' to refer to the belief containing it. So B*Orcutt is a spy* *is* the belief that Ralph would explicitly express, 'Ortcutt is a spy'. And let us use '*Ortcutt*' to refer to the part (or aspect) of *Ortcutt is a spy* that refers to Ortcutt.

We have noted that it is partly in virtue of the semantic properties of mental representations, their contents, that thoughts have their causal roles. So just as the person Ortcutt has his causal role in virtue of being, say, intelligent and sly, so does the representation *Ortcutt* have its causal role in virtue of its content.[4] Clearly, then, we have to explain the nature of these contents that play such an important role. What is it about *Ortcutt is a spy* that explains why Ralph behaves as he does toward Ortcutt. Why does he *say* 'Ortcutt is a spy', stalk Ortcutt, and so on? And what is it about *Oscar is a spy* that might enable Ralph's acquaintances to learn from it about Ortcutt and spies? These are not easy questions, of course, but, if the Occamist considerations of the last section are correct, we should expect answers in terms of the relations that this mental representation has to Ortcutt, to spies (and, perhaps, to other thoughts). So, we do not expect explanations in terms of relations to 'new' objects posited especially for semantics but rather in terms of relations to 'old' objects like Ortcutt and spies that we already had good reasons for believing in, reasons having nothing to do with semantics.

5 Thoughts Without Propositions

This idea that semantics can get by with such 'old' objects is at odds with the consensus. The semantic investigation of thought ascriptions is dominated by philosophers who think that the reality consists also of 'propositions', objects introduced simply to do semantics. Now, if talk of propositions was just a technical device, or model, for throwing light on the actual properties of concrete thoughts and utterances but not to be taken seriously when the ontological chips are down, then we should have only the minor objection that it seems to be unnecessary and misleading. But the talk usually involves a serious commitment to Platonic objects of some sort, perhaps sets of possible worlds, that are separate from the concrete spatio-temporal world of meaningful thoughts.

A commitment to such Platonic propositions would be appropriate, Occam advises us, only if these propositions do real explanatory work. And it is hard to see how entities that are outside space-time could do any such work. Thoughts and the utterances that express them are parts of the natural physical world. How, then, *could* they be related to entities outside space-time? Even if they could, how *could* their being so related do any work?

[4] My talk of 'properties' here and elsewhere is just a convenience. To say that Ortcutt or *Ortcutt* has a causal role in virtue of its property *F-hood* is just to say that it has that role because it is *F*. So there is no commitment to an *entity F-hood*.

Our task is to ascribe properties to thoughts and utterances that can explain their causal role in the spatio-temporal world. Relations to objects outside the causal order surely could not do this. How could a relation to a Platonic object help explain the way *Ortcutt is a spy* causes Ralph's behavior and informs us about the world? If there are no nonsemantic reasons for believing in nonactual possible worlds, how could positing sets of them explain the role of thoughts in the actual world?

Apart from being explanatorily idle entities, Platonic propositions have another problem: They are deeply mysterious.

Now it might be objected that if these considerations against Platonic propositions were good, they should count equally against talk of numbers in physics. Yet physics is committed to numbers. I think that this commitment should be much more a source of discomfort about physics than it should be a source of comfort about propositions. We should seek some way of understanding physics that is not committed to Platonic objects, perhaps following Field (1980) in eliminating numbers altogether.

I am arguing that we should start semantics with a prejudice against Platonic propositions. But perhaps we will discover that they do explanatory work after all. I aim to show that they don't.

6 Some Particular Thoughts

6.1 Quine's Ortcutt

Let us start with Quine's actual Ortcutt case in his classic discussions of thought ascriptions.[5] Ralph has observed a man in a brown hat lurking suspiciously in the campus bushes and comes to a belief he would express 'The man in the brown hat is a spy':

(1) B*The man in the brown hat is a spy*.

On another occasion, Ralph has observed someone at the beach who he thinks of as a pillar of society and who, unbeknownst to Ralph, is that same man, namely Ortcutt. So, Ralph does *not* hold a belief he would express 'The man in the brown hat is the man seen at the beach':

(2) B*The man in the brown hat is the man seen at the beach*.

When we want to explain Ralph's behavior, we have an obvious interest in distinguishing (1), the belief that he has, from another one he does not,

[5] Quine 1953: 139–59; 1960: 141–51, 166–9; 1966: 183–94. My references to Quine are all to these discussions. My views reflect the influence of Quine but are in many respects quite unQuinean. My discussion of Ortcutt draws on more detailed earlier discussions, particularly 1996: 141–54.

(3) B*The man seen at the beach is a spy*,

even though both beliefs concern the same man. For, (1) explains some of Ralph's campus behavior but is irrelevant to his beach behavior whereas (3) would be irrelevant to his campus behavior and quite at odds with his beach behavior. Similarly, it is easy to see that an interest in explaining Ralph's behavior will want to distinguish both (1) and (3) from other beliefs that Ralph might have had,

(4) B*Orcutt is a spy*,

(5) B*You are a spy* (where Ortcutt is the person addressed).

Although all these beliefs contain representations that refer to Ortcutt, the different ways in which they refer to him, their different 'modes of reference', are obviously relevant to an explanation of Ralph's behavior, even an explanation by someone who knows that all these representations refer to Ortcutt. And were Ralph to come to hold (2), its different modes would be relevant to explaining his behavior in a way that the trivial belief,

(6) B*The man in the brown hat is the man in the brown hat,

would not.[6]

Far from having belief (3), Ralph in fact has the following belief,

(7) B*The man seen at the beach is not a spy*.

But there is nothing in the least irrational about Ralph having both (1) and (7) and there is nothing in the least puzzling that he does have both. Even though *the man in the brown hat* and *the man seen at the beach* refer to the same man, they do so in different ways and the beliefs containing them play different roles in Ralph's mental life.

Given the importance of a thought's mode of reference to the explanation of behavior, we should expect there to be a conventional way of conveying that mode in our ordinary ascriptions of thoughts. And, when we get to our discussion of thought ascriptions, we shall see that there is: We have what Quine calls 'opaque' thought ascriptions (sec. 9.1).

Modes matter when our interest in a person's beliefs are to explain her behavior. But they don't matter when our interest in her beliefs is to gather information about the world. Thus, we would of course all be concerned if any of our acquaintances were a spy. Now, suppose we think that Ralph is a good judge of spies. Then we would be interested in any belief that Ralph had of the form, B**a* is a spy*, where '*a*' refers to one of our acquaintances,

---

[6] I have discussed identity beliefs in some detail elsewhere, particularly 1984: 403–7; 1996: 171–9; 1997b: 382–6.

whatever Ralph's mode of referring to that individual. Should the individual be Ortcutt, it would not matter to us whether Ralph represented him by *Ortcutt*, *the man in the brown hat*, or whatever. We need to be able to identify the subject of Ralph's suspicions ourselves, of course, but it doesn't matter to us how *Ralph* identifies him. When our concern is to gather pertinent information about the entities in our world from the beliefs of another, her modes of representing those entities are not important.[7]

Given that the modes of reference of beliefs are not important to our gathering information from beliefs, we should expect there to be a conventional way of conveying the information in our ordinary ascriptions of thoughts without specifying a mode. And when we get to our discussion of thought ascriptions, we shall see that there is: We have what Quine calls 'transparent' thought ascriptions (9.1).

The above mental representations, *the man in the brown hat*, *the man seen at the beach*, *Ortcutt*, and *you* have 'fine-grained' contents referring to Ortcutt in various different ways, contents that are important to the representations' roles in explaining behaviors. But, of course, if they have those contents, they must *also* have the 'coarse-grained' content of simply referring to Ortcutt, a content that is important to their role of conveying information: To refer to him in a certain way is to refer to him. And there is no theoretical point in insisting that one of these layers of content is the *only true* content.[8] Lapsing into proposition-speak for a moment, there is no theoretical point in insisting that the object of a thought containing one of these representations is either a fine-grained or coarse-grained proposition: It has both objects.

6.2 Kripke's Paderewski

The same points can be made about a famous case of Saul Kripke's:[9]

> Peter . . . may learn the name 'Paderewski' with an identification of the person named as a famous pianist. Naturally, having learned this, Peter will assent to 'Paderewski had musical talent'. . . . Later, in a different circle, Peter learns of

---

[7] This is a bit of an overstatement (1996: 152). Modes do not matter to the informational content we want from the beliefs of another but they may do to our assessment of the reliability of the information. Thus, we may think that Ralph is reliable about Ortcutt under the mode of *the man in the brown hat* but not under the mode of *the man seen at the beach*.

[8] Similarly, I argue, there is no theoretical point to insisting that the linguistic tokens that express these mental representations have only one layer of 'meaning' or 'semantic value' (1996: 140–54). The idea that a name like 'Ortcutt' has a fine-grained meaning is, of course, rejected by 'direct reference'. In arguing against direct reference, I have claimed that names have meanings that are *causal* modes of referring rather than Fregean descriptive modes (1989; 1996: 179–86, 240–4; 2012).

[9] My discussion of this case draws on more detailed earlier discussions, particularly 1984: 407–12; 1996: 228–40. The latter discussion also concerns Kripke's case of Pierre and London.

> someone called 'Paderewski' who was a Polish nationalist leader and Prime Minister. Peter is skeptical of the musical abilities of politicians. . . . Using 'Paderewski' as a name for the *statesman*, Peter assents to, 'Paderewski had no musical talent'. (1979: 265)

Now clearly Peter has two different mental representations of Paderewski, two modes of referring to Paderewski, one he associates with *famous pianist*, the other with *Prime Minister*, and both of which he expresses using 'Paderewski'. If we name both representations '*Paderewski*' we will fail to distinguish them. So, let us name them, '*Paderewski$_1$*' and '*Paderewski$_2$*', respectively. Then we can say that Peter has the following two beliefs:

(8) B*Paderewski$_1$ has musical talent*

(9) B*Paderewski$_2$ has no musical talent*.

Peter has made a mistake in failing to hold,

(10) B*Paderewski$_1$ is Paderewski$_2$*.

But this is no more a sign of irrationality in Peter than is Ralph failing to hold (2) a sign of irrationality in Ralph. However, whereas there is no problem using ordinary thought ascriptions to describe Ralph's beliefs, Kripke pointed out that there is such a problem with Peter's beliefs (9.2).

6.3 Richard's Phone Booth

Next consider a nice case invented by Mark Richard:[10]

> *A* ... both sees a woman, across the street, in a phone booth, and is speaking to a woman through a phone. He does not realize that the woman to whom he is speaking—*B*, to give her a name—is the woman he sees. He perceives her to be in some danger—a run-away steamroller, say, is bearing down upon her phone booth. *A* waves at the woman; he says nothing into the phone. (1983: 439)

A has the following false belief,

(11) B*She is not you*,

where *she* is prompted by his seeing the woman across the street and *you*, by his conversation with the woman over the phone. He is led to wave by his belief,

(12) B*She is in danger*.

However, he says nothing into the phone because he believes

---

[10] My discussion of this case draws on a more detailed earlier discussion, 1996: 218–23.

(13) B*You are not in danger*.

Even though *A* wrongly holds (11), he is not in the least irrational. He has two distinct mental representations of *B*, just as Ralph did of Ortcutt and Peter did of Paderewski. These two representations have different modes of referring to *B*, reflecting different observational perspectives. And these differences are crucial in explaining *A*'s behavior. But, once again, there is an ascription problem (9.3).

6.4 De Se Thoughts

Finally, we consider *de se* thoughts. When Perry first notices the trail of sugar he comes to the belief,

(14) B*The shopper with a torn sack is making a mess*.[11]

Later, when he observes himself in the mirror without realizing that it is himself, he comes to believe,

(15) B*That man is making a mess*.

But this doesn't cause him to stop following the trail and rearrange the torn sack. For that, he needed the belief,

(16) B*I am making a mess*.

This story vividly demonstrates the importance of beliefs under the first-person mode of reference to the explanation of behavior. Perry's earlier failure to form the belief,

(17) B*I am the shopper with a torn sack*,

was a mistake, of course, but not a sign of any irrationality. He has three distinct mental representations, *the shopper with a torn sack*, *that man*, and *I*, all referring to Perry himself but all playing distinct roles in his cognitive life.

Given the importance of *de se* thoughts to the explanation of behavior we should expect there to be a conventional way of conveying that mode in our ordinary ascriptions of thoughts. And when we get to our discussion of thought ascriptions, we shall see that there is (9.4).

[11] My discussion of this case draws on more detailed earlier discussions, particularly 1984: 397–400; 1996: 218–23

6.5 General Comments

Now this discussion of thoughts leaves much work to be done. In particular, it rests heavily on modes of referring. We would like to know much more about them. And there are, of course, many proposals on that score. First, it has long been noted that the representation 'in subject position' may have a 'singular' mode like *Ortcutt* or *you* or it may have a 'general' or 'quantificational' mode like *all spies*, *few shoppers*, or Perry's *the shopper with a torn sack*. When we have a representation under a singular mode, we have, as the folk say, some particular object 'in mind'; we are, as David Kaplan (1968) says, 'en rapport' with the object. So, one challenge is to say what this amounts to. Influenced by Kripke (1980), some have proposed causal modes of referring for singular representations like *Ortcutt*. Some hold that a certain sort of causal-perceptual link to an object is central to the modes of referring of other singular representations like *that man*, *she*, and *you*. And some, influenced by Keith Donnellan, go against the Russellian tradition and hold much the same for the likes of the 'referential' *the man in the brown hat* in (1). All of these views amount to explaining having-an-object-in-mind, being *en rapport* with it, in terms of an appropriate direct causal link to the object[12] What about the mode of *I*? In a way, this singular mode seems simpler than the others. It is a special way that *I* has of referring to a person that is explained solely in terms of *I*'s functional role in the very mind containing it. And because the mode for *I* is so explained, a *de se* thought in one person's mind must differ from such a thought in any other person's mind. And because of this, no other person can *express* a person's de se thought. Given the nature of an *I* representation, this is not puzzling but just what we should expect.

So there is plenty to be done on modes of referring. But, *there is nothing essentially puzzling about modes of referring in general nor about that for *I* in particular*. With acceptance of RTM goes an acceptance of mental representations of the world. For each such representation, there must *be* some way in which it refers to that world, for it doesn't refer by magic. So, it must *have* a mode of referring. And it is not surprising that modes will *differ* from representation to representation. Indeed, given the differing causal roles of thoughts we have very good evidence of certain differences; for example, of the difference between the general ('attributive') *the shopper with a torn sack* and the singular *that man*; of the difference between the two singulars, *that man* and *I*. None of these modes of co-referential representations can be 'reduced' to another.[13] That should really go without saying.

---

[12] I have made proposals along these lines; see, e.g. 1974; 1981a,b; 2004; 2007.

[13] Cf. Boer and Lycan 1980: 432.

In sum, far from being a 'great puzzle' in contemporary philosophy, the *de se* should not be a puzzle at all. At least, it should not be a puzzle at the level of thoughts. Perhaps the situation is different at the level of ascriptions of thoughts. In Section 9, we shall see that it is not.

We have found no need to talk of propositions. I suggest that this is *why* we have found nothing particularly problematic about *de se* thoughts.[14]

It is time to turn from thoughts to language.

7 Languages in General

Languages are as much part of the natural world as are thoughts. What are they and why do we posit them?

It is helpful to look at nonhuman animals to answer these questions. Cognitive ethologists posit languages to explain communication in some species. The honey bee provides a famous example: Karl von Frisch won a Nobel Prize for discovering a language in the bee's 'waggle dance', a dance used to communicate the direction and distance of a food source. Prairie dogs provide another example: They have a language of 'barks' that convey information about which sort of predator is threatening and about the characteristics of a particular predator of that sort (Slobodchikoff 2002).[15] So what are these languages of dances and barks? They are *representational, or symbolic, systems*. And they are clearly of great use: Getting reliable information about food or predators is very beneficial.

Now consider humans. It is a truism that they have languages which they use to communicate 'messages': As the folk say, 'language expresses thought'. This idea seems irresistible once one has accepted intentional realism, accepted that humans have thoughts (Devitt 2006a: 127–8). As Fodor, Bever, and Garrett say, 'there is much to be said for the old-fashioned view that speech expresses thought, and very little to be said against it' (1974: 375). So, just as the bees and the prairie dogs have representational systems used for communicating with each other, so do we.[16]

---

[14] Mind you, we could talk of propositions without harm by conceiving of them as sets of modes of reference, many of them nondescriptive and causal modes. We could then capture the differences between, say, thoughts about Perry that include *Perry*, *the shopper with the torn sack*, *that man*, and *I* by taking these thoughts to be related to propositions containing different modes of referring to Perry. But these are not the way propositions are usually conceived. And there is no point in this maneuver.

[15] And it is worth noting that sometimes we posit an animal language because we have *taught* it; think of some dolphins and primates that have been taught surprisingly complex languages.

[16] Strangely, this view of human language is rejected by Chomskians; see, e.g. Chomsky 1986 and 1996; Dwyer and Pietroski 1996; Laurence 2003; Collins 2008a,b; Antony 2008. They see a human language as an internal state not a system of external symbols that represent the world. I have argued against this view: 2003; 2006a: chs 2 and 10; 2006b; 2008a,b,c; 2009.

Return to our example of Mark and the ascription to him of B*It is raining*. Suppose that the people present ascribe this belief because Mark uttered the sound, /It is raining/. This sound means that it is raining. If the people assume that Mark is being literal and straightforward, they will take that meaning to be the message the speaker intentionally communicates, his 'speaker meaning'. As a result, they have evidence of his thoughts. Taking him to be sincere in his expression, they conclude that he has a belief with that meaning (content), ascribing B*It is raining*. In this way, language is an extraordinarily effective way of making the thoughts of others accessible to us, thoughts that otherwise would be largely inaccessible; and of making our thoughts accessible to others, often in the hope of changing their thoughts and hence their behavior. Even though the thoughts of others are sometimes accessible to us without language, they mostly are not.

The language of the bee is very likely entirely innate, that of humans is largely conventional.[17] As Lewis points out at the beginning of his classic, *Convention*, it is a 'platitude that language is ruled by convention' (1969: 1).[18] In any case, whatever the source of a language that is used for communication, we have a powerful theoretical interest in that language and its rules. Serious scientists work to discover the natures of the representations in these systems.

In sum, human languages, like all other natural languages, are parts of the causal world posited to explain behavior. And the properties in virtue of which they play their causal roles are natural ones, which should be explained accordingly.

8 Thought Ascriptions Without Propositions

The semantic task is to explain the nature of those natural properties, to explain their 'meanings'. According to the Occamist methodological proposal in Section 3, we should expect to do this for a language that concerns a certain reality in terms of the objects we already suppose constitute that reality, 'old' objects. Thoughts are, of course, the reality that concerns thought ascriptions. So, the semantics of thought ascriptions should be explained in terms of their relations to the reality described in Sections 4–6 (assuming, of course, that we have gotten that reality more or less right). This reality does not include propositions. So we should not expect the semantics of thought ascriptions to posit them. Yet the standard view does posit them.

---

[17] I say 'largely' because I do not reject the Chomskian view that some syntax is innate. The qualification should be taken as read in future.

[18] A platitude that is, nonetheless, rejected by Chomsky (1996: 47-8) and Laurence (1996). See also Collins 2006, 2008a,b, and Devitt 2008a,b, for an exchange on the issue.

Mark Richard provides an argument for the standard view. He starts his book, *Propositional Attitudes*,

> from the assumption that attitude ascriptions are what they appear to be: . . . two-place predicat[ions] . . . This assumption—that at a certain level of generality
>
> Iago hopes that Desdemona will betray Othello
>
> is on a syntactic and semantic par with
>
> Iago kissed Desdemona
>
> —saddles us immediately with t-clauses as names of entities of some sort. That is, it saddles us immediately with propositions. (1990: 5)

So, Richard's implicit response to my Occamist objection to positing propositions is that semanticists do need to posit them because the meanings of ordinary thought ascriptions require them. And Richard surely speaks for many here.

We should note first that positing propositions solely to give meaning to ordinary thought ascriptions smacks of the Meinongian procedure of positing golden mountains solely to give meaning to 'the golden mountain'. We found no need for propositions in the psychological reality that is the concern of thought ascriptions and so we should be very reluctant to posit them to give meaning to those ascriptions.

Are ordinary thought ascriptions really committed to propositions anyway? The apparent commitment arose from taking the 'logical form' of the above hope ascription to be on a par with 'Iago kissed Desdemona', which has the *definite* singular term 'Desdemona' in object position. But there is an attractive alternative: taking the ascription to be on a par with 'Iago kissed a woman', which has the *indefinite* singular term, or quantifier, 'a woman' in object position. So, just as this sentence commits us to a token object with the property specified by 'woman', the hope ascription commits us to a token mental state with the property specified by 'that Desdemona will betray Othello'. The ascription does not commit us to propositions. Indeed, it commits us to just the sort of reality we are already committed to by our discussion of thoughts: mental states with representational properties. And, despite what Richard says, an attitude ascription no more appears to have the logical form of 'Iago kissed Desdemona' than it appears to have that of 'Iago kissed a woman'.[19]

---

[19] 1996: 56–7, 211–2. I took this alternative view in my 1981a, unaware that it goes back at least to Sellars 1963; see also Davidson 1984: 93-108; Lycan 1988: 7–9.

The case for propositions is stronger when we consider general thought ascriptions that seem to *quantify over* propositions. But I think this case can be met too (1996: 212–14).

I have been arguing that putting metaphysics first spares us propositions in semantics. It has another advantage: Propositions are sometimes largely responsible for *generating* puzzles about belief ascriptions. This seems to be the case with *de se* ascriptions.

9 Some Particular Thought Ascriptions

We shall consider the ascription of the thoughts discussed in Section 6.

9.1 Quine's Ortcutt

We noted there (6.1) that a belief's mode of reference matters to its role in causing behavior. So, in Quine's Ortcutt story,[20] the fact that Ralph has the singular belief

(1) B*The man in the brown hat is a spy*

explains his campus behavior in a way that his having

(3) B*The man seen at the beach is a spy*

would not. So we would expect to have a conventional way in our language of specifying the mode in ascribing a belief. And we have:

(18) Ralph believes that the man in the brown hat is a spy.

Given its logical form, (18) attributes to Ralph a belief state with a property specified by 'that the man in the brown hat is a spy'. According to one conventional reading of (18), that property includes the mode of *the man in the brown hat* but not the mode of *the man seen at the beach*: (18) is made true by Ralph having (1) but would not be made true by his having (3). In contrast, the similar reading of

(19) Ralph believes that the man seen at the beach is a spy

specifies the mode of *the man seen at the beach* and would not be made true by Ralph having (1). Quine calls this reading 'opaque', pointing out that on this reading of (18) 'the man in the brown hat' is not used as a means simply of specifying its object and is not subject to 'the law of substitutivity of identity'.

---

[20] See notes 5–6 and 9–11 for references to more detailed discussions of this case and the ones that follow.

Quine notes further that ordinary thought ascriptions of this form are *ambiguous*, having another conventional reading that he calls 'transparent'. For these, the law of substitutivity does hold. Transparently construed, Ralph's mode of referring to Ortcutt does not matter to the truth of (18): (18) simply specifies that Ralph's belief state includes a representation that does refer to Ortcutt. This reference must of course be under some mode, but it does not matter to the truth of (18) which mode.

Suppose that Ralph has told me of the experiences that led him to (1) but, unlike Ralph, I know that his suspect is Ortcutt. I am concerned to pass on to others this information about a possible spy (not to explain Ralph's behavior). I might well convey this information to an acquaintance of Ortcutt by saying,

(20) Ralph believes that Ortcutt is a spy,

even though I am well aware that Ralph does not hold

(4) B*Ortcutt is a spy*,

he does not have a singular belief he would express, 'Ortcutt is a spy'. Indeed, after a day at the beach where a certain man I recognize as Ortcutt was particularly salient, I might use (19) to convey that same information to a companion who does not know Ortcutt, even though I am aware that Ralph does not have belief (3) but rather

(7) B*The man seen at the beach is not a spy*.

In sum, we can replace 'Ortcutt' in the transparently construed (20) with any co-referential term and the resulting ascription will still be true on the strength of Ralph holding (1).

Just as Ralph's holding (1) licenses the transparently construed (20), so too does Ralph's holding (7) license the transparently construed

(21) Ralph believes that Ortcutt is not a spy.

We should follow Quine in noting that (20) and (21) do not convict Ralph of irrationality, for he has the beliefs in question under different modes of referring to Ortcutt.

Ralph's mental state, B*The man in the brown hat is a spy*, has (at least) two contents of theoretical interest: the fine-grained content of referring to Ortcutt in a certain way, the way of *the man in the brown hat*; and the coarse-grained content of simply referring to Ortcutt (sec. 6.1). Construed opaquely, (18) specifies that fine-grained content. Construed transparently, it specifies that coarse-grained content, as do (19) and (20).[21] There is no theoretical basis for claiming that one of these is the *only true* content.

Finally, it is worth noting that the distinction between transparent ascriptions and opaque ascriptions *has nothing to do with* the distinction between singular (en rapport) thoughts and general (quantificational) thoughts described in Section 6.5. (This bears on the problems of '*de re*' and '*de dicto*', discussed in Appendix.)

Consider opaque ascriptions. Some obviously ascribe general thoughts, but *many ascribe singular ones*. The Donnellan-influenced should see the opaquely construed (18) and (19) as examples. But if those examples are unacceptable, consider (20), now *opaquely* construed. It ascribes B*Ortcutt is a spy* to Ralph which requires for its truth that Ralph refer to Ortcutt under the singular mode of *Ortcutt*. To do this Ralph must have Ortcutt particularly in mind; he must be en rapport with him.

Consider transparent ascriptions. Some are obviously made true by singular thoughts. The *transparently* construed (20) being made true by (1) is an example for the Donnellan-influenced, but it is easy to come up with others. What is really interesting is that *general thoughts* can also make the transparently construed (20) true. Thus, suppose that a copy of the University's secret admissions policy is left on a library table and then leaked to the press. Ralph is very suspicious of whoever left that copy but does not know his identity: He holds the general belief, B*The person who left the copy on the table is a spy*. Unlike Ralph, I know that Ortcutt is the culprit. I might well convey Ralph's suspicions to someone who knows nothing about the leak by using the transparently construed (20). (20) would be true even though Ralph is not en rapport with Ortcutt.[22]

In sum, some opaque ascriptions ascribe singular beliefs, some, general. Transparent ascriptions are not specific on that score: They can be made true by either a singular or general beliefs.

So far then, there is no puzzle at the level of thought ascriptions. There is a nice match between what we earlier saw was explanatorily interesting

[21] The view that thought ascriptions have a transparent-opaque ambiguity, well-supported by Quine, plays strangely little role in discussions. Those who are struck by the way interpretations of these ascriptions can vary in context prefer rather to think of them as containing 'hidden indexicals'. I argue that there is no evidence for this more extreme context-dependency view of thought ascriptions: The Quinean ambiguity view can accommodate all cases (1996: 196–208).

[22] This example is inspired by Schiffer's nice one of Big Felix (1979: 67), which I have discussed in some detail (1996: 145–154). My discussion is at odds with another of Quine's suggestions (which I once accepted: 1981a; 1984): that the transparently construed (20) is equivalent to the *unambiguously* transparent 'Ortcutt is such that Ralph believes him to be a spy'. With this suggestion went the vexed idea of the 'exportation' of 'Ortcutt' from the opaque to the explicitly transparent forms.

about thought contents and what we find ordinary thought ascriptions conventionally ascribing. Still there are puzzles at the level of ascriptions.

9.2 Kripke's Paderewski

Consider Kripke's ingenious case of Peter and Paderewski. We saw (6.2) that Peter has the following two singular beliefs:

(8) B*Paderewski$_1$ has musical talent*

(9) B*Paderewski$_2$ has no musical talent*.

Peter has made a mistake, of course, but there is no puzzle about his cognitive life. Still, there is a puzzle about our ordinary descriptions of that life. The fact that Peter holds (8) seems sufficient for the truth of the opaquely construed

(22) Peter believes that Paderewski has musical talent.

Yet the fact that Peter holds (9) seems sufficient for the truth of the opaquely construed

(23) Peter believes that Paderewski has no musical talent.

These conventional opaque ascriptions seem to ascribe irrationality to Peter by failing to distinguish his representation *Paderewski$_1$* from his representation *Paderewski$_2$*. As a result, neither ascription is adequate to explain the very different behaviors caused by these two representations. It is not hard to distinguish these representations—indeed I have done so using subscripts—but it is not something that we, who have not made Peter's mistake, can do using conventional ascriptions. For we, unlike Peter, have only one mode of referring to Paderewski by 'Paderewski'. To convey the very fine-grained contents that are relevant to explaining Peter, we would likely resort to something unconventional like

(25) Peter believes that Paderewski, *qua pianist*, has musical talent.

With Kripke's example there is a breakdown in the nice match between what we earlier saw was explanatorily significant about thought contents and what we find ordinary thought ascriptions conventionally ascribing.

9.3 Richard's Phone Booth

There is a breakdown in the match again with Richard's example (6.3). *A* has two singular beliefs about the one person:

(12) B*She is in danger* (as a result of seeing a woman across the street)

(13) B*You are not in danger* (as a result of talking to a woman on a phone)

There is no more puzzle about *A*'s cognitive life than about Ralph's or Peter's but there is, once again, a puzzle about our ordinary descriptions.

Suppose that *C* is with *B* in the phone booth. Before observing *A* waving, *C* had already figured out that *B* is talking to *A* on the phone. On the strength of the waving, he concludes that *A* holds (12), which is sufficient for saying to *B*:

(26) *A* believes that you are in danger.

At the same time, on the basis of information supplied to him by *B*, he concludes that *A* holds (13), which is sufficient for saying to *B*:

(27) *A* believes that you are not in danger.

Yet, manifestly, neither of these conventional ascriptions is adequate to explain *A*'s behavior. The problem here is not that ascriptions like these—ones with a deictic pronoun or demonstrative in the subject position of the content clause—lack an opaque construal:[23] We have as much reason to believe in an opaque construal of these ascriptions as in those involving names or definite descriptions. The problem is that, in their opaque construal, they ascribe to the belief state the property of referring to *B* under some 'demonstrative' mode or other but not under any *particular* one; thus the mode might be that of *she*, *you*, or even *that woman*. So neither (26) nor (27) specifies under which demonstrative mode *A* has his belief. And asserting both of them no more convicts *A* of irrationality than did asserting both of the transparent (21) and (22) convict Ralph of it. Yet the modes of *she* and *you* cause very different behaviors in *A*. To convey the very fine-grained contents that are relevant to explaining *A*, we would likely resort to something unconventional like

(28) *A* believes that you, *qua person he is waving at*, are in danger.

With Richard's example, as with Kripke's, there is a breakdown in the nice match between what we earlier saw was explanatorily significant about thought contents and what we find ordinary thought ascriptions conventionally ascribing. But a mismatch in these cases is not surprising. The situations described by Kripke and Richard are not normal: It took ingenuity to

---

[23] Although I once thought otherwise (1981a: 245).

invent them. It is not surprising that our standard ways of ascribing thoughts are not adequate to explain behavior in these abnormal situations.

9.4 De Se Thoughts

Finally, we consider the ascription of *de se* thoughts, a special sort of singular thought. In the version of Perry's story that we adopted (6.4), he starts with belief (14), gains (15) when he sees himself in the mirror, then finally comes to (16), having realized (17):

(14) B*The shopper with a torn sack is making a mess*

(15) B*That man is making a mess*

(16) B*I am making a mess*

(17) B*I am the shopper with a torn sack*,

The striking thing about the story is that the change from simply holding (14) and (15) to holding the *de se* (16) dramatically changes Perry's behavior: He stops following the sugar trail and rearranges the torn sack. Situations like this are not rare, as the literature shows. So we should expect there to be a conventional way of ascribing *de se* thoughts. Hector-Neri Castaneda (1966; 1967; 1968) argued convincingly that there is such a way, using pronouns that are explicitly or implicitly reflexive. Thus we can explicitly ascribe (16) with

(29) Perry believes that he himself is making a mess

or implicitly ascribe it by replacing 'he himself' with 'he'. (Other explicit examples use 'I myself', 'you yourself', and so on.) None of the other forms of ascription that we have been considering can be used to ascribe this *de se* belief.

I am here construing (29) as opaque: The position of 'he himself' is not open to substitutivity. (29) is, of course, a special sort of opaque, ascribing a first-person belief. But then (26) is a special sort of opaque too, ascribing a demonstrative belief. And (20) is a special sort, ascribing an *Ortcutt* belief. It should go without saying that none of these can be 'reduced' to another: They are ascribing different sorts of thoughts playing different causal roles.

Is there a transparent construal of the likes of (29)? Ernest Sosa produced an ingenious example that suggests that there is (1970: 893). If so, it should also go without saying that the opaquely construed (29) cannot be reduced to this transparent construal any more than any opaque construal can be reduced to its corresponding transparent one.

Attention has recently been drawn to another conventional way of ascribing *de se* thoughts where, as James Higginbotham says, 'the subject of the complement clause is understood'; the subject is, in Chomskian terms, the element PRO, a pronoun that has 'no phonetic realization' (2003: 497). Consider this example:

(30) John expects to win.

(30) ascribes to John a *de se* expectation involving the representation *I will win*.

We noted above that although there is a standard form for ascribing a thought under some demonstrative mode or other, illustrated by the opaquely construed (26) and (27), there is not one for ascribing a thought under the particular mode of *she* or *you*. Yet there are ones, illustrated by (29) and (30), for ascribing a thought under the mode of *I*. And the reason for the difference is clear. Only in rather rare cases like Richard's do we need to distinguish among demonstrative modes to explain a person's behavior, whereas we frequently have to distinguish the mode of *I* from all other modes of referring to a person in order to explain her behavior.

9.5 General Comments

I concluded my discussion of thoughts by stating the obvious: That discussion leaves plenty to be done (6.5). And it is just as obvious that the discussion of thought ascriptions in this section leaves plenty to be done. But the issue that concerns this paper is whether there is anything *particularly* problematic and puzzling about the *de se*. I concluded that, so far as *de se* thoughts are concerned, there is not. I take this section to have shown that just the same is true of the ascription of *de se* thoughts. Indeed, if there is anything puzzling about ascriptions, rather than simply work to be done, it is to be found in Kripke's and Richard's examples not the *de se*. In those examples there is a mismatch between what is theoretically significant about thought contents for the explanation of behavior and what conventional thought ascriptions ascribe. With the *de se* there is no mismatch: Ascriptions like (29) and (30) conventionally ascribe precisely what we are theoretically interested in, namely *de se* beliefs like (16).

So, we have found nothing particularly problematic about the *de se*, neither with the thoughts nor their ascriptions. We have also found no need to talk of propositions. In my view, such talk generates the alleged problem of the *de se*.

10 Conclusion

The received wisdom is that *de se* thoughts and their ascriptions are particularly problematic. My aim in this paper has been to show that this is a myth.

A theory of thoughts and a theory of their ascriptions must be related. Appealing to Quinean naturalism and Occam, I argued in Section 3 for the explanatory priority of the theory of thoughts. So I started with that theory in Sections 4 to 6. Assuming RTM, I take mental representations to be the 'objects of thoughts'. From this basis, I offered suggestions about thoughts in standard and 'puzzle' situations. These suggestions are far from a complete theory of thoughts, of course, but they are sufficient, I argue, to show that there is nothing particularly problematic about *de se* thoughts. In light of this, I considered ascriptions of thoughts in Sections 7 to 9. I concluded that there is nothing particularly problematic about the ascription of *de se* thoughts either.

Throughout I have emphasized that languages and minds are parts of the natural world, interacting causally with other parts of that world. It is hard to see how Platonic propositions, the root of the myth, could be a part of that world. In any case, I found no need to posit them.

Appendix: '*De Dicto*' and '*De Re*'

In discussing thoughts and their ascriptions, use of the terms '*de dicto*' and '*de re*' is ubiquitous. I have argued elsewhere that this talk is (i) confusing, (ii) often confused, and (iii) unnecessary (1984: 388–90, 392–4). My argument, briefly, is as follows.[24]

(i) The talk is confusing for several reasons. First, '*de dicto*' and '*de re*' are often unexplained. This would not matter if the terms were unambiguous and had clear and generally accepted meanings. But, second, this is far from the case, as I shall now indicate. Third, the terms have misleading associations from their uses in discussing modalities.

(ii) The talk is often confused. First, authors slip back and forth between applying the terms to ascriptions of thoughts and applying them to the thoughts themselves. This reflects a general tendency to confuse thoughts with their ascriptions. Thus, one famous article has the title 'A Puzzle about Belief' (Kripke 1979), and another, the subtitle 'Reporting Puzzling Beliefs' (Crimmins and Perry 1989), and yet neither show *beliefs* to be puzzling; they show some *ascriptions* of beliefs to be.[25] There seems to be an assumption that the application of '*de dicto*' and '*de re*' to thoughts is an obvious consequence of their application to thought ascriptions. Yet it clearly is not. Con-

[24] I earlier found evidence for the problems described here in: Sosa 1970: 883–5; Pastin 1974; Chisholm 1976: 1–4, 9-10; Burge 1977: 340; Donnellan 1979: 54; Kripke 1979: 242; Lewis 1983: 151–6; Schiffer 1979: 62–6; Boer and Lycan 1980: 427–31, 447–9; Fitch 1981: 25; Perry 1993: 39–42. For some more recent evidence, see: Maier 2009, Ninan 2010, and several papers in the present volume.

[25] See also my discussion (1996: 118-20) of Stephen Stich's argument for holism (1983).

sider, for example, love ascriptions: Particular ones like 'Tom loves Dick' differ from general ones like 'Tom loves someone', but this does not entail that there are particular lovers and general lovers.

The talk is confused, second, because the application of '*de dicto*' and '*de re*' to both thoughts and their ascriptions conflates two distinctions that, as noted (9.1), have nothing to do with each other: (a) the distinction between transparent ascriptions and opaque ascriptions; and, (b) the distinction between singular (en rapport) thoughts and general (quantificational) thoughts. In particular, on the one hand, en rapport thoughts can be ascribed by opaque ascriptions; for example, by the opaquely construed

(20) Ralph believes that Ortcutt is a spy

(26) *A* believes that you are in danger.

(27) *A* believes that you are not in danger

and, for the Donnellan-influenced,

(18) Ralph believes that the man in the brown hat is a spy

(19) Ralph believes that the man seen at the beach is a spy.

On the other hand, transparent ascriptions do not ascribe en rapport thoughts: They can be made true by general thoughts; for example, the transparently construed (20) was made true by Ralph's holding B*The person who left the copy on the table is a spy*. One pair of terms cannot capture the two important distinctions that have emerged in this area: distinction (a), which is about ascriptions of thoughts, and distinction (b), which is, in the first instance, about the thoughts themselves.

Talk of *de dicto*, *de re*, and *de se* has generated issues about whether one can be 'reduced' to another. Yet there is no issue here worthy of attention, whether the concern is with thoughts or their ascriptions. There are singular and general thoughts, and there are different sorts of each, and they all play different causal roles. No sense can be made of reducing any one to any other (6.5). There are transparent and opaque ascriptions of these different thoughts and no sense can be made of reducing one sort of ascription to another (9.4).

(iii) Finally, the talk is unnecessary because we have other, relatively clear, terminology to mark the distinctions, as we have seen: Thus we have the Quinean terms 'transparent' and 'opaque' to distinguish ascriptions; and the terms 'singular' ('en rapport') and 'general' ('quantificational') to distinguish the modes of reference of thoughts.[26]

---

[26] A version of this paper was delivered at Arché, St. Andrews in July 2011. I am indebted to the lively comments of the audience for several improvements.

References

Antony, L. 2008. Meta-Linguistics: Methodology and Ontology in Devitt's *Ignorance of Language*. *Australasian Journal of Philosophy* 86: 643–56.

Barber, A., ed. 2003. *Epistemology of Language*. Oxford: Oxford University Press.

Boer, S, and W. G. Lycan. 1980. Who Me? *Philosophical Review* 89: 427–66.

Burge, T. 1977. Belief *De Re*. *Journal of Philosophy* 74: 338–62.

Castaneda, H. N. 1966. He*: A Study in the Logic of Self-Consciousness. *Ratio* 8: 130–57.

Castaneda, H. N.. 1967. Indicators and Quasi-Indicators. *American Philosophical Quarterly* 4: 1–16.

Castaneda, H. N. 1968. On the Logic of Attributions of Self-Knowledge to Others. *Journal of Philosophy* LXV: 439–56.

Chisholm, R. 1976. Knowledge and Belief: '*De Dicto*' and '*De Re*'. *Philosophical Studies* 29: 1–20

Chomsky, N. 1986. *Knowledge of Language: Its Nature, Origin, and Use*. New York: Praeger Publishers.

Chomsky, N. 1996. *Powers and Prospects: Reflections on Human Nature and the Social Order*. Boston: South End Press.

Collins, J. 2006. Between a Rock and a Hard Place: A Dialogue on the Philosophy and Methodology of Generative Linguistics. *Croatian Journal of Philosophy* VI: 469–503.

Collins, J. 2008a. Knowledge of Language Redux. *Croatian Journal of Philosophy* VIII: 3–43.

Collins, J. 2008b. A Note on Conventions and Unvoiced Syntax. *Croatian Journal of Philosophy* VIII: 241–7.

Crimmins, M., and J. Perry. 1989. The Prince and the Phone Booth: Reporting Puzzling Beliefs. *Journal of Philosophy* 86: 685–711.

Davidson, D. 1984. *Inquiries into Truth and Interpretation* Oxford: Clarendon Press.

Davis, W. A. 2013. Indexicals and *De Se* Attitudes. This volume.

Devitt, M. 1974. Singular Terms. *Journal of Philosophy* 71: 183-205.

Devitt, M. 1981a. *Designation*. New York: Columbia University Press.

Devitt, M. 1981b. Donnellan's Distinction. *Midwest Studies in Philosophy Vol. 6, The Foundations of Analytic Philosophy*, eds. P. A. French, T. E. Uehling, Jr., and H. K.Wettstein , 511-24. Minneapolis: University of Minnesota Press.

Devitt, M. 1984. Thoughts and Their Ascription. *Midwest Studies in Philosophy Vol. 9, Causation and Causal Theories*, eds. P. A. French, T. E. Uehling, Jr., and H. K.Wettstein French, Uehling, and Wettstein, 385-420. Minneapolis: University of Minnesota Press.

Devitt, M. 1989. Against Direct Reference. *Midwest Studies in Philosophy Vol. 13, Contemporary Perspectives in the Philosophy of Language II*, eds. P. A. French, T. E. Uehling, Jr., and H. K.Wettstein, 206–40. Notre Dame: University of Notre Dame Press

Devitt, M. 1990. On Removing Puzzles about Belief Ascription. *Pacific Philosophical Quarterly* 71: 165–81.

Devitt, M. 1996. *Coming to Our Senses*. Cambridge: Cambridge University Press.

Devitt, M. 1997a. *Realism and Truth*. 2nd edn. with Afterword. 1st edn. 1984, Princeton: Princeton University Press.

Devitt, M. 1997b. Responses to the Maribor Papers. *The Maribor Papers in Naturalized Semantics*, ed. D. Jutronic, 353–411. Maribor: Pedagoska fakulteta.

Devitt, M. 2003. Linguistics is not Psychology. Barber 2003: 107–39.

Devitt, M. 2004. The Case for Referential Descriptions. *Descriptions and Beyond*, eds. M. Reimer and A. Bezuidenhout, 280–305. Oxford: Clarendon Press.

Devitt, M. 2006a. *Ignorance of Language*. Oxford: Clarendon Press.

Devitt, M. 2006b. Defending *Ignorance of Language*: Responses to the Dubrovnik Papers. *Croatian Journal of Philosophy* VI: 571–606.

Devitt, M. 2007. Referential Descriptions and Conversational Implicatures. *European Journal of Analytic Philosophy* 3: 7–32.

Devitt, M. 2008a. Explanation and Reality in Linguistics. *Croatian Journal of Philosophy* VIII: 203–31

Devitt, M. 2008b. A Response to Collins' Note on Conventions and Unvoiced Syntax. *Croatian Journal of Philosophy* VIII: 249–55.

Devitt, M. 2008c. Methodology in the Philosophy of Linguistics. *Australasian Journal of Philosophy* 86: 671–84.

Devitt, M. 2009. Psychological Conception, Psychological Reality: A Response to Longworth and Slezak. *Croatian Journal of Philosophy* 9: 37–46.

Devitt, M. 2010. *Putting Metaphysics First: Essays on Metaphysics and Epistemology*. Oxford: Oxford University Press.

Devitt, M. 2011. Methodology and the Nature of Knowing How. *Journal of Philosophy* CVIII: 205–18.

Devitt, M. 2012. Still Against Direct Reference. *Prospects for Meaning*, ed. R. Schantz. Berlin: Walter de Gruyter, 61–84.

Donnellan, K. S. 1979. The Contingent *A Priori* and Rigid Designation. French, Uehling, and Wettstein 1979: 45–60.

Dwyer, S., and P. Pietroski. 1996. Believing in Language. *Philosophy of Science* 63: 338–73.

Feit, N. 2013. Belief Reports and the Property Theory of Content. This volume.

Field, H. 1980. *Science Without Numbers: A Defense of Nominalism*. Princeton. Princeton University Press.

Fitch, G. W. 1981. Names and the '*De Re-De Dicto*' Distinction. *Philosophical Studies* 39: 25–34.

Fodor, J. A., T. G. Bever, and M. F. Garrett. 1974. *The Psychology of Language: An Introduction to Psycholinguistics and Generative Grammar*. New York: McGraw-Hill Book Company.

French, P. A., T. E. Uehling, Jr., and H. K. Wettstein, eds. 1979. *Contemporary Perspectives in the Philosophy of Language.* Minneapolis: University of Minnesota Press.

Higginbotham, J. 2003. Remembering, Imagining, and the First Person. Barber 2003: 496–533.

Kaplan, D. 1968. Quantifying In. *Synthese* 19: 178–214.

Kripke, S. A. 1979. A Puzzle About Belief. *Meaning and Use*, ed. A. Margalit, 239–83. Dordrecht: Reidel.

Kripke, S. 1980. *Naming and Necessity*. Cambridge, MA: Harvard University Press.

Laurence, S. 1996. A Chomskian Alternative to Convention-Based Semantics. *Mind* 105: 269–301.

Laurence, S. 2003. Is Linguistics a Branch of Psychology? Barber 2003: 69–106.

Lewis, D. K. 1969. *Convention: A Philosophical Study*. Cambridge, Mass.: Harvard University Press.

Lewis D. K. 1983. *Philosophical Papers*. New York. Oxford University Press.

Lycan, W. G. 1988. *Judgement and Justification*. Cambridge: Cambridge University Press.

Maier, E. 2009. Presupposing Acquaintance: A unified Semantics for *De Dicto*, *De Re* and *De Se* Belief Reports. *Linguist and Philosophy* 32:429–47

Ninin, D. 2010. *De Se* Attitudes: Ascriptions and Communication. *Philosophical Compass* 5: 551–67.

Pastin, M. 1974. About *De Re* Belief. *Philosophy and Phenomenological Research* 24: 569–75.

Perry, J. 1993. *The Problem of the Essential Indexical and Other Essays*. New York: Oxford University Press.

Quine, W. V. 1953. *From a Logical Point of View*. Cambridge, MA: Harvard University Press.

Quine, W. V. 1960. *Word and Object*. Cambridge, MA: MIT Press.

Quine, W. V. 1966. *Ways of Paradox and Other Essays*. New York: Random House.

Recanati, F. 2009. *De Re* and *De Dicto*. *Dialectica* 63: 249–69.

Richard, M. 1983. Direct Reference and Ascriptions of Belief. *Journal of Philosophical Logic* 12: 426–52.

Schiffer, S. 1979. Naming and Knowing. French, Uehling, and Wettstein 1979: 61–74.

Schiffer, S. 1992. Belief Ascription. *Journal of Philosophy* 89: 499–521.

Sellars, W. 1963. *Science, Perception, and Reality*. New York: Humanities Press.

Slezak, P. 2009. Linguistic Explanation and 'Psychological Reality'. *Croatian Journal of Philosophy* 9: 3–20.

Slobodchikoff, C. N. 2002. Cognition and Communication in Prairie Dogs. *The Cognitive Animal: Empirical and Theoretical Perspectives on Animal Cognition*, eds. M. Bekoff, C. Allen, and G. M. Burchardt, 257–64. Cambridge MA: MIT Press.

Sosa, E. 1970. Propositional Attitudes *de Dictu* and *de Re*. *Journal of Philosophy* 67: 883–96.

Stanley, J., and T. Williamson. 2001. Knowing How. *Journal of Philosophy* 98: 411–44.

Stich, S. P. 1983. *From Folk Psychology to Cognitive Science: The Case Against Belief.* Cambridge, MA: MIT Press.

6

In Defense of Propositions: A Presuppositional Analysis of Indexicals and Shifted Pronouns

DENIS DELFITTO AND GAETANO FIORIN

In this contribution, we strive towards a propositional account of indexicality. As a strictly intertwined result, we also purport to derive the propositional nature of the *de re* / *de dicto* ambiguity (crucially including *de se* readings).

1 Indexicals and propositions

In the philosophical and linguistic tradition, two main effects are tied to indexicality: (i) the fact that indexicals cannot be treated as concealed descriptions ("I" is not equivalent to "the speaker in the context of utterance"); and (ii) the fact that indexicals are referentially 'rigid' (in the sense that they refer to the same object in all possible worlds). These two facts have been typically seen as the two sides of the same coin: the descriptive content of indexicals is used to fix their reference in the world of evaluation, with this reference keeping constant in all relevant possible worlds (see Kaplan 1989; Recanati 2008 for a recent assessment). In other words, indexicals are special because their 'descriptive' content is not part of their 'propositional' content. Suppose I am Ortcutt and that I utter (1):

(1) I am Ortcutt

Attitudes De Se: Linguistics, Epistemology, Metaphysics.
Neil Feit and Alessandro Capone (eds.).

If the reference of "I" is fixed rigidly, the sentence (1), as uttered by Ortcutt, has the same truth-conditions of the sentence *Ortcutt is Ortcutt*, a necessary truth. In a possible world semantics a necessarily true statement is not informative as it does not restrict the set of worlds which are plausible candidates for being the actual world. It is intuitively clear, however, that (1) can be informative. For example it can be used by Ortcutt to introduce himself. Yet, such informativeness cannot be expressed by the sentence's truth-conditions, otherwise we would have to admit that the sentences *I am Ortcutt* and *Ortcutt is Ortcutt*, having the same truth-conditions, express the same informational content. To solve this problem, Kaplan proposes that the informativeness of indexical sentences is provided by their *character*, a property of the context, rather than by their truth-conditions. That is, according to Kaplan the informativeness of indexical terms is to be kept apart from the sentence's truth conditions (this raises the issue of 'subjective' meaning, see Haas-Spohn 1994). This consequence could be avoided if indexicals were given a descriptive, non-rigid content such as 'the speaker of this utterance'.

However, if this were the case,we should get the logical equivalence between (2) and (3) in counterfactuals, deriving – wrongly, it seems – that (2) is interpreted in the same way as (3):

(2) If I were not speaking, …

(3) If the speaker in the context of utterance were not speaking, …

Conditionals are in fact standardly analyzed as expressing that the set of possible worlds corresponding to the propositional content of the antecedent is included in the set of worlds corresponding to the proposition expressed by the consequent. If we assume that "I" is a concealed definite description, (2) ends up expressing something on these lines: All the possible worlds *w* (accessible from the world of evaluation according to some accessibility relation) such that the speaker in *c* in *w* is not speaking in *w* are included in the proposition expressed by the consequent. However, there can be no world *w* such that the speaker in *c* in *w* is not speaking in *w*. Of course, the problem is avoided if the reference of "I" is rigid: in this case, the possible worlds we should consider are simply those where Ortcutt is not speaking, if (2) is uttered by Ortcutt. Arguably, thus, this strengthens the conceptual foundations of Kaplan's proposal that the descriptive content of indexicals should correspond to an independent parameter of evaluation (*context*): once the context of utterance has enabled us to identify the referent of the description (say, Ortcutt in the described circumstances), this semantic value should be kept constant across all relevant possible worlds. In this way, (2) comes up as propositionally equivalent to (4), which is true if the set of possible worlds where Orcutt is not speaking is included in the set of worlds expressed by the consequent:

(4) If Ortcutt were not speaking, …

If we adopt Kaplan's approach, the meaning of (2) is a function from contexts to propositions (again, what Kaplan called the *character* of a given sentence). From this perspective, indexicals are not mere descriptions, but special descriptions activating the context-parameter *c*. Their informativeness consists thus in establishing one of the values tied to *c* (in the case under discussion, i.e. the semantics of the first-person, the speaker in *c*). The price to pay is however very high, from a theoretical perspective: meaning is no longer propositional in nature, in the sense that sentences containing indexicals cannot be reduced to functions from worlds to truth-values. In other words, indexicals are special descriptions that force us to add 'context' as an independent parameter of evaluation of the meaning content of sentences. It is important to realize, in this respect, that Kaplan's enrichment of the model-theoretic apparatus (both worlds and contexts as two independent parameters of model-theoretic interpretation) should be regarded as a conceptual conclusion on the irreducibility of indexicals to descriptions and of sentences containing indexicals to propositions, and not simply as a technical move for which there might be viable alternatives. There are in fact technical alternatives, but there seems to be no radical conceptual alternative. Stalnaker's notion of 'propositional concept' represents a nice exemplification of this state of affairs. In his bi-modal approach, worlds play both the role of contexts and the role of arguments of the function corresponding to propositional content. However, the two roles have to be kept carefully apart, and a certain amount of technicalities is called for (Stalnaker's 'diagonalization') in order to show that the 'indexical constructs' satisfy the strict requirements Stalnaker defines for 'asserted' propositions. On these grounds, it is no surprise that indexicals have played a major role in the recent debate about 'insensitive semantics' (cf. Cappelen and Lepore 2005) and the possibility to build propositional meaning as a function of purely linguistic structure (i.e. lexical meaning and syntactic structure). It is namely quite evident that the role we assign to extra-linguistic context in the determination of propositional meaning will largely depend on the way we model the semantic contribution of indexical elements. Significantly however, everybody seems to agree that the role of context has to be acknowledged at least for indexicals (the matter of the debate being actually the role of context once one has settled, one way or another, the issue of indexicals). We should immediately emphasize that, while remaining neutral on the issue of the (a-)contextual nature of propositional meaning, we wish to modify one important aspect of the received wisdom on propositions, i.e. the fact that they are insufficient to account for the semantic contribution of indexical elements. We endeavor to show that indexicals turn out to be not "that special", after all, under a 'presuppositional' analysis of the descriptions to which they are associated and a syntactic approach to presupposition resolution.

Finally, notice that the 'indexicals as concealed descriptions' analysis seems to be confuted by the grammatical observation that if (3) could be conceived as equivalent to (5), we should not find third-person agreement on the verb. In fact, if the description 'the person who is speaking in the present context of utterance' represents the content of the indexical value 'first-person', this description should trigger first-person agreement on the verb, contrary to facts (6):

(5) The speaker in the context of utterance is Ortcutt

(6) *The speaker in the context of utterance am Ortcutt

2 Propositions and *de re/de dicto* ambiguities

There is a distinct phenomenon that has been largely taken to pledge for the insufficiency of a propositional analysis. It concerns the *de re/de dicto* ambiguities, as arising in cases like (7) below (cf. Quine 1956):

(7) Jonas believes that the man wearing a brown hat is a spy

If I utter (7) I am in no way committed to the belief that there is actually a man wearing a brown hat in the world of evaluation of (7). This is the *de dicto* reading and should not be confused with Donnellan's distinction between a 'referential' and an 'attributive' reading of the definite description in (7) (as emphasized most notably by Kripke), that is, with the further ambiguity arising from the fact that Jonas might have (or have not) a specific individual in mind as the bearer of the property of wearing a yellow hat. The reading we are interested in is the *de re* reading of (7), according to which I am willing to assert the actual existence of a man with a yellow hat when I utter (7). It has long been believed that the ambiguity at stake can be dealt with propositionally, in terms of a straightforward scope ambiguity, whose syntactic representation is offered in (8) below:

(8) a. $\exists!x.MBH(x)$ [believe (J, $^\wedge Spy(x)$)] (*de re*)
b. believe [(J, $^\wedge\exists!x.MBH(x) \wedge Spy(x)$)] (*de dicto*)

However, Quine noticed that representing the *de re* reading of (7) in terms of (8a) leads to unacceptable consequences. This happens if we suppose that there is a unique individual with the habit of running on the beach daily in the early morning, of whom Jonas definitely thinks that he is not a spy. We might describe this situation by means of (9a) and the logical representation in (9b):

(9) a. Jonas believes that the man who runs on the beach is not a spy
b. $\exists!x.ROB(x)$ [believe (J, $^\wedge\neg Spy(x)$)] (*de re*)

Now suppose that the individual with a brown hat and the individual who daily runs on the beach are actually the very same person. Since (8a) and (9b) would then boil down to asserting that there is a unique person (wearing a brown hat and running on the beach) of whom Jonas believes that he is a spy and that he is not a spy, we cannot avoid attributing contradictory beliefs to Jonas. More precisely, interpreting (7) and (9a) *de re* has the undesirable consequence (under the given circumstances) of attributing contradictory beliefs to Jonas, if we represent the two relevant readings as (8a) and (9b). This is undesirable (or simply mistaken) for the very reason that I can certainly utter (7) and (9a) while believing that the unique individual at stake really exists (*de re*) and still without necessarily entailing that Jonas is consciously entertaining contradictory beliefs. Quine's objections to the use of a propositional style of representation for *de re* undoubtedly led to increased skepticism about the possibility of analyzing predicates of propositional attitudes in terms of relations between individuals and propositions. It was deemed that a more adequate expression of *de re* readings should have recourse to tripartite structures of the sort of (10), where the predicate *believe* is analyzed as a three-place relation involving the belief-holder, the object of belief and the property ascribed to the object of belief:

(10) believe [J, ιx.MBH(x), λx.spy(x)]

This view was strongly corroborated by Lewis' observation that a propositional analysis clearly fails in the special case of *de re* that involves self-representation, that is, the ascription of a property to an individual that is identified with the belief-holder (*de se* readings). More particularly, Lewis observed that one might have a complete knowledge of all true propositions in the universe without knowing which properties to ascribe to himself. Lewis proposed a radical view according to which self-representation is semantically encoded through property-ascription (this amounting to a sort of semantic primitive), providing in fact a deep conceptual motivation for the recourse to a non-propositional style of representation for propositional attitudes that are not interpreted *de dicto*. Later on, Chierchia offered non-trivial syntactic evidence that *de se* readings can be syntactically encoded and are compelling in cases where the alleged propositional object arguably involves an empty category to which abstraction could be applied, providing thus a strong argument in favor of the empirical adequacy of the tripartite structure in (10). So, while an English sentence like (11a) is ambiguous between a *de re* and a *de se* reading (the pronoun providing a variable that can be optionally abstracted over), its Italian equivalent (11b) can be read only *de se*, since the infinitival complement of *credere* (a control structure in current syntactic terminology) obligatorily expresses a property:

(11) a. Jonas believed that he was in danger
b. Jonas credette [di PRO essere in pericolo]

However influential this view might have been, there are rather compelling empirical arguments against it (Reinhart 1990). Here are two of them. First, suppose that Lili and Greta are two broadcast managers in search of the perfect female voice; their voice is recorded by one of their associates and they do not recognize it, simply finding it too aggressive. Suppose further that we utter (12) to describe the situation above:

(12) Lili thought that she sounded too aggressive, and Greta thought the same thing

(12) gives rise to a variety of readings, in particular to a 'strict' and 'sloppy' reading of the second conjunct. What interests us is the observation that there is a sloppy reading which is perfectly compatible with a *de re* reading. This is the interpretation according to which Lili thought of her voice that it was too aggressive without recognizing that it was her voice, and Greta thought that Greta's voice was too aggressive without recognizing that it was Greta's voice. Since sloppy readings in ellipsis contexts necessarily involve logical forms where the pronoun is interpreted as a bound-variable (that is, a variable bound by a lambda-operator), property-ascription necessarily follows, and a *de se* reading should be compulsory. The fact that we easily get a *de re* reading as well casts then serious doubts on the tenability of the analysis of *de se* as property-ascription. Second, consider the fact that according to the Lewis/Chierchia's analysis the complement of a propositional attitude predicate should always contain a linguistic element that can be abstracted over, such as a pronoun or an empty category like PRO in control structures. We predict thus that the passive structures in (13) should give rise to a strong contrast, since abstraction can take place in (13a) (the pronoun *he* can be abstracted over) but not in (13b) (the definite description *the president* cannot be abstracted over). In other words, the analysis of *de se* as property-ascription predicts that a *de se* reading is possible in (13a) and not possible in (13b). Clearly, the prediction is not borne out, since *de se* is easily accessible for both structures:

(13) a. That he will be remembered as a hero is strongly believed by the president
b. That the president will be remembered as a hero is strongly believed by him

All in all, we are strongly inclined to share Reinhart's insight that the theory of *de se* as property-ascription is hardly adequate and that we should look for a propositional alternative. In the next section, we will try to elucidate how a presuppositional approach to definite descriptions is a key to a viable propositional alternative for the analysis of *de se*.

3 Descriptions as presuppositions

Consider again the two sentences that gave rise to Quine's 'Ortcutt's problem', restated below as (14a) and (14b):

(14) a. Jonas believes that the man wearing a brown hat is a spy
b. Jonas believes that the man who runs on the beach is not a spy

We intend to show that if we interpret the descriptive content of the definite descriptions in (14) as presuppositional, the alternative between local and global resolution of the presupposition constitutes a viable way to dissolve 'Ortcutt's puzzle', often referred to as Quine's 'double vision' argument against *de re*. In order to see this with a sufficient degree of technical precision, let us adopt some clear-cut hypotheses on definite descriptions (DDs). We propose that the property expressed by a description corresponds to a specific mode according to which a subject of propositional attitude is acquainted with an object. In the case of "the man wearing a brown hat", the DD refers to an individual with whom someone is acquainted as the individual who satisfies the property MBH. However, we also propose that reference goes through only if the presupposition is satisfied that the individual with whom someone is acquainted as MBH is also actually endowed with the property MBH. The relevant logical form is given in (15):

(15) ιx: MBH(x). $\exists e$ R(e) $\wedge$ $\exists y$ Experiencer(y, e) $\wedge$ Acquainted-as-MBH(y, x), with R a predicate of propositional attitude

Although we will not engage in a detailed discussion of this issue, it is intuitive that the referential part of (15) offers a straightforward solution to the problem of 'incomplete' descriptions: in a context where the uniqueness requirement is not satisfied (there are more individuals satisfying MBH), it may still be the case that only one of those individuals is such that someone is acquainted with him as MBH, under a broad interpretation of 'acquaintance' in terms of 'cognitive salience' or some related notion. Moreover, the presuppositional part of (15) captures the fact that the property expressed by the description not only fixes the nature of a subjective acquaintance relation but also determines an objective mode of presentation: reference is not successful if I use "the MBH" to refer to an individual *a* with whom I am acquainted as 'the individual with a brown hat' (due to some distortion of my perception system) while *a* is actually wearing a yellow hat. In terms of (15), this would simply be a case where the presupposition "MBH(x)" is not satisfied. As the informed reader will certainly have noticed, (15) is an attempt to generalize the classical answer to Quine's 'double-vision' argument against *de re* beliefs in terms of 'acquaintance' (originally due to Kaplan and Lewis) to the theory of descriptions. The original insight was in fact that *de re* beliefs involve relations of 'vivid acquaintance' between a subject and an object. A sentence like (14a) would thus receive an analysis according the lines of (16):

(16) $\exists R\ R(j, \iota x.MBH(x)) \wedge Bel\ (j, {}^\wedge Spy\ (\iota x.\ R(j, x)))$

In a nutshell, (16) says that in the real world *w* there is a relation of acquaintance R between Jonas and the MBH and that in the doxastic worlds *w'* the individual Jonas is acquainted with in terms of R is a spy. On these grounds, (14a-b) turn out to be *de re* since there is an actually existing individual with whom Jonas is objectively acquainted in terms of some relation R; at the same time, no contradictory belief is ascribed to Jonas, since the two individuals Jonas is differently acquainted with need not be the same individual in the doxastic worlds *w'* (as is the case in the real world *w*). However, this analysis is based on the insight that the indirect report of a *de re* belief necessarily involves the expression of a contextually determined relation of acquaintance between the believer and the object of belief. If the acquaintance relation corresponds to the linguistic content of the description, we obtain, for (14a), that the sentence is true iff in the real world *w* Jonas is acquainted with the MBH as MBH, and in the doxastic worlds *w'* the individual he is acquainted with as MBH is a spy. We doubt that this insight is entirely correct. Many indirect reports of *de re* beliefs are simply about an object that is identified in the real world according to a certain acquaintance relation that involves the author of the sentence and not the believer, and that in fact abstracts away from the acquaintance relation that may hold between the believer and the object of belief (let's call this case 'pure' *de re*). Consider for instance the context in (17):

(17) Nowadays we know that the morning star (MS) and the evening star (ES) are the planet Venus. But the ancients contradictorily believed that the MS (i.e. Venus) appeared only in the morning and that the ES (i.e. the very same planet) appeared only in the evening

There is a reading of (17) in which we are not interested in justifying the ancients' contradictory belief by presenting 'the MS' and 'the ES' as the ways the ancients were acquainted with Venus. We are rather interested in pointing to the contradiction, by assuming that 'the MS' and 'the ES' correspond to two ways WE (i.e. the author of (17)) are acquainted with the planet Venus. It is not clear how one can capture this reading in the contextualist approach we are discussing, where the acquaintance relation triggered by the *de re* reading necessarily involves the believer. In the rest of this paragraph we intend to show that a presuppositional account based on

(15) is empirically equivalent to the contextualist approach, while still retaining the possibility of a 'pure' *de re* reading.

Given (14a), consider first the case where both the referential and the presuppositional part of (15) are resolved locally, i.e. at the level of the embedded clause. The sentence is true iff in the doxastic worlds *w'* the individual Jonas is acquainted with as 'the MBH' is a spy, provided the presupposition is satisfied that that individual satisfies MBH in *w'*. In particular, notice that according to this construal, the requirement concerning the existence of a bearer of propositional attitude being acquainted with the object of belief as MBH is naturally satisfied by Jonas. This clearly amounts to a *de dicto* reading of (14a). Consider now the construal according to which both the referential part of (15) and the presuppositional part of (15) are interpreted globally, that is, outside the intensional context corresponding to the embedded clause (for the sake of explicitness, we assume that the referential part of the DD undergoes Quantifier Raising). The sentence is true iff in the real world *w* the author of (14a) is acquainted with the individual that satisfies the property MBH in *w* as 'the MBH', and in the doxastic worlds *w'* that individual is a spy. According to this construal, the requirement concerning the existence of a bearer of propositional attitude being acquainted with the object of belief as MBH cannot be satisfied by Jonas, and is thus naturally satisfied by the author of the whole sentence. Clearly, this amounts to a 'pure' *de re* reading of (14a), where we are reporting a belief that Jonas has with respect to an object identified by means of its mode of presentation in the real world, and we are thus abstracting away from the modes Jonas himself may be acquainted with that object. If both sentences in (14) are interpreted in this way, uttering these sentences would amount to ascribing a contradictory belief to Jonas, as when we say, in (17), that the ancients had a contradictory belief about Venus. Consider finally the construal in which the referential part of (15) does not undergo QR, but the presupposition is resolved globally. The sentence is true iff in the doxastic worlds *w'* the individual Jonas is acquainted with as MBH is a spy, provided that individual satisfies MBH in the real world *w*. This correctly renders the *de re* nature of the belief (since the belief is about an actually existing object), while still retaining the possibility that the different modes of presentation corresponding to the different acquaintance relations identify two distinct individuals in the doxastic worlds *w'*, thus accounting for the observation that we are not ascribing, by uttering the two sentences in (14), a contradictory belief to Jonas. Quine's argument against *de re* is thus neutralized.

Given this presuppositional analysis of descriptions, we might wonder whether it can be extended to names and pronouns. Leaving the treatment of names for a future occasion, the case of pronouns is rather straightforward. Pronouns provide indexes interpreted by means of an assignment function, and the presupposition they encode corresponds to what is normally regarded as grammatical features. For gender, a presuppositional analysis is quite common (cf. Cooper 1983 a.o.). In a sentence such as 'she is a hero', the feminine pronoun 'she' can be associated with the representation in (18):

(18) ιx: female(x). g(i) = x

Conceptually, this proposal becomes interesting if we consider the possibility that grammatical features are in fact 'grammaticalized' descriptions, involving the mapping of full-fledged descriptions into certain dedicated formal features that enter the endowment of pronominal DPs. In this sense, 'feminine' would be a morphological shortcut for the description 'is a female', and first-person would be a morphological shortcut for the description 'is the speaker in the context of utterance'. The question that naturally arises is whether the presuppositions associated to 'gender' and to 'person' have to be resolved globally or locally. For gender, consider the relevant examples in (19):

(19) Jonas believes that she is a man

Clearly, this sentence cannot be used to express Jonas' belief that a certain individual who is a woman is a man: this belief would clearly be contradictory, whereas the belief held by Jonas according to (19) is not contradictory. The correct reading can be derived by resolving the presupposition at a global level: in the doxastic worlds *w'*, g(i) is a man, provided g(i) is a woman in the real world *w*. This is – by the way – the reason why Cooper 1983 refers to 'gender' as an 'indexical' feature. His observation is descriptively correct. However, we suggest that the perspective should be reversed: we should not elucidate the behavior of gender by referring to allegedly 'primitive' properties of indexicals; rather, we should elucidate the behavior of indexicals by referring to the properties of the grammatical features the indexicals express. In particular, given the behavior of 'gender', a natural hypothesis comes to mind: 'grammaticalizing' a description means actually 'freezing' it, that is, subtracting it to the standard cyclic procedures of compositionality. In a nutshell, the 'frozen' presupposition is put into storage and is resolved at the end of the semantic computation (local resolution is thus excluded). In this way, we – tentatively – come to the conclusion that the possibility of local presupposition resolution for standard DDs – as in the discussion above - depends on the fact that their descriptive content is not grammaticalized. This obviously raises the question concerning the behavior of other grammatical features such as 'person', which constitute the standard feature endowment of indexical elements. We will see that the envisaged presuppositional treatment can be indeed successfully extended to 'person' and constitutes the essential ingredient of a descriptive and propositional treatment of indexicals. This will be the aim of the next two sections.

4 First-person indexicals and presupposition resolution

In section 1, we have seen that Kaplan regarded the behavior of first-person indexicals in counterfactuals as a decisive argument against a descriptive analysis of indexicals. Given (2) (restated here as (20)), we would derive a contradiction if (2) were interpreted as in (3) (restated here as (21)):

(20) If I were not speaking,...

(21) If the speaker in the context of utterance were not speaking,...

However, suppose we extend the presuppositional analysis of grammatical features tentatively adopted in the preceding section to person-features. The semantics of a first-person pronoun would then be correctly expressed by the logical format in (22):

(22) ιx: speaker-in-c(x). g(i) = x

Does (22) provide us with a solution to Kaplan's objections to a descriptive analysis of indexicals? To see whether this is the case, let us consider again the semantics of conditionals. Stalnaker (1975; 1999) proposes that all conditional statements, indicative and subjunctive, are assertions that the consequent is true not necessarily in the world as it is, but in the world as it would be if the antecedent were true. More formally, Stalnaker introduces a function f mapping the proposition expressed by the antecedent and the world of evaluation into the world, maximally similar to the world of evaluation, in which the antecedent holds:

(23) A conditional *if A, B* is true in w iff B is true in f(A,w).

The difference between indicative and counterfactual conditionals depends on whether the value of f(A,w) must or must not be a world included in the context set C. In the case of indicative conditionals, if the conditional is evaluated at a world that is a member of C, then the value of f(A,w) must be a member of C too. This constraint accounts for the fact that an indicative conditional statement of the form *if A, B* requires that all is presupposed in the world of evaluation is also presupposed in the hypothetical world in which B is true. In the case of subjunctive conditionals, the selection function can reach outside C to select a counterfactual world. The subjunctive mood is a conventional device 'for indicating that the presuppositions are being suspended, which means in the case of subjunctive conditional statements that the selection function is one that may reach outside of the context set' (Stalnaker 1999:70). However, Heim (1992) notices that if the selection function of counterfactuals could select any logically accessible possible world outside C, this would not explain why the antecedents of counterfactuals can carry presuppositions. The antecedent of (24), to consider an example, presupposes that John smokes, both in C and in the counterfactual world. This means that the presupposition not only can, but must be entailed by the modal base of f.

(24) If John had quit smoking, ...

To solve this problem, Heim proposes that in counterfactuals, the modal base of the selection function f is a revised version of C: the biggest superset of C such that A (the proposition expressed by the antecedent) is compatible with it. Informally, the revision of C is a context where some assumptions have been suspended, in such a way that the antecedent is consistent with it, but the presuppositions of the antecedent have remained.

Notice, however, that there are cases in which also the presuppositions of the antecedent need be suspended in the counterfactual world for the antecedent to be compatible with it. In (25), *the king of Spain* is normally assumed to presuppose the existence of a unique king of Spain; and in fact the sentence does presuppose that there is a unique king of Spain in C; yet, the counterfactual world must be such that there is no king of Spain in it. Similarly, as we have seen above, *she* presupposes that its referent is female in (26); and in fact the sentence does presuppose that *she* denotes a female individual in C; yet, the counterfactual world must be such that the referent of *she* is not female in that world.

(25) If the king of Spain did not exist,...

(26) If she were a man,…

A plausible solution to this problem is that in cases such as (25) and (26) the presupposition is interpreted *de re*. Geurts (1999) and Maier (2006) propose that the ambiguity *de re/de dicto* depends on the point of resolution of the presuppositions of the relevant noun phrase. Consider an example:

(27) John thinks that the king of Spain is smart

According to Geurts and Maier the *de dicto* reading of (27) results from resolving the presupposition of *the king of Spain* at the level of the embedded clause (John thinks that there exists a unique king of Spain and that the king of Spain is smart); the *de re* reading results from resolving the same presupposition at the level of the matrix clause (there exists a unique king of Spain and John thinks that he is smart).

Now, let us go back to (25). If the presuppositions of *the king of Spain* are resolved at the level of the matrix clause, we derive the following truth conditions: There is a unique king of Spain in C and there is a world w such that: (i) w is the world most similar to the world of evaluation that belongs to the revision of C obtained by suspending the proposition *there exists a king of Spain*; (ii) the proposition *there exists no king of Spain* holds in w; (iii) w belongs to the consequent. Under this interpretation, (25) requires that there is a king of Spain in C but not in the counterfactual world. A similar reasoning can be applied to (26) and, most importantly, to (20), the case involving a first-person indexical. Given (22), and the divide between a referential and a presuppositional part encoded by (22), the semantics of (20) roughly expresses that (i) the world w that is maximally similar to the world of evaluation is such that the assignment function g assigns to the index i an individual who is not speaking in w; in other words, we treat the referential part of the DD (i.e. $\iota x.g(i)=x$) as a constant that picks up a certain individual who is not speaking in w; (ii) the presupposition associated to the constant is satisfied in the world of evaluation; in other words, the individual to whom $\iota x.g(i)=x$ refers satisfies the property of being 'the speaker in c' in the world of evaluation; (iii) w belongs to the set of worlds expressed by the consequent in (20).

All in all, we have seen that Kaplan's objections against a descriptive analysis of first-person indexicals can be overruled. We have proposed a view according to which *person* shares with *gender* the property of expressing a 'grammaticalized' presupposition that has to be resolved globally. Global presupposition resolution allows us to avoid contradictions in counterfactuals, on partial analogy with a *de re* treatment of presuppositional DDs in counterfactuals, as extensively discussed above. However, in the next section we will see that there are strong reasons to believe that the person feature is not necessarily bound to global presupposition resolution.

5 Person-features and syntactically-driven presupposition resolution

As we have seen, it is standardly believed that indexicals are rigid designators whose descriptive content is not relevant propositionally but only triggers the activation of the context-parameter. First-person pronouns, for instance, would invariably refer to the author of sentence S, and would be insensitive to the presence of levels of embedding introduced by predicates of propositional attitude within S, corresponding to independent speech acts. In fact, a sentence such as (28) cannot be interpreted, in English, as in (29), but only as in (30):

(28) Jonas said that I am right

(29) Jonas said that the speaker in the reported speech act (i.e. Jonas) is right

(30) Jonas said that the author of (28) (say, the utterer of (28)) is right

However, this may well be true for Indo-european, but there is by now rather extensive evidence that sentences of the sort of (28) can unequivocally be interpreted along the lines of (29) in many other language families (like Semitic (Amharic) and Dravidian (Tamil); see Schlenker 2003; Delfitto and Fiorin 2011 a.o.). In previous work, we have proposed a compositional semantics of these pronoun-shift phenomena along neo-Davidsonian lines, according to which first-person pronouns activate a syntactic dependency with a dedicated position in the left-periphery (Rizzi's *Force*), and the alternation between the 'shifted' and the 'deictic' interpretation is essentially due to syntactic locality effects. We have further proposed that the reason why the shifted reading of first-person pronouns is blocked in English depends on the availability, in English, of a more economical construal, in which a third-person pronoun replaces the first-person pronoun. In a nutshell, this means that (28) cannot be interpreted as in (29) for the very reason that (31) is (whereby the third-pronoun *he* is linked to the DP referring to the author of the speech act expressed by the embedded clause, that is, Jonas):

(31) Jonas said that he is right

English pronouns (contrary to pronouns in Amharic or Tamil) can have an underspecified referential index, along the lines of (32) (cf. Elbourne 2005), and it is the process of resolution of index underspecification that triggers linking:

(32) [the ∅ [NP]]

Linking is interpreted as thematic inheritance, to the effect that (31) is roughly read as follows: "Jonas believes that the holder of this very same belief is right", which is, intuitively, the very same first-personal (i.e. *de se*) reading expressed by the Amharic or Tamil equivalent of (28) (cf. also Higginbotham 2003). The reason why we propose that (31) is more economical than (28) is that we assume that the so-called third-person pronouns are actually devoid of person-features, and feature-expression is minimized by grammar whenever possible. Let us see how the system works by considering the sentence in (33):

(33) I am a hero

The L(ogical) F(orm) (that is, the level of syntactic representation that feeds the semantic computation) we proposed for a sentence like (33) is something along the lines of (34), where the arrows represent the syntactic dependency between "I" and the functional head *Force* (technically, this dependency is implemented in terms of covert movement; the interested reader is referred to Delfitto and Fiorin 2011). The dependency indicates that "I" is interpreted as the speaker in the event of uttering the sentence selected by *Force*.

(34) $[_{ForceP}$ Force $[_{CP}$ [I am a hero]
↑_____↑

As we have seen, there are languages in which the first-person pronoun is not necessarily evaluated with respect to the event of utterance corresponding to uttering the whole sentence. In English, sentence (35) can only have the interpretation according to which John says that the speaker in the event of uttering (35) is a hero. However, in Amharic a sentence such as (35) can also mean that John says that the speaker in the event of uttering the embedded sentence is a hero. That is, the sentence can also mean that John says that John, in as much as he qualifies as the speaker in the event of uttering the embedded sentence, is a hero.

(35) John says I am a hero

We proposed that the ambiguity of Amharic "I" depends on whether the pronoun enters a dependency with the *Force* of the matrix sentence or the *Force* of the embedded sentence. The first reading is derived from the LF in (36). Here the dependency indicates that "I" is interpreted as the individual uttering the sentence corresponding to the CP selected by the matrix *Force*:

(36) $[_{ForceP}$Force $[_{CP}$ John says $[_{ForceP}$ Force $[_{CP}$I am a hero]]]]
↑_________________________↑

Force restricts the set of events of propositional attitude potentially associated with the propositional content expressed by the sentence in (35) to the unique event of propositional attitude that consists in uttering S. The utterer of (35) is thus correctly predicted to be the referent of the first-person pronoun. The second reading is derived from the LF in (37). Here the dependency indicates that "I" is interpreted as the individual uttering the sentence corresponding to the CP selected by the embedded *Force*:

(37) $[_{ForceP}$ Force $[_{CP}$ John says $[_{ForceP}$ Force $[_{CP}$I am a hero]]]]
↑____↑

This second reading is available in Amharic (and a number of other languages) and is not available in English, for the reasons indicated above.

The issue that interests us here is why the presupposition introduced by the first-person feature is necessarily interpreted *de re* (i.e. involves global resolution, on a par with what we observed for the gender feature). Consider the case of the English sentences (38) and (39):

(38) If I were not speaking,...

(39) John thinks that I am smart

In the frame of Geurts' and Maier's theories, the question boils down to why the presupposition of "I" must be resolved at the level of the matrix clause. Capitalizing on the analysis in Delfitto and Fiorin (2011), we propose that the dependency between "I" and *Force* does not only define the relevant event of utterance (by singling out the unique event of propositional attitude selected by *Force*) but also, and crucially in the present perspective, the point of resolution of the presupposition introduced by the first-person feature. Consider then the LFs that we would assign to (38) and (39):

(40) $[_{ForceP}$ Force [If I were not speaking][...]]
↑____↑

(41) $[_{ForceP}$ Force [John thinks $[_{ForceP}$ Force [I am smart]]]]
↑________________________↑

Our proposal is that the dependency between "I" and *Force* determines (i) the relevant event of utterance and (ii) the point of resolution of the presupposition of "I". This correctly derives the fact that, at least in English, the presupposition of first-person pronouns must be resolved at the level of the matrix clause, as the only way a first-person pronoun can be interpreted is through a dependency with *matrix Force*. At the same time, the system correctly predicts the possibility that the presupposition encoded by first-person be resolved locally, as a matter of syntactic parameterization: local presupposition resolution is possible if nothing in the grammar rules out a dependency between "I" and embedded *Force*.[1]

This account needs not stipulate that the first-person feature is an 'indexical' feature, in the sense of Cooper (1983). Rather, it derives 'indexicality' (which is equivalent, in the present terms, to global presupposition resolution) from independently established syntactic considerations. More particularly, the proposed explanation holds that the point of resolution of the first-person feature is determined syntactically and corresponds to the *Force* projection encoding the relevant event of utterance.

The conceptual advantages are evident. First, indexicality is not a primitive feature of first-person pronouns, and this paves the way to an elegant account for the cases of pronoun-shift, in terms of a syntactically-triggered process of local presupposition resolution. Second, for the languages that express *de se* by means of first-person shifted pronouns, we come close to the same analysis envisaged in Maier (2006), according to which this variety of *de se*, involving local resolution of the person presupposition, is actu-

[1] In this perspective, the reason why first-person cannot be linked to embedded *Force* in conditional clauses is necessarily that conditional clauses are devoid of a *Force*-position. In fact, L. Haegeman convincingly argued, on independent grounds, for exactly this conclusion (Haegeman 2006).

ally a particular case of *de dicto*. We also agree with Maier on the observation that *de se* covers thus a whole class of different semantic processes in different languages, but differ from him in suggesting that this sort of interpretive variation is not arbitrary, but rather linked to a well-defined form of syntactic parameterization. Moreover, it should be emphasized that the two analyses (Cooper's and ours) also make different predictions with respect to the shifted use of the first-person pronoun attested in Amharic. As we saw above, the Amharic counterpart of (35), repeated here as (42), can have a reading according to which "I" is interpreted as referring to the speaker in the event of uttering the embedded sentence. In Delfitto and Fiorin's framework this reading is derived from the LF in (43).

(42) John says I am a hero

(43) $[_{ForceP}$ Force $[_{CP}$ John says $[_{ForceP}$ Force $[_{CP}$I am a hero]]]]
↑____↑

Now notice that the analysis according to which the presupposition of "I" is indexical in nature predicts that the presupposition must be satisfied at the level of the matrix clause. On the other hand, the analysis according to which the point of resolution of "I" is determined by the dependency with Force predicts that the presupposition must be satisfied at the level of the embedded clause. The embedded interpretation of "I" in the Amharic counterpart of (44) should prove that the latter analysis is to be preferred.

(44) John does not say that I_i am a hero

If the presupposition is resolved at the matrix level it takes scope over the negation and the sentence ends up presupposing that g(i) is the speaker in the event of uttering the embedded sentence and asserting that there is no event of John asserting the embedded sentence. For g(i) = John, the presupposition ends up contradicting the assertion. If the presupposition is interpreted at the level of the embedded clause, as predicted by our analysis, the sentence expresses the meaning according to which that there is no event of John saying that g(i) is a hero while presupposing that g(i) is the speaker in the event of uttering the embedded clause. No contradiction arises, and this is of course a desirable result.[2]

---

[2] Under the locality approach that we are suggesting here, we expect that first-person pronouns are syntactically dependent on the closest occurrence of *Force*, if no other condition blocks this dependency, as is for instance the case in English, where dependencies on embedded *Force* are blocked by Economy, as argued above. Now, it is well-known that in languages such as Amharic, first-person pronouns are ambiguous between an anaphoric interpretation (corresponding to the predicted dependency on embedded *Force*) and a deictic interpretation (corresponding to a de-

Before closing this section, we would like to briefly address an important issue implicitly raised by our analysis. If we are right, person-features (that is, first- and second-person) trigger a process of syntactically-driven presupposition resolution. This is not the case for the gender-features. That is, we have seen that the presuppositions encoded by gender are always resolved globally. The question that arises is: why should it be the case? There is – we believe – a quite interesting answer to this question, essentially based on the kind of syntactic asymmetry between *gender* and *person* features that was recently discussed in Baker (2008). Basing himself on a sample of more than one hundred languages, Baker observes that subject-verb agreement is the only configuration that licenses person-agreement, to a quite significant cross-linguistic extent. For instance, person-agreement is rarely (if at all) found in modification configurations, where an adjective modifies a noun. First of all, Baker provides a suitable structural foundation for agreement phenomena, by hypothesizing that each lexical category (nouns, adjectives and verbs) has a functional category F in its extended projection, which is the locus of agreement. Agreeing features are base-generated on nouns, and can show agreement with adjectives and verbs by exploiting the F-position inside these categories. Noun-noun agreement is excluded on principled grounds (in nouns, the NP-complement of F blocks external agreement with other NPs), and adjective-noun agreement is limited to number and gender. Person agreement only arises in strictly local noun-verb configurations, as when a nominative first-person pronoun agrees with T. Moreover, Baker makes sense of this set of data by proposing the Structural Condition on Person Agreement (SCOPA), which basically restricts person-agreement to strictly local configurations:

---

pendency on main *Force* that should be excluded by locality). However, the problem dissolves under a Relativized Minimality account of locality, according to which the deictic construal is made possible by the fact that embedded *Force* does not qualify as a closer attractor for the pronoun when the latter is interpreted deictically (i.e. as dependent on main *Force*). The reason is that a given occurrence of *Force* does not necessarily expresses the person-features that function as an attractor for the pronoun (see the discussion below in the text). We contend that this move is empirically corroborated by the observation that there are languages where the use of logophoric pronouns in the embedded clause triggers the presence of special complementizers (see a.o. Sells 1987). Since logophoric pronouns are strictly tied to 'shifted' first-person pronouns (see Delfitto and Fiorin 2011 for a detailed discussion), the idea is that the use of a 'normal' complementizer corresponds to the case where *Force* is devoid of person-features. This situation rules out the occurrence of a logophor in the embedded clause and enforces the deictic reading of a first-person pronoun. We leave an in-depth discussion of this interesting issue for a future occasion.

(45) SCOPA: F can agree with XP in a first- or second-person only if a projection of F merges with a first- or second-person element and F projects.

Now, Baker himself observes that there is an interesting parallelism between the locality of person-agreement and the locality of the syntactic dependencies observed with shifted-pronouns. In our terms, the latter sort of locality can be described by saying that the shifted first-person pronoun obligatorily depends on the closest *Force*, unless the latter does not qualify as a binder of the pronoun on principled syntactic grounds, essentially concerning feature-endowment (cf. fn. 2) or, as is the case in English, the local configuration is excluded by principles governing the economy of computation. On these grounds, what we need is an explanation for two related facts: (i) why *person* needs be licensed by this sort of A-bar dependency; and (ii) why licensing of *person* needs be strictly local. The obvious hope is that the answer to these questions might elucidate the reason why *person* – and not *gender* – tolerates local presupposition resolution. Baker's proposal is that Person inherently triggers an A-bar dependency. The reason is that person-features are not inherently generated on the agreeing noun but are basically induced from outside by means of a sort of operator-variable agreement (see also Kratzer 2009). In our terms, Baker's idea would read as follows: the syntactic locus of person features is the syntactic position in the left periphery that we identified as Rizzi's *Force*. Person-features are base-generated there, and copied by Agree on the agreeing pronoun by means of an operator-variable dependency (that is, an A-bar-dependency). This form of Agree is strictly local (in particular, it does not tolerate the presence of any intervening head) and this explains the locality effects we discussed above. Of course, this only holds for pronoun-shift languages: in English the route to 'dependent' first-personal readings is not based on person-feature agreement, since English third-person pronouns may be generated with an underspecified referential index and trigger as such A-dependencies involving thematic inheritance (linking).

In this way, the two questions asked above are tentatively answered. And in fact, this provides a principled answer to the question concerning the different behavior of *gender* and *person* in presupposition resolution. Gender-features are base-generated on (pronominal) DPs. Person-features are base-generated in a dedicated position in the left-periphery (as is quite natural on compositional grounds, given their semantics; see Delfitto and Fiorin 2011 for a full discussion). They are transmitted to pronominal DPs by means of Agreement, and the locality of this type of agreement explains both the SCOPA and the locality effects observed in pronoun-shift languages.

Summarizing, we have seen that the view we proposed of grammatical features as 'frozen' presuppositions has far-reaching consequences. It derives the 'indexical' behavior of gender but it also derives, on independently established syntactic grounds, the non-indexical behavior of person. Frozen-descriptions are featurally expressed, and features are the natural input of the syntactic computation. No surprise that we have discovered an interesting domain in which the process of resolving presuppositions is syntactically-driven.

6 Conclusion

In this contribution, we have endeavored to provide the philosophical foundations of the semantics of first-person pronouns developed in Delfitto and Fiorin 2011. Essentially, these foundations lie in an analysis of indexicals as grammaticalized definite descriptions and in a propositional analysis of sentences that contain indexicals. There are far-reaching consequences, some of them partially discussed in the present contribution, some of them to be explored in future work: (i) we have proposed a presuppositional analysis of both descriptions and pronouns; (ii) we have refused the analysis according to which rigid designation is a primitive property of indexicals; (iii) we have argued that the process of presupposition resolution is the crucial ingredient of a descriptive analysis of indexicals; (iv) we have argued that this process may be syntactically triggered.

If the analysis proposed here is on the right track, it is not the principles of language use but syntax itself that provides some of the keys for the resolution of the mysteries of indexicality.

References

Baker, M. 2008.The syntax of agreement and concord. Cambridge: CUP.

Cappelen, H. and Lepore, E. 2005. Insensitive semantics: A defense of semantics minimalism and speech act pluralism. Oxford: Wiley-Blackwell.

Chierchia, G. 1989. Anaphora and attitudes *de se*. In Semantics and contextual expressions, ed. by Renate Bartsch, Johan van Benthem, and Peter van Emde Boas, 1–31. Dordrecht: Foris.

Cooper, R. 1983. Quantification and syntactic theory. Dordrecht: Kluwer.

Delfitto, D. and Fiorin, G. 2011. Person features and pronominal anaphora. Linguistic Inquiry 42:193-224.

Elbourne, P. 2005. Situations and individuals. Cambridge (Mass.): MIT Press.

Fodor, J. D. 1970.The Linguistic Description of Opaque Contexts. Ph.D. dissertation, MIT.

Geurts, B. 1999. Presuppositions and pronouns (Current research in the semantics/pragmatics interface,3). Oxford, London: Elsevier.

Haas-Spohn, U. 1994.Versteckte Indexicalität und subjective Bedeutung. Ph. D. thesis, Universität Tübingen. English translation at http://www2.sfs.nphil.uni-tuebingen.de/Alumni/Dissertationen/ullidiss/

Haegeman, L. 2006. Conditionals, factives and the left-periphery. Lingua 116/10: 1651-1669.

Heim, I. 1992. Presupposition projection and the semantics of attitude verbs. Journal of Semantics 9:183–221.

Higginbotham, J. 2003. Remembering, imagining, and the first-person. In Epistemology of language, ed. by Alex Barber, 496–533. Oxford: Oxford University Press.

Kaplan, D. 1969. Quantifying. In Words and objections, ed. by Donald Davidson & Jaakko Hintikka. Dordrecht: D. Reidel Publishing Company.

Kaplan, D. 1989. Demonstratives. In Themes for Kaplan, ed. by Joseph Almog, John Perry, and Howard Wettstein, 581–663. Oxford: Oxford University Press.

Kratzer, A. 2009. Making a pronoun: Fake indexicals as a window into the properties of pronouns. Linguistic Inquiry 40:187-237.

Lewis, D. 1979. Attitudes *de dicto* and *de se*. The Philosophical Review 88: 513–543.

Maier, E. 2006. Belief in context: Towards a unified semantics of *de re* and *de se* attitude reports. Ph.D. thesis, Radboud University Nijmegen.

Quine, W. V. 1956. Quantifiers and propositional attitudes. In Reference and modality, ed. by Leonard Linsky, 1971, 101-111. Oxford: Oxford University Press

Recanati, F. 2008. Philosophie du langage (et de l'ésprit). Paris: Gallimard.

Reinhart, T. 1990. Self-representation. Lecture delivered at Princeton Conference on Anaphora, October.

Rizzi, L. 1997. The fine structure of the left periphery. In Elements of grammar: A handbook of generative syntax, ed. by Liliane Haegeman, 281–337. Dordrecht: Kluwer.

Schlenker, P. 2003. A plea for monsters. Linguistics and Philosophy 26:29–120.

Sells, P. 1987. Aspects of logophoricity. Linguistic Inquiry 18:445-479.

Stalnaker, R. 1975. Indicative conditionals. Philosophia 5: 269-286.

Stalnaker, R. 1999. Context and content: Essays on intentionality in speech and thought. Oxford: Oxford University Press.

7

De Se Attitude/Belief Ascription and Neo-Gricean Truth-Conditional Pragmatics: Logophoric Expressions in West African Languages and Long-Distance Reflexives in East, South, and Southeast Asian Languages[1]

YAN HUANG

1 *De Se* versus *De Re* Attitudes/Beliefs

In the philosophy of language, two types of attitudes/beliefs about oneself are commonly distinguished: (i) attitudes/beliefs held about oneself in a first-person way, and (ii) attitudes/beliefs held about oneself in a third-person way. As an example of type (i), consider my belief that I am healthy. This is a belief I hold about myself from a first-person perspective. In other words, it is a belief about myself which I would normally use a first-person personal pronoun or what Perry (1979) called an essential indexical *I* to encode, as in (1).

[1]An earlier draft of this essay was presented at the University of Auckland DALSL research seminar and the International Workshop on Semantics, Pragmatics and Rhetoric (SPR-11), held at the University of the Basque Country, Donostia, Spain. I have benefited from the comments received on both occasions. Special thanks go to Frank Lichtenberk, Eros Corazza and Kepa Korta. I am particularly grateful to John Perry for the kind words he said about this paper in his plenary closing speech at the workshop. I also wish to thank the two editors of this volume Neil Feit and Alessandro Capone for their encouragement and patience.

Attitudes De Se: Linguistics, Epistemology, Metaphysics.
Neil Feit and Alessandro Capone (eds.).

(1) I am healthy. (said by Yan Huang)

Next, suppose, unbeknownst to me, I have just been awarded a research prize. I believe that the recipient of the prize is intelligent. While this belief of mine is also about me, it is not a belief which I would normally use the first-person personal pronoun or essential indexical *I* to express. Instead, I would normally use (2) to represent this belief of mine.

(2) The recipient of the prize is intelligent.

Attitudes/beliefs of the former type - self-locating attitudes/beliefs - are considered to be *de se* (Latin 'of oneself'), and attitudes/beliefs of the latter type, to be *de re* (Latin for 'about a/the thing') (see e.g., Castañeda 1966, 1967, 1968, 1989, Lewis 1979, Perry 1979, 2000, Stalnaker 1981, Feit 2008).

2 *De Se* Attitude/Belief Ascription

How, then, can the attribution of *de se* attitudes/beliefs from a third-person point of view be represented? Castañeda (1966, 1967) created an artificial pronoun *he*/she*/it** to encode the attribution of *de se* attitudes/beliefs from a third-person perspective. Thus, (3) represents (4).

(3) Yan Huang said that he* is healthy.

(4) I am healthy. (said by Yan Huang)

In other words, (3) is used to mark the self-conscious self-reference on the part of the reported speaker Yan Huang, who uttered (4).

Castañeda called the artificial pronoun a 'quasi-indicator' and claimed that it is the only device that allows the marking of a *de se* attitude/belief from a third-person viewpoint. Furthermore, he pointed out that a quasi-indicator is characterised by the properties in (5).

(5) Characteristics of a quasi-indicator
   (i) A quasi-indicator does not express an indexical reference made by the speaker;
   (ii) It occurs in *oratio obliqua* (Latin for 'indirect speech');
   (iii) It has an antecedent, which it refers back;
   (iv) Its antecedent is outside the *oratio obliqua* containing the quasi-indicator; and
   (v) It is used to attribute, so to speak, implicit indexical reference to the referent of its antecedent.

Do quasi-indicators exist in natural language? The answer is yes. Regarding English, Castañeda suggested *he himself* is a quasi-indicator, as in (6). More recently, Chierchia (1989) pointed out that PRO is also a quasi-indicator, as in (7). This proposal is further echoed by Higginbotham (2003) and Schlenker (2003) (but see e.g., Safir 2004 for counterevidence and counterarguments, and Capone 2010 for further comments).

(6) John claimed that he himself was an expert on eye photography.

(7) John claimed PRO to be an expert on eye photography.

By contrast, the attribution of *de re* attitudes/beliefs from a third-person point of view can be encoded by a regular personal pronoun in English. Thus, from a third-person perspective, (2) can be reported as (8). In other words, (8) can be understood as a *de re* report.[2]

(8) Yan Huang said that he is intelligent.

In addition, as pointed out by Corazza (2004, this volume), an attitude/belief ascription can also be partly *de se* and partly *de re*. Imagine that Stephen Levinson has overheard me say (9). He can then make a report like (10).

(9) Steve and I have just been awarded a research prize. (said by Yan Huang)

(10) Yan believes that we have just been awarded a research prize. (said by Stephen Levinson)

(10) can then be elaborated as (11).

(11) Yan believes that he himself has just been awarded a research prize and that I have just been awarded a research prize.

(10) is a mixed report because on the one hand, it attributes an 'I'-thought to Yan, hence it is *de se*; and on the other hand, the use of the regular personal pronoun *we* selects the current external speaker, hence it is *de re*.

The aim of this paper is twofold. First, I shall take a look at two types of linguistic expressions: (i) logophoric expressions in West African languages and (ii) long-distance reflexives in East, South, and Southeast Asian languages, showing that both can function as a quasi-indicator in the sense of Castañeda. My second goal is that given that quasi-indicators are largely a pragmatic phenomenon (see e.g., Perry 2000), I shall provide a formal pragmatic analysis of the marking of *de se* attribution by logophoric expressions in West African languages and long-distance reflexives in East, South, and Southeast Asian languages and the related use of regular expressions/personal pronouns in these languages in terms of the version of

---

[2] A regular personal pronoun like *he/she/it* in English is claimed to be ambiguous between a *de re* and *de se* reading.

the neo-Gricean pragmatic theory of anaphora developed by Huang (e.g., 1991, 1994/2007, 2000a, b, 2007, 2010a, forthcoming, see also Chiou and Huang 2010), using the three general pragmatic principles proposed by Levinson (1987, 1991, 2000), namely the Q-, I- and M-principles.

2.1 Logophoric Expressions *qua De Se* Markers in West African Languages

Logophoric expressions are expressions that can be used to mark logophoricity or logophora. By logophoricity or logophora is meant the phenomenon whereby the perspective of an internal protagonist of a sentence or discourse, as opposed to that of the current, external speaker, is being reported by using some morphological and/or syntactic means. In West African languages, logophoricity may be morphologically and/or syntactically expressed by one or more of the following linguistic mechanisms: (i) logophoric pronouns, as in (12); (ii) logophoric addressee pronouns, as in (13); (iii) logophoric verbal affixes, as in (14), (iv) logophoric cross-referencing, as in (15); and (v) first-person logophoric marking, as in (16) (see e.g., Huang 1994, 2000a, 2001, 2002, 2010a, forthcoming).

(12) Logophoric pronoun
(Donno Sɔ, Culy 1994)

Oumar	Anta	inyemɛñ	waa	be	gi.
Oumar	Anta	LOG-ACC	seen	AUX	said[3]

‘Omar$_1$ said that Anta$_2$ had seen him$_1$.’

(13) Logophoric addressee pronoun[4]
(Mapun, Frajzyngier 1985)

n-	sat	n-wur	taji	gwar	dim	n	Kaano.
I	say	BEN-3SG	PROHB	ADDR	go	PREP	Kano

‘I told him$_1$ that he$_1$ may not go to Kano.’

[3] Main abbreviations: ACC, accusative; ADDR, addressee pronoun ; AUX, auxiliary; COMP, complementiser: DAT, dative; DUR, durative aspect; INDIC, indicative; LOG, logophoric; NOM, nominative; PAST, past tense; PL, plural; REL, relative clause; RP, report particle; SBJV, subjunctive; SG, singular; SUBJ, subject; TOP, topic.

[4] Logophoric addressee pronouns are in general second-person. It is known that second person can sometimes be actually represented as a function of first person. This raises the issue of whether the logophoric complement should be treated as *oratio recta* (direct speech) or *oratio obliqua* (indirect speech).

(14) Logophoric verbal affix
(Gokana, Hyman and Comrie 1981)

à	nyíma	kɔ	aè	dɔ-ɛ.
he	knows	that	he	fell-LOG

'He$_1$ knows that he$_1$ fell.'

(15) Logophoric cross-referencing
(Akɔɔse, Curnow 2002)

a-hɔbe	a	mə-kag
he-said	RP	LOG-should go

'He$_1$ said that he$_1$ should go.'

(16) First-person logophoric marking
(Karimojong, quoted in Curnow 2002)

abu-papa	tolim	ɛbe	alozi	iŋez	moroto.
AUX-father	say	that	1SG-go	3SG	Moroto

'The father$_1$ said that he$_1$ was going to Moroto'

Out of these logophoric marking devices, (i) and (ii) represent a (pro)nominal strategy, and logophoricity is marked overtly by a pronoun in syntax. By contrast, (iii), (iv) and (v) display a verbal strategy, and logophoricity is indicated morphologically. Notice that the verbal strategy constitutes a violation of categorical iconicity, because the function of reference-tracking is indicated on the verb rather than on the noun (see e.g., Huang 2000a: 175). A further point of interest is that a West African language may use a combination of the logophoric marking mechanisms, mentioned above, to encode logophoricity. For example, Mapun has both logoporic pronouns and logophoric addressee pronouns (Frajzyngier 1985). Donno Sɔ is a language which contains both logophoric pronouns and first-person logophoric marking. In Moru, there are both logophoric pronouns and logophoric cross-referencing (Curnow 2002).[5]

Next, a number of implicational universals relating to logophoric marking in West African languages can be set up.

[5] In some cases, the distinction is not clear-cut. Curnow (2002), for example, is of the view that logophoric pronouns that are cliticised to verbs, as in (i) below, are intermediate between logophoric pronouns and logophoric cross-referencing.

(i) (Ewe, Clements 1975)

Kofi	be	ye-dzo.
Kofi	say	LOG-leave

'Kofi$_1$ said that he$_1$ left.'

(17) Person hierarchy for logophoric marking

$3 > 2 > 1$

First-person logophoric marking implies second-person logophoric marking, and second-person logophoric marking implies third-person logophoric marking.

Given (17), it is predicted that in all West African languages with logophoric marking, logophoric marking can be third-person; in some, they can also be identified as second-person; in a few, they can be distinguished on first-person as well. For example, the logophoric pronoun *ni* in Sango can be third-person only. By contrast, in Mundani, the logophoric pronoun *ye* is used for third- and second-, but not for first-person. Finally, in languages like Lele, logophoric marking can be done in all three persons (see e.g., Huang 2000a, 2001, 2002). A further piece of supporting evidence for (17) comes from Gokana. In this language, whereas third-person logophoric marking is obligatory, second-person logophoric marking is optional but preferred, and first-person logophoric marking is optional but dispreferred, as in (18) – (20) (Hyman and Comrie 1981).

(18) a. aè kɔ aè dɔ-ɛ.
he said he fell-LOG
'He$_1$ said that he$_1$ fell.'

b. aè kɔ aè dɔ.
he said he fell
'He$_1$ said that he$_2$ fell.'

(19) a. oò kɔ oò dɔ-ɛ.
you said you fell-LOG
'You said that you fell.'

b. oò kɔ oò dɔ.
you said you fell
'You said that you fell.'

(20) a. mm kɔ mm dɔ-ɛ.
I said I fell-LOG
'I said that I fell.'

b. mm kɔ mm dɔ.
I said I fell
'I said that I fell.'

Clearly, there is a functional/pragmatic explanation for (17): for referential disambiguity, the third-person distinction is the most, and the first-person distinction, the least useful, with the second-person distinction sitting in between, for third-person is closer to non-person than either first- or second-person. It follows therefore that the fact that first-person logophoric marking is very rare, if not non-existent, in natural language, is hardly surprising, given that logophoric expressions are one of the (most common) devices the current, external speaker (which is encoded usually in terms of a first-person personal pronoun/essential indexical) utilises in attributing a *de se* attitude/belief to an attributee (usually an internal protagonist) but him- or herself. In other words, when embedded in a self-ascription such as (20), the Gokana unmarked, regular first-person personal pronoun *mm* can function as a quasi-indicator to self-ascribe the making of first-person reference. This has the consequence that the logophoric marking by using the marked logophoric verbal suffix becomes unnecessary, hence dispreferred. Next, we have the number hierarchy for logophoric marking.

(21) Number hierarchy for logophoric marking

Singulars > plurals

Logophoric marking on plural logophoric expressions implies that on singular logophoric expressions.

The implicational universal in (21) summarises the general pattern of number specification for logophoric marking in West African languages. While all logophoric languages allow singular logophoric expressions to be marked, only some permit plural logophoric expressions to be marked as well. Babungo, Igbo, Mundang, and Songhai, for instance, are languages which have only singular logophoric marking. By contrast, Ewe, Gbandili, and Ngwo permit both singular and plural logophoric markings. Once again, from the viewpoint of the *de se* attitude/belief ascription, singulars are more prototypical than plurals.

What is of further interest is that a plural logophoric expression can be used for a singular antecedent, provided that the antecedent is properly included in the set denoted by the plural logophoric expression, and that the singular antecedent and the plural logophoric expression accord to the universal of conjunction of different persons. This is illustrated in (22).

(22) (Ewe, Clements 1975)

Kofi	kpɔ	be	yèwo-do	go.
Kofi	see	COMP	LOG-PL-come	out

'Kofi$_1$ saw that they$_{\{1+2\}}$ had come out.'

The same is true of Donno Sɔ, Eleme, Gokana, Lele and Mapun.

Thirdly, mention should be made of logocentric triggers, namely those NPs that can act as an antecedent for a logophoric expression. In the first place, logocentric triggers are generally constrained to be a core-argument of the logocentric predicate (to be elucidated later) of the matrix clause. Secondly, they are typically subjects.

But logocentric triggers can also be some other, non-subject argument, provided that this argument represents the 'source' of the proposition or the 'experience' of the mental state that is being reported. Two types of construction are particularly common in West African languages. The first involves the predicate 'hear from', as in (23).

(23) (Ewe, Clements 1975)

Ama	se	tso	Kofi	gbɔ	be	yè-xɔ	nunana.
Ama	hear	from	Kofi	side	COMP	LOG-receive	gift

'Ama$_1$ heard from Kofi$_2$ that she$_1$/he$_2$ had received a gift.'

Similar examples have been found in Donno Sɔ, Gokana and Tuburi.

The second involves 'psychological' predicates expressing emotional states and attitudes, of which the 'experiencer' frequently acts as direct object or object of preposition. This is shown by (24).

(24) (Gokana, Hyman and Comrie 1981)

à	kyɛ	lébàrè	kɔ	aè	dɔ-ɛ.
It	angers	Lébàrè	that	he	fell-LOG

'It angers Lébàrè$_1$ that he$_1$ fell.'

The same pattern can be located in Eleme, Ewe, and Mundani. All this shows that a logophoric expression can also be identified with a hearer and/or an experiencer, in addition to the usual speaker, thinker and believer.

In fact, there seems to be an implicational universal for logocentric triggers.

(25) Hierarchy for logocentric triggers

Surface structure: subject > object > others

Semantic role: agent > experiencer/benefactive > others

The higher an NP is on the hierarchy in (25), the more likely it will function as an antecedent for a logophoric expression. Given that the subject of the matrix clause is typically the NP that is highest on the hierarchy (and incidentally most animate), it is hardly surprising that it is the typical antecedent for a logophoric expression.

Taken together, the above three hierarchies predict that the most basic, unmarked pattern of logophoric and *de se* attitude/belief ascription marking in West African languages is one which encodes logophoricity and *de se* attitude/belief ascription by the use of a third-person, singular, logophoric expression which refers to a human subject whose e.g. speech, thought and belief is being reported.

Finally, it should be pointed out that a logophoric expression usually occurs in a logophoric domain, namely a sentence or a stretch of discourse in which the internal protagonist's or the attributee's perspective is being represented. As can be seen in the examples above, in general a logophoric domain constitutes an indirect or reported speech or *oratio obliqua*. In other words, it starts in a clause that is subordinate to the clause in which the logocentric trigger or the antecedent of the logophoric expression is identified either explicitly or implicitly. Two types of logphoric domain can be found: (i) sentential logophoric domain which operates within a sentence, and (ii) discourse logophoric domain that operates across sentence boundaries. Discourse logophoric domains are found in a number of West African languages including Angas, Bwamu, Donno Sɔ, Ewe, Fon, Gokana, and Tuburi. There is, thus, another parallelism between a logophoric expression and a quasi-indicator, namely both appear in an indirect or reportive speech (see Huang 2000a for illustration).

The logophoric domain is commonly set up by a logocentric licenser. Two varieties can be identified: (i) logocentric predicates and (ii) logocentric complementisers. Logocentric predicates can largely be distinguished on a semantic basis. The most common types of logocentric predicates are predicates of speech and thought. But other types of predicates such as those of mental states, knowledge and direct perception can also license a logophoric domain. Cross-linguistically, an implicational universal for logocentric predicates can be established.

(26) An implicational universal for logocentric predicates

> Speech predicates > epistemic predicates > psychological predicates > knowledge predicates > perceptive predicates

Some of the logocentric predicates in West African languages are listed in (27).

(27) Logocentric predicates
Speech: 'say', 'ask'
Epistemic: 'think', 'want'
Psychological: 'seem good', 'be happy'
Knowledge: 'know'
Perceptive: 'see', 'hear'

What (26) basically dictates is this, if a language allows (some) predicates of one class to trigger a logophoric domain, then it will also allow (some) predicates of every class higher on the hierarchy to do the same. Thus if a language has logophoric marking with predicates of, say, psychological states, then it will necessarily have it with predicates of thought and communication. Out of the five types of logocentric predicates listed in (26), the first four types constitute what is traditionally called propositional attitude verbs, i.e. verbs such as *say*, *claim*, *tell*, *think*, *believe*, *realise*, *know*, and *hope*, which are used in a *de se* attitude/belief ascription report. The second type of logocentric licenser is what Stirling (1993) called 'report-opening' complementizer such as *be* in Ewe, *se* in Mundang and *ga* in Tubiri. These complementizers are frequently homophonous with the verb 'say' and are often developed out of it. In many logophoric languages, a complementizer of this kind plays an important role in logophoric/*de se* attitude/belief ascription marking in that it opens an indirect or reported context. By contrast, in other logophoric languages, logophoric/*de se* attitude/belief ascription marking can occur without such a complementizer (see e.g., Huang 2000a, 2001, 2002, forthcoming for further discussion).

2.2 Long-Distance Reflexives *qua De Se* Markers in East, South, and Southeast Asian Languages

We move next to *de se* attitude/belief ascription marking in East, South, and Southeast Asian languages. Since there are no special, logophoric expressions in these languages, marking of *de se* attitude/belief ascriptions in East, South, and Southeast Asian languages is accomplished syntactically in terms of a long-distance reflexive (see also Pan 1995 with regard to Chinese).

By long-distance reflexive is meant a reflexive that can be bound outside its local syntactic domain. Languages that systematically allow long-distance reflexives are called 'long-distance reflexivization' languages. Cross-linguistically, central cases of long-distance reflexivization involve binding of a reflexive out of an NP, out of a small clause, across an infinitival clause, across a subjunctive clause, across an indicative clause, across sentence boundaries into discourse, and across speakers/turns in a conversation (see e.g., Huang 2000a for illustrations from a wide range of languages). Needless to say, languages differ in precisely which types of complement out of which a long-distance reflexive can be bound. However, cross-linguistically the variation in the distribution of long-distance reflexives appears to manifest itself in a relatively clear, uniform and consistent manner. This consistency can be captured in an implicational universal in (28).

(28) An implicational universal for long-distance reflexivization complement types
  (i) At the sentence level
    NPs > small clauses > infinitives >subjunctives > indicatives
  (ii) At the discourse level
    Discourse > different speakers/turns in a conversation
  (iii) Sentence and discourse
    Sentence > discourse

What (28) basically predicts is this: if a language allows long-distance reflexivization into one type of complement, then it will also permit it into every type higher on the hierarchy. Thus, if a language has long-distance reflexivization with indicatives, then it will necessarily have it with (if relevant) subjunctives, infinitives, small clauses and NPs. This is the case with Icelandic. Next, while Italian is a language in which 'binding' of a long-distance reflexive is normally up to subjunctives, Russian allows long-distance reflexivization at most out of infinitives. Still next, if a language allows 'binding' of a reflexive across different speakers/turns in a conversation, then it will also permit 'binding' of it across sentence boundaries into discourse. Finally, if a language allows long-distance reflexivisation at the discourse level, then it will also allow it at the sentence level. In general, at the sentence level, East, South, and Southeast Asian languages permit long-distance reflexivization with up to indicatives, and at the discourse level, they have long-distance reflexivization up into different speakers/turns in a conversation.

Long-distance reflexivisation exhibits a number of universal tendencies, notably those listed in (29).

(29) Universal tendencies of long-distance reflexivization

a. Subject orientation:
Antecedents for a long-distance reflexive tend to be subjects.

b. Maximality effect:
Possible antecedents of a long-distance reflexive can in principle be the subject of any matrix clause, but the root clause subject tends to be preferred to any intermediate clause subjects.

c. Morphologically simplicity:
Long-distance reflexives tend to be morphologically simplex.

d. Referential optionality:
Long-distance reflexives tend to be referentially optional, and consequently they are not in complementary distribution, with regular personal pronouns.

Having outlined the basics of long-distance reflexivization, let me turn to East, South, and Southeast Asian languages to show how long-distance reflexives in these language can act as a quasi-indicator in the sense of Castañeda. In the first place, long-distance reflexives in these languages may be morphologically simplex or complex. They may or may not be specified for person, number or gender. But what is of relevance to us here is that its pattern of person and number distinctions does not run counter to the person and number hierarchies in (17) and (21) set up for the other type of quasi-indicator, namely, logophoric expressions in West African languages.

Next, antecedents for long-distance reflexives in East, South, and Southeast Asian languages also run parallel to those for logophoric expressions/quasi-indicators in West African languages. First, they are normally limited to be a core-argument of the predicate of the matrix clause. Secondly, they are typically subjects, as is shown in (30).

(30) (Chinese)

Xiaoming	gaosu	Xiaohua	Xiaolan	xihuan	ziji.
Xiaoming	tell	Xiaohua	Xiaolan	like	self

'Xiaoming$_1$ tells Xiaohua$_2$ that Xiaolan$_3$ likes self$_{1/*2/3}$.'

In other words, as with a logophoric expression in West African language, a long-distance reflexive in East, South, and Southeast Asian languages is normally 'bound' by the agent of, or the perspectival operator introduced by, a propositional attitude verb. However, once again, as in the case of logocentric triggers for logophoric expressions/quasi-indicators in West African languages, antecedents for long-distance reflexives in East, South, and Southeast Asian languages can also be some non-subject argument, provided that this argument represents the 'source' of the proposition or the 'experience' of the mental states that is being described. Once more, the two most common types of construction are (i) those involving the predicate 'hear from', as in the Korean example (31), and (ii) those involving psychological predicates, as in the Tamil example (32).

(31) (Korean, quoted in Huang 2000a)

John-un	Bill-loputhe	caki-ka	tayhak
John-TOP	Bill-from	self-NOM	college

iphaksihem-ey	hapkyekhayssta-nun
entrance examination-at	passed-that

iyaki-lul	tulessta.
story-ACC	heard

'John$_1$ heard from Bill$_2$ that self$_{1/2}$ passed the college entrance examination.'

(32) (Tamil, Annamalai 2000)

taan	toottadu	kumaare	romba	paadiccadu.
self	defeat-PAST-it	Kumar-ACC	much	affect-PAST-it

'That self$_1$ was defeated affected Kumar$_1$ very much.'

Putting it another way, a hearer and/or an experiencer can also be the antecedent of a long-distance reflexive in East, South, and Southeast Asian languages provided that he or she is the perspective-holder.

Turning next to the syntactic and discourse environments in which a long-distance reflexive in East, South, and Southeast Asian languages is used, we can see that they typically constitute a logophoric domain or an indirect/reported speech. The 'binding' domain for long-distance reflexives in these languages is usually triggered by a logocentric predicate. The first four types of predicate listed on hierarchy (26) are allowed in South, and all the five types are permitted in East Asian, languages to act as a logocentric licenser. This explains why long-distance reflexivization occurs predominantly within the sentential complements of predicates of speech, thought, mental state, knowledge and perception in these languages. The Chinese example below shows that even perceptive predicates can be used as logocentric licensers.

(33) (Chinese)

Xiaoming	tingjian	Xiaohua	zai	biaoyang	ziji.
Xiaoming	hear	Xiaohua	DUR	praise	self

'Xiaoming$_1$ hears Xiaohua praising self$_1$.'

Furthermore, as with logophoric domains in West African languages, long-distance reflexive domains in East and South Asian languages are not restricted to clausal complements of a logocentric predicate, either. Firstly, they can be extended to other types of syntactic construction such as the topic-comment construction and the relative construction. Secondly, they can also operate across sentence boundaries, extending over an arbitrarily long stretch of discourse, provided that this portion of discourse falls under the scope of the NP which antecedes the long-distance reflexive. This is exemplified in (34)

(34) (Korean, quoted in Huang 2000)

Kokayt	malu-ey	olla-se-ni	kuliwun	caki	cip
hill	slope-at	rise-stand-as	lovely	self	house

tungpul-i	poinita.
lamplight-NOM	visible

Sekpong-i-nun ...	transwum-e	kokay-lul	ttwie
Sekpong-TOP	in one breath	hill-ACC	run

naylye	kassupnita.
down	went

'Upon standing on the slope, the lamplight from self's$_1$ lovely home is visible. Sekpong$_1$ ... ran down the hill in one breath.'

So far I have been showing that there are strong parallels in the use of logophoric expressions in West African languages and in that of long-distance reflexives in East, South, and Southeast Asian languages to report on a *de se* attitude/belief to an attributee. But there is one pattern of long-distance reflexivization in East Asian languages which has not been attested for logophoric expressions in West African languages. This is concerned with the use of deictically-oriented directional predicates such as 'come/go' and 'bring/take'. As can be shown by the Chinese example (35) below, while the use of 'come' in (35a) allows long-distance reflexivization, the use of 'go' in (35b) does not. Furthermore, note that this contrast is independent of whether or not a logocentric predicate occurs in the matrix clause.

(35) (Chinese)

a.

Yinwei	tongxue	lai	kan	guo	ziji	le,
because	classmate	come	see	EXP	self	PFV

suoyi	Xiaohua	hen	gaoxing.
so	Xiaohua	very	happy

'Xiaohua$_1$ was very happy because his classmates have come to see self$_1$.'

b.

?Yinwei	tongxue	qu	kan	guo	ziji	le,
because	classmate	go	see	EXP	self	PFV

suoyi	Xiaohua	hen	gaoxing.
so	Xiaohua	very	happy

'Xiaohua$_1$ was very happy because his classmates have gone to see self$_1$.'

The same is true of Japanese, Korean and Turkish.

This contrast seems to be attributed to the fact that the use of 'come' in (35a) makes clear what is reported on is from the space-location of the matrix subject, therefore the matrix subject is the pivot or the relativized 'centre of deixis' in the long-distance reflexive domain, hence the possibility of long-distance reflexivization. In other words, 'come' must be interpreted as describing movement towards the matrix subject. On the other hand, the use of 'go' in (35b) is an indication that what is described is not from the 'camera angle' of the matrix subject, rather it indicates movement away from the matrix subject, therefore the matrix subject cannot be the pivot, hence long-distance reflexivization is bad. Perhaps this can be seen as an extended case of the attribution of a *de se* attitude/belief from a third-person viewpoint.

3 A Neo-Gricean Pragmatic Analysis

I have now come to the stage at which I can outline a neo-Gricean pragmatic analysis of *de se* attitude/belief ascriptions by means of logophoric expressions in West African languages and long-distance reflexives in East, South, and Southeast Asian languages and the related use of regular expressions/personal pronouns in these languages. Let me start with the three neo-Gricean pragmatic principles proposed by Levinson (1987, 1991, 2000, see also e.g., Grice 1989 and Huang 1991, 1994/2007, 2000a, b, 2007, 2010b, 2011).

(36) Levinson's Q-, I-, and M-principles (simplified)

a. The Q-principle
Speaker: Do not say less than is required (given I).
Addressee: What is not said is not the case.

b. The I-principle
Speaker: Do not say more than is required (given Q).
Addressee: What is generally said is stereotypically and specifically exemplified

c. The M-principle
Speaker: Do not use a marked expression without reason.
Addressee: What is said in a marked way is not unmarked.

Each of these three principles has two sides: a speaker's maxim, which specifies what the principle enjoins a speaker to say, and a recipient's corollary, which dictates what it allows an addressee to infer. The speaker's maxim is normally concerned with production and is a prohibition. By contrast, the recipient's corollary or the addressee's maxim is usually about comprehension and is an obligation.

The basic idea of the Q-principle is that the use of an expression (especially a semantically weaker one) in a set of contrastive semantic alternates Q-implicates the negation of the interpretation associated with the use of another expression (especially a semantically stronger one) in the same set. In other words, the effect of this pragmatic strategy is to give rise to an upper-bounding conversational implicature: from the absence of a semantically stronger expression, we infer that the interpretation associated with the use of that expression does not hold. Schematically (I use the symbol +> to indicate 'conversationally implicate'):

(37) Q-scale: <x,y>
y +>$_{Q}$ ~ x

(38) Q-scalar: <all, some>
Some of John's friends like roast chestnuts.
+> Not all of John's friends like roast chestnuts.

Next, the basic idea of the I-principle is that the use of a semantically general linguistic expression I-implicates a semantically specific interpretation. In other words, the operation of the I-principle induces an inference to a proposition that is best in keeping with the most stereotypical and explanatory expectation given world knowledge. Schematically:

(39) I-scale: [x,y]

$y +>_I x$

(40) (Conjunction buttressing)

p and q +> p and then q

+> p therefore q

+> p in order to cause q

John turned the key and the drawer opened.

+> John first turned the key and then the drawer opened.

+> John turned the key and therefore the drawer opened.

+> John turned the key in order to cause the drawer to open.

Finally, the basic idea of the M-principle is that the use of a marked expression M-implicates the negation of the interpretation associated with the use of an alternative, unmarked expression in the same set. In other words, from the use of a marked expression, we infer that the stereotypical interpretation associated with the use of an alternative, unmarked expression does not hold. Schematically:

(41) M-scale: {x,y}

$y +>_M \sim x$

(42) a. The tram comes frequently.

+> The tram comes, say, every ten minutes.

b. The tram comes not infrequently.

+> The tram comes not as frequently as the uttering of (a) suggests, say, every half an hour

Taken together, the I-, and M-principles give rise to complementary interpretations: the use of an unmarked expression tends to convey an unmarked message, whereas the use of a marked expression, a marked message. Furthermore, inconsistencies arising from the Q-, I-, and M-principles are resolved by an ordered set of precedence.

(43) Levinson's resolution schema

a. Level of genus: Q > M > I

b. Level of species: e.g. $Q_{\text{-clausal}} > Q_{\text{-scalar}}$

This amounts to saying that genuine Q-implicatures tend to precede I-implicatures, but otherwise I-implicatures take precedence until the use of a marked expression triggers a complementary M-implicature to the negation of the applicability of the pertinent I-implicature (see e.g., Huang 1991, 1994/2007, 2000a, b, 2007, 2010b for further discussion).

We move next to the version of the neo-Gricean pragmatic theory of anaphora advanced by Huang (e.g., 1991, 1994/2007, 2000a, b, 2004, 2007, 2010a) (see also Levinson 1987, 1991, 2000). The underlying idea is that the interpretation of certain patterns of anaphora can be made using pragmatic enrichment, parasitic on a language user's knowledge of the range of options available in the grammar and of the systematic use or avoidance of particular linguistic expressions or structures on particular occasions.

Applying the Q-, I- and M-principles, sketched above, to the domain of anaphoric reference, we can derive a general pragmatic apparatus for the interpretation of zero anaphors, pronouns, reflexives, and lexical NPs in (44).

(44) A revised neo-Gricean pragmatic apparatus for anaphora (e.g., Huang 2000a, 2004, 2007, 2010a)

(a) Interpretation principles

(i) The use of an anaphoric expression *x* I-implicates a local coreferential interpretation, unless (ii) or (iii).

(ii) There is an anaphoric Q-scale <x, y>, in which case, the use of *y* Q-implicates the complement of the I-implicature associated with the use of *x*, in terms of reference.

(iii) There is an anaphoric M-scale {x, y}, in which case, the use of *y* M implicates the complement of the I-implicature associated with the use of *x*, in terms of either reference or expectedness.

(b) Consistency constraints

Any interpretation implicated by (a) is subject to the requirement of consistency with

(i) The revised DRP.

(ii) Information saliency, so that

(a) implicatures due to matrix constructions may take precedence over implicatures due to subordinate constructions, and

(b) implicatures to coreference may be preferred according to the saliency of antecedent in line with the following hierarchy:

topic > subject > object, etc.; and

(iii) General implicature constraints, namely,

(a) background assumptions,

(b) contextual factors

(c) meaning$_{\text{-nn}}$, and

(d) semantic entailments.

(45) The revised disjoint reference presumption (DRP) (see e.g., Huang 2000a, 2004, 2007)

The co-arguments of a predicate are intended to be disjoint, unless one of them is reflexive-marked.

Coming back to the use of logophoric expressions in West African languages and long-distance reflexives in East, South, and Southeast Asian languages to encode the *de se* attitude/belief ascription, the interpretation of them and their associated regular personal pronouns can be determined by (44).

Let me start with logophoric expressions *qua de se* markers in West African languages. Notice that referentially, the use of logophoric expressions in these languages is in complementary distribution with that of regular expressions (such as regular personal pronouns), and that logophoric expressions are the only option available in the grammar of these languages to encode coreference in a logophoric domain.[6] Now contrast (46a) with (46b).

(46) (Donno Sɔ, Culy 1994)

a. (Logophoric pronoun)
Oumar Anta inyemɛñ waa be gi.
Oumar Anta LOG-ACC seen AUX said
'Omar$_1$ said that Anta$_2$ had seen him$_1$.'

b. (Regular pronoun)
Oumar Anta woñ waa be gi.
Oumar Anta 3SG-ACC seen AUX said
'Omar$_1$ said that Anta$_2$ had seen him$_3$.'

As a result, any speaker of these languages who intends coreference will also have to use a logophoric expression. This has the consequence that if a

[6] However, more recently Adésolá (2004) has reported that in addition to the logophoric pronoun, Yoruba has a non-logophoric pronoun that can be used to mark coreference with the matrix subject of the sentence in which the pronoun occurs. This is illustrated in (ib).

(i) a. Olu gbagbo pé ilé oun ti wo.
Olu believe that house LOG ASP fall
'Olu$_1$ believes that his$_1$ house has collapsed.'

b. Olu gbagbo pé ilé ré ti wo.
Olu believe that house 3SG ASP fall
'Olu$_1$ believes that his$_{1/2}$ house has collapsed.'

But as pointed out by Adésolá (2004) and Safir (2004), the logophoric pronoun has to be used if a *de se* attitude/belief ascription is intended. This pattern can be grouped together with the long-distance reflexive versus regular personal pronoun pattern in East, South, and Southeast Asian languages, for the neo-Gricean pragmatic analysis of which see below.

logophoric expression is not employed but a regular personal pronoun is used instead, a Q-implicature will arise, namely neither the marking of *de se* attitude/belief ascription nor coreference is intended. In other words, we have a Q-scale <logophoric expression, regular pronoun> here, such that the use of the semantically weaker regular pronoun Q-implicates that the use of the semantically stronger logophoric expression cannot be truthfully entertained, that is to say, both the *de se* reading and the coreferential interpretation which are associated with the use of a logophoric expression should be avoided. Schematically:

(47) <logophoric expression [+de se, +coreference], regular pronoun [-de se, -coreference]>

regular pronoun +>Q ~ logophoric expression

We move next to the use of long-distance reflexives to represent a *de se* attitude/belief ascription in East, South, and Southeast Asian languages. Note that unlike in West African languages, in these languages, long-distance reflexives are not in referential complementary distribution with regular pronouns. In other words, there is usually a referential overlap between long-distance reflexives and regular personal pronouns, as the examples in (48) – (50) indicate.

(48) (Chinese)

a. Xiaoming yiwei Xiaohua bu ai ziji.
Xiaoming think Xiaohua not love self
'Xiaoming$_1$ thinks that Xiaohua$_2$ does not love self$_{1/2}$.'

b. Xiaoming yiwei Xiaohua bu ai ta.
Xiaoming think Xiaohua not love 3SG
'Xiaoming$_1$ thinks that Xiaohua$_2$ does not love him$_{1/3}$.'

(49) (Bangla, Sengupta 2000)

a. babli bolo nije kaj-Ta korbe.
Babli-NOM said self work-CL-ACC will do
'Babli$_1$ said self$_1$ would do the job.'

b. babli bolo se kaj-Ta korbe.
Babli-NOM said she work-CL-ACC will do
'Babli$_1$ said she$_{1/2}$ would do the job.'

(50) (Malay, quoted in Huang 2000a)

a.

Timah	memberitahu	Rohani		bahawa
Timah	tell	Rohani		that
Ali	memandang	rendah	akan	dirinya.
Ali	look	low	to	self-3SG

'Timah$_1$ told Rohani$_2$ that Ali$_3$ looked down on herself$_1$.'

b.

Timah	memberitahu	Rohani		bahawa
Timah	tell	Rohani		that
Ali	memandang	rendah	akan	nya.
Ali	look	low	to	3SG

'Timah$_1$ told Rohani$_2$ that Ali$_3$ looked down on her$_{1/2/4}$.'

While a long-distance reflexive is used for the purpose of encoding *de se* attitude/belief ascriptions, for coreference, a regular personal pronoun can be employed. Put another way, whereas the use of a long-distance reflexive encodes both a *de se* attitude/belief ascription and coreference, the use of a regular personal pronoun may or may not encode coreference, but normally not *de se* attitude/belief ascriptions. This is sufficient enough to form a Q-scale <long-distance reflexive, regular pronoun> to the effect that the unavailability of the semantically stronger long-distance reflexive will Q-implicate the speaker's intention to avoid at least one of the features associated with its use, namely the *de se* reading. Long-distance reflexives are semantically stronger than regular personal pronouns in that (i) syntactically they usually require to be somewhat bound, and (ii) semantically they typically have to be referentially dependent. Schematically:

(51) <long-distance reflexive [+de se, +coreference], regular pronoun [-de se, +/- coreference]>

regular pronoun +>Q ~ long-distance reflexive

Alternatively, the use of long-distance reflexives and regular pronouns in East, South, and Southeast Asian languages can be accounted for in terms of the systematic interaction between the I- and M-principles. Since the grammar of these languages allows the unmarked regular personal pronoun to be used to mark coreference, a speaker will use it if such an interpretation is intended. On the other hand, if the unmarked regular personal pronoun is not used, but the marked (morphologically more complex) long-distance reflexive is used instead, then an M-implicature is created, namely not only coreference but *de se* construal/interpretation as well is intended. Schematically:

(52) {regular pronoun [-de se, +/-coreference], long-distance reflexive [+de se, +coreference] }

long-distance reflexive +>M~ regular pronoun[7]

Also worth noting is that if relevant, the choice between long-distance reflexives on the one hand and regular personal pronouns on the other, is correlated with that between subjunctive and indicative mood: it is common for the use of a long-distance reflexive to go with subjunctive mood and for

---

[7] Note that in Chinese, Japanese and Korean, while a regular personal pronoun cannot admit of a quantifier-variable interpretation, a reflexive can.

(i) (Chinese)

a. Mei ge ren dou shuo ta xihuan gudian yinyue.
every CL person all say 3SG like classic music
'Everybody$_1$ says that he$_2$ likes classic music.'

b. Mei ge ren dou shuo ziji xihuan gudian yinyue.
every CL person all say self like classic music
'Everybody$_1$ says that self$_1$ likes classic music.'

(ii) (Japanese, quoted in Huang 2000)

a. Daremo-ga kare-ga Mary-ni kirawareteiru to
everyone-NOM he-NOM Mary-by be-disliked COMP
omoikondeiru (koto).
be convinced fact
'Everyone$_1$ is convinced that he$_2$ is disliked by Mary.'

b. Daremo-ga zibun-ga Mary-ni kirawareteiru to
everyone-NOM self-NOM Mary-by be-disliked COMP
omoikondeiru (koto).
be convinced fact
'Everyone$_1$ is convinced that self$_1$ is disliked by Mary.'

(iii) (Korean, quoted in Huang 2000)

a. amuto ku-ka Mary-lul cohahanta-ko malhaci
anyone he-NOM Mary-ACC like-COMP say
anhassta.
did not
'Nobody$_1$ said that he$_2$ liked Mary.'

b. amuto caki-ka Mary-lul cohahanta-ko malhaci
anyone self-NOM Mary-ACC like-COMP say
anhassta.
did not
'Nobody$_1$ said that self$_1$ liked Mary.'

This can also be accounted for in terms of our M-principle; the use of a marked reflexive M-implicates a quantifier-variable interpretation. For more discussion, see Huang (2000a).

the employment of a regular personal pronoun to go with indicative mood, as (53) shows (see also Coulmas 1986 for the observation that subjunctives are commonly used to mark indirect speech or discourse).

(53) (Icelandic, Sigurðsson 1990)

a.	Jón	segir	að	María	elski	sig.
	John	says-INDIC	that	Mary	loves-SBJV	self

'John$_1$ says that Mary loves self$_1$.'

b.	Jón	veit	að	María	elskar	hann.
	John	knows-INDIC	that	Mary	loves-INDIC	him

'John$_1$ knows that Mary loves him$_1$.'

Once again, the correlation seems to be a reflection of a semantic/pragmatic choice made by the external speaker about the responsibility he or she assumes for the truthfulness of what he or she is reporting. If a regular personal pronoun and indicative mood are used, as in (53b), it shows that the speaker asserts that the report is true, because the report is *de re*. He or she cannot go on to deny it because doing so will give rise to Moore's paradox. If on the other hand, a long-distance reflexive and subjunctive mood are deployed, as in (53a), it indicates that the speaker does not take the responsibility for the truth of the report, because he or she simply attributes an 'I'-thought to an attributee. He or she can then go on to deny it. Thus, the optionality of long-distance reflexives/regular personal pronouns and of subjunctives/indicatives provides the speaker with a useful means of expressing his or her attitudes toward the truth of what he or she is reporting, or more broadly, of expressing evidentiality (see e.g., Huang forthcoming for a discussion of the relationship between logophoricity and evidentiality).

4 Summary

In this article, I have provided a description of the marking of *de se* attitude/belief ascriptions by means of logophoric expressions in West African languages and long-distance reflexives in East, South, and Southeast Asian languages. I have also outlined a pragmatic analysis of it and the related phenomenon in these languages utilising my version of the neo-Gricean pragmatic theory of anaphora.

References

Adésolá, O. 2004. Null operators and pronouns: A-bar dependencies and relations in Yoruba. PhD dissertation, Rutgers University.

Amritavalli, R. 2000. Lexical anaphors and pronouns in Tamil. In Lust B. et al (eds.) 169-216.

Capone, A. 2010. Between Scylla and Charybdis: the semantics and pragmatics of attitudes *de se*. *Intercultural Pragmatics* 7: 471-503.

Castañeda, H.-N. 1966. 'He': a study in the logic of self-consciousness. *Ratio* 8 (2): 130-157.

Castañeda, H.-N. 1967. Indicators and quasi-indicators. *American Philosophical Quarterly* 4 (2): 85-100.

Castañeda, H.-N. 1968. On the logic of attributions of self-knowledge to others. *The Journal of Philosophy* 65 (15): 439-56.

Castañeda, H-N. 1989. *Thinking, Language, and Experience*. Minneapolis: University of Minnesota Press.

Chierchia, G. 1989. Anaphora and attitudes *de se*. In Bartsch, R., van Bentham, J. and van Emde Boas, P. (eds.), *Language in Context*. Dordrecht: Foris, 1-31

Chiou, M. and Huang, Y. 2010. NP-anaphora in Modern Greek: a partial neo-Gricean pragmatic approach. *Journal of Pragmatics* 42: 2036-2057.

Clements, George N. 1975. The logophoric pronoun in Ewe: its role in discourse. *Journal of West African Languages* 10: 141-177.

Corazza, E. 2004. Essential indexicals and quasi-indicators. *Journal of Semantics* 21:1-34.

Corazza, E. 2011. Empathy as a psychological guide to the *de se/de re* distinction. This volume.

Coulmas, F. (ed.) 1986. *Direct and Indirect Speech*. Berlin: Mouton de Gruyter.

Culy, C. 1994. Aspects of logophoric marking. *Linguistics* 32: 1055-1094.

Curnow, T. 2002. Three types of verbal logophoricity in African languages. *Studies in African Linguistics* 31:1-25.

Feit, N. 2008. *Belief about the self*. Oxford: Oxford University Press.

Frajzyngier, Z. 1985. Logophoric systems in Chadic. *Journal of African Languages and Linguistics* 7. 23-37.

Grice, H. P. 1989. *Studies in the Way of Words*, Cambridge, MA: Harvard University Press.

Hagège, C. 1974. Les pronoms logophoriques. *Bulletin de la Société de Linguistique de Paris* 69 : 287-310.

Higginbotham, J. 2003. Remembering, imaging, and the first person. In Barber, A. (ed.) *Epistemology of Language*. Oxford: Oxford University Press. 496-535.

Huang, Y. 1991. A neo-Gricean pragmatic theory of anaphora. *Journal of Linguistics* 27: 301-335.

Huang, Y. 1994/2007. *The Syntax and Pragmatics of Anaphora: A Study with Special Reference to Chinese*. (Cambridge Studies in Linguistics 70) Cambridge: Cambridge University Press.

Huang, Y. 2000a. *Anaphora: A Cross-linguistic Study*. (Oxford Studies in Typology and Linguistic Theory) Oxford: Oxford University Press.

Huang, Y. 2000b. Discourse anaphora: four theoretical models. *Journal of Pragmatics* 32:151-176.

Huang, Y. 2001. Marking of logophoricity in West African, East and South Asian languages. In *Proceedings of the 6th International Conference on the Languages of East, Southeast Asia and West Africa*. St Petersburg: University of St Petersburg Oriental Press. 224-238.

Huang, Y. 2002. Logophoric marking in East Asian languages. In T. Güldemann and M. von Roncador (eds.) *Reported Discourse: A Meeting Ground for Different Linguistic Domains*. Amsterdam: John Benjamins. 213-224.

Huang, Y. 2004 Anaphora and the pragmatics-syntax interface. In L. Horn and G. Ward (eds.) *The Handbook of Pragmatics*. Oxford: Blackwell. 288-314.

Huang, Y. 2007. *Pragmatics*. (Oxford Textbooks in Linguistics) Oxford: Oxford University Press.

Huang, Y. 2010a. Switch-reference in Amele and logophoric verbal suffix in Gokana: a generalized neo-Gricean pragmatic analysis. In Shu, D. F. and Turner, K. (eds.) *Contrasting Meaning in Languages of the East and West*. Berlin: Peter Lang. 75-101.

Huang, Y. 2010b. Neo-Gricean pragmatic theory of conversational implicature. In B. Heine and H. Narrog (eds.) *The Oxford Handbook of Linguistic Analysis*. Oxford: Oxford University Press. 607-631.

Huang, Y. 2011. Types of inference: entailment, presupposition, and implicature. In Bublitz, W. and Norrick, N. (eds.), *Foundations of Pragmatics*. Berlin: Mouton de Gruyter. 397-421.

Huang, Y. (Forthcoming). Logophoricity and neo-Gricean truth-conditional pragmatics. In Capone, A., Piparo, F. L. and Carapezza, M, (eds.) *Perspectives on Pragmatics and Philosophy*. Heidelberg: Springer.

Hyman, L. and Comrie, B. 1981. Logophoric reference in Gokana. *Journal of African Languages and Linguistics* 3:19-37.

Levinson, S. C. 1987. Pragmatics and the grammar of anaphora. *Journal of Linguistics* 23:379-434.

Levinson, S. C. 1991. Pragmatic reduction of the Binding Conditions revisited. *Journal of Linguistics* 27:107-161.

Levinson, S. C. 2000. *Presumptive Meanings*. Cambridge, MA: The MIT Press.

Lewis, D. 1979. Attitudes *de dicto* and *de se*. *The Philosophical Review* 88: 513-543.

Lust, B., Wali, K., Gair, J. and Subbarao, K. V. (eds.) 2000. *Lexical Anaphors and Pronouns in Selected South Asian Languages*. Berlin: Mouton de Gruyter.

Pan, H.-H. 1995. Locality, self-ascription, discourse prominence, and Mandarin reflexives. PhD dissertation, University of Texas at Austin.

Parker, E. 1986. Mundani pronouns. In Wiesemann (ed.), 131-166. Tübingen: Narr.

Perry, J. 1979. The problem of the essential indexical. *Nous* 13: 3-21.

Perry, J. 2000. Castañeda on *he* and *I*. In Perry, J., *The Problem of the Essential Indexical and Other Essays*. Stanford: CSLI. 77-100.

Safir, K. 2004. Person, context and perspective. *Rivista di Linguistica* (Italian Journal of Linguistics)16.

Schlenker, P. 2003. A plea for monster. *Linguistics and Philosophy* 26: 29-120.

Sengupta, G. 2000. Lexical anaphors and pronouns in Bangla. In Lust, B. et al (eds.), 277-332.

Sigurðsson, H. A. 1990. Long-distance reflexives and moods in Icelandic. In Maling, J. and Zaenen, A. (eds.) *Syntax and Semantics 24: Modern Icelandic Syntax*. London: Academic Press. 309-346.

Stalnaker, R. 1981. Indexical belief. *Synthesis* 49:129-151.

Stirling, L. 1993. *Switch-reference and Discourse Representation*. Cambridge: Cambridge University Press.

Wiesemann, U. (ed.) 1986. *Pronominal Systems*. Tübingen: Narr.

8

Empathy as a Psychological Guide to the *De Se/De Re* Distinction

EROS CORAZZA

1 Introduction

In this paper I discuss some linguistic data favoring the *de re/de se* distinction. To do so I focus on the different way epithets (e.g.: 'the bastard', 'the imbecile', ...) and quasi-indicators (e.g.: 's/he her/himself') behave when appearing in psychological characterizations. I argue that they often work like attributive anaphors. The quasi-indicator 'she herself' in "$Jane_1$ believes that *she (herself)*$_1$ is rich" inherits its value from 'Jane' and *attributes* an 'I'-thought to Jane. The epithet 'the bastard' in "Jane planned to marry Jon_1, but *the bastard*$_1$ ran away" also inherits its value from 'Jon' and *attributes* the property of being a bastard to Jon. I shall further show how the ungrammaticality of sentences like "*Jon_1 claimed/ said/ thinks/... that *the bastard*$_1$ was honest") does not threaten the view that epithets can be understood as anaphoric pronouns. Their ungrammaticality rests on the fact that the epithet is embedded in what should be a *de se* attribution (e.g. "Jon_1 claimed/ said/ thinks/... that *he (himself)*$_1$ was honest") while its nature is to contribute to the expression of a *de re* attribution. This also helps to understand the ungrammaticality of "*$Jane_1$ said/ thinks/ promised/... that *the imbecile*$_1$ will come" *vs.* the grammaticality of "$Jane_1$ said/ thinks/ promised/... that *she (herself)*$_1$ will come" on the one hand, and the ungrammaticality of "*Jon_1 ran over a man who was trying to give *him (himself)*$_1$ directions", *vs.* the grammaticality of "Jon_1 ran over a man who was trying to give *the idiot*$_1$ directions" on the other hand. These linguistic data will ultimately be accounted for in referring to discourse consideration involving

Attitudes De Se: Linguistics, Epistemology, Metaphysics.
Neil Feit and Alessandro Capone (eds.).

the notions of point of view, perspective and empathy. I argue that empathy is central when we come to distinguish between *de se* and *de re* construals, and that the difference in behavior between an epithet and a quasi-indicator is best accounted for in focusing on such a notion. When the reporter empathizes with the attributee s/he is unlikely to use an epithet in characterizing the attributee. Empathy is also relevant when we come to defend the view that in a psychological characterization an epithet forces the *de re* reading while a quasi-indicator triggers the *de se* one.

2 Some Data and the Framework

Quasi-indicators and epithets display the following interesting features: they can act either as anaphoric pronouns or as bound variables:

(1) a. Jane$_1$ said that she would come but *the idiot*$_1$ will probably miss the train
b. Every student$_1$ promised to come but *the idiots*$_1$ missed the train

(2) a. Jane$_1$ believes that *she herself*$_1$ is clever
b. Every student$_1$ believes that *she herself*$_1$ is clever

In (1a) and (2a) the epithet 'the idiot' and the quasi-indicator 'she herself' are anaphoric on 'Jane', while in (1b) and (2b) they are bound by 'every student'. In constructions such as (1) and (2), both the epithets and the quasi-indicators are attributive in addition to being anaphoric/bound variables. In (1a) and (2a) they attribute a particular property to the referent of the NP (Jane) from which they inherit their value. While the epithet 'the idiot' in (1a) attributes the property of being an idiot to Jane, the quasi-indicator 'she herself' in (2a) attributes an 'I'-thought to her.[1]

In this chapter I propose a picture that handles the anaphoric characteristic of quasi-indicators and epithets without giving up their attributive nature. To do so, I introduce the notion of *attributive anaphora*. I shall further argue that the difference between epithets and quasi-indicators parallels the *de se*/*de re* distinction. A quasi-indicator like 's/he (herself)' attributes an egocentric (*de se*) thought to the referent of the NP it inherits its value from. That is to say, 's/he (herself)' attributes to the attributee a thought s/he

[1] It is worth stressing, though, that the attribution of a thought differs from the attribution of a property. With a quasi-indicator one attributes a thought while with an epithet one attributes a property. As we shall see, this difference helps to stress that a quasi-indicator like 'she herself' contributes to a *de se* attribution while an epithet like 'the idiot' implies a *de re* characterization.

would express in using 'I'. On the other hand, epithets are always transparent (*de re*) and, as such, do not characterize the attributee's mental state. Actually, when an epithet is used as an attributive anaphora it is used by the narrator to attribute a particular property to someone without suggesting that the latter would use the epithet to characterize her/himself. The use of an epithet suggests that the attributee would not accept the epithet as a characterization of her/himself. This is not surprising, since not many people would seriously characterize themselves using derogatory language.

The general framework I am working with can be summarized as follows. Since empathy corresponds to the speaker's identification (in varying degrees) with the person participating in the event described, empathy helps to explain how we capture someone else's perspective. In other terms, empathy is a key feature of our mindreading capacity: we are, one could say, empathetic organisms and we are hard wired to be so. Furthermore, empathy can be understood as the root of our thoughts, for it is only insofar as one is capable of taking another's person's perspective that one can be credited with the kind of thoughts normal human being are capable of.[2] This picture is in accordance with the Wittgensteinian view that the perception and understanding of other people's mental attitudes and the attribution of mental properties to others does not work on an inferential basis. In particular, it does not work on the model of analogy, i.e. on the model that one understands, say someone else's pain, because one relates someone's pain to her own:

> "We see emotion."—As opposed to what?—We do not see facial contortions and *make the inference* that he is feeling joy, grief, boredom. We describe a face immediately as sad, radiant, bored, even when we are unable to give any other description of the features.—Grief, one would like to say, is personified in face. This is essential to what we call "emotion". (Wittgenstein *RPP II*: § 570)

As I understand it, empathy can be considered as one of the main, if not the main, feature underlying our intersubjective interaction and communication. As such it should also help explain how we attribute intentional states to others. For empathy can be characterized both as the cognitive awareness of someone else's mental state and as the vicarious affective response to

---

[2] "Thinking becomes possible because the child separates out one person's perspective from another's ... thinking arises out of repeated experiences of *moving* from one psychological stance to another in relation to things and events. Critically important is the kind of mental movement involved. It is not enough that the baby shifts perspectives by herself. In order to grasp that she can move in her attitudes to the world, the movements need to happen *through someone else*" (Hobson 2002: 105). For an interesting treatment of empathy, its history and its role in mindreading, see Stueber (2006).

someone else (see Hoffman 2000: 29). In short, we are capable of interpreting someone's intentional states insofar as we are able to empathize with him/her.[3] Given these general remarks concerning our empathetic faculty and the role it plays in mindreading, it should not come as a surprise to hear that empathy plays a central role in the understanding and explanation of attitude ascriptions as well.

The empathy-based picture I have in mind is also reminiscent of Quine's view that, when a reporter attributes a belief/desire/... to someone else, the former often puts him/herself in the latter situation and a mimicking act thus occurs.[4] When one describes someone's state of mind one can either assume the perspective of the individual described or maintain her own perspective. In the first case one empathizes with the individual described while in the latter one does not. When a narrator empathizes with someone, the former assumes the latter's viewpoint. Thus if one hears Mary saying: "I think that I'll visit London" one can report Mary's utterance by either assuming Mary's viewpoint or not. If one reports "Mary thinks that she herself will visit London", the narrator describes Mary's state of mind from Mary's perspective. In that case the narrator empathizes with Mary: were the narrator in Mary's shoes s/he would say "I think that I'll visit London". For this reason the report is *de se*. On the other hand, if one were to report "Mary thinks that the imbecile will visit London" (with 'the imbe-

---

[3] It is worth mentioning that the lack of the empathetic faculty goes hand in hand with the lack of mindreading capacity. This is particularly evident among autistic people. For a book-length treatment of empathy *vis-à-vis* autism see Hobson (1993).

[4] "[I]n indirect quotation we project ourselves into what, from his remarks and other indications, we *imagine* the speaker's state of mind to have been, and then we say what, *in our language*, is natural and *relevant for us* in the state thus feigned. An indirect quotation we can usually expect to rate only as better or worse, more or less faithful, and we cannot even hope for a strict standard of more and less; what is involved is evaluation, relative to special purposes, of an essentially dramatic act. Correspondingly for other propositional attitudes, for all of them can be thought of as involving something like quotation of one's own imagined verbal response to an imagined situation.

Casting our real selves thus in unreal roles, we do not generally know how much reality to hold constant. Quandaries arise. But despite them we find ourselves attributing beliefs, wishes, and strivings even to creatures lacking the power of speech, such is our dramatic virtuosity. We project ourselves even into what from his behavior we imagine a mouse's state of mind to have been, and dramatize it as a belief, wish, or striving, verbalized as seems relevant and natural to us in the state thus feigned" (Quine 1960: 219, italics mine). Although Quine's characterization seems to embrace a form of simulation theory, the position I am defending should be regarded as neutral on whether one embraces *simulation theory* (roughly, the view that when we come to read someone else's' mind we do so by putting ourselves into other people's shoes) or *the modularity view* (roughly, the view that our mind is designed to read other people's minds insofar as we're equipped with a mindreading specialized organ or module). As often the right picture would probably be a hybrid of the tow positions. For recent accounts and defense of these two positions see Goldman (2006) and Carruthers (2006).

cile' coreferential with 'Mary'), the narrator would not assume Mary's viewpoint. For, the presence of the epithet 'the imbecile' makes it clear that the narrator does not suppose that Mary would use the epithet in characterizing herself. In that case the report is *de re*.

The general point I shall end up defending goes as follows. A quasi-indicator is used when the reporter is empathizing with the attributee, while an epithet is used when the narrator does not empathize with the attributee. This phenomenon, I claim, is what underlies the *de se/de re* distinction.

With this framework in place we can easily, or so I am going to argue, account for some interesting linguistic phenomena involving quasi-indicators and epithets without giving up the intuitive view that they often work as (attributive) anaphors.

Before going further, it is worth stressing that I focus on epithets mainly for pedagogical reasons. It is an open question whether a similar story could be told about the anaphoric use of descriptions. There are, though, some differences between epithets and descriptions *qua* anaphoric terms. In several contexts the replacement of an epithet by a description renders the sentence ungrammatical:

(3) a. Igor$_1$ has been charmed by a woman who tried to sell *the idiot*$_1$ a new car
  b. * Igor$_1$ has been charmed by a woman who tried to sell *the director*$_1$ a new car

(4) a. Bush convinced Berlusconi$_1$ that in supporting the invasion of Iraq *the buffoon*$_1$ would become a popular leader in Europe
  b. * Bush convinced Berlusconi$_1$ that in supporting the invasion of Iraq *the patron of Mediaset*$_1$ would become a popular leader in Europe

Since the grammatical structure of (3a)/(4a) and (3b)/(4b) does not differ, no grammatical rule can be invoked to understand why one is grammatical and the other is not. Discourse considerations must enter the scene. For this very reason the notion of empathy plays center stage when we come to characterize the behavior of epithets and quasi-indicators understood as attributive anaphors.[5]

[5] As far as I know, the first who appealed to the notion of empathy to characterize linguistic phenomena are Kuno & Kaburaki (1977). They do not use this notion, though, to discuss the similarities and differences between quasi-indicators and epithets and to distinguish between *de se* and *de re* contexts.

3 *De Se* Reports and Quasi-Indicators

Castañeda (1966, 1967, 1968) claims that the only way to attribute an indexical thought is by means of a quasi-indicator. From a third-person perspective, for instance, a use of the first-person pronoun can be attributed, in English, only by using an expression like 's/he (her/himself)'. Imagine that Jon, an amnesiac, has forgotten his name. In reading an article reporting his abominable behaviour during the Iraq war Jon comes to entertain the belief that Jon did not abide by the Geneva Conventions. Given this situation the following three attributions can be true together:

(5) a. Jon believes that Jon did not abide by the Geneva Conventions
b. Jon_1 believes that he_1 did not abide by the Geneva Conventions
c. I do not believe that I did not abide by the Geneva Conventions *[said by Jon]*

For these reports to capture Jon's attitudes, (5b) must be *de re*. As such the pronoun 'he' does not attribute to Jon a particular way of thinking about himself. Actually (5b) could continue as:

(5) d. Jon_1 believes that he_1 did not abide by the Geneva Conventions but he_1 does not realize/does not believe that he $(himself)_1$ did not abide by the Geneva Conventions

On the other hand, a self-attribution like (5c) specifies the way Jon thinks about himself, i.e., that he thinks in the first-person way and thus that he entertains an 'I'-thought. It is, therefore, *de se*. From a third-person perspective, Jon's self-ascription (5c) should be rendered as:

(5) e. Jon_1 does not believe that he $(himself)_1$ did not abide by the Geneva Conventions

If 'he' in (5b) were understood as a quasi-indicator, (5e) would contradict (5b).

Castañeda creates an artificial pronoun, 's/he*', to represent the (possibly implicit) use of the first-person pronoun in an attitude ascription: "Sue says that she* is rich" represents Sue as saying "I am rich". 'S/he*' stands for 's/he (her/himself)'. Castañeda claims that quasi-indicators are the only mechanism enabling the attribution of indexical reference from the third-person perspective. They are, therefore, the only tools allowing one to capture someone's egocentric perspective. It is an accident of English that a single pronoun, 's/he', can play very different logical roles and thus can be used to perform very different speech acts (see Castañeda 1967: 207). In an *oratio recta* construction, it usually works as a demonstrative while in an *oratio obliqua* construction it can work either as a demonstrative, a bound variable, an anaphoric pronoun or a quasi-indicator. The following examples instantiate the different logical roles that the pronoun 'she' can play when embedded in an attitude ascription:

(6) Jane$_1$ said that *she*$_2$ [pointing to Pauline] is F ***[demonstrative use]***

(7) Jane$_1$ said that *she*$_1$ is F, but she did not know that she herself was F ***[anaphoric use]***

(8) Jane$_1$ said that *she herself*$_1$ *(she*$^*_1$*)* is F ***[quasi-indexical use]***

(9) Every woman$_1$ will tell a man that *she*$_1$ is in love with him ***[bound variable use]***

The quasi-indicator 's/he*' concurs in the attribution of a *de se* attitude. A *de se* attribution, though, need not present an explicit quasi-indicator. Actually, a powerful argument in favor of *de se* reports without explicitly mentioning quasi-indicators can be proposed (see Chierchia 1989). It concerns some occurrences of the unpronounced subjects of infinitive clauses, which linguists call PRO.[6] The following scenario should highlight how PRO can contribute in the attribution of *de se* attitudes. Jane enters a young composer's competition with a song she wrote a couple of years earlier. The night before the members of the jury meet to decide who will win the competition, Jane listens to various competing songs. When Jane hears her own song she does not realize that that very song is the one she submitted. Since Jane's musical taste changed drastically in the last few months, she dislikes the song (her song) she is now hearing. Jane finds this song particularly tasteless and comes to hope that its author will not win the competition. Yet, Jane believes that another, more recent song of hers, is competing and she hopes to bring home the reward. In this scenario, a self-attribution like (10a) will be appropriate, while a self-attribution like (10b) would not:

(10) a. I hope that she will lose the competition
b. I hope to lose the competition

From a third-person perspective (10a) and (10b) could be rendered as:

(11) a. Jane hopes that she will lose the competition
b. Jane hopes to lose the competition

---

[6] PRO represents the null pronominal element acting as the syntactic subject of infinitives and gerunds. In other words, PRO is viewed as the null analogue of lexical pronouns. Actually, an attribution like "Pavarotti very much wants to get help" entails "Pavarotti very much wants for Pavarotti to get help" but not conversely. That is, a *de se* attribution entails a *de re* one, but a *de re* ascription does not necessarily entail a *de se* one (cf. Chierchia 1989).

While (11a) captures Jane's mental state, (11b) does not.

The unpronounced subject (PRO) in (10b) and (11b) can only be understood as attributing an 'I'-thought to the attributee, Jane. On the other hand, (10a) and (11a) must be understood *de re*. Adopting Castañeda's notation, a *de se* report like (11b) can be represented as:

(11) c. Jane$_1$ hopes [*PRO*$_1$* to lose the competition][7]

In favor of the view that a *de se* interpretation may be grammatically forced, we can also mention cross-linguistic evidence. Actually, some languages (so-called pure logophoric languages) morphologically mark the distinction between the deictic use, the anaphoric use and the quasi-indexical use of a pronoun appearing in an *oratio obliqua* construction.[8] In these languages logophoric pronouns appear in reportive contexts and are used to capture the words or thought of an individual or individuals other than the narrator. Furthermore, personal logophoric pronouns, like quasi-indicators and unlike many personal pronouns, cannot be used without a discourse antecedent (see Culy 1997: 851-2). Like quasi-indicators, they are syncategorematic terms. Pure logophoric languages are languages in which these pronouns are used *only* as logophors and not as other reflexives or in emphatic uses. Tabury, for instance, distinguishes between the third person pronoun *qua* anaphoric pronoun, '*à*', and the third person pronoun *qua* quasi-indicator (logophoric pronoun), '*sɛ́*' (see Hagège 1974: 299):

(12) a. á Dík lí māy mà:gā à kó n sú: mònò
[He$_1$ thinks of the young girl that he$_1$ saw yesterday]

---

[7] Chierchia (1989) proposes another argument in favor of the view that the *de se* interpretation can be grammatically forced. It focuses on the strict/sloppy understanding of inferences like:

(i) a. Jane believes she won the lottery
b. Sue believes whatever Jane believes
c. Therefore, Sue believes she won the lottery

Assuming that there is coreference between 'Jane' and 'she' in the first premise (and thus that they are coindexed), the conclusion can be understood in different ways, meaning either that Sue believes that Jane won the lottery (strict inference) or that Sue believes that she herself won the lottery (sloppy inference). Chierchia argues that with the strict inference the belief attribution to Sue is understood *de re* while, with the sloppy inference, it must be *de se*. As I understand this, the pronoun 'she' in a sloppy inference must be understood as a quasi-indicator attributing an 'I'-thought to Sue.

[8] Among the logophoric languages we can cite some African languages (mainly of the Eastern branches of Niger-Congo) such as Dogon, Ewe, Tupuri, etc. The term 'logophoric pronoun' was first introduced by Hagège (1974). As Culy points out: "In pure logophoric languages, there are always environments in which coreferring with the logophoric trigger can only be done by a logophoric pronoun" (Culy 1994: 1080). See also Clements (1975) and Culy (1994a, 1997).

b. á Dík lí māy mà:gā sɛ́ kó n sú: mònò
[He$_1$ thinks of the young girl that he (himself)/he$_1$* saw yesterday]

Furthermore, in Ewe the pronoun 'yé' is used exclusively as a logophoric pronoun and appears merely in attitude reports (see Clements 1975: 152):

(13) a. Kofi be yé-dzo
[Kofi say LOG-leave]
(Kofi$_1$ said that he (himself)/he*$_1$ leaves)
b. Kofi be me-dzo
[Kofi say I-leave]
(Kofi$_1$ said that I$_2$ leave)
c. Kofi be e-dzo
[Kofi say s/he-leave]
(Kofi$_1$ said that she/he$_2$ leaves)

As a first approximation we could say that, while ascriptions like (13b) and (13c) represent *de re* attributions, ascriptions like (13a) are *de se*. This classification, though, is far from exhaustive. Actually, we can have attributions that are partly *de re* and partly *de se*. Overhearing Jon saying: "Jane and I are the joint winners of the musical competition", Jane can report:

(14) a. Jon believes that we won the musical competition[9]

A report like this attributes to Jon an 'I'-thought and, as such, it is *de se*. At the same time, though, the pronoun 'we' also works as a deictic. As such, it picks out the reporter in a transparent way. It is thus *de re*. In other words, a report like (14a) is a mixed report insofar as it specifies the attributee's, Jon's, attitude *vis-à-vis* himself, yet it is silent on the way Jon thought about Jane, the reporter. To understand this difference we could argue that a report such as (14a) is a shortcut of:

(14) b. Jon$_1$ believes that he$_1$* won the musical competition and that I$_2$ won the musical competition

'I' makes it clear that the reporter does not specify the way in which Jon thought about the attributer, Jane. That is to say, 'I' does not attribute to Jon a specific mechanism of reference he used or would be disposed to use in

---

[9] Plurals with split antecedents, such as "Igor told Jane that they are rich", are represented as:
(i) Jgor$_1$ told Jane$_2$ that they$_{1 \oplus 2}$ are rich
where '1 ⊕ 2' signals that the index of the plural is the fusion of the indices of its antecedents. It is an open question whether in our example the predicate of being rich holds of the antecedents individually or collectively, i.e., whether the plural reference is distributive or collective (see Fiengo & May 1994: 39).

thinking about Jane. This phenomenon can be characterized as *the attribution indeterminacy phenomenon.* This indeterminacy can easily be explained with the notion of empathy. In using the pronoun 'we' the narrator of (14a), Jane, stresses that she empathizes with herself. Actually, when one refers to oneself using either 'I' or 'we', one empathizes with oneself, and when one empathizes with oneself one cannot at the same time take someone else's viewpoint. In a report like "Mary said that I am F", the narrator empathizes with her/himself and in so doing it is impossible for her/him to empathize with Mary as well. In short, it is because of the self-empathy involved in the use of 'we' that a report like (14a) should be understood along the lines of (14b) and is, thus, indeterminate *vis-à-vis* the way Jon thought about the narrator, Jane. To put it into a nutshell: it is because 'we' encapsulates an 'I' that reports in which it occurs are indeterminate. Multiple embedded reports bring in indeterminacy as well. Consider:

(15) Jane_1 believes that Jon_2 knows that she*_1 won the competition

where the quasi-indicator 'she*' attributes an 'I'-thought to Jane. As such, it specifies the way Jane thought about herself. Yet, it is silent on the way Jon thought about Jane. All we can stipulate is that there is *a* way Jon referred/thought about Jane. The report, though, does not specify which one. For this reason, the report is indeterminate. Reports can be more or less indeterminate, depending on how much information regarding the attributee is left unspecified.[10] In a multiple embedded report involving quasi-indicators, whatever is unspecified is often easily noticed. It is a matter of grammar that a report like (15), for instance, is silent on the way in which Jon thought about Jane. Once again, using the notion of empathy we can easily explain the indeterminacy involved in (15). The quasi-indicator stresses that the narrator empathizes with Jane. Since the narrator empathizes with Jane s/he cannot also empathize with Jon. Thus the report is silent on how Jon thought about Jane. Other reports, though, are far more enigmatic, for indeterminate reports do not always present themselves under the (*de re*) mantel: "Of *NN, A* believes/wishes/... that she/he/it is *F*". A report like "Pizarro thought that Peru must be conquered", for instance, does not specify the

[10] Besides, multiple-embedded reports containing quasi-indicators can be ambiguous with regard to the antecedent they are coreferential with. "Jane thought that Mary believes that she* is rich" licenses both (i) and (ii):

(i) Jane_1 thought that Mary_2 believes that she_1* is rich

(ii) Jane_1 thought that Mary_2 believes that she_2* is rich

Curiously enough, a similar phenomenon occurs with the logophoric pronoun 'yé' in Ewe: "Kofi xɔ-e se be Ama gblɔ be yé-ƒu-i" can be translated either as (iii) or (iv) (see Clements 1975: 173):

(iii) Kofi_1 believes that Ama_2 said that he_1 beat her_2

(iv) Kofi_1 believes that Ama_2 said that she_2 beat him_1

way in which Pizarro thought about Peru, for we assume that Pizarro did not have the name 'Peru' in his idiolect to refer to the region he visited. Reports that present themselves under the (*de dicto*) guise "*A* believes that *NN* is *F*" may be indeterminate as well. The highlight so far, seems to be that grammar alone may not determine the *de re/de dicto/de se* nature of a report.

4 *De Re* Reports and Epithets

An epithet—from the ancient Greek '*epíthetos'*, meaning added—"is a word or phrase expressing an attribute or quality regarded as characteristic of the person or thing mentioned; a significant appellation; a suitable descriptive term" (*New Shorter Oxford English Dictionary*: 839). Under the same entry we also read that an epithet is "an offensive or derogatory expression used of a person; a term of abuse, a profanity". Epithets are often used to characterize the nature of a subject and they may be stereotypical.[11] From a grammatical viewpoint, epithets are NPs which typically consist of the definite article (in which case they are like definite descriptions; 'the idiot', 'the bastard', 'the buffoon', …) or a demonstrative coupled with a noun (in which case they are like complex demonstratives; 'this/that idiot', 'this/that bastard', 'this/that buffoon', …). The latter contributes mainly affective (often negative) meaning. For this very reason they help us to appreciate the importance of empathy when we come to the task of understanding the use of epithets and when we deal with the *de se/de re* distinction. When the reporter takes the attributee's viewpoint, and thus empathizes with her/him, a use of a quasi-indicator is licensed, while when the reporter does not empathize with the attributee a use of an epithet can occur.

In order to stress how epithets can be anaphoric, let us consider:

(17) a. Mary$_1$ promised to come, but *she*$_1$ missed the train
b. Mary$_1$ promised to come, but *the imbecile*$_1$ missed the train[12]

[11] In the Greek epic literature epithets used to be words or phrases accompanying or taking the place of proper names. Thus in the *Odyssey*, for instance, Athena the goddess is firstly introduced as 'grey-eyed Athena' (book 1) and she is subsequently often referred to as merely 'the grey-eyed'. Nowadays many epithets are racially or sexually abusive (e.g.: 'the nigger', 'the fag', 'the queer', etc.). For this very reasons, the *Columbia Guide to Standard American English* (1993) under the label 'offensive epithets and dispraising labels' states that 'the best advice is to call people only what they *want* to be called. Apply sharp-pointed epithets only to yourself'.

[12] A similar example is found in Huang (2000: 48) who quotes Lasnik (1989) as the one who first claimed that epithets, unlike names, can take antecedents from previous clauses and can participate in left dislocation on a par with a pronominal, but not with names, as in: "John: everyone thinks that he/the idiot should be demoted". As far as I know, the first person to

(18) a. Jon_1 and Joe_2 played poker all night and *they*$_{1\oplus2}$ lost all their money

b. Jon_1 and Joe_2 played poker all night and *the idiots*$_{1\oplus2}$ lost all their money

(19) a. Jon_1 saw $Jane_2$ and *he*$_1$ ignored *her*$_2$

b. Jon_1 saw $Jane_2$ and *the bastard*$_1$ ignored *the sweetheart*$_2$

In (17b), for instance, the epithet 'the imbecile' is anaphoric on 'Mary'—its semantic value is inherited from the semantic value of 'Mary'. In (17a), the pronoun 'she' is merely an anaphoric pronoun, i.e. it goes proxy for its antecedent, 'Mary' (adopting Geach's terminology, it *can* be viewed as a pronoun of laziness).

One could object that in (17b), for instance, 'the imbecile' is not anaphoric but works as a description picking out, as Russell taught us, the unique object satisfying it. Hence, as far as reference fixing is concerned, 'the imbecile' in (17b) would not differ from 'the train' in (20):

(20) Mary promised to come but *the train* was delayed

If so, 'the imbecile' in (17b) does not work like an anaphora. It should be stressed that 'the train' in (20) does not express or attribute a quality to the person mentioned and, as such, it cannot be an epithet. In (17b), though, 'the imbecile' attributes a quality to the person mentioned, Mary. As such, it must be viewed as coreferential with 'Mary'. Hence, 'the imbecile' in (17b) and 'the train' in (20) cannot be treated on a par. Yet one can go on arguing that though 'the imbecile' is coreferential with 'Mary', it picks up Mary because the latter has been previously made salient. Its semantic value is not determined in an anaphoric way. It rather works like a referring expression, i.e., an expression which does not inherit its value from an antecedent it is linked with. It would work like a definite description picking up the unique individual which, in the relevant domain, happens to be an imbecile. I have some difficulties, though, in seeing how a definite description works in selecting an object previously made salient. To do this job the description should be understood to work in the referential way, i.e. to work like a singular term.[13] I do not follow this interpretation. It seems to me that the epi-

stress that epithets can work as anaphors was Jackendoff (1972: 110). The examples he proposes are, "I wanted Charlie to help me, but *the bastard* wouldn't do it", "Irving was besieged by a horde of bills and *the poor guy* couldn't pay them", "Although *the bum* tried to hit me, I can't really get too mad at Harry". Jackendoff writes: "These 'pronominal epithets' can occur in some subset of the environment in which pronominalization is possible, and they function semantically more or less as specialized pronouns" (Jackendoff 1972: 110).

[13] It may be worth mentioning that the strategy of explaining away unbound anaphora as referential expressions referring to a previously made salient object has been introduced by Kripke

thetical nature of 'the imbecile' in (17b) forces its anaphoric reading. Furthermore, if we replace the epithet 'the imbecile' with a non-epithetical definite description we generate ungrammaticality:

(21) a. * Mary$_1$ promised to come, but *the student*$_1$ missed the train
b. * Mary$_1$ promised to come, but *the daughter of Jon*$_1$ missed the train

As I understand it, the ungrammaticality of (21a-b) is triggered by the non-epithetical nature of the descriptions. In other words, it is triggered by the fact that the descriptions do not convey affective meaning and are thus empathically neutral. This seems to furnish further evidence in favor of the theses that: (i) epithets like 'the imbecile' in (17b) should be interpreted to work in an anaphoric way; and (ii) since epithets convey affective meaning, the notion of empathy is crucial in explaining when and how they can be used. In other words, since epithets express affective meaning, the notion of empathy should help determine the reportive contexts in which the presence of an epithet generates grammaticality or ungrammaticality, i.e. whether the report is *de re* or *de se*. To further highlight the importance of empathy in understanding how epithets *qua* attributive anaphors work, we can consider:

(22) a. Jon$_1$ and I$_2$ played poker all night and *we*$_{1\oplus2}$ lost a fortune
b. * Jon$_1$ and I$_2$ played poker all night and *the idiots*$_{1\oplus2}$ lost a fortune

The ungrammaticality of (22b) can be explained by the fact that one cannot use an epithet in characterizing someone one is empathizing with. The presence of the first-person pronoun indicates that the narrator empathizes with her/himself. Thus, the epithet cannot be coindexed with a NP standing for an individual the narrator empathizes with, in our case the narrator her/himself. This phenomenon can be further stressed if we consider the grammaticality of:

(22) c. Jon$_1$ and I$_2$ played poker all night and *that idiot*$_1$ lost a fortune
d. Jon$_1$, Ivan$_2$ and I played poker all night and *the idiots*$_{1\oplus2}$ lost a fortune

These reports are grammatical for the epithet is not used to characterize an individual the narrator empathizes with.

(1977) in his well documented criticism of Donnellan's referential/attributive distinction. It is a bit ironic that if one appeals to this strategy to explain away the anaphoric nature of an epithet, one ends up assuming that the epithet *qua* description should be understood as a singular term, i.e. a description used referentially.

When an epithet works like an anaphora, there is an implicit argument at work, which takes charge of the anaphoric link. This implicit argument works like a bound variable. Hence the analysis of (17b) should be:

(17) c. Mary$_1$ promised to come but the imbecile(x_1) missed the train

The same analysis can be proposed for quantified utterances; thus, (21a) will be analyzed as (21b):

(21) a. All the students$_1$ promised to come, but the imbeciles$_1$ missed the train

b. All the students$_1$ promised to come, but the imbeciles(x_1) missed the train

The underlying structure of (21b) can be represented as:

(21) c. $\forall x$ [x is a student $\rightarrow$ (x promised to come & imbecile(x) missed the train)]

The same story can be told for:

(22) a. Jon blames *each orator*$_1$ in private while praising *him*$_1$ in public

b. Jon blames *each orator*$_1$ in private while praising *the charlatan*$_1$ in public

The underlying structure of (22b) can be represented as:

(22) c. $\forall x$ [x is an orator $\rightarrow$ (Jon blames x in private & Jon praises charlatan(x) in public)]

In favor of this regimentation we can further mention that in Lebanese Arabic epithets can behave like pronominals only when they appear with a pronominal morpheme, 'ha' (this), that can be used anaphorically (see Aoun & Choueiri 2001). Thus in Lebanese Arabic an epithet like 'ha-I-maz3duub' (this-the idiot) can function in an anaphoric way or as a bound variable because of the presence of the pronominal morpheme 'ha' (this).

5 Epithets *vs.* Quasi-Indicators; *De Re vs. De Se*

I now turn to discuss an attempt to dismiss the view that epithets can work as anaphoric pronouns. This exercise will help me to further stress how we ultimately have to bring in the notion of empathy to handle the data and to show how the latter is relevant in characterizing the *de re*/*de se* distinction. The attempt I have in mind is found in Lasnik (1976). According to this view, epithets in utterances like (1)[Jane$_1$ said that she would come, but *the idiot*$_1$ will probably miss the train] are best viewed as descriptions referring to an individual previously made salient.[14] This position focuses on the fact that in many cases an anaphoric interpretation of the epithet makes the utterance ungrammatical:

(23) a. * Malvin$_1$ claims that the bastard$_1$ was honest
b. * John$_1$ thinks that I admire the idiot$_1$

On the basis of examples like these, Lasnik argues that epithets are not anaphoric pronouns at all, but referential expressions. According to Lasnik (cf. 1976: 93), the ungrammaticality of (23) parallels the ungrammaticality of:

(24) a. * Oscar finally realized that Oscar is unpopular
b. * It surprised John that John was so well liked
c. * Harry was really surprised that Harry lost the race
d. * Nixon hates people who criticize Nixon

(24a-d) are ungrammatical because the second occurrence of the noun phrase is bound.[15] The moral Lasnik draws is that epithets, like referential expressions, cannot be bound. To stress this point, let us contrast the ungrammaticality of (24a-d) with the grammaticality of:

(25) a. Oscar finally realized that he is unpopular
b. It surprised John that he was so well liked
c. Harry was really surprised that he lost the race
d. Nixon hates people who criticize him

Since pronouns can be bound, (25a-d) are grammatical. In (25a), for instance, 'he' is bound by 'Oscar'. According to Lasnik, epithets are *free in*

---

[14] This view comes close to the view of unbound anaphora defended by Kripke (1977) and Lewis (1979).

[15] Following the traditional wisdom of the Government and Binding Theory (see Hageman 1994: ch. 4), anaphoric pronouns differ from the indexical use of pronouns because of the following three principles of *Binding Theory:*

- *Principle A*: anaphors must be bound in their governing category.
- *Principle B*: pronouns must be free in their governing category.
- *Principle C*: other NPs must be free in all categories.

A governing category (GC) is defined as:

- A is a GC for B if A is the minimal category (i.e. the smallest NP or S) containing B, a governor of B, and a subject accessible to B.

Roughly, the minimal GC is the S or NP node immediately dominating the antecedent and the anaphor. The element which governs is called the *governor* while the element that is governed is the *governee*. A pronoun is *bound* iff it is c-commanded by a co-indexed element, while a pronoun is *free* iff it is not c-commanded by a co-indexed element. The notion of C-command is defined as:

- *C-command:* Node A c-commands node B iff:
  (i) A does not dominate B and B does not dominate A; and
  (ii) the first branching node dominating A also dominates B.

their governing category. Thus, epithets are not anaphoric and, as coreference is concerned, they should be understood in a similar way to pronouns like 'they' in:

(26) As soon as Jon met Mary, they left the room

Since there is no single NP designating Jon and Mary in (26), no formulation of a transformational rule linking 'they' to 'John' and 'Mary' can account for the coreferentiality of 'they' with 'Mary + John'. That is to say, 'they' in (26) is unbound. But this, Lasnik claims, is not a problem, for "no coreference rule is needed to explain [26], because there is nothing to explain. *They* in [26] can be used to refer to any group of entities; under many discourse situations, however, John and Mary are the only likely candidates" (Lasnik 1976: 98-9).

Dubinsky & Hamilton (1998) challenge Lasnik's prediction and show that epithets can be bound:

(27) John_1 ran over a man (who was) trying to give *the idiot*$_1$ directions

(28) Through a number of slipups, John_1 (inadvertently) led his students to conclude that *the idiot*$_1$ couldn't teach

In (27), for instance, 'the idiot' is both c-commanded and coindexed with 'John'. It is, therefore, bound by 'John'. On the basis of these data Dubinsky & Hamilton argue that the ungrammaticality of (23a-b) is not triggered, *pace* Lasnik, by condition C, i.e., by the fact that referring terms must be free in all categories. This contrasts with pronouns (which must be free in their governing category) and anaphors (which must be bound in their governing category). The ungrammaticality comes from the fact that "the non local antecedent is the perspective-bearer (i.e. one from whose perspective the attributive content of the epithets is evaluated)", while the grammaticality of (27) and (28) is granted "precisely because the antecedent of the epithet is not the perspective-bearer. Put differently, epithets are antilogophoric" (Dubinsky & Hamilton 1998: 687).

The thesis that epithets are antilogophoric gains further credence when we focus on examples like the following pairs, in which each (a) sentence is ungrammatical precisely because the epithet's antecedent is the perspective-bearer:

(29) a. * It was said by John_1 that the idiot_1 lost a thousand dollars on the slots
b. It was said of John_1 that the idiot_1 lost a thousand dollars on the slots

(30) a. * According to John_1, the idiot_1 is married to a genius
b. Speaking of John_1, the idiot_1 is married to a genius

(31) a. * $John_1$ told us of a man (who was) trying to give the $idiot_1$ directions

b. $John_1$ ran over a man (who was) trying to give the $idiot_1$ directions

The moral is, *pace* Lasnik, that "epithets are not subject to condition C and must be bound by nonlocal antecedents so long as antilogophoricity is respected" (Dubinsky & Hamilton 1998: 688). This is in direct contrast with referential expressions, like proper names and unbound descriptions, for instance:

(32) * $John_1$ ran over a man who was trying to give the $president_1$ directions

(33) * Through a number of slipups, the $teacher_1$ inadvertently led his students to conclude that $John_1$ couldn't teach

These data confirm what I said at the beginning when I argued that there are differences between epithets and descriptions: while in some contexts the former suggest an anaphoric interpretation, the latter cannot. Bearing in mind that epithets often convey affective meaning, this should not come as a surprise. Once again, this should bring to mind the idea that considerations pertaining to discourse representation must be taken on board when characterizing the use of epithets *qua* attributive anaphors and that the notion of empathy is crucial in understanding their use. Furthermore, like logophoric pronouns and quasi-indicators, epithets cannot be bound locally:

(34) * $John_1$ shaved the $idiot_1$

(35) * $John_1$ embarrassed the $idiot_1$

The general moral seems to be that the counterexamples proposed by Lasnik do not jeopardize the view that epithets can be anaphoric.

As I suggested at the beginning, the thesis that epithets can work in an anaphoric way is best defended if we analyze epithets in the way we analyze quasi-indicators. We should now be in a position to appreciate that epithets are best understood against the background of quasi-indicators or, to borrow Dubinsky & Hamilton's terminology, to be antilogophoric. The following examples should illustrate this fact. The presence of the quasi-indicator 'he himself' makes the sentence grammatical, whereas a substitution of an epithet for the quasi-indicator makes it ungrammatical:

(36) a. Jon_1 said that *he (himself)*$_1$ is rich

b. * Jon_1 said that *the idiot*$_1$ is rich

a. Jon_1 asked Jane whether *he (himself)*$_1$ is rich

b. * Jon_1 asked Jane whether *the idiot*$_1$ is rich

a. Jon$_1$ told Jane that he$_1$ wonders whether *he (himself)*$_1$ is rich
b. * Jon$_1$ told Jane that he$_1$ wonders whether *the idiot*$_1$ is rich

a. After last night's lottery draw, Jon$_1$ thinks that *he (himself)*$_1$ is rich
b. * After last night's lottery draw, Jon$_1$ thinks that *the idiot*$_1$ is rich

a. Jon$_1$ may not know that *he (himself)*$_1$ is rich
b. * Jon$_1$ may not know that *the idiot*$_1$ is rich

The general moral that we can draw so far is that a quasi-indicator must appear within the scope of a logophoric predicate, whereas an epithet may not—as I understand it, a logophoric predicate is a predicate suggesting that the narrator empathizes with the attributee while an antilogophoric predicate suggests that the narrator does not empathizes with the attributee. The broad structures in which quasi-indicators and epithets can appear can be summarized as follows:

- NP$_1$ + logophoric predicate + *quasi-indicator*$_1$ + VP
- NP$_1$ + antilogophoric predicate + *epithet*$_1$ + VP

If we consider a factual predicate, for instance, an epithet can work as an anaphoric pronoun, but if a quasi-indicator is substituted for the epithet, the sentence becomes ungrammatical:

(37) a. John$_1$ ran over a man (who was) trying to give *the idiot*$_1$ directions
b. * John$_1$ ran over a man (who was) trying to give *him (himself)*$_1$ directions

(38) a. Through a number of slipups, John$_1$ (inadvertently) led his students to conclude that *the idiot*$_1$ couldn't teach
b. * Through a number of slipups, John$_1$ (inadvertently) led his students to conclude that *he (himself)*$_1$ couldn't teach

If we understand epithets against the background of quasi-indicators, it emerges that: (i) like the latter they can be attributive anaphors; and (ii) they cannot participate in the same kind of attributions as quasi-indicators. While a quasi-indicator like 's/he her/himself' contributes in making a *de se* attribution, an epithet is transparent and can only contribute in making a *de re* attribution. That is, a quasi-indicator *qua* attributive anaphora attributes an indexical thought to the referent of the NP it inherits its semantic value from. An epithet *qua* attributive anaphora stresses that the referent of the NP from which it inherits its value is unlikely to accept the property that the narrator attributes to him/her in using the epithet. To put it slightly differently, we can say that while quasi-indicators reveal the attributee's egocentric perspective, epithets reveal the narrator's perspective—it is because there is a switch of perspective that in (37) and (38) the replacement of a quasi-indicator by an epithet makes the resulting sentence ungrammatical. In a nutshell, while quasi-indicators are intrinsically opaque, epithets are intrinsically transparent. To stress this feature, let us consider a report such as:

(39) Jane$_1$ said that *she*$_1$ would like to visit us but *the idiot*$_1$ was not sure if she could catch the last train

Contrast this report with:

(40) Jane$_1$ said that *she*$_1$ would like to visit us but that *she (herself)*$_1$ was not sure if she could catch the last train

In (39) the epithet 'the idiot' does not attribute a specific mechanism of reference to Jane. It certainly does not suggest that she referred (or thought about) herself using 'the idiot'. The epithet is used by the reporter to characterize Jane and, as such, it is transparent. On the other hand, 'she herself' in (40) attributes to Jane an 'I'-thought. This is the main difference between epithets and quasi-indicators.

The following diagram should summarize the main similarities and differences between epithets, quasi-indicators and simple anaphors.

	Quasi-indicator	Epithet	Simple anaphora
Anaphoric	+	+	+
Attributive	+	+	—
De se	+	—	—
De re	—	+	+

As I already suggested (section 1), attributive anaphors, either quasi-indicators or epithets, are best understood as obeying constraints which should be stated in terms of discourse considerations involving notions such as *point of view*, *perspective* and, in particular, *empathy*. Since empathy corresponds to the speaker's identification (in varying degrees) with the person participating in the event described, we can easily appreciate its importance in the explanation of attributive anaphors and, in particular, in understanding why epithets force a *de re* reading while quasi-indicators trigger a *de se* one.

Further evidence in favor of the view that empathy plays a crucial role when we come to the task of distinguishing between *de re* and *de se* ascriptions is furnished by so-called picture noun reflexives (see Pollard & Sag 1992: 274). Picture noun reflexives inherit their value from an individual whose viewpoint or perspective is reported, i.e., from the individual the speaker empathizes with. Pollard & Sag (1992: 274) invite us to consider the following:

(41) $John_1$ was going to get even with Mary. That picture of $himself_1$ in the paper would really annoy her, as would the other stunts he had planned

The picture noun phrase is naturally interpreted as coreferential with 'John' insofar as the narrator has taken on John's viewpoint and thus empathizes with him. For this very reason the report is *de se* and as such it attributes to John an 'I'-thought. Actually, if John were to express the attitude the narrator attributes to him with (41), he would come out with something like: "That picture of *myself* in the paper would really annoy Mary". If we compare this discourse with the following—in which the narrator empathizes with Mary and thus takes on her viewpoint—where the picture name reflexive is coindexed with 'John', we generate ungrammaticality:

(42) * Mary was quite taken aback by the publicity $John_1$ was receiving. That picture of $himself_1$ in the paper had really annoyed her, and there was not much she could do about it

Pollard & Sag's moral is that, when a reflexive is exempt from Principle A, discourse considerations should enter the picture: the reflexive must take as its antecedent a NP selecting the agent whose viewpoint is presented in the text. Pollard & Sag (1992: 277-8) also note that psychological verbs such as 'bother' make evident how the notion of viewpoint can be crucial in determining the antecedent of an anaphora. In the case of 'bother', for instance, it is natural to assume that the agent whose viewpoint is being reflected is the direct object of the verb. This can be highlighted in considering:

(43) a. The picture of $himself_1$ in *Newsweek* bothered $John_1$
b. * The picture of $himself_1$ in *Newsweek* bothered $John_1$'s father

The ungrammaticality of (43b) is explained by the fact that the viewpoint represented is that of John's father, rather than John's. That is to say, (43a) is grammatical because the reflexive stands for the individual, John, the narrator empathizes with. On the other hand, (43b) is ungrammatical because the narrator is empathizing with John's father while the reflexive stands for John. In a nutshell, the reflexive must be coindexed with the NP selecting the individual the narrator empathizes with. This phenomenon is further highlighted if we consider (43c-d) which, though structurally equivalent to the ungrammatical (43b), are grammatical precisely because they reflect John's viewpoint, i.e., because the narrator is empathizing with him:

(43) c. The picture of $himself_1$ in *Newsweek* dominated $John_1$'s thoughts

d. The picture of himself$_1$ in *Newsweek* made John$_1$'s day

Furthermore, the fact that one cannot empathize with someone more than one empathizes with oneself helps us to explain the difference between reports like:

(44) a. Jane hopes to win the tournament
[Jane hopes PRO* to win the tournament]
b. I expect Jane to win the tournament
[I expect Jane PRO to win the tournament]
c. * Talking of Jane, I expect herself to win the tournament

As we saw, (44a) receives a *de se* interpretation, and this can be explained by the fact that the reporter empathizes with the attributee, Jane. On the other hand, (44b) forces the *de re* reading, and this is explained by the fact that the reporter does not (and cannot) empathize with Jane; the speaker cannot empathize with someone more than she empathizes with herself, and this is pointed out by the presence of 'I'. This peculiarity should also explain the ungrammaticality of (44c): the reflexive 'herself' suggests that the speaker empathizes with Jane while the first-person pronoun underlines the speaker empathizing with herself. This generates a conflict of empathy focus and, thus, ungrammaticality. The ungrammaticality of (44c) can thus be explained by the reporter's use of the first person pronoun 'I'. Because of this very fact, the reporter cannot take Jane's perspective.

The general lesson seems to be that if we take the notion of empathy as a reliable guide we can easily explain the difference between *de se* and *de re* ascriptions. For the notion of empathy—understood as the cognitive awareness of someone's mental state—enables us to distinguish between logophoric and anti-logophoric contexts and, ultimately, to distinguish between *de se* and *de re* structures.

As a general approximation we can propose the following:

- *Reflexives* which are not locally bound must stand for an individual the narrator empathizes with; the latter is the individual whose viewpoint is being assumed.

- *Epithets* cannot be coindexed with a NP standing for an individual the narrator empathizes with.

This general approximation should capture the working of epithets and reflexives in English. When a reflexive is grammatically forced—i.e., it has a local antecedent (e.g. "Jon$_1$ shaved him$_{*1/2}$/himself$_{1/*2}$")—it does not represent a particular point of view (cf. Culy 1997: 851). When a reflexive is not grammatically forced, though, it represents the point of view of the individual the narrator empathizes with. The latter can be either the individual(s) selected by the NP the reflexive is coindexed with or the value of an unbound reflexive like in (cf. Reinhart & Reuland 1991: 311):

(45) a. This paper was written by Ann and *myself*
b. Apart from *myself* only three members protested
c. Physicists like *yourself* are a godsend

The narrator of (45a) and (45b) empathizes with her/himself while the narrator of (45c) empathizes with the addressee. Hence, according to the analysis I am proposing, (45a-c) are *de se.* While in (45a-b) the narrator, in using 'myself', stresses that s/he empathizes with her/himself, in (45c) the narrator empathizes with the addressee and, were the narrator in the addressee's shoes, s/he would say "Physicists like *myself/me* are a godsend".

Summing up. When one makes an attribution using a quasi-indicator, one puts oneself into the attributee's shoes and represents the world from this adopted perspective. Thus the reporter uses the quasi-indicator 's/he (her/himself)' when, were s/he in the attributee's position, s/he would have used the first person pronoun. That is, she would use 'I' to express the mental life of the agent the reporter is assuming the perspective. On the other hand, one cannot use an epithet when one takes the attributee's perspective, i.e., when one empathizes with the latter. This should explain the fact that when we have a psychological verb (a logophoric predicate) suggesting that the reporter is taking the attributee's perspective (as in the 36b series) followed by an epithet characterizing the latter, the sentence is ungrammatical.

6 Conclusion

I hope that I have been able to show that:

- Epithets can work as anaphoric pronouns and, like quasi-indicators, are best viewed as *attributive* anaphors;
- When epithets *qua* anaphors appear in an *oratio obliqua* construal they are transparent insofar as, unlike quasi-indicators, they do not attribute a property the attributee would use in characterizing herself;
- Epithets *qua* anaphors, unlike quasi-indicators, are anti-logophoric insofar as they are coreferential with a NP referring to an agent who is not the perspective-bearer of the attribution, i.e. is not the individual the narrator empathizes with;
- Epithets and quasi-indicators rest on, and contribute in stressing, the *de se*/*de re* distinction;
- Empathy should be a key notion in explaining the difference between *de se* and *de re* structures.

Acknowledgements

For comments and discussion on these issues I'd like to thank: Jérôme Dokic, Pierre Jacob, Kepa Korta, María Ponte, John Perry, Stefano Predelli, and François Recanati. Research for this paper has partly been sponsored the Spanish Ministry of Science and Innovation (FFI2009-08574), the University of the Basque Country (GIU 08/23), and a Social Sciences and Humanities Research Council of Canada (SSHRC 410-2010-1334) grant.

References

Aoun J. & Coueri L., 2001. "Epithets". University of Southern California, ms.

Carruthers P. 2006. *The Architecture of Mind.* Oxford: Oxford University Press

Castañeda, H.-N., 1966. "'He': A Study in the Logic of Self-Consciousness". *Ratio* 8 (2), 130-157

Castañeda, H.-N., 1967. "Indicators and Quasi-Indicators". *American Philosophical Quarterly* 4 (2), 85-100. Reprinted in Castañeda, H-N., 1989. *Thinking, Language, and Experience*. Minneapolis: University of Minnesota Press, 206-31

Castañeda, H.-N., 1968. "On the Logic of Attributions of Self-Knowledge to Others". *The Journal of Philosophy* 65 (15), 439-56

Castañeda, H-N., 1989. *Thinking, Language, and Experience*. Minneapolis: University of Minnesota Press

Chierchia, G., 1989. "Anaphora and Attitudes *De Se*". In Bartsch, R., Van Bentham, J., & Van Emde, P. (eds.), 1987. *Language in Context.* Dordrecht: Doris, 1-31

Clements, G., 1975. "The Logophoric Pronoun in EWE: Its Role in Discourse". *Journal of West African Languages* 10, 141-77

Culy, C., 1994. "Aspects of Logophoric Marking". *Linguistics* 32, 1055-1094

Culy, C., 1994a. "A Note on Logophoricity in Dogon". *Journal of African Languages and Linguistics* 15, 113-125

Culy, C., 1997. "Logophoric Pronouns and Point of View". *Linguistics* 35, 845-59

Fiengo R. & May R., 1994. *Indices and Identity*. Cambridge Mass: MIT Press

Goldman A., 2006. *Simulating Minds.* Oxford: Oxford University Press

Dubinsky, S. & Hamilton, R., 1998. "Epithets as Antilogophoric Pronouns". *Linguistic Inquiry* 29, 685-93

Hagège, G.N., 1974. "Les Pronoms Logophoriques". *Bulletin de la Société de Linguistique de Paris* 69, 287-310

Haegeman, L., 1994. *Government and Binding Theory*. Oxford: Blackwell

Hobson, R.P., 1993. *Autism and the Development of Mind.* Trowbridge: Psychology Press

Hobson, P., 2002. *The Cradle of Thought: Exploring the Origin of Thinking.* Macmillian: London

Hoffman, M. L., 2000. *Empathy and Moral Development: Implications for Caring and Justice*. Cambridge: Cambridge University Press

Huang, Y., 1994. *The Syntax and Pragmatics of Anaphora: A Study with Special Reference to Chinese*. Cambridge: Cambridge University Press

Huang, Y., 2000. *Anaphora: A Cross-linguistic Study*. Oxford: Oxford University Press

Jackendoff, R., 1972. *Semantic Interpretation in Generative Grammar*. Cambridge Mass: MIT Press

Kripke, S., 1977. "Speaker's Reference and Semantic Reference". In French, A., Ueling T.E. and Wettstein, H.K. (eds.). *Contemporary Perspectives in the Philosophy of Language*,. Minneapolis: University of Minnesota Press, 6-27

Kuno, S. & Kaburaki, E., 1977. "Empathy and Syntax". *Linguistic Inquiry* 8, 627-72

Lasnik, H., 1976. "Remarks on Coreference". *Linguistic Analysis* 2, 1-22. Reprint in Lasnik, H., 1989. *Essays on Anaphora*. Dordrecht: Kluver, 90-109

Lewis, D., 1979. "Scorekeeping in a Language Game". *Journal of Philosophical Logic* 8, 339-59. Reprinted in Lewis, D., 1983. *Philosophical Papers, Vol. 1*. Oxford: Oxford University Press, 233-49

Pollard, C. & Sag I., 1992. "Anaphors in English and the Scope of Binding Theory". *Linguistic Inquiry* 23, 261–303.

Quine, W. v. O., 1960. *Word and Object*. Cambridge Mass: MIT Press

Reinhart, T. & Reuland E., 1991. "Anaphors and Logophors: An Argument Structure Perspective". In Koster, J. & Reuland, E. (eds.). *Long Distance Anaphora*. Cambridge: Cambridge University Press, 283-321

Stueber, K., 2006. *Rediscovering Empathy: Agency, Folk Psychology, and the Human Sciences*. Cambridge Mass: MIT Press

Wittgenstein, L., 1980. *Remarks on the Philosophy of Psychology; Volume II*. Oxford: Blackwell

9

Consequences of the Pragmatics of 'De Se'[1]

ALESSANDRO CAPONE

1 Introduction

'De se' attitudes (beliefs and other similar attitudes about the (possibly unnamed) thinking subject) constitute a very interesting, intriguing and hot philosophical and linguistic topic. Since Perry's seminal article, it has been clear that the 'de se' mode of presentation of the reference, like other modes of presentation in general, has profound consequences on action. A universal truism about 'de se' modes of presentation is that they are irreducibly indexical. Despite the appeal of this topic to philosophers, a number of linguists have been attracted by its aura of mystery and have tried to discipline its ineffability under a set of linguistic concepts (mainly drawn from the theory of anaphora or from logophoricity), trying to systematize the behavior of 'de se' under logical inference. The slide from philosophical to linguistic treatments is certainly laudable, as the systematicity of a linguistic treatment that disciplines the behavior of 'de se' from the point of view of logical inference is certainly welcome. In this paper, my fundamental claim is that the most successful linguistic treatment, which I take to be that of Higginbotham (2003), needs supplementation by specific inclusion of the 'I' (or EGO) mode of presentation at the level of (interpreted) logical form. The main reasons for this are given in my paper in Capone (2010), follow-

[1] Having clarified that all defects and errors are my own, I would like to express a profound sense of gratitude to the scholars who most encouraged me: Igor Douven, Neil Feit Wayne Davis, Istvan Kecskes, Jim Higginbotham, Michel Seymour, K. Jaszczolt, Jacob L. Mey, Keith Allan, Louise Cummings, and Franco Lo Piparo.

Attitudes De Se: Linguistics, Epistemology, Metaphysics.
Neil Feit and Alessandro Capone (eds.).

ing Feit (personal communication) and in Feit (this volume) as supplemented by considerations of parsimony and other inferential behaviors. In this paper, I want to open up again this discussion and examine the bifurcation between a strand of research (Castañeda 1966) which tries to eliminate the view that 'he*' can be reduced to the first-person pronominal and another strand that favors the identification of the essential indexical with 'I' or anyway properties of the first-person pronominal (Perry 1979). I will also find it useful to let the discussion interact with considerations by Jaszczolt (this volume), which seem to lead away from Perry's considerations.

The views by David Lewis (1979) on 'de se' are not discussed in the following section Suffice it to say that for Lewis a 'de se' ascription could be expressed as a self-attribution of a property. In the main body of this paper, I only take up this view to discuss Higginbotham's influential and interesting objections to it.

The structure of my paper is the following:

a. A resume of the classical papers on 'de se', including recent papers by Higginbotham (2003) and Recanati (2009).
b. A discussion of the recent pragmatics literature on 'de se' attitudes (linguistics);
c. A discussion of pragmatic intrusion in connection with the first-person pronoun;
d. A discussion of the logical connection between the first-personal dimension, the internal dimension and immunity to error through misidentification. Is immunity to error through misidentification dependent on the intrusion of the EGO concept in a 'de se' construction? What kind of relationship is there between immunity to error through misidentification and the internal dimension of 'de se'?
e. Pragmatics and the internal dimension (whether partial or full);
f. Immunity to error through misidentification: semantic (Higginbotham 2003) or pragmatic (Recanati 2009)? Or how to diffuse the dichotomy. (Modularity and pragmatic intrusion).

PART I

2 'De Se' in Philosophy

In this section I shall present what I take to be the most influential theories on 'de se'. Higginbotham's view is philosophical/linguistic, but I have decided to include it in this philosophical section because it is the only one that has the merit of unifying the first-personal character of 'de se', with phenomena such as the internal dimension of PRO and immunity to error through misidentification. I will mainly use the perspective outlined in

Higginbotham (2003), because it is linguistically explicit, in making recourse to anaphoric concepts and to concepts taken from Fillmore's theory, and I will supplement it with considerations by Perry (the idea that the essential indexical needs to make use of the concept 'I' at some level of (pragmatic) interpretation). After articulating this section in a relatively neutral way, I shall discuss the dichotomy in the views of Castañeda and Perry, opting for Perry's views, and I will make connections between Higginbotham's view of immunity to error through misidentification and Recanati's novel treatment, which is, if I understand it well, pragmatically biased.

2.1 Castañeda

In his seminal paper, Castañeda (1966) discusses uses of the pronominal 'he' in attributions of self-knowledge – hence his use of the term 'S-uses of he*'. Self-knowledge attributions normally have the following linguistic structure:

(1) John knows he* is happy.

Castañeda claims that 'he' is an essential indexical in that it cannot be replaced a) by a pronominal which refers to some x; b) by a description used to refer to x; c) by a Proper Name used to refer to x; d) by a deictic; e) by the pronominal 'I'.

The claim by Castañeda is valid for verbs of psychological attribution, in addition to being applicable to verbs such as 'say', 'assert', 'deny' (assertive or quasi assertive verbs; this class of verbs is not discussed in depth by anyone; but my impression is that the link between these verbs and verbs of genuine propositional attitude is only a derivative one).

What should be emphasized is the claim that we cannot replace 'he*' in (1) with e.g. a definite description or with a demonstrative pronoun (the extension of the reasoning to genuine pronominals and Proper Names is straightforward).

Suppose we consider (2):

(2) The editor of Soul believes he* is a millionaire.

In case we know that X is the just appointed editor of Soul but x does not yet know that, we may report (2) but not (3)

(3) The editor of Soul believes that the editor of Soul is a millionaire.

The reason for this is that x does not recognize himself through the mode of presentation 'the editor of Soul'.

Analogously, we should not be inclined to use (4) with a deictic use of 'he' to express (2):

(4) The editor of Soul believes he is a millionaire.

The editor of Soul may look at himself in a mirror, without recognizing himself and would assent to 'He is a millionaire' without having the disposition to assent to 'I am a millionaire'.

The second part of the paper is devoted to the discussion of the deictic 'I' in connection with the claim that there is a close relationship between 'de se' attributions and attributions using 'I'.

Given that Castañeda denies that the essential indexical can be expressed through 'I', it is not clear what the aim of the second part of the paper is. My speculation is that, despite the alleged falsity of Carl Ginet's claim that 'de se' is reducible to 'I', somehow Castandeda thinks it is plausible that someone else will try to establish the connection between the essential indexical and 'I'.

Despite the complexity of the second part of the paper, we can single out some essential discussions. Castañeda claims that 'I' has **ontological** priority as well as epistemic priority. The ontological priority is based on the consideration that a correct use of 'I' cannot fail to refer to the object it purports to refer. This property is not shared by definite descriptions.

Epistemic priority consists in the consideration that a person cannot remember facts about himself, without using in his memory the word 'I'. Castañeda, however, claims that the word 'I' only has partial epistemic priority. In fact, when people distinct from the person who would use 'I' to refer to herself have to remember some facts, they have to make use of 'he' or 'he*' as in 'John knows that he* was happy'. The fact that definite descriptions, proper names, pronominals have to be eliminated to remember self-knowledge is counterbalanced by the fact that these descriptions are not eliminable when the same facts are reported from the outside.

The last, possibly decisive point Castañeda wants to establish is that he* is ineliminable, while 'I' can be eliminated. Consider what happens in (5)

(5) I believe that I am a millionaire and Gaskon believes he* is a millionaire.

We can replace this with:

(6) Each of two persons, Gaskon and me, remembers that he* is a millionaire.

It appears that 'I' is eliminated from the 'that' clause; however, it is shifted to the main clause. So this is not really a case of complete eliminability.

Another case in which a use of 'I' is eliminable in favor of a use of 'he*' is when we make a report of what someone asserts. For instance, suppose Privatus asserts 'I believe that I am a millionaire'. For everybody else, Privatus' first token of 'I' must yield some description of Privatus, but the second token of 'I' must be replaced by a token of 'he*'.

However, Castañeda does not mention the fact that the use of 'I' could be implicit in a use of 'he*'. In this case, eliminability is not clearly established.

Before closing this section on Castañeda, I want to discuss Castañeda's discussion of a suggestion by Carl Ginet, according to which 'he*' can be replaced by using 'I'. The proposal by Ginet is the following:

For any sentence of the form "X believes that he* is H" there is a corresponding sentence that contains no form of 'he*' but that would in most circumstances make the same statement. The corresponding sentence that will do the job, I suggest, is the one of the form "X believes (to be true) the proposition that X would express if X were to say 'I am H' or perhaps more clearly "If X were to say 'I am H', he would express what he (X) believes".

Castañeda objects to this formulation on pragmatic grounds. He thinks that 'Saying' must be replaced with 'assertively uttering'. Even this, according to him , does not suffice given that one who says 'I am H' may express in context something completely different from 'I am H'.

2.2 John Perry

Perry (1979) deals with the problem of the essential indexical in relation to utterances such as:

(7) I am making a mess.

Perry takes utterances such as (7) as having a motivational force which utterances corresponding to (7) where 'I' is replaced by a definite description (e.g. the messy shopper) do not have.

There are at least two examples Perry uses to show what is distinctive about the essential indexicals. The first one is that of the messy shopper. I am at the supermarket; I see a trail of sugar on the floor and I follow the messy shopper who caused it. However, when I realize that I am the messy shopper, I stop and I rearrange the torn sack of sugar. Clearly, the thought 'I am making a mess' has a motivational force which the equivalent 'The messy shopper is making a mess' does not have. The other example Perry uses is the following. A professor has a meeting at noon. He knows all the while that he has this meeting at noon; however, it is only when he thinks 'The meeting is now' that he goes to the meeting. Again, the use of the essential indexical has motivational force.

Perry tries to solve this problem by discussing a theory of propositions along the lines of Frege. He takes belief to be a relationship between a person and a proposition. The proposition believed consists of an object and a predicate which is attributed to the object. Perry focuses on the idea that the proposition may contain a **missing conceptual component**, say a Mode of Presentation of an object. Then he wonders if the essential indexical corresponds to some concept that fits the speaker/thinker uniquely when he thinks/says 'I am making a mess'. Perry's answer is that recourse to a concept that fits the referent uniquely will not do the job required. For example, even if I was thinking of myself as the only bearded philosopher in a Safeway Sore West of the Mississippi, the fact that I came to believe that the only such philosopher was making a mess explains my action only on the assumption that I believed that I was the only such philosopher, which brings in the problem of the essential indexical again.

At this point, Perry considers if a treatment in terms of 'de re' belief can offer a solution to the problem of the essential indexical. Perry says that the most influential treatments of 'de re' belief have tried to explain it in terms of 'de dicto' belief. The simplest account of 'de re' belief in terms of 'de dicto' belief is the following:

> X believes of y that he is so and so
> Just in case
> There is a concept α such that α fits y and X believes that α is so and so.

This is problematic because I can believe that I am making a mess even if there is no concept α such that I alone can fit α and I believe that α is making a mess. Another possible solution Perry considers is that of relativized propositions. Now, on a Relativized Proposition view, 'I am making a mess' is true or false at a time and at a person. The problem is, how do we individuate the person at which the proposition is true? If we individuate it through a description, then the motivational force of 'I am making a mess' is lost, since one can say that the statement is true relative the time t and the person 'the messy shopper', which is a description of the person who refers to himself through 'I'.

The solution which Perry offers is that we should distinguish between objects of belief and **belief states**. Belief states are more abstract than fully articulated objects of belief and they should include a perspective or a context as well as the inclination to describe the belief by making use of an essential indexical such as 'I' or 'now'. Such states are recognizable because they have motivational force. Suppose various people have used the sentence 'I am making a mess'. What is it that all these belief states have in common? They have in common the same motivational force (this is a functional characterization, as Chalmers (1996) would say), as well as an abstract structure in which the believer identifies himself through the use of the word 'I' in describing his belief and the context is enough for giving full articulation to this belief. We do not expect all thoughts entertained by use of 'I am making a mess' to be isomorphic, because they are identified in virtue of contexts that are different from one another.

Most importantly, we have shown that 'I' cannot be reduced to the α or to 'This α'. In other words, Perry has demonstrated the same properties which Castañeda attributed to he*. It follows that Castañeda's 'he*' and Perry's 'I' are somewhat related.

2.3 Higginbotham (2003)

Higginbotham recognizes that there is something special about first-personal uses of pronominals such as those discussed by Castañeda. The merits of his discussion lie in his pointing out that constructions with PRO may even be more first-personal than uses of 'he himself' and in linking the issue of immunity to error through misidentification to the issue of the internal perspective in connection with PRO (in cases of verbs like 'remember', 'imagine', etc.). He claims that the propositional analysis articulated through the notion of anaphora and thematic roles is superior to the property-based view of Lewis and Chierchia. In fact, according to him, the property-based analysis of beliefs and attitudes 'de se' does not allow the theorist to explain 1) immunity to error through misidentification; 2) the internal dimension of PRO in complements of verbs such as 'remember', or 'imagine'. (We'll test this in a later section).

Higginbotham accepts Perry's idea that 'de se' attitudes involve a first-personal mode of presentation (involving sometimes the word 'I' or some related notion) and reformulates such a view through considerations based on anaphora and thematic relations.

Higginbotham also accepts Peacocke's (1981) consideration that a 'de se' thought involves the use of a mode of presentation 'self' which only the thinker and nobody else can use in reporting such a thought.

Higginbotham considers cases with PRO such as:

(8) John remembers PRO going to Paris

which is contrasted with (9) and (10)

(9) John remembers that he went to Paris;

(10) John remembers that he himself went to Paris.

The first-personal nature of (8) is expressed through a notation which involves self-reflexive thought:

(11) For x = John, ∃e, remember [x, e, ^ ∃e': go to Paris (σ (e), e')]

(8) is different from (9) because it involves an internal dimension. It is the internal dimension which apparently causes immunity to error through misidentification. We can capture this 'internal dimension' through the expression in logical form of a thematic role: the person who undergoes the action in question. So we can reformulate (8) through (12)

(12) For X = John, ∃e, remember [x, e, ^ ∃e': go to Paris (σ (e) & θ (e'))].

With this elucidation in mind, we can explain the following facts:

Only Churchill gave the speech
Churchill remembers giving the speech
:
Only Churchill remembers giving the speech.

Surely someone who listened to the speech remembers that Churchill gave the speech or remembers his giving the speech. But are the speeches which Churchill remembers giving and which another person remembers hearing the same kind of thought? At some level of abstraction they are. At some deeper level, however, there are not. What validates the inference in the deduction above is the fact that Churchill remembers giving his speech from the inside. So in case he has forgotten giving the speech and someone else informs him that, in fact, he gave the speech, Churchill cannot (truthfully) say that he remembers giving the speech. Memory involves an internal perspective in case PRO is used in the complement clause. Thus, if one remembers falling downstairs, one must certainly have memories of sensations of pain; something which one need not have in case memory is reconstructed through an external narration.

Higginbotham discusses an interesting question. He asks whether mad Heimson who believes that he is Hume has numerically the same belief as Hume. The question, put crudely, is whether the belief Heimson has in believing that he himself is Hume is the same as the one which Hume has in believing that he himself is Hume. The answer by Higginbotham is ambivalent. On the one hand, their beliefs are different, so much so that we must say that, in believing he is Hume, Heimson has a false belief while in case Hume believes he is Hume, we shall say that he has a true belief. This is nicely expressed through an anaphoric treatment:

(13) For x = Heimson, ∃e, believe [x, e, ^ (∃e') identical ((σ (e) & θ (e')), Hume,) e'].

Since σ (e) is anaphorically related to Heimson, there is clearly an **external** component to that thought. However, Higginbotham says that at some level of generality, we can say that Heimson and Hume have the same thought

^ (∃e') identical (σ (e), Hume, e')

Higginbotham illustrates this through an analogy to two collapses of bridges. Of course, in one sense two collapses of bridges cannot be the same event, unless the bridges are the same. In another sense, we could say that the collapses of two distinct bridges are the same type of event provided that the bridges have similar characteristics.

2.4 Recanati and immunity to error through misidentification

Recanati expatiates on the nature of 'de re' thoughts and subsequently reflects on the relation between 'de re' and 'de se' thoughts. First of all, Recanati clarifies that in order to have a 'de re' thought, one must think of the object through a mode of presentation. However, the mode of presentation is irrelevant to truth-evaluation of the thought. To have a thought 'de re' about object x, there must be an **information link** between the object and the subject. Consider the thought that 'That man is drunk'. Here there is a demonstrative link between the subject of the thought and the object and the object is determined through a demonstrative mode of presentation – that is a relation of acquaintance with object x based on perception. However, as Recanati says, the property of being seen by the subject (that is the particular relation of acquaintance) does not appear in the content of the thought. According to Recanati, 'de re' modes of presentation involve contextual relations to the object. The object the thought is about is the object which stands in the right contextual relations to the thinking subject. In general, 'de re' thoughts are based on relations in virtue of which the subject can gain information about the object. We call these 'acquaintance relations'. The subject can be related to the object through a **perception relation** or through a **communicative chain**.

What determines the reference (the particular relation of acquaintance with the referent) is something external, not represented by the content of the thought. Recanati clarifies that, by this, he means that no constituent of the thought stands for that relation of acquaintance. Recanati finds an analogy between the acquaintance relations that determine a referent for a pronominal or a definite description and the conventional meaning that determines the referent of the indexical 'I'. It would be mistaken to identify the referent of 'I' (of a token of 'I') with the character of this word.

Recanati identifies modes of presentations with **files** opened up when one is in the appropriate contextual relationship to an object. The file can also contain information about the properties of the object made available through a relation of acquaintance. The file is a mental particular that bears certain relations to an object. A file may be opened by encountering a particular object.

Demonstratives involve the creation of temporary files. When the situation one encounters is no longer available, one will have to replace this file with a new one, identifiable through a definite description. The file is merely a mode of presentation that allows one to provide solutions to Frege's puzzle, among other things.

A specific file is the 'self' file. A self-file contains properties which one is aware of through proprioception, which provides information available to nobody else.

Recanati clearly states that a 'de se' thought is a thought about oneself that involves the mode of presentation EGO. To make clear the distinction between 'de se' and 'de re' thoughts which are accidentally 'de se', Recanati uses an example by Kaplan (1977). When I say 'My pants are on fire' I am having a thought about myself (as determined by proprioception, e.g. the feel of burning on the skin). However, if I look at a mirror and I see a person who looks like somebody else, I may say 'His pants are on fire' with no implication that I am having a thought about myself determined by proprioception.

Recanati relates the property of immunity to error through misidentification to 'de se' thoughts and arrives at the conclusion that it is not the case that all 'de se' thoughts share this property.

Recanati discusses examples that are due to Wittgenstein, showing that proprioception determines 'de se' thoughts displaying immunity to error through misidentification. When I say 'My arm hurts' I say this because I have an inner experience about which I cannot be mistaken. Instead, if I say 'My arm is broken' basing this on visual experience of a broken arm which I mistake for my own, it is clear that my statement relies on the premise d is broken; d = that arm; d = c (my arm). Since the premises on which my statement rests involve identification (d = c), then I can be mistaken about c = d and the resulting statement can be mistaken too. Following Evans (1982), Recanati claims that 'de se' statements can also involve bodily properties. Since the attribution of bodily properties can be determined either through proprioception or visual experience, it turns out that a statement such as 'My legs are crossed' is ambiguous. On one interpretation, it shows immunity to error through misidentification. On the normal visual perception reading, it is vulnerable to error through misidentification.

Suppose I say 'My legs are crossed' on the basis of visual experience. Then I can fail to note that these are John's legs. My statement a is F rests on the identification a = b and on the judgment b is F. Since there is a misidentification component, misidentification can occur.

Recanati focuses on one kind of statements which is implicitly 'de se'. When we say 'Pain' or 'There is pain', we are saying that there is a pain which the subject is experiencing even if we are not explicitly representing the subject in the content. We can say that the content of the conscious state is not a complete proposition but the property of being in pain.

Implicit 'de se' statements are clearly immune to error through misidentification, since they are based on proprioceptive experience. Immunity is retained because the statement does not rest on premises such as b is F and a = b. It is not based on an identification act.

In the conclusive section of his paper, Recanati discusses the ideas by Lewis (1979), in particular the reduction of 'de re' to 'de se' thoughts and its relation to an egocentric perspective on the attitudes. First of all, it should be noted that, when discussing 'de re' thoughts, Lewis incorporates the acquaintance condition into the 'de re' thought. So 'John believes that Mary is pretty' comes out as

> ∃x = John , ∃y = Mary, such x is acquainted with Mary, who has the property of being pretty.

The reason why this is done is that Lewis wants to reduce all belief to belief 'de se'. Now, while in case of belief that is genuinely 'de se' (Mary believes she is pretty), belief 'de se' can be reduced to attribution of a property to the self, this cannot be done in the case of belief 'de re', unless the acquaintance condition is incorporated into the content of the thought. In other words, this is due to a conception of the attitudes that is too egocentric.

PART II

3 Pragmatic treatments

In this section, I will report three types of pragmatic treatments. Capone (2010) is a treatment based on Relevance Theory considerations. Jaszczolt (this volume) is based on her general theory of Default Semantics and merger representations and seems to be a step forward towards a contextualist theory of 'de se'. Huang (this volume) is based on a neo-Gricean theory of anaphora and assimilates 'de se' and logophoricity.

3.1 Capone (2010) and the pragmatics of 'de se'.

Capone (2010) is an eclectic treatment combining linguistic, cognitive and philosophical considerations in order to predict pragmatic results. His approach is eclectic and is a rethinking of pragmatic scales à la Levinson/Horn/Huang in terms of considerations based on Relevance Theory. His ideas, in essentials, are very simple. If one accepts Higginbotham's considerations on the logical forms of 'de se' and 'de re' beliefs (to pick up just the most representative of the attitudes), it goes without saying that the logical forms of 'de se' beliefs entail the logical forms of 'de re' beliefs. Hence the possibility of pragmatic scales. On a strictly Relevance Theory line of thinking, the ranking of 'de se', 'de re' in terms of entailment entails a ranking in terms of informativeness. Then it goes without saying that a 'de se' interpretation of a pronominal (where both interpretations are possible) is informationally richer and, thus, following the Principle of Relevance, greater Cognitive Effects, with a parity of cognitive efforts, are predicted. One may also concoct stories in which a 'de se' interpretation leads to some kind of action which the 'de re' interpretation would never cause (See Perry; see also Capone 2010, the pill story). If this line of thought is accepted, then we can easily explain why

(14) John believes he is clever

tends to be associated with a 'de se' interpretation. As Jaszczolt (1999) would say, this interpretation tends to be 'default'. Of course, its default status derives from the way the mind is predisposed to calculate inferences and also from the human tendency to standardize or short-circuit familiar inferences that are probabilistically high.

According to Capone, one may also investigate scales such as the following:

(15) John wants to go away;

(16) John wants him to go away;

(17) John remembers going away;

(18) John remembers his going away.

The use of the marked pronominal, instead of less marked PRO, tends to invite an interpretation which is complementary to that associated with PRO. This can be explained in terms of M-scales in the framework of Levinson/Horn/Huang or in terms of cognitive efforts, which tend to pick up an interpretation disjoint from the one associated with the expression involving least amount of cognitive efforts.

Capone also explains certain interesting examples by Perry, which seem to illuminate further the boundary between semantics and pragmatics. Readers are referred for these to Capone (2010).

Perhaps the most interesting discussion found in Capone (2010) concerns the internal dimension of PRO, which is connected by Higginbotham to immunity to error through misidentification. Capone argues that, in connection with certain verbs, such as 'remember' the internal dimension of PRO is guaranteed by semantic effects up to a certain point, and that at least part of the internal dimension associated with PRO is due to pragmatic effects driven by typical scenarios. With some other verbs, such as 'expect', Capone argues that it is less likely that the internal dimension of PRO is a semantic inference and opts for the view that it is a pragmatic increment. Other verbs such as, e.g. 'knows how' are examined.

The most radical part of Capone's ideas is that Higginbotham's semantic elucidations for verbs such as 'remember', 'imagine' etc., refined and important though it is, suffers from a certain weakness, which cannot be remedied semantically, but only pragmatically. Leaving aside formal notation, Higginbotham's treatment of (19)

(19) John remembers walking in Oxford

comes out as 'The agent of the remembering/John remembers that the agent of the walking was walking in Oxford'. But then John should know that he is the agent of the remembering, a grammatical expertise which may not be acquired by anyone at all (See also Davis (this volume) on this problem). Furthermore, this analysis presupposes that there is a unique thinker of this thought and thus it is incompatible with the possibility that someone else, say God, is having the same thought. (This difficulty was raised by Neil Feit (personal communication), and is to be taken seriously). The third kind of problem is that, despite the fact that Higginbotham says that these constructions are first-personal, there is nothing in their logical form that makes them first personal, unless one allows as normative the inference 'I = the believer of this thought' (and here endless discussions could arise on how obvious, normative or natural this inference is or should be).

My own view is that the first personal element EGO must somehow be incorporated into the propositional form, *not* at the level of semantics, but at the level of pragmatics. EGO can be taken to be a concept of mentalese, a mode of presentation through which the thinking subject thinks of himself. It is not necessarily a word used or a deictic requiring interpretation, since the EGO concept can be used in two cases. It can be used when the subject thinks of himself, in which case EGO requires no interpretation procedure, but is essentially a concept of mentalese linked anaphorically with previous acts of thinking (and the question of reference is not of any importance for the thinking subject or is at most a question of presuppositions). Otherwise, it can be used when a subject is attributed a 'de se' thought, in which case interpretation needs an anaphoric chain of interpretation linked to a thinking subject and the question of reference is of some crucial importance. We need pragmatic intrusion – and here the theories due to Levinson (2000), Carston (2002), Sperber and Wilson (1896) come to our aid. Accepting that semantics can be underdetermined, we may incorporate certain elements through pragmatic intrusion. Considerations of parsimony may even lead us to think that pragmatic intrusion, in this case, is to be preferred to incorporation of the component EGO at the level of Higginbotham's logical form.

What reasons have we got against incorporating EGO into Higginbotham's logical forms (say through identification)? There are constructions such as the following where EGO would not be required, although they may well be captured by Higginbotham's analysis of 'de se':

(20) Anyone who thought that the believer of this thought was happy was certainly happy: anyone who thinks he is happy, is happy.

Now, I want to dwell on the possible replies to Neil Feit's objection to Higginbotham. First of all, I voice Neil Feit's opinion:

> Another reason why I do not think Higginbotham's account can handle 'de se' cases adequately is this. It seems possible that somebody could believe (correctly or mistakenly, it does not matter) that he is not the only thinker of a certain thought, for example he might believe that God is thinking it too. More generally, he might think that he is not the only thinker of any of these thoughts. But, even with this, it seems he could have a 'de se' belief. But on Higginbotham's view - and other similar views – such a belief amounts to 'the believer of this thought is F'. This cannot be what the belief amounts to, however, since he does not think there is a unique believer, the believer of his thought. Moreover, if someone else (God perhaps) really is having the same thought, then all Higginbotham-style beliefs are false, but he could surely have some true 'de se' beliefs (personal communication in Capone (2010)).

Now, of course, when I say 'John believes he is not crazy' I do not have in mind believers of this thought other than John. And, if it is somehow in the background that God and I are the only believers of this thought, it is not the case that I thereby express or intend to express that John believes that he and God are not crazy. Nor does Higginbotham think so (presumably). The examples by Higginbotham, such as 'John remembers walking in Oxford', are less vulnerable to Feit's objection. Higginbotham's tacit reply could be that, given the anaphoric properties of PRO, it goes without saying that the unique believer of this thought (the agent of the remembering) is John and not God (Is not anaphoric coindexation enough to make this clear?). It is not even necessary to resort to the more complicated story that makes the subject of the walking plural: the believers of this thought, assuming a kind of metaphysics in which wherever one is, God is there too. (And if talk of God is infused into Higginbotham's story, then certain metaphysical consequences would not be completely absurd).

Of course, the problem raised by Neil Feit becomes more cogent not in the cases of constructions dear to Higginbotham, but to the more interpretatively ambiguous:

(21) John thinks he is happy.

Here pragmatics is abundantly involved, as even Higginbotham has to admit, and it goes without saying that if Feit's objection has some cogency, this goes up to some point, because if, by pragmatic intrusion, we create an anaphoric identity link between the thinker of this thought and John, the uniqueness condition is valid and thoughts about God's having the same thought are out of the question. (So either we assume that some pragmatic linking between 'John' and 'the believer of this thought' is presupposed, making Feit's considerations otiose, or one needs to insert the anaphoric link explicitly into the semantics).

3.2 Jaszczolt on 'De Se'

Jaszczolt's views about 'de se' need to be discussed with reference to her framework based on Default Semantics. Her view is based on a rigorously parsimonious acceptance of only those levels of meaning that are necessary (indispensable), in line with **Modified Occam's Razor**. Accordingly, she posits compositionality at the level of merger representations, rather than at the level of sentential meaning. Since sentential meaning is part of merger representations, this parsimony ensures that compositionality is calculated only once and that, when compositionality seems to break down at the level of sentential meaning, it percolates down to the sentential components from the merger representations, where pragmatics ensures compositionality. Now, the question which Jaszczolt tackles, one which is not devoid of theoretical interest, is whether 'de se' meanings belong to the grammar component (or the level of semantics) or, otherwise, to the contextualist level of meaning. Which attitude should prevail, in this case: Minimalism or Contextualism? The emerging attitude is the one that is found in Jaszczolt (2005). Jaszczolt, in fact, believes that minimalism, properly construed, is compatible with contextualism. In particular, she takes grammar (the grammatical resources that are taken to be responsible for 'de se' interpretations) to provide defaults which are either promoted at the level of the contextualist component of meaning or, otherwise, abrogated through cancellation, costly thought this can be. Jaszczolt takes issue with scholars like Chierchia who claim that pronominals (e,g, PRO) are fundamentally responsible for 'de se' interpretations, and she clarifies that other types of constructions can be responsible for first-personal meanings as in the following examples (used in a first-personal way):

(22) Sammy wants a biscuit;

(23) Mummy will be with you in a moment.

Jaszczolt also proposes examples that divest grammar from its non-monotonic status based on cases in which an NP that is not a pronominal can be invested with pronominal, first-personal meaning, thanks to inferences accruing in context:

(24) I believe I should have prepared the drinks for the party. In a way I also believed that I should have done it when I walked into the room. The fact is, the person appointed by the Faculty Board should have done it and, as I later realized, I was this person.

Now, this example can be taken in an ambivalent way. On the one hand, 'I' used in the first two sentences takes on the value of a definite description, once we arrive at the final sentence (The fact is....). Alternatively, on re-interpretation the NP 'The person appointed by the Faculty Board' could acquire a first-personal meaning. The fact that various potential reinterpretations are latent does not deprive the example from the significance that it has for Jaszczolt: in other words it is not the level of grammar that can guarantee the first-personal dimension of a pronominal, but contextual interpretation is required as well.

So, the upshot of all this is that grammar only provides **defaults**, which can be overridden, even if with some cost, but they can also be reinforced at the level of the contextual component of meaning, where they can be fully promoted as utterance interpretations.

There are, nevertheless, some disturbing problems raised by Jaszczolt for my views expressed in Capone (2010). If grammatical resources, such as pronominals (PRO, I, etc.) can only provide defaults capable of being overridden in context, my view that Higginbotham's considerations need to be supplemented by an explicitly first-personal constituent like EGO seem to go by the board. If we follow Jaszczolt, EGO is not, by itself, sufficient to guarantee a first-personal interpretation, as we saw through example (24) (the pronominal 'he' here could very well be taken to mean 'The person appointed by the Faculty Board' on a suitable reinterpretation). Furthermore, as Jaszczolt claims, many NPs normally disjoint in interpretation from pronominals, can take first-personal readings ('Mummy', 'Sammy' etc.).

Furthermore Jaszczolt takes the view that a pronominal like 'he*' is associated with a first-personal reading by cancellable pragmatic inference, which is somehow contrary to the notion of pragmatic intrusion I have developed through many publications. I usually claimed that pragmatic intrusions that are indispensable to rescue an utterance from a logical problem (take for example the problem raised by Feit in connection with uniqueness) are not cancellable. I agree with Jaszczolt to some extent, as she also finds that the cancellability of the 'de se' inference is very costly, as in:

(25) John Perry believes that he is making a mess but doesn't realize it is him.

(25) by Jaszczolt, however, cannot be a serious problem for my views, first of all because she grants that cancellability (abrogating the 'de se' inference) is a costly move. Secondly, the 'de se' interpretation arises only on condition that we identify 'he' with 'John Perry' by an anaphoric link and, thus, the first-personal reading is accessed only on top of this, let us say, possible interpretation. The cases like 'Mummy', 'Sammy' which Jaszczolt discusses in order to eliminate the view that 'de se' is a concept that is entrenched in the grammar, interesting though they are, only show that there are alternative expressive possibilities, which may very well be **parasitic** on the forms which grammar provides. Furthermore, the fact that there are constructions which are **interpretatively** ambiguous at least potentially,

such as 'John believes he is clever' does not preclude the possibility that certain forms of pronominals encode first-personal meanings. It is probably the discussion which Feit and I proposed in the section above which opens the way for the possibility of 'de se' constructions needing a pragmatic increment involving the concept 'EGO'. Unfortunately, the radical question which Jaszczolt poses – a question which I find extremely intriguing – is that the concept EGO alone is not sufficient in articulated linguistic texts to ensure the grasp of a first-personal concept (see the interesting example by Jaszczolt reported in (24)). However, I want to defend myself by saying that even if we grant that in the articulated linguistic texts words can be ambiguous and can be interpreted in different ways and, therefore, there is nothing that can prevent EGO from being interpreted as a description (an ordinary descriptive NP), the concept EGO which I propose to use in inference must belong to some language of thought, some kind of **Mentalese**, which is completely disambiguated. And since pragmatic inference need not be dependent on written or articulated words, the words used in inferences (pragmatic or not) are words of mentalese that can be fully made explicit. What ensures that EGO and EGO are the same word of mentalese both for the speaker and the hearer and for the speaker and the many hearers is that such an inference is indispensable in rescuing the statement from the problems raised by Feit. If the speaker and the hearer had different EGOs in mind, by extending the interpretation work, the aim of this pragmatic explicature would be defeated. On the contrary, I assume that the speaker and the hearer share the task of making interpretations plausible by obeying a normative principle of Charity imposing that they amend possible logical deficiencies such as absurd interpretations or patent contradictions. Some cooperation and coordination work goes on between the speaker and the hearer and, thus, the multiple reinterpretations which the word EGO may undergo in articulated speech cannot be assumed in a pragmatic inferential work, which does not act only on explicit words, but on what is strictly required to make the interpretation work plausible (occurrences of Mentalese, in other words). Re-contextualizations leading us away from the concept EGO to NPs with various descriptive force are therefore not necessary and extremely costly. This is why hearers do not go for them.

Before closing this section on Jaszczolt, it is fair to point out that she manages to reconcile both minimalism and contextualism, by adding a level of merger representations where compositionality is operative, Modified Occam's Razor preventing compositionality from operating at the level of sentential meaning. Now, if these considerations make sense, it is clear that compositionality also works to combine components that are the result of pragmatic inference (the EGO concept I was in fact discussing) with components that are present in the sentential level. Thus a pronominal like 'he' that is potentially ambiguous at the level of semantics becomes an essential indexical (he*) in the sense of Castañeda only after some basic compositional operations, like, for example, establishing an anaphoric link with some previous subject within the sentence (as Jaszczolt says, following van der Sandt, local accommodation is preferred and, thus, the anaphoric linkage occurs within the minimal syntactic projection (the matrix sentence usually) and then by gluing the EGO concept to the pronominal 'he'). The essential indexical is fundamentally the result of two logical operations; a) an anaphoric link within the minimal projected category; gluing the EGO concept onto 'he'. These operations occur at the level of the merger representations and thus allow the compositionality effects to percolate down the level of sentence. These operations occur at an inferential level; thus it is not to be excluded that pragmatic principles like for the example the Principle of Relevance are at work; yet it appears that Jaszczolt prefers to admit only a level of standardized inference and, thus, legitimately talks about defaults.

3.3 Yan Huang on 'De Se'

Yan Huang's treatment of 'de se' and pragmatics does not belong properly to the philosophy of language, being rooted in cross-linguistic analysis, a theory of anaphora and, also a theory of logophoricity. This discussion is, therefore, necessarily brief. I will nevertheless, try to sum up the essentials of this paper because they point to how a pragmatic treatment of 'de se' should be handled. Huang starts with the characteristics of a quasi-indicator to establish obvious analogies with long-distance reflexives and logophoric elements which he takes to be the counterparts of quasi-indicators in West African languages and in Asian languages:

(i) A quasi-indicator does not express an indexical reference made by the speaker;

(ii) It occurs in *oratio obliqua*;

(iii) It has an antecedent, to which it refers back;

(iv) Its antecedent is outside the *oratio obliqua* containing the quasi-indicator;

(v) It is used to attribute implicit indexical reference to the referent of its antecedent.

Huang agrees that expressions like 'he himself' or PRO are quasi-indicators in English and also mentions the presence of attitude ascriptions that can be partly 'de se' and partly 'de re'. The author discusses logophoric expressions in West-African languages and long-distance reflexives in East and South Asian languages showing that they can both function as quasi-indicators in the sense of Castañeda. Logophoric expressions are expressions that can be used to mark logophoricity or logophora. By logophoricity one means the phenomenon whereby the perspective of the internal protagonist of a sentence or discourse, as opposed to that of the current external speaker, is being reported by using some morphological/syntactic means. According to Huang, it is hardly surprising that logophoric expressions are one of the most common devices the current, external speaker uses in attributing a 'de se' attitude to an internal protagonist. Huang points out that a logophoric expression usually occurs in a logophoric domain, namely a sentence or a stretch of discourse in which the internal protagonist is represented. In general, a logophoric domain constitutes an indirect speech. Logophoric domains are usually set up by logophoric licensers: logophoric predicates and logophoric complementisers (such complementisers being often homophonous with the verb 'say').

In Asian languages, since there is no special logophor, the essential indexical can be expressed by resorting to long distance reflexives. Long-distance reflexives in East and South Asian languages can be morphologically simple or complex. Marking of 'de se' attitude ascriptions is accomplished syntactically in terms of long distance reflexives. A long-distance reflexive is one that can be bound outside its local syntactic domain. Long-distance reflexivization occurs usually within the sentential complements of speech, thought, mental state, knowledge and perception.

In West African languages, the use of logophoric expressions is in complementary distribution with that of regular expressions like pronouns. As a result, any speaker of these languages intending coreference will also have to use a logophoric expression. If a logophoric expression is not employed, but a regular pronoun is, a Q-implicature will arise, namely neither a 'de se' interpretation nor a coreferential interpretation is intended.

Concerning Asian languages, while the use of a long-distance reflexive encodes both a 'de se' attitude and coreference, the use of a regular pronoun may or may not encode coreference, but *not* 'de se' ascriptions. So there is a scale <long distance reflexive, regular pronoun> modeled on Q-scales. The effect is that the unavailability of the semantically stronger long-distance reflexive will Q-implicate the speaker's intention to avoid at least one feature associated with it, namely the 'de se' reading. If the unmarked regular pronoun is not used, but the marked long-distance reflexive is used instead, an M-implicature is created, that is not only coreference but a 'de se' interpretation is intended.

A different paper would be required to cast such considerations in the framework of Relevance Theory. Suffice it to say that Huang's considerations work on the ranking of informativeness, which is also what Relevance Theory does. According to RT an interpretation that yields greater contextual effects is to be preferred to one which does not yield the same amount of effects, cognitive costs remaining equal. Implicatures/explicatures due to the use of marked expressions can be predicted by Relevance Theorists by paying due attention to cognitive effort, marked expressions usually requiring greater cognitive efforts.

4 EGO or not EGO? (A Discussion of Castañeda and Perry)

While Castañeda (1966) in his seminal papers disseminated original ideas about 'de se' attitudes, and provided the basic examples alimenting the theoretical discussion, he was clearly at a fork in having to decide whether 'he*' was completely irreducible (a clearly radical and original claim) or whether it could be partially reduced, say by making use of the concept EGO, to appear somehow in the semantic/pragmatic analysis of uses of the essential indexical. The other horn of the dilemma is certainly constituted by Perry's ideas that beliefs 'de se' amount to specifications of mental states in which the concept EGO appears somehow (even if it could not be shown to be semantically present, it could be shown to be indispensable for a pragmatic type of analysis). While the considerations by Perry are quite straightforward and presumably presuppose the at least partial reducibility of 'de se' to the EGO concept, Castañeda's considerations about the irreducibility of 'de se' are fully articulated and explicitly deny that recourse to the concept EGO, even if invoked through pragmatic machinery, could be useful.

Consider, first of all, the claim that 'I' has **ontological** priority (such a priority consisting in the fact that a correct use of 'I' cannot fail to refer to the object it purports to refer). This claim is, in my opinion, reminiscent of the claim of immunity to error through misidentification; however, Castañeda limits this claim just to the first person pronominal and does not extend it, in the way Higginbotham does, to 'he*'. If Castañeda is right, 'I' is immune to error through misidentification. However, if Higginbotham (based on Shoemaker 1968) is correct, 'He*' is also immune to error through misidentification. This provides 'prima facie' evidence that 'I' and 'he*' are related (though we certainly do not want to say that 'I' is identical with 'He*'. Is it possible that the relation between 'I' and 'He*' is due to the fact that either 'I' should be expressed in terms of the concept 'He*' or that 'He*' should be expressed in terms of the concept 'I'? While, on the basis of these considerations alone, we cannot establish which direction we should go, we have at least established that it is implausible to think, the way Castañeda does, that 'He*' and 'I' are NOT related.

Feit (personal communication) in response to this, says:

> I am not sure these are the same kinds of immunity to error. One kind is this: you cannot fail, or 'I' cannot fail, to refer. But the kind Shoemaker was interested in is different. It is this: you cannot be wrong in believing some-

> thing because you misidentified somebody else as yourself. One problem with Higginbotham's paper, as I see it, is that he does not clearly distinguish these two different phenomena.
>
> For example, consider my statement: "I was born on Corsica." There is immunity here in the first sense above, since my use of 'I' cannot fail to refer to me. However, there is no immunity in the second sense. That is, there is vulnerability to error through misidentification in Shoemaker's sense. For suppose I make my statement because I have just learned that Napoleon was born on Corsica, and because I mistakenly believe that I am Napoleon. This example is from Pryor (1999).

In reply to Feit's considerations, I need to say that my approach is, like Shoemaker's, both a semantic and an epistemological approach. In particular, the epistemological approach is taken to be supervenient on the semantic approach. The case discussed by Feit (taken from Pryor 1999) is a case of an inferential extension to human knowledge.

But the central cases of Immunity to Error through Misidentification are clearly not those where the subject (in the third person) is logically independent of a verb of propositional attitude but one which is embedded in the object of an attitude ("I remember I was walking in Oxford": the question of IEM is about the second subject). Clearly I cannot say 'I remember I was born in Corsica' because I believe I am Napoleon and I just learned that Napoleon was born in Corsica. The reason why I cannot remember facts deduced through logical deductions is that remembering involves an internal dimension, as you remember from the inside; instead, logical deductions involve a dimension which is external to the event remembered. The internal dimension may be partly semantic, partly pragmatic; but whatever it is, it contributes to excluding the magic tricks of deduction and most importantly the idea that the thought cannot be first-personal or that the subject can fail to refer to himself. In any case, a person who thinks of himself as 'I', even if he does attribute himself the property 'I = Napoleon", still may think of himself as himself, despite the additional identification 'I = Napoleon". The example by Feit can only serve to illuminate the question of whether identification is always primary or whether there may be two types of identification: 'primary' and 'secondary' identification. My claim would still be that primary identification, being independent of secondary identification, can work well to ensure that IEM occurs even in sentences like the one Feit brought to my attention. Furthermore, we need to consider what happens when we replace 'remember' with 'believe'. Consider the statement 'I believe that I was born in Corsica'. Suppose I believe this as a result of someone having led me to a misidentification of myself. I was led to believe I am Napoleon and then I deduced that I was born in Corsica. Since belief does not imply an internal dimension, the magic tricks of logical deduction cannot be excluded. Yet, paradoxically, to use some apparatus on the pragmatics of belief by Igor Douven (2010), after learning that I am Napoleon and after deducing that I was born in Corsica, I may well continue to remember that I was born in Corsica, but forget that I am Napoleon. IEM in this case occurs and shows that the identification I= Napoleon in only secondary and cannot in any way prevent the thinker from thinking of himself under a neutral mode of presentation such as 'EGO'. Second, Castañeda argues that 'I' has only **partial epistemic priority**. In other words, in order to remember things that happened to me or statements about me (the kind of statements that are found in encyclopedias, history books, etc.), I should eliminate modes of presentation of myself other than 'I', because this is the only way to be sure that I do not lose sight of the connection (of identity) between such modes of presentation and the mode of presentation 'I'. (If I forget that Julius Caesar was my name I may very well forget most of what history books say about me (I being Julius Caesar). To ensure transmission of memories in my mind, I must reduce all other modes of presentation of myself to the bare 'I'.[2] Now while this has some cogent plausibility (given all the other considerations Castañeda said to induce us to believe that 'de se' attitudes have a special status, distinct from 'de re' attitudes), Castañeda refuses to accept that eliminability of modes of presentation of 'I' is necessary to ensure that memories are retained when we report such states of the world in the third person, through statements such as (26)

(26) Caesar believes he* conquered Egypt.

Yet, on the one hand it is clear that sentences such as (27) are transformations of sentences such as (27):

(27) Caesar: I conquered Egypt.

Sentences like (26) are parasitic on the logical properties of sentences such as (27). Furthermore, preserving memories of facts such as 'Caesar conquered Egypt' may very well depend, even if in exceptional cases, on what Caesar may be able to report himself. Since, in cases of amnesia, he may not be able to report 'Caesar conquered Egypt' but he may only report 'I conquered Egypt' it is clear that transmission of memories through utterances such as 'Caesar remembers conquering Egypt' ultimately depends on eliminability of any other modes of presentation of 'Caesar' in favor of 'I'. Thus, it is demonstrated that 'he*' preserves all the logical features of 'I', as far as the eliminability of modes of presentation other than 'I' are concerned and, therefore, is shown to be closely related to the use of 'I' (whether in thought or in speech).

[2] This consideration is of great importance. It appears to follow independently from Igor Douven's (2010) paper on the pragmatics of belief.

Third, Castañeda wants to establish that 'he*' is ineliminable, while 'I' can be (logically) eliminated. He claims that (28)

(28) I believe that I am a millionaire and Gaskon believes he* is a millionaire

is logically equivalent to (29)

(29) Each of two persons, Gaskon and me, remembers that he* is a millionaire.

However, all Castañeda has shown that the first person has been removed from the embedded proposition to ascend to the root clause. This result is not particularly cogent and does not prove that 'I' can be easily eliminated.

Fourth, Castañeda takes issue with Carl Ginet who transforms 'X believes that he* is ill' into the (presumably equivalent statement) 'X believes the proposition that X would express if X were to say 'I am ill'. Castaneda objects that the notion of 'saying that' would have to be enriched pragmatically. But the real objection to be raised is that one moves from an indicative sentence to a sentence that is heavily modal; and this is counterintuitive. However, Castañeda does not consider the possibility of pragmatic enrichments such as:

(30) John believes that he is ill (John thinks of himself under the mode of presentation 'Ego').

After all, it is this pragmatic enrichment which Castañeda's famous asterisk indicates. Castañeda wants to opt for a more radical thesis, according to which he* cannot be reduced to a simpler semantic/pragmatic analysis, but by doing so he ends up in trouble because he ends up giving up the possibility that immunity to error through misidentification which is notoriously associated with 'he*' depends on some pragmatic enrichment of 'he' (that is related to 'I') and, thus, makes it impossible to transfer at least the concept of immunity to error through misidentification associated with use of 'I' to the use of 'he'.

5 Immunity to Error through Misidentification is the Result of Pragmatic Intrusion

If my considerations on what Castaneda says are correct, immunity to error through misidentification is a property which 'de se' constructions inherit from the property of the 'first-person'. However, if my claim that 'de se' constructions involve use of an implicit EGO component through pragmatic intrusion, it cannot be true that immunity to error through misidentification is a semantic property of 'de se' constructions, although we can legitimately say that it is a pragmatic property of 'de se' constructions, being derivative from the EGO component incorporated into 'de se' constructions through pragmatic intrusion.

Before proceeding, I want to cast aside some considerations which may jeopardize my discussion so far. Feit (personal communication) says:

> The speaker of a 'de se' attribution (such as 'John believes that he* is clever') can fail to refer to the alleged believer, so there does not seem to be the kind of immunity in which 'I' cannot fail to refer. But the other kind of immunity (e.g. Shoemaker's) does not seem to be at all linguistic. One and the same belief can be immune to error when it is believed on first personal grounds (like introspection etc.), and yet vulnerable to error when it is believed on other grounds. So, it seems to me that nothing in the semantics or even pragmatics should guarantee immunity. On this point see Pryor 1999 and Recanati 2009. (Neil Feit, personal communication)

My reply to Feit is brief. Concerning the fact that the speaker of 'de se' attributions can fail to refer to the believer does not worry me. IEM is only limited to the relationship between the subject of the belief and himself. Concerning the second worry, I note that in this paper I try to reconcile epistemology and semantics claiming that IEM reconciles both dimensions. However, I want to bring out the consideration that epistemology is supervenient on the semantics. How can one introspect without using the first person? Is it plausible that there can be a phenomenon called 'introspecting' without first person attributions and the IEM which it can guarantee? My answer is negative.

Now, after this detour, I want to stress that my idea that IEM derives from pragmatic intrusion is not an implausible speculation. However, before taking a definitive commitment, I want to explore further the consequences of Higginbotham's claim that Lewis' property-based treatment does not do justice a) to the internal dimension of PRO/de se constructions; b) to immunity to error through misidentification. Let us put this claim to the test immediately. Lewis, and Feit after him, claim that a sentence such as:

(31) John believes he is clever

can be represented as:

(32) John attributes to himself the property: being clever.

Can (32) vindicate the idea of an internal dimension being associated with PRO? If (32) is interpreted, as is most plausible, as (33):

(33) John attributes himself the property: PROarb being clever

it is clear that PROarb cannot be associated with an internal dimension. There is some inter-subjective property which anyone at all can have, and which is not specific to anyone at all: hence there can be no internal dimension attached to this property. However, Lewis or Feit could insist that although there is no internal dimension associated with PRO, internalization can occur through attribution of the property (perhaps a sort of semantic effect of the predicate on the object). The doubt remains that if PROarb expresses an intersubjective dimension, even by a relation of self-attribution, it will end up expressing an intersubjective dimension and NOT an internal dimension. The situation becomes more complicated when verbs such as 'remember' are considered. Consider (34)

(34) John remembers falling down the stairs.

Now, undoubtedly it is difficult to transpose this through a Lewis-style analysis; the most we can say is that John attributes himself the property: PRO arb falling down the stairs. But PROarb deprives the property of any internal dimension at all.

I propose that we leave this undoubtedly complicated task to the followers of Lewis. (one way to solve this problem would be to resort to radical pragmatic intrusion and claim that the internal dimension is grafted pragmatically to the semantics). For the time being, the most we can make of this discussion is to decide whether we should derive immunity to error through identification from the internal dimension of PRO (or of a 'de se 'construction) or whether we should derive the internal dimension of PRO (or 'de se') from immunity to error through misidentification. This is not a trivial question. We can make this question even more complicated by asking whether the internal dimension is derivable from the implicit use of EGO in 'de se' constructions. After all, we could have the following logical chain:

EGO > Internal dimension > immunity to error through misidentification.

If the logical chain above has some validity, and we can establish without doubt that EGO is a pragmatically enriched component of the 'de se' construction, then we 'ipso facto' show that the internal dimension of 'de se' and immunity to error through misidentification are consequences of pragmatic intrusion and, in particular, the incorporation of EGO in 'de se' constructions.

Have we got independent support for such a line of thought? Recanati (2009) has insisted that not all 'de se' constructions involve immunity to error through misidentification and that proprioception is involved in guaranteeing immunity to error through misidentification. What is proprioception? While the discussion is undoubtedly complicated, Recanati distinguishes between feeling that something is the case and seeing that something is the case. For example, I can feel that my arm is broken or I can see that my arm is broken. In case I feel that my arm is broken, proprioception is involved and there can be no case for error due to misidentification (it is proprioception that guarantees immunity to error through misidentification). If I see that my arm is broken, but I mistake your arm for my arm and I make an identification mistake, then immunity to error through misidentification is not guaranteed. While there is some truth in this discussion, it deserves deepening. However, unlike Recanati, instead of placing the burden on the distinction between perception and proprioception, I want to make immunity to error through misidentification depend (at least in basic cases like 'John thinks he is clever') on the awareness of the subject of the thinking experience. Of course, awareness of the subject of experience involves some kind of self-awareness and not proprioception proper or only perception, as the kind of immunity to error through misidentification in cases like 'John thinks he is clever' is different from the cases discussed by Recanati and does not concern objects of experience but subjects of experience. Thus proprioception may not be the right concept in this case, because it is not the case that the thinking subject is engaged in proprioception in thinking (with some appropriate exceptions, of course: This thought makes me nervous; this thought makes me sad; this thought made me tremble; this thought made me faint). Thinking is the essential relation necessary for establishing a thinking subject. It is the act of thinking that establishes the subject and the identity between the subject of thinking and the subject of the thought. While the person who thinks (35)

(35) I think I am clever

is not particularly engaged in an interpretation process but provides the appropriate EGO concept by the act of thinking and this is enough to ensure immunity to error through misidentification, something different occurs in (36)

(36) John thinks he is clever.

Here the hearer/reader must simulate (as noted by Igor Douven in this volume) an act of thinking and in simulating this act she supplies an EGO concept through inference. Of course, pragmatic inference, utilizing the principle of relevance, independently supports the simulation process and establishes the anaphoric link between John and 'he' and also supplies the EGO concept which is incorporated into the thought by pragmatic enrichment. Having done so, having established that John thinks of himself as Ego and that this is guaranteed by the act of thinking in itself, the hearer can simulate John's mental state and, in particular, the internal dimension of the thought (he thinks he is clever or happy because he experiences cleverness or happiness) and the internal dimension of the thought serves to reinforce immunity to error through misidentification, already supplied through the EGO component pragmatically. If the EGO component has been supplied by the simulation of the act of thinking, one can also simulate that John **cannot** be mistaken about his own identity, that is to say about EGO.

From the above, I have deduced that the first-personal dimension of 'de se', as pragmatically implicated, is logically responsible for immunity to error through misidentification (we could also see this case as a case of immunity of error through misidentification being supervenient (in the sense of Chalmers 1996) on the ego-component of 'de se').

If, as I claimed, the EGO component of a 'de se' thought, is due to pragmatic intrusion, immunity to error through misidentification is a consequence of a pragmatic attribution in **reports** of 'de se' thoughts. In naturally occurring 'de se' thoughts which are not reported, it is the act of thinking and the identity between consequential acts of thinking that guarantees the EGO component, and, consequently immunity to error through misidentification. An opponent, at this point, may plausibly say:

> But of course there is no pragmatic intrusion here, since the thought is not reported. In what sense, then, is immunity to error the "result" of pragmatic intrusion – as in the title of this section?

While I grant that my answer to this stimulating and provocative question is tentative, and possibly needs further refinement, provisionally I am content with the idea that what binds the EGO concept to the thinker of the thought is a pragmatic process of coindexation. This process is made more visible when we have anaphoric chains (embeddings with multiple uses of 'I'). While surely the question of interpretation does not arise when the speaker speaks, the question of interpretation arises when the speaker remembers what he said. When the speaker remembers what he said he turns into someone equivalent to an over-hearer; and then matters of interpretation are relevant. Furthermore, the concept EGO becomes vacuous if it is not coindexed with some person in particular. And the coindexation process has some sense when the conversation makes use of other EGO concepts which are coindexed to different speakers. Furthermore, when the speaker tries to remember what he said, it is clear that pragmatics of belief as conceived by Igor Douven is applicable.

6 Why Immunity to Error through Misidentification is Logically Independent of the Internal Dimension of PRO/de se

Admittedly, the reasons I furnish in this section against making a logical connection between the internal dimension of PRO/de se and immunity to error through misidentification depend on some previous considerations on the inferential behavior of de se/PRO, discussed in Capone (2010). There I wanted to make the provision/expression of the internal dimension of

PRO/'de se' a pragmatic constituent of the report of the thought. However, after some discussion I moved towards the more balanced view that, in general, especially with verbs such as 'remember', the internal dimension of PRO is semantically associated with the specific construction (PRO, in our case). Then I have speculated that the internal dimension (constituent) supplied through the semantics is only partial or gappy (in line with views by Carston (2002) on semantic underdetermination) and that pragmatics is responsible in part for supplying a partial internal dimension. For certain other verbs, such as 'expect', 'know how', etc. I have speculated that the internal dimension constituent is fully provided through pragmatics.

Now, what are the consequences of the acceptance of the views above for the plausibility of the view that immunity to error through misidentification depends on the internal dimension of PRO/de se? The most immediate consequence would be that, in the most straightforward cases, like 'expect', or 'imagine' 'de se' constructions ('he*' or 'she*') should not be associated with immunity to error through misidentification. Thus, someone who expects to leave for Rome tomorrow may legitimately hold some doubts as to whether he himself is involved in the thought that he will leave for Rome tomorrow. But this is absurd. Immunity to error through misidentification must be granted for cases such as 'expect' and 'imagine' as well and this shows that immunity is not logically dependent on the internal dimension (which is implicated in these cases, if my view in Capone (2010) is correct.

In this connection, Neil Feit (personal communication) comments that:

> This is absurd, given one kind of immunity to error, but not absurd given another. So you need to be clear which kind is at issue. If I read about somebody, whom I take to be myself, but mistakenly, and what I read reports that this person will leave for Rome tomorrow, then I will expect to leave for Rome. But this expectation is not immune to error in the Shoemaker sense.

Let us see how one can reply to Feit. Suppose that I am at the airport and that in the waiting hall there is a big mirror. There is someone who resembles me closely (same clothes, same type of hair, same type of nose) and I take him (say John) to be myself. Suppose I read the information on the ticket he has in his hand that is about to leave for Rome. Then, considering that that person is to leave for Rome and has got a ticket in his hand and take him to be myself, I conclude that I can leave for Rome tomorrow and thus I expect to leave for Rome tomorrow. Then I expect to be able to leave for Rome tomorrow. Surely this is a false belief, one that crucially relies on misidentification. However, despite there being a secondary misidentification, there is not a primary misidentification, in the sense that I am attributing myself the property 'about to leave for Rome'. The property misattribution does not jeopardize the process of referring to oneself in the right way.

What other consequences follow from the fact that the internal dimension of PRO/'de se' is only partially semantically expressed and partially pragmatically articulated in cases such as 'remember'? If we grant the logical dependence between immunity to error through misidentification and the internal dimension of PRO, we paradoxically arrive at the conclusion that the greater the pragmatic enrichment in connection with the internal dimension of PRO/'de se', the greater the immunity to error through misidentification. However, I think nobody says or is willing to accept that immunity to error through misidentification is a gradable notion.

The internal dimension of PRO is useful in establishing immunity to error through misidentification only in those cases where there can be some doubt because a sentence is ambiguous. Consider, again an ambiguous sentence similar to one example by Recanati:

(37) He thought his legs were crossed.

Depending on whether he was only seeing his legs crossed or was also feeling them (proprioception being involved), (37) presents (or does not) a case of immunity to error through misidentification. The internal dimension of the pronominal 'his' is clearly projected through a pragmatic enrichment and, thus, proprioception is responsible for promoting immunity to error through misidentification. The pragmatically enriched internal dimension and proprioception go hand in hand and serve to reinforce immunity to error to misidentification in the sense of disambiguating a sentence which is interpretatively ambiguous.

7 Wayne Davis and the Pragmatics of Belief

In this short section, I cannot do full justice to Davis' (this volume) important and intriguing considerations on 'de se' attitudes. I merely point out that they show a similarity to my considerations, even if I am more explicit on certain matters that are of concern to the semantics/pragmatics debate.

Some disturbing problems are introduced when we accept, as is natural to do, Davis' distinction between 'thinking' and 'believing' or 'thinking' and 'knowing'. The problem of 'de se' seems to be related to double concepts or parallel concepts such as 'thinking/believing' or 'thinking/knowing'. In fact, a sleeping person, surely knows something like the proposition that say he teaches at Cornell University but we are reluctant to say that in the file where the belief is stored there is any mode of presentation of the referent/knowing subject that is particularly relevant say to action. What kind of action could the thinking subject be involved in? The undreaming subject has knowledge files that are indexed to himself without recourse to any particular mode of presentation. The fact that the referent is identical with the knowing mind is enough to ensure that knowledge is identified in the right way and then put to use in the right way when the sleeping subject becomes awake again. We do not need special words such as 'I' or 'Alessandro Capone' or 'the experiencer' or 'the knowing subject'. Identity in the knowing mind is established by the fact that memories are stored in the same mind. It is the files where knowledge is stored that establish identity and it is not even necessary to name those files. The files are in my mind and not in yours.

The sleeping subject, when he is not dreaming or when he is unaware of his dreams, cannot be an experience, a thinking subject, and cannot be involved in any real or mental action. Thus there is no reason to suppose that a special mode of presentation of the reference may be relevant to action or may be involved in different kinds of actions or be causally relevant to any action.

It follows that all cases of 'de se' thoughts that are genuinely philosophically interesting are those where we are faced with two coupled propositional attitudes: thinking and believing, thinking and remembering, thinking and expecting. Now I cannot clearly draw all implications of this new line of thinking inaugurated by Davis' genial remarks, but I can point out that something new may come out of this.

Davis thinks (in essentials) that 'de se' attitudes are to be explained by reference to deictic concepts. The thinking subject thinks of himself through a deictic. This is similar to what I have claimed myself, although Davis is more detailed. I was content with an 'I' concept, while Davis distinguishes between a deictic, a demonstrative and an anaphoric use of 'I'. The deictic use of 'I' is probably what is involved in 'de se' thoughts, deictic uses being licensed by what Davis calls 'presentations'. The thinker thinks of himself and has a presentation of himself that gives interpretation to his use (whether mental or verbal) of 'I'. I would probably depart from Davis in recognizing a dichotomy between the thinker's use of 'I' in thought, and the hearer's interpretation of 'I' or 'he*' in an ascription of thought. The thinker's use of 'I' in thought needs no special act of interpretation and involves immunity to error through misidentification in that no identity is needed or established, as there is no interpretation problem from the point of view of the thinker, who surely has a 'presentation' of himself which is perhaps tacit and who keeps track of himself and his identity through the act of thinking, rather than through the act of interpretation. The ascription of 'de se' attitudes (to someone else) involves an interpretation problem and tracking of the referent and mode of presentation used by the thinker either through a simulation process or through a pragmatic act of interpretation guided through the Principle of Relevance or both. The two perspectives are different and surely the use of 'I' in ascription of 'de se' attitudes involves both an internalized dimension and an external dimension. The deictic use discussed by Davis may be suitable to both dimensions, provided that we are clear that a 'presentation' or 'self-presentation' is involved in the thinker's awareness of ego, while a simulation or pragmatic interpretation is involved in understanding the presentation which the thinking subject experiences. Perhaps it would not even be incorrect to say that we can speak of a deictic use when referring to the hearer's interpretation problem, while from the point of view of the thinker there is no interpretation problem and thus it is not a matter of establishing the content of the deictic thanks to contextual coordinates. All that is required is the thinking act and the thinking act is its own context and also its own content.

Before closing, should we be content with Davis's exposition? While surely Davis' story resolves the problems he himself raised to Higginbotham's theory (along the lines of the problems I myself discussed), he does so in an ambiguous way. Is the use of the deictic a semantic or a pragmatic component? I was clear that pragmatics was involved in establishing the ego concept in 'de se' attitudes – even in cases of PRO, which are particularly problematic for Davis since PRO does not receive content from a context and thus is not easily assimilated to a first-personal concept). If we accept the considerations by Davis, we should have a double interpretation process. The provision of an Ego concept and, then, the interpretation relevant to a context of use (but this I admitted through lavish use of anaphora). From the point of view of the thinking subject, however, there is no pragmatics, since he has direct introspective access to his/her own thoughts. Pragmatics is involved only from a third person perspective, that of a hearer who tries to reconstruct the speaker's thoughts and self-awareness.

8 'De Se' and Modularity of Mind: Cancellability?

Finally it is time to examine the issue of the cancellability or non-cancellability of the 'de se' inferences I have discussed at length. Non-cancellability *per se*, as Grice was well aware, does not militate against the pragmatic nature of an inference. I have claimed elsewhere that explicatures are non-cancellable and the motivation I gave for this is that explicatures tend to be motivated by problems in the logical form, when a sentence is perceived to be blatantly false or a logical absurdity and pragmatics is there to help and remedy the problem. Since the explicature is the *Deus ex machina* of the semantics, I have claimed in a number of publications that it is and should be non-cancellable. This seems to fit in with a modular view of pragmatic processes, as argued in a number of publications. (See Capone 2010, Capone 2011 for detailed arguments).

We saw that the incorporation of the Ego concept was the Deus-ex-Machina of the semantic treatment à la Higginbotham, protecting this treatment from all the objections raised by e.g. Davis (this volume). But we also saw that various contextual considerations especially those invoked by

Jaszczolt (this volume) could be used to show the contextual variability of 'de se' inferences.

One further reason for opting for a pragmatic treatment of 'de se' is, of course, the parsimony of levels that it affords us, as we can eliminate at least an important meaning component from the semantics, obtaining it for free from pragmatics.

One last reason for opting for a pragmatic level of meaning in 'de se' attributions is the differential mechanisms of 'de se' thoughts in view of what happens in the mental processes of the thinker and of what happens in the mental processes of the hearer. The hearer is in a different position, both with respect to calculation of the Ego component and of the anaphoric links within the 'de se' ascription and with respect to the attribution of immunity to error through misidentification. The disparity between the position of the thinker and the position of the speaker/hearer in connection with pragmatic inferences was noted in an article by Jeff Speaks (2006), in which the author by reflecting on such a disparity arrived at very surprising conclusions (one of these being the following, which I do not endorse: "The fact that a sentence S may be used in conversation to communicate (convey, assert) p can be explained as a conversational implicature only if S cannot be used by an agent in thought to judge (think) p (Speaks 2006, 6)). The disparity between the thinker and the speaker/hearers stance to the inference is due to the fact that luminosity is available in thought, introspection being a guide to one's intended meanings, while the meanings projected by the speaker and understood by the hearer in conversation do not rely on luminosity but on an explicit effort to get intentions across through contextual clues and cues.

While immunity to error through misidentification is presupposed for the thinker in virtue of the continuity afforded by the act of thinking (thus immunity seems to be an 'a priori' category of first-personal thought) and by the fact that in thinking the question of misidentification cannot arise; for the hearer, immunity is a logical consequence of the pragmatic inference involved in assigning an ego component to the 'de se' thought. Simulation and, also pragmatic interpretation flowing from the Principle of relevance are clearly involved.

The disparity between the speaker's perception of himself as himself and the hearer's ascription of 'ego' to the thinker has interesting consequences concerning cancellability. The speaker's perception of himself as himself is clearly non-cancellable; the hearer's ascription of EGO to the thinker of the 'de se' thought is driven by contextual clues which lead the interpretation process in a certain direction, from which it is impossible to go back. So both from the speaker's and the hearer's perspectives it is impossible to cancel the EGO component of the thought.

Implicitly, I have replied to qualms by Coliva (2003) about the idea that immunity to error through misidentification depends on the ego concept incorporated in 'de se' attitudes. Her main objection to this idea is that the use of 'I' in 'de se' thoughts (whether explicit or implicit) is not enough to guarantee a first-personal thought. Coliva speaks of the split between speaker's reference and semantic reference. Given this split (which has emerged especially in the discussions of Donnellan's attributive/referential distinction), it may not be correct to say that immunity to error through misidentification depends on the presence of a pronominal like 'I' in logical form. The case discussed by Bezuidenhout (1997) (Bill Clinton: The Founding Fathers invested me with the power to appoint Supreme Court justices) does justice to the ideas and doubts exposed by Coliva. In the example by Bezuidenhout 'me' is used attributively, and not referentially. Of course Coliva does well to address the issue of the pragmatic nature of the incorporation of the EGO-component in 'de se' attitudes. However, we get the impression that her skepticism on the idea of deriving immunity to error through misidentification is not completely justified, given the heavy presence of pragmatic intrusion in propositional forms. Given the non-cancellable character of the pragmatic inference which I posited in 'de se' thoughts, it should not be a problem that 'I' can be interpreted attributively, rather than referentially. Of course, my claim that immunity to error through misidentification follows from the Ego-like nature of 'de se' should be confined to cases where Ego is interpreted referentially. But this is, of course, presupposed by the 'de se' semantic/pragmatic analysis. Again, we should distinguish between the interpretation of the construction (e.g. I believe I am happy) on the part of the speaker, which heavily relies on Mentalese (the speaker has direct access to her own thoughts, and, thus, ego as used in 'de se' constructions is clearly and directly referential), and the hearer. When we examine the dimension of the hearer, we see that the interpretative problem of 'de se' constructions consists in assigning, through pragmatics, an inferential increment that makes the logical form more plausible than it would otherwise be. The pragmatic enrichment, thus, could not make use of an un-interpreted EGO component, but has to make use of an interpreted EGO component, a component that is referential and not attributive. Of course, if we accepted a view in which the EGO component were assigned at the level of the semantics (say by identifying PRO with 'I' or an EGO-concept), then Coliva's objections could be certainly and dramatically applicable. But this is one more reason for opting for a semantic/pragmatic treatment, rather than for opting for a semantic treatment only. In a sense, we owe to Coliva the intuition that pragmatic intrusion resolves problems that would otherwise be insuperable.

9 Conclusion

This paper has been loaded with theoretical considerations and their consequences. Presumably we have reached a stage in which, pragmatics, which originated in philosophy and was propagated outside philosophy giving impetus to communication-oriented linguistic views, can serve to throw light on philosophical topics. I cannot exaggerate the importance of seeing the phenomenon of immunity to error through misidentification as a consequence of pragmatic intrusion. It is true; we have reached a stage in which the theory has become loaded with various consequences of previously accepted views. However, it is the nature of interconnected considerations and interlocking ideas one finds in this paper, that makes it rich, by provoking novel and perhaps radical discussions of phenomena of which we knew little or nothing, before putting some thought to pragmatic intrusion.

References

Bezuidenhout, A. 1997. Pragmatics, semantic underdetermination and the referential/attributive distinction. *Mind* 106 (423): 375-407.

Capone, A. 2010. What can modularity of mind tell us about the semantics/pragmatics debate? *Australian Journal of linguistics* 30/4: 497-522.

Capone, A. 2010. "Between Scylla and Charibdis": The semantics and pragmatics of attitudes 'de se'. *Journal of Intercultural Pragmatics* 7/3: 471-503.

Capone, A. 2011. The attributive/referential distinction, pragmatics, modularity of mind and modularization. *Australian Journal of Linguistics* 31/2: 153-186.

Carston, R. 2002. *Thoughts and Utterances*. Oxford: Blackwell.

Castañeda, H. 1966. 'He': a study in the logic of self-consciousness. *Ratio* 8: 130-157.

Chalmers, D. J. 1996. *The conscious mind.* Oxford, OUP.

Coliva, A. 2003. The First Person: Error through Misidentification, the Split between Speaker's and Semantic Reference and the Real Guarantee. *Journal of Philosophy* 100/8: 416-431.

Davis, W. 2013. Indexicals and *De Se* attitudes. *Attitudes De Se: Linguistics, Epistemology, Metaphysics*, ed. N. Feit, A. Capone. Stanford: CSLI Publications.

Van Der Sandt, R. 1992. Presupposition projection as anaphora resolution *Journal of Semantics* 9: 333-377.

Douven, I. 2010. The pragmatics of belief. *Journal of Pragmatics* 42: 35–47

Douven, I. 2013. The epistemology of *De Se* beliefs. *Attitudes De Se: Linguistics, Epistemology, Metaphysics*, eds. N. Feit, A. Capone. Stanford: CSLI Publications.

Evans, G. 1982. *The varieties of reference*. Ed. J. McDowell. Oxford: OUP.

Feit, N. 2008. *Belief about the self.* Oxford: Oxford University Press.

Feit, N. 2013. Belief Reports and the Property Theory of Content. *Attitudes De Se: Linguistics, Epistemology, Metaphysics*, eds. N. Feit, A. Capone. Stanford: CSLI Publications.

Grice, H. P. 1989. *Studies in the way of words*. Cambridge, Mass.: Harvard University Press.

Higginbotham, J. 2003. Remembering, Imagining, and the First Person. *Epistemology of Language* ed. A. Barber. 496-535. Oxford: Clarendon Press.

Huang, Y. 2013. *De Se* Attitude/Belief Ascription and Neo-Gricean Truth Conditional Pragmatics: Logophoric Expressions in West African Languages and Long-Distance Reflexives in East, South, and Southeast Asian Languages. *Attitudes De Se: Linguistics, Epistemology, Metaphysics*, eds. N. Feit, A. Capone. Stanford: CSLI Publications.

Jaszczolt, K. 1999. *Discourse, Beliefs, and Intentions*. Oxford: Elsevier.

Jaszczolt, K. 2005. *Default semantics: foundations of a compositional theory of acts of communication*. Oxford: Oxford University Press

Jaszczolt, K. Contextualism and Minimalism on *De Se* Belief Ascription. *Attitudes De Se: Linguistics, Epistemology, Metaphysics*, eds. N. Feit, A. Capone. Stanford: CSLI Publications.

Kaplan, D. 1977. Demonstratives. An Essay on the Semantics, Logic, Metaphysics, and Epistemology of Demonstratives and Other Indexicals. *Themes from Kaplan*, eds. J. Almog, J. Perry, H. Wettstein, 481-564. Oxford: Oxford University Press

Levinson, S.C. 2000. *Presumptive Meanings*. Cambridge, Mass.: MIT Press.

Lewis, D. 1979. Attitudes 'De Dicto' and 'de se'. *The Philosophical review* 88/4: 513-543.

Peacocke, C. 1981. Demonstrative thought and psychological explanation. *Synthese* 49/2: 187–217.

Perry, J. 1979. The problem of the essential indexical. *Noûs* 13/1: 3-21.

Pryor, J. 1999. Immunity to error through misidentification. *Philosophical Topics* 26/1-2: 271-304.

Recanati, F. 2009. 'De re' and 'de se'. *Dialectica* 63/3: 249-269

Sperber, D., Wilson, D.. 1986. *Relevance (second ed)*. Oxford: Blackwell.

Shoemaker, S. 1968. Self-reference and self-awareness. *The Journal of Philosophy* LXV/19: 555–567.

Speaks, J.. 2006. Conversational implicature, thought and communication. *Mind & Language* 23/1: 107-122.

Stalnaker, R. 1981. Indexical belief. *Synthese* 49/1: 129-151.

Part II

Epistemology and Metaphysics

10

The Epistemology of *De Se* Beliefs

IGOR DOUVEN

Some of my beliefs about myself I hold in an essentially first-person way. They are the beliefs I express, or would express, by using a first-person pronoun. Examples are the beliefs that I am employed by the University of Groningen, that my name is Igor Douven, and that Patricia holds a grudge against me. Philosophers have come to distinguish such beliefs—beliefs *de se*, or self-locating beliefs, as they are now commonly called—from beliefs that I hold about myself in a third-person way.[1] If, unbeknownst to me, I have just won the State Lottery, then my belief that the person who actually won the State Lottery is a lucky devil is about me, but it is not a belief I would express by using the indexical "I." Beliefs of the latter kind are often said to be merely *de re*.

There is a venerable tradition in philosophy of modeling propositions as sets of possible worlds; for instance, the proposition that snow is white is identified with the set of all possible worlds in which snow is white. There is an equally venerable tradition in philosophy of conceiving belief as a two-place relation, relating a subject—the believer—to the object of his or her belief, typically taken to be a proposition. In tandem, these traditions seem to leave no room for distinguishing between beliefs about myself that are *de se* and beliefs about myself that are merely *de re*. If I happen to be the winner of the State Lottery, but I am still unaware of this happy fact, then my believing that the person who actually won the State Lottery is a

[1] Castañeda (1967), Perry (1977), (1979), and Lewis (1979) brought the distinction to prominence in the literature.

Attitudes De Se: Linguistics, Epistemology, Metaphysics.
Neil Feit and Alessandro Capone (eds.).

lucky devil relates me to the set of worlds in which I am a lucky devil.[2] But that is precisely what the *de se* belief that I am a lucky devil does, too.

This problem has prompted some to model propositions not as sets of worlds simpliciter but as sets of *centered* worlds, thought of as sets of triples consisting of a world, a time, and a world inhabitant existing at the given world and time. In a variant of this proposal, *de se* beliefs have properties instead of propositions as their content; for instance, to believe *de se* that one is a lucky devil is to ascribe to oneself the property of being a lucky devil.[3] Other authors have attributed the problem to the traditional conception of belief rather than to that of a proposition. For them, the existence of *de se* beliefs indicates that belief is not a two-place but a three-place relation, relating a subject, a proposition, and a "way" in which the subject believes the proposition, or a "guise" under which he or she believes it.[4]

It is fair to say that these newer conceptions of propositions and of the belief relation do not quite have the alluring simplicity of the traditional views they are meant to replace. That is not a decisive argument against them, nor do I know of any such argument. Moreover, there may be reasons independent of the problem of distinguishing *de se* from mere *de re* belief that warrant adopting an alternative conception of propositions, or of belief (or of both).[5] But—I would like to argue—proper reflection on the epistemology of belief reports suggests that the problem in itself gives reason neither to abandon the classical conception of propositions nor to revise the standard view of belief as a two-place relation.

Before we begin, it is important to be clear about what exactly the task at hand is. It is decisively *not* to *define* the *de se* / *de re* distinction. By way of definition, the informal characterization of the two types of belief about oneself given in the opening paragraph above—a characterization that is also customary in the literature—suffices perfectly. No one has ever complained that the *de se* / *de re* distinction is vague or ambiguous or otherwise hard to make. Instead, the task before us is to give a satisfactory theoretical account of this distinction while keeping aboard the traditional conceptions of propositions and belief. That is what cannot be done, according to most theorists. My goal here is to challenge this near consensus.

---

[2] I am assuming, with the mainstream, that the actuality operator rigidifies the description "the person who won the State Lottery."

[3] See Lewis (1979). Feit (2008) contains a generalized and greatly expanded defense of this position.

[4] See, e.g., Perry (1979). For a recent proposal in this vein, see Maier (2006).

[5] For instance, Fodor (1994, Ch. 2) takes Frege's puzzle cases stemming from unknown identities as a motivation to conceive of propositions not simply as sets of worlds but as ordered pairs of such sets and syntactic objects. I am sympathetic to the proposal, if only because it helps us explain how pragmatic phenomena of the kind addressed by Gricean pragmatics can occur also in thought, and not only in speech; see Douven (2010).

I

The proposal is to account for the *de se* / *de re* distinction by focusing on a specific *epistemological* difference between the types of belief at issue. This is not to suggest that there is but one way to characterize the distinction in epistemic terms. However, I do believe that the difference to be highlighted below is both simple and phenomenologically plausible.

Central to the proposal are so-called belief reports, sentences of the schematic form "*S* believes that *P*," which we use to ascribe beliefs to people. More specifically, we shall be concerned with the question of what it takes to justify such reports, or what counts as evidence for these reports, and ultimately with what it takes to justify the propositions they express. The claim is that there is a marked difference between the sort of justification—or the sort of evidence—needed to warrant propositions expressed by reports of *de se* beliefs and the sort of justification—or the sort of evidence—needed to warrant propositions expressed by reports of beliefs that are merely *de re*. To flesh out this claim, I will rely on work in simulation theory, which I will now first briefly summarize.

In an influential article on the nature and status of folk psychology, Gordon (1986) argues that folk psychology is not a theory but rather a "capacity for practical reasoning" (1986: 171). Part of this capacity consists of our ability to "simulate" states of mind, both our own—in hypothetical situations—and those of others. Simulation here is understood as a kind of pretend play, in which one projects oneself into an imagined situation, or into the situation of another person, and then pretends to judge or decide a given matter in that situation. Such acts of simulation enable us to predict our own behavior in nonactual situations as well as to predict the behavior of others (in actual and nonactual situations). Imagining that I am in a situation in which I have to tell Jenny that her thesis still needs another round of revision and pretending to decide how to break the news to her enables me to predict how I will break the news tomorrow when I meet Jenny. Based on the assumption that other people are not too different from me in most respects, the same type of procedure enables me to predict how Jenny will respond to the news. And tomorrow, after my meeting with Jenny, it will help me to explain why she responded to the news the way she did.[6]

In the final part of his paper, Gordon tries to exploit his ideas about simulation to provide a semantics for belief reports. According to Gordon (1986: 167), by asserting

---

[6] A related proposal is made in Goldman (2006). Goldman offers a wealth of behavioral data and data from neuroscience in support of the hypothesis that simulation plays a key role in the practice of belief attribution and, more generally, mindreading. There are important differences between Gordon's and Goldman's proposals, but these need not detain us here.

(1) Let's do a Smith simulation. Ready? Dewey won the election.[7]

one says the same thing as by asserting

(2) Smith believes that Dewey won the election.

This claim may well be too strong. For instance, it is unclear whether, by uttering (1), one is claiming anything *about* Smith. One would rather seem to be claiming something about *Dewey*, albeit under the pretense that one is in Smith's state of mind. By contrast, (2) does appear to be about Smith; it says that Smith has a certain property, to wit, that of believing Dewey to have won the election.

Be this as it may, something is patently correct about the idea that simulation is closely connected to belief reports. In my view, however, the connection is to be found not so much in the *semantics* of belief reports, but rather in their *epistemology*, in particular, in what it takes to justify a belief report.[8] Gordon might in fact agree, even though he does not discuss the issue of justification in his article.[9] For, as he presents matters, the practice of simulation is not just *somehow* involved in our predicting the behavior of others; it is what *warrants* us in making such predictions.[10] And it is hard to see how that could be the case if the practice did not warrant the belief reports that it issues, and on which the said predictions rest.

It is to be stressed that simulation will not always be *sufficient* for the justification of belief reports: it is not as though pretending to be in someone else's position is guaranteed to give you enough information for making a warranted judgment about the other person's belief. More importantly for our present concerns, simulation is not always *necessary* for the justification of belief reports either. Another important source of justification is testimony, broadly speaking: a reliable person may have told you what he or she believes, or what some third person believes, or you may have read about a person's beliefs in a reliable written source. Such cases do not seem to call for any kind of simulation.

---

[7] By "doing a Smith simulation," Gordon means the act of hypothetically putting oneself into Smith's state of mind.

[8] Or, to be more cautious, the connection is *also* to be found in the epistemology of belief reports. Krzyżanowska (2013) develops a semantics for belief reports on the basis of something like mental simulation (actually, the kind of hypothetical thinking that is meant to be captured by the so-called Ramsey Test for conditionals) that is more promising than Gordon's proposal mentioned in the text.

[9] Nor does Gordon discuss the justification of belief reports in his [1995], which is more directly than the older paper concerned with epistemological issues surrounding simulation.

[10] See more explicitly in this vein Fuller (1995, Sect. 1). Various passages in Goldman (2006) suggest that he would also concur with this assessment of the epistemic import of simulation.

It might be added that, obviously, simulation is not necessary for the justification of reports of our *own* beliefs. For such reports, introspection may appear to be the authoritative source of justification. And even if the nature of introspection is still not fully understood, it is safe to say that introspection does not rely on the practice of mental simulation, nor, for that matter, on consulting external sources.[11] We do not put ourselves in our own current position (whatever that might mean) in order to consider what we would or would not believe in this position, nor do we consult others or books or news media for the said purpose.[12] One might mark the distinction terminologically by saying that the justification of reports of our own beliefs is *direct*, relying on introspection, while that of other belief reports is *indirect*, relying either on simulation or on trustworthy external sources (or on both).[13]

Obvious though this may seem, it is not quite true. To see why not, suppose that Hank Smith is with a friend in a bar which is smokey, overcrowded, and is not very well lit. Hank sees a person sitting directly opposite who seems to be staring back at him. Hank tells his friend:

(3) The man I am watching believes that he is being watched.

As it happens, however, there is no person sitting opposite to Hank. Hank is looking at himself in a mirror; he is staring himself in the face. Before and after he discovers this (which, suppose, he does at some point), he may believe that the person he is watching believes that he is being watched, and in either case this may be construed as a relation Hank bears to the proposition that Hank Smith believes that Hank Smith is being watched. However, the routine he will have to go through to justify (3) is very different before and after the discovery. Before the discovery, justification of that belief report requires embarking on a mental simulation, while after the discovery, doing a mental simulation is no longer necessary, and would even no longer make sense, given that then Hank can simply ask himself whether he believes that he is being watched. So, even though (3) reports a belief of his own, he cannot warrantedly report it on the basis of introspection, at least not initial-

---

[11] This assessment of the status of introspection was famously disputed by behaviorist psychologists. See, most notably, Bem (1967), who claims that we learn about our own attitudes (including, in our terminology, our *de se* attitudes) in the same way we learn about the attitudes of others. His "self-perception theory" has long gone out of favor, however, along with the rest of behaviorist psychology; see specifically for criticisms of Bem's theory, Jones and Nisbett (1972) and Storms (1973).

[12] We may consult external sources to find out what we believed (say) a year ago. But that is another matter.

[13] According to some theorists, simulation *also* involves introspection (but see Gordon (1995) for an argument against this). These might prefer to say that direct justification, but not indirect justification, relies *only* on introspection.

ly. Only after he discovers that the person seemingly sitting across him is none other than himself can he directly justify (3)—supposing he then still believes that he is being watched.[14]

By way of further illustration, consider Perry's (1977: 492 f) celebrated hypothetical case of Rudolf Lingens, the amnesiac who is lost in the Stanford library. The library has a copy of a biography of Lingens, which Lingens reads while he is lost in the library. One of the things he reads in his biography is that Lingens is the cousin of a spy. He thereby comes to believe that Lingens is the cousin of a spy, but, not knowing that he is Lingens, does not come to have the corresponding *de se* belief that he himself is the cousin of a spy. However, the amnesiac Lingens can ask himself whether Lingens, the subject of the biography, believes that he is the cousin of a spy. Perhaps the biography says as much. Or else Lingens may, helped by what he has read in the biography, try to put himself into the subject's shoes and consider in that hypothetical situation whether he believes that he is a spy. Nothing of this may yield an answer to his question. The important point, however, is that what Lingens will *not* do, or at least what certainly would not warrant an answer to his question, is just ask himself whether he believes that he is the cousin of a spy; introspection is simply not enough for Lingens to warrantedly report

(4) Lingens believes that Lingens is the cousin of a spy.

Naturally, once Lingens has regained his memory, he *can* warrantedly report (4) on the basis of introspection—supposing he then still believes that he is the cousin of a spy.

These examples suggest a way to differentiate formally between beliefs *de se* and beliefs that are merely *de re*. Consider again

(3) The man I am watching believes that he is being watched.

There is nothing in the grammar of this sentence that prevents it from reporting a *de se* belief. If Hank Smith were to use (3) to report a *de se* belief of his, then that might be unusual, but it would not be wrong, nor would it necessarily be misleading; for instance, all those around him might be aware that Hank is in a fanciful mood and means to designate himself by the phrase "the man I am watching."[15] Nor is there, in the proposal to be made, anything to the structure of the proposition that Hank Smith is being watched, or to the relation referred to by "believes" in (3), or the "way" that relation holds between Hank and the proposition that Hank Smith is being watched, that determines whether (3) reports a belief held *de se* or one that

---

[14] Which may well be: some other guests may be watching Hank, and he may be aware of that fact.

[15] Nor would it be unprecedented. In *De Bello Gallico*, Julius Caesar consistently refers to himself in the third person, also in relating his contemplations during the military campaigns.

is merely *de re*. Whether (3) reports the one or the other is a matter of whether Hank's being justified in believing the proposition expressed by (3) requires an act of mental simulation or the consultation of external sources, or whether introspection will do. If the former, then (3) reports a belief that Hank holds merely *de re*; if the latter, then (3) reports a *de se* belief of his. Similarly for the other example: depending on the conditions that hold for Lingens' warrantedly believing that Lingens believes that Lingens is the cousin of a spy, Lingens believes that he is the cousin of a spy *de se* or merely *de re*.

To make this suggestion precise, it is first to be clarified that the justification conditions of the proposition expressed by a belief report are not necessarily those of that report. Based on what he reads in what is, unbeknownst to him, his own biography, Lingens may be justified in reporting (4); introspection would certainly not do for that purpose. However, Lingens can also ask himself whether he—whoever he is—is the cousin of a spy. If he answers the question in the positive, he has thereby obtained direct justification for the belief report

(5) I believe that I am the cousin of a spy.

In Lingens' mouth, (4) and (5) both express the proposition that Lingens believes that Lingens is the cousin of a spy. So, we would end up with an inconsistent view if we were to take the justification conditions that hold for that proposition to be identical to those that hold for the reports that express it. It would mean that for Lingens to be justified in believing the proposition, it is necessary that he go through a process of mental simulation or consult external sources *and* that introspection will do for him to be justified in believing the proposition. But if both cannot be the case, which is it? The natural thing to say here, I believe, is that introspection is enough for Lingens to be justified in believing the proposition that he is the cousin of a spy, even though there are reports expressing that proposition that Lingens cannot justify on that basis. Indeed, it would seem odd to say that a belief report can be warranted on the basis of introspection but the proposition expressed by it cannot. And it is nothing short of a truism that if a proposition can be warrantedly held on the basis of introspection, then simulation or the consultation of external sources are not necessary for its warrant—even if they *are* necessary for warranting some *belief reports* expressing the proposition.

The proposal, then, is as follows: For any person *S* and any proposition that is believed by *S* and that attributes a property *P* to a person *S**,[16] if for *S* to be justified in holding the proposition that ascribes to *S** the belief that

[16] It will be noted that this is the only kind of proposition for which the question can arise of whether the proposition is believed *de se* or *de re*.

S^* is P it is a necessary (though perhaps not sufficient) condition that S go through a process of mental simulation, or consult external sources, then S believes *de re* of S^* that he or she is P. Thus in particular, if $S = S^*$, S believes merely *de re* of him- or herself that he or she has property P. If, on the other hand, introspection suffices for S to be justified in ascribing to S^* the said belief, S believes *de se* of S^* that he or she is P, which means that S believes *de se* that he himself or she herself has the property.[17]

I have five comments on this. First, it will be remembered that our task was explicitly not to *define* the *de se / de re* distinction. Instead, it was to account for this distinction within a framework that keeps to the traditional conceptions of proposition and belief. The above proposal is meant to show that this poses a problem only if one assumes that the designated distinction must be accounted for *solely* in terms of propositions and the belief relation. The proposal casts doubt on that assumption by pointing at the practice of reporting beliefs and, in particular, the justification conditions of belief reports and, via those, of the propositions expressed by belief reports, which do not appear to be definable strictly in terms of propositions and belief.[18] Specifically, it invokes an independently motivated distinction between ways of justifying belief reports and, derivatively, the propositions they express and uses that distinction to characterize the already informally understood distinction between beliefs *de se* an beliefs merely *de re*. Put very generally, in the current proposal the status *qua* being believed *de se* or being believed merely *de re* (if believed at all) of a proposition gets reflected by the justification conditions that attach to a *different* but *related* proposition, to wit, the proposition which ascribes the first proposition as a belief to the subject of that proposition.

Second, it is to be emphasized that the proposal does not boil down to a triadic view of belief as favored by Perry and other theorists. As far as the proposal goes, there is only one way of believing. It is just that belief reports as well as the propositions expressed by them may be associated with different justification conditions. These claims are obviously compatible with one another.

---

[17] Jonathan Adler (personal communication) brought to my attention that the tenability of the proposal depends on the contingent fact that we cannot directly inspect the contents of other people's "belief boxes." After all, a person with the right sort of science fiction equipment could introspect our beliefs as well as we can. However, if the proposal stands as long as the said kind of equipment has not been developed, I believe we are good for some time to come.

[18] This is already so because the concept of justification seems irreducible to the concepts of proposition and belief. Admittedly, on some versions of coherentism justification *is* to be understood purely in terms of propositions and the belief relation. But it is no exaggeration to say that *no* version of coherentism, however sophisticated, enjoys much popularity anymore. Even BonJour, who for many years was the main advocate of coherentism, came to regard the position as rather hopeless; see his (1999).

Third, while this paper focusses on only one self-locating attitude—to wit, that of belief *de se*—the above proposal for representing the *de se* / *de re* distinction for beliefs generalizes swiftly to other self-locating attitudes. For any person S and any proposition that attributes a property P to a subject S^* and that S hopes to be the case, if S can only be indirectly justified in holding the proposition that ascribes to S^* the hope that S^* is P, then S hopes *de re* of S^* that he or she is P. So, here too, if $S = S^*$, then S hopes merely *de re* of him- or herself that he or she has property P. If introspection suffices for S to be justified in ascribing to S^* the said hope, S hopes *de se* of S^* that he or she is P, that is, S hopes *de se* that he himself or she herself has the property. Similarly for the other propositional attitudes.

The fourth comment addresses a worry that one might have about the proposal. The worry is that the proposal makes every belief one holds *de re* about oneself come out as a *de se* belief. Given that *de se* belief is generally conceived as a particular kind of *de re* belief, that would imply a collapse of the distinction between beliefs held about oneself *de re* and beliefs *de se*. The argument for the worry would be that every proposition which attributes to oneself a belief that one holds merely *de re* can be expressed by a first-person belief report; for instance, the first-person belief report (5) expresses the same proposition as the third-person belief report (4). And surely—it might be said—introspection will suffice to obtain warrant for any first-person belief report. Thus, any belief that one may hold *de re* about oneself one holds, on the above proposal, also *de se*.

This argument is fallacious, however. It is a mistake to suppose that introspection will always suffice for warranting a first-person belief report. Consider that as long as I have not been informed that I won the State Lottery, introspection may not suffice to warrant reporting

(6) I believe that I am a lucky devil.

even if I do believe that the man who actually won the State Lottery is a lucky devil and thus, given our assumptions about propositions and the belief relation, do believe that I am a lucky devil. For if I engage in introspection and ask myself whether I am a lucky devil, the answer may well be negative (even if it would be positive were I to know that I won the lottery). If it is, then obviously that fails to warrant me in reporting (6) and hence it does not follow that I believe *de se* of myself that I am a lucky devil, although (by supposition) I do believe this *de re* of myself.

The final comment concerns another possible worry. I am directly justified in holding the proposition that I believe that I am a human being. This means that I have direct justification for standing in the belief relation to the set of possible worlds in which Igor Douven stands in the belief relation to the set of worlds in which he is a human being. Suppose, as seems plausible, that I am *essentially* a human being. Then the set of worlds in which I am a human being is the set of all worlds in which I exist. But that set is the same set of worlds in which I possess *any* essential property, like—let us say—the set of worlds in which I have the DNA characteristics that make up the essence of being human. Thus, the set of possible worlds in which Igor Douven stands in the belief relation to the set of worlds in which he is a human being is the set of possible worlds in which Igor Douven has certain DNA characteristics. And so, given that I am directly justified in standing in the belief relation to the former set, I must be directly justified in standing in the belief relation to the latter set. So, finally, it must be that I believe *de se* that I have such-and-such DNA characteristics. But surely that is absurd. I may not believe at all that I have such-and-such DNA characteristics, whether *de se* or *de re*. In fact, based on what happens to be a false theory, I may be mistaken about the essence of being human and believe that I have very different DNA characteristics. This problem may occur for any two necessarily co-extensive properties.

The proper response to the problem is to recall the point made by Frege, Kripke, and others that people who would appear to be eminently rational in a pre-theoretical sense may have contradictory attitudes toward one and the same proposition (as standardly conceived); they may believe that Venus appears only in the morning and that Venus appears only in the evening, that London is pretty and that London is not pretty, and that Paderewski had musical talent and that Paderewski did not have musical talent. As I see it, the above problem is nothing but another manifestation of that older problem. And no one should have expected that accounting for the *de se* / *de re* distinction automatically yields a solution to the Frege–Kripke puzzles.

This is not to deny the possibility that, once we have a solution to those puzzles, that solution will also furnish a theoretically adequate answer to the question of what distinguishes *de se* from mere *de re* belief. Indeed, if we take Frege's puzzle cases as a motivation to conceive of propositions not simply as sets of worlds but as ordered pairs of such sets and syntactic objects,[19] then that may also help with the current problem concerning *de se* belief. And Feit (2008, Ch. 6) argues that his property theory of content not only allows us to answer the question of what distinguishes belief *de se* from belief merely *de re* but also to solve Kripke's (1979) puzzle about belief. Three things are to be noted, however. First, the Frege–Kripke cases only present us with a *problem* if consistency is postulated as a necessary condition for rationality. Why is the lesson to be learned from these cases not simply that rationality does not mandate consistency?[20] Second, the possible advantages of the alternative solutions that were just mentioned

[19] As, for instance, Fodor does; see note 5.

[20] For a defense of a conception of rationality that does not require consistency, see Cherniak (1981).

will have to be balanced against the fact that these proposals are highly revisionary, imploring us to abandon well-entrenched conceptions of proposition and, respectively, belief. And third, it is to be recalled that the claim I am arguing for is *not* that we should stick to the traditional conceptions of proposition and belief at all costs. It is the weaker claim that the phenomenon of *de se* belief does not by itself provide reason for abandoning either of them.

II

Thus, the proposal is to account for the distinction between beliefs that are *de se* and those that are merely *de re* in terms of the justification conditions that attach to particular belief-ascribing propositions; some of those propositions can be justified on the basis of introspection, and others only by means of a mental simulation procedure or by consulting external sources (if they can be justified at all). It may be said, however, that this can at best be part of the story. For as it stands, the proposal naturally invites the question of how we *determine* which of those propositions do, and which do not, require either an act of mental simulation or consultation of external sources (or both) and which can be justified on the basis of introspection. If the answer forces us to take on board centered propositions after all, or to distinguish between ways of believing, or otherwise to revise our conception of belief, we clearly have failed to reach the goal we set for ourselves.

In the remainder of this paper, I would like to argue that our proposal does account for the *de se* / *de re* distinction in a way that permits us to maintain the traditional conceptions of proposition and belief. It will be seen, though, that how one will want to respond to the above question may depend on one's stand in the externalism / internalism debate about justification; that is to say, on whether one holds that justification requires some kind of awareness of the justification conditions being fulfilled—as internalists do—or whether one holds that a belief can be justified in the absence of such awareness, as long as the belief is connected in the right way to what it is about, or is formed in the right way, as externalists do.[21]

Externalists may well be in a position to dismiss the said question without much ado. If all it takes for a belief to be justified is its being connected in the right way to what it is about, or to be formed in the right way, then, it would seem, a person may be justified in holding the proposition expressed by a given belief report on the basis of introspection, regardless of whether she is able to determine that introspection is enough to justify her in holding that proposition. For instance, externalists may argue that as long as Hank

---

[21] Not all who call themselves "internalist" insist on the awareness requirement for justification. But see Bergmann (2006, Chs. 1 and 3) for a compelling argument to the effect that the requirement *is* an essential feature of internalism.

Smith is unaware that he is watching himself in a mirror, introspection may not be enough to connect in the requisite way his belief expressed by (3) with the truth of that report; he may have to embark on a simulation in order to be justified in holding the said belief. If, or as soon as, he becomes aware of the identity, introspection is enough to establish the requisite connection (supposing, as said above, that he then still believes that he is being watched). For that to be the case, Hank Smith need not first *determine* whether holding the belief expressed by (3) requires going through a mental simulation or whether an act of introspection will do. If he realizes that he is the man he is watching, then introspection will do; if not, simulation may be called for.[22]

Naturally, this response can be sustained only if introspection connects the belief expressed by a belief report in the right way to the corresponding fact if the reported belief is *de se* but not if the reported belief is held merely *de re*. While there is some disagreement among externalists about what counts as "right" here, the majority view is that rightness is to be understood in terms of reliability. Specifically, a belief is said to be justified iff it has been formed by use of a method that reliably produces true beliefs.[23] It seems that, in the case at hand, externalists can argue indeed that introspection is a reliable method for arriving at true belief-ascribing beliefs if the ascribed beliefs are ones held *de se*, and that it is not a reliable method if the ascribed beliefs are ones held *de re*, regardless of whether the latter beliefs are about us or about others. From our present post-behaviorist standpoint, the former is not contentious. And the latter should not raise any eyebrows either. It is not just that, being unable to distinguish between *de re* beliefs about ourselves and *de re* beliefs about others, we should expect to make many false reports of, and to come to hold many false beliefs about, other people's beliefs were we to form these reports, respectively beliefs, on the basis of introspection. As we saw above in the example involving (6), introspection is not even a reliable method for forming beliefs about what we believe merely *de re* about ourselves.

While externalists may thus reject the question posed in the first paragraph of this section as being based on a false presupposition, internalists will have to confront it head on. As stated earlier in the paper, for them justification requires some appreciation by the believer of the fulfillment of the justification conditions associated with the given belief, and thus appreciation of those justification conditions. It would be blatantly *ad hoc* to make an exception for the justification conditions of belief-ascribing propositions.

[22] "May," because Hank may believe *de se* that he is being watched even if he fails to realize that he is watching himself, for reasons explained earlier.

[23] See Goldman (1986) for the canonical statement of this view.

From an internalist perspective, a seemingly natural answer to the designated question might be that we determine justification conditions on the basis of some sort of "meta-beliefs," in this case beliefs about which propositions expressed by belief reports require indirect justification (simulation or the consultation of external sources), and which can be justified directly. But that way a regress threatens. For, on the conception of propositions we are supposing, a meta-belief of the relevant kind would consist of the relation between a believer and a set of worlds in which the proposition that a given person believes that he or she is such-and-such can be warrantedly held via direct justification, *casu quo*, requires indirect justification. So, for instance, Lingens could stand in the belief relation to the set of worlds in which Lingens can directly justify the belief expressed by (4). But given that (or as long as) Lingens does not realize that he is Lingens, it is unclear how this meta-belief could help him determine what is or is not needed for justifiably holding the said belief.

This might be taken as a (possibly further) reason for preferring externalism. However, here I would like to point out a possible response on behalf of the internalist that may just help to avoid the threatening regress. The response starts with the observation that, while largely ignored by mainstream epistemology, there is a role to be played in our epistemic lives by what one might call *epistemic directives*: directives telling us how to check, store, process, and more generally handle beliefs or candidate-beliefs under various circumstances. For instance, I take to be an important fact about myself as an epistemic agent that I tend to heed my old mathematics teacher's advice to double check the results of my calculations when several arithmetical operations are involved. It makes me fairly reliable in coming up with correct arithmetical truths (at least of the sort we encounter in daily practice) and thereby helps me to justifiably believe and even know such truths, which in turn makes me for others a reliable informant about (at least some) arithmetical truths. Other examples of directives are to resist the temptation to stereotype, not to rely on wishful thinking, to prefer expert advice to lay advice, not to accept testimony from known liars, to repeat in silence from time to time important information that is hard to memorize (like one's PIN code), and not to trust color judgments when lighting conditions are poor. Directives need not all be so general. For instance, a directive may tell me not to trust Alfie anymore, or just not to trust him on matters concerning Latin grammar.[24]

Internalists may be able to exploit this observation by arguing that the said justification conditions need not be specified by meta-beliefs—with the ensuing regress problem—but may be encoded in our mind in the form of

[24] Still further examples may be what Peterson and Riggs (1999) call "modification instructions," which, in their account of mindreading, guide the process of mental simulation.

directives. In particular, the suggestion could be that, if a person *S* holds a given belief merely *de re*, then there is something like the directive "Do a mental simulation, or defer to external sources" to be found in *S*'s mind associated with the proposition that ascribes the given belief to *S*. By contrast, if the belief is held *de se*, there is something like the directive "Introspect" associated with the said proposition. So, for instance, while Lingens still suffers from memory loss, we should expect to find in his mind something like the former directive associated with the proposition expressed by (4). Once he has regained his memory, that directive will be replaced by the directive dictating Lingens to introspect. To see how this may help with the problem in question, note that directives *address* us, are commands *directed* at us, but do not *refer* to us. In other words, they address us no matter how mistaken we may be about who we are. Put in yet another way, there is, in these directives, no constituent that one will first have to identify as being oneself if one is to comply to the directives. As a result, there is no regress problem.

Admittedly, there is presently not much to be found in the literature that could be adduced in support of the above suggestion,[25] and there are many fundamental questions to be answered concerning both the metaphysical status and the exact functioning of epistemic directives. One would want to know, for instance, whether directives are *sui generis* or derive from things we believe.[26] Also, how exactly do they get associated with and dissociated from propositions? I am happy to leave these questions, and more generally a defense of the suggestion made here, to those more drawn to internalism than I am. Meanwhile, I would like to argue that the idea of how epistemic directives relate to the issue of *de se* belief should have some appeal to all—externalists included—who wish to maintain the traditional conceptions of propositions and beliefs.

The point to be made is that, granting the conception of propositions as sets of possible worlds, directives of the kind assumed in the foregoing offer

---

[25] However, directives would evidently count as procedural knowledge in the terminology of researchers active in the fields of cognitive science and artificial intelligence. In epistemology, there has been some discussion of this in the writings of Pollock; see, e.g., his (1986, Ch. 5) and (1999).

[26] For instance, the directive to double check more complicated calculations might derive from my belief that people have some tendency to make mistakes in such calculations. However, I doubt that it does. As far as I remember, I simply adopted this directive on the basis of my teacher's say so. In particular, he did not (again, as far as I remember) try to motivate the advice, for instance, by telling the class that people easily get confused and are prone to make mistakes when they have to apply a number of different arithmetical operations in succession. And although presently I do believe that the advice was well-motivated precisely by the aforementioned reason, for a long time I simply heeded the advice without there being a proposition I believed that somehow explained why I heeded the advice. Yet even then, I think, the fact that I heeded the advice was a significant fact about me as an epistemic agent.

a distinctive theoretical advantage in modeling the kind of shift that occurs when we come to believe something *de se* about ourselves that previously we believed merely *de re* about ourselves (*de re*-to-*de se* shifts, for short). In the standard way of thinking about how our epistemic states evolve over time, our initial belief state is characterized by the smallest set of possible worlds that are compatible with everything we know; these worlds are also referred to as the "epistemically possible worlds." As we acquire new information, we eliminate more and more worlds from that set, namely, all those worlds that are incompatible with the newly acquired information. A crucial feature of this way of modeling the dynamics of belief states is that eliminating worlds is the *only* operation that is permitted on the set of epistemically possible worlds. This creates a problem for representing *de re*-to-*de se* shifts. For instance, it is hard to see how my coming to believe *de se* that I am a lucky devil after I have been informed that I am the person who actually won the State Lottery can be modelled by eliminating worlds that I previously deemed epistemically possible. Surely the information that leads to this shift is compatible with all epistemically possible worlds. (While there are worlds in which I did not win the State Lottery, there are no worlds in which I did not *actually* win the State Lottery, given that, as we are supposing, I won the State Lottery in the actual world.) And yet my coming to believe *de se* that the person who won the State Lottery is a lucky devil is a dramatic change in my epistemic perspective, a change that one would like to be able to represent. Note that this problem is neutral as regards the internalism–externalism divide.

If we take the idea of epistemic directives seriously, that does give us a tool for modeling *de re*-to-*de se* shifts. For instance, in that case my coming to believe *de se* that I am a lucky devil can be represented as my coming to associate a directive dictating to introspect with the proposition expressed by

(7) The person who actually won the State Lottery believes that he is a lucky devil.

and, correspondingly, dissociating from that proposition a directive dictating to simulate or to consult external sources. This way of modeling *de re*-to-*de se* shifts is open to internalists and externalists alike.

It might be thought that externalists have no use for directives when it comes to modeling such shifts, given that they can simply take *de re*-to-*de se* shifts to be reflected by changes in the conditions on how the belief relation between the subject and the propositions expressed by particular belief reports must come, or must have come, to hold if the subject is to be justified in believing these propositions. For example, my coming to believe *de se* that I am a lucky devil in the above example may be formally taken to consist of a shift in the justification conditions for the proposition expressed by (7). However, precisely because, in standard externalist thinking, such conditions may obtain, and so may presumably also change, without the subject appreciating their obtaining (or their changing), modeling *de re*-to-*de se* shifts purely as changes in the justification conditions pertaining to particular belief-ascribing propositions would fail to do justice to the fact that when we undergo a shift of the said kind, there is something manifestly "internal," something that we do appreciate, that changes. That much will have to be acknowledged by externalists as well. In order to model this internal aspect of *de re*-to-*de se* shifts, they may well want to go along with the above proposal and countenance epistemic directives in the role the proposal attributes to them. Surely externalists can do so without jeopardizing their position. It is one thing to admit that people are aware of the justification conditions of certain belief-ascribing propositions, and of changes therein; it is quite another thing to make awareness a general requirement for justification.

To sum up, the *de se* / *de re* distinction can be satisfactorily accounted for in a representational framework that keeps to the standard conceptions of proposition and belief. Doing so requires that we admit to the framework justification conditions that may attach to propositions, but that is something we will want to do anyway, for reasons obviously independent of the *de se* / *de re* problematique: we will not just want to represent which propositions are believed by a given person, but also which propositions that person is *justified* in believing, and even which propositions that person *knows*. Focusing on how we go about justifying belief reports led us to distinguish between different kinds of justification conditions that obtain for the propositions expressed by such reports. And that difference, it was argued, aligns exactly with the difference between those beliefs that we do and those that we do not hold *de se*.[27]

References

Bem, D. J. 1967. "Self-perception: An Alternative Interpretation of Cognitive Dissonance Phenomena," *Psychological Review* 74: 183–200.

Bergmann, M. 2006. *Justification without Awareness*, Oxford: Oxford University Press.

BonJour, L. 1999. "The Dialectic of Foundationalism and Coherentism," in J. Greco and E. Sosa (eds.) *The Blackwell Guide to Epistemology*, Oxford: Blackwell, pp. 117–142.

Castañeda, H.-N. 1967. "Indicators and Quasi-indicators,"*American Philosophical Quarterly* 4: 85–100.

[27] I am grateful to Jonathan Adler, Karolina Krzyżanowska, Emar Maier, and Jennifer Nagel for helpful comments on a previous version.

Cherniak, C. 1981. "Minimal Rationality," *Mind* 90:161–183.

Douven, I. 2010. "The Pragmatics of Belief," *Journal of Pragmatics* 42: 35–47.

Feit, N. 2008. *Belief about the Self: A Defense of the Property Theory of Content*, Oxford: Oxford University Press.

Fodor, J. A. 1994. *The Elm and the Expert*, Cambridge MA: MIT Press.

Fuller, G. 1995. "Simulation and Psychological Concepts," in M. Davies and T. Stone (eds.) *Mental Simulation*, Oxford: Blackwell, pp. 19–32.

Goldman, A. I. 1986. *Epistemology and Cognition*, Cambridge MA: Harvard University Press.

Goldman, A. I. 2006. *Simulating Minds*, Oxford: Oxford University Press.

Gordon, R. M. 1986. "Folk Psychology as Simulation," *Mind and Language* 1: 158–171.

Gordon, R. M. 1995. "Simulation without Introspection or Inference from Me to You," in M. Davies and T. Stone (eds.) *Mental Simulation*, Oxford: Blackwell, pp. 53–67.

Jones, E. E. and Nisbett, R. E. 1972. "The Actor and the Observer: Divergent Perceptions of the Causes of Behavior," in E.E. Jones, D. E. Kanouse, H. H. Kelley, R. E. Nisbett, S. Valins, and B. Weiner (eds.) *Attribution: Perceiving the Causes of Behavior*, Morristown NJ: General Learning Press, pp. 79–94.

Kripke, S. 1979. "A Puzzle about Belief," in A. Margalit (ed.) *Meaning and Use*, Dordrecht: Reidel, pp. 239–283.

Krzyżanowska, K. 2013. "Belief Ascription and the Ramsey Test," *Synthese*, 190: 21-36.

Lewis, D. K. 1979 "Attitudes *De Dicto* and *De Se*," *Philosophical Review* 88: 513–543.

Maier, E. 2006. *Belief in Context: Towards a Unified Semantics of* De Re *and* De Se *Attitude Reports*, PhD dissertation, Radboud University Nijmegen.

Perry, J. 1977. "Frege on Indexicals," *Philosophical Review* 86: 474–497.

Perry, J. 1979. "The Problem of the Essential Indexical," *Noûs* 13: 3–21.

Peterson, D. M. and Riggs, K. J. 1999. "Adaptive Modelling and Mindreading," *Mind and Language* 14: 80–112.

Pollock, J. L. 1986. *Contemporary Theories of Knowledge*, Lanham MD: Rowman and Littlefield.

Pollock, J. L. 1999. "Procedural Epistemology—At the Interface of Philosophy and AI," in J. Greco and E. Sosa (eds.) *The Blackwell Guide to Epistemology*, Oxford: Blackwell, pp. 383–414.

Storms, M. D. 1973. "Videotape and the Attribution Process: Reversing Actor's and Observer's Points of View," *Journal of Personality and Social Psychology* 27: 165–175.

11

Dynamic Beliefs and the Passage of Time

DARREN BRADLEY

1 Introduction

How should our beliefs change over time? Much has been written about how our beliefs should change in the light of new *evidence*. But that is not the question I'm asking. Sometimes our beliefs change without new evidence. I previously believed it was Sunday. I now believe it's Monday. In this paper I discuss the implications of such beliefs for philosophy of mind. I will argue that two-dimensionalism (e.g. Perry 1979) about the objects of belief are supported over one-dimensionalism (e.g. Lewis 1979) for two related reasons. First, two-dimensionalism gives us a more natural account of belief retention. Second, the extra complexity of two-dimensionalism turns out to be independently motivated by confirmation theory. So if the argument is correct, it will be an instance where our epistemology informs our philosophy of mind.

2 The Propositional Theory of Belief

The propositional theory of belief states that when an agent believes something, he is standing in a certain relation to a proposition; namely, the relation of believing it. This theory has two features that are in tension.[1]

First, the objects of belief, propositions, are eternally true or false. That is, if true at a time, they are always true, and if false at a time, they are al-

[1] These features are drawn from Perry 1979 who attributes them to Frege.

Attitudes De Se: Linguistics, Epistemology, Metaphysics.
Neil Feit and Alessandro Capone (eds.).

ways false. They do not vary in truth-value like the sentence 'It is Tuesday', which is true one day, false another.

Second, if a rational agent believes proposition P, but doesn't believe proposition P', then P and P' are different propositions. This feature individuates propositions in terms of their *cognitive significance*, which can be thought of as the role the belief plays in the life of the agent.

The tension between these features is brought out by self-locating beliefs. John Perry (1979) tells the story of how he followed a trail of sugar around the supermarket looking for the person who was making a mess. After walking in a circle he realized that he was the person making a mess and bent down to fix the bag of sugar. But what was this belief that he discovered? It can be expressed as 'I am making a mess'. But this straightforward belief presents a problem for the propositional theory of belief.

The sentence 'I am making a mess' doesn't have the first feature mentioned above – it is not eternally true or false. Instead, it is true for one person and false for another. So the belief Perry discovered is not completely expressed by this sentence.

Advocates of the propositional theory of belief might respond that 'I' is short for some concept which always picks out John Perry. Suppose this concept is expressed by *John Perry*. The proposition learnt would then be completely expressed by '*John Perry* is making a mess'. But here we run into of the second feature of belief – that if a rational agent agrees with proposition P, but doesn't agree with proposition P', then P and P' are different propositions. Imagine John Perry had amnesia and didn't remember who he was. Then he might believe the proposition expressed by '*John Perry* is making a mess' while not believing the proposition expressed by 'I am making a mess'. So rather than expressing the proposition believed, adding a concept that always picks out John Perry would turn it into a different one.

Perry argues convincingly that there is no way to turn the belief expressed by 'I am making a mess' into something that fits the propositional theory of belief. Although Perry focusses on indexicals, they are not needed for the problem to be raised. Take Salmon's (1989) example 'Frege is writing'. This sentence changes in truth value as time passes, so the sentence alone cannot completely express a proposition. And adding a concept that picks out a specific time – Frege is writing at t – changes it into a different proposition, for someone who has lost track of the time may accept 'Frege is writing' but not accept 'Frege is writing at t'.

So there is no point trying to fix the problem by trying to get rid of the indexicals. The problem is due to a fundamental tension between taking the objects of belief to have eternal truth-values and taking them to be individuated by cognitive significance. The cognitive significance of a proposition varies according to where the agent is located, but the truth-value does not. Most philosophers have given up one of the features mentioned above.

Temporalists hold that some beliefs have a truth-value only relative to a time. So for example 'it is Tuesday' could completely express a belief – the belief being true relative to Tuesday. So temporalists keep the second feature, that beliefs are individuated by cognitive significance, but give up the first, that they have eternal truth-values. Eternalists hold that all beliefs have eternal truth-values. So eternalists keep the first feature (eternal truth-values) but give up the second (individuation by cognitive significance). Two-dimensionalists[2] posit both types of objects of belief.

It is widely agreed that we need a notion of beliefs individuated by cognitive significance, so in practice, and in this paper, eternalism gives way to two-dimensionalism. So the debate is between two-dimensionalists who posit both temporal and eternal beliefs, and one-dimensionalists who posit only temporal beliefs. This paper argues for two-dimensionalism and against one-dimensionalism.

I think we need the eternal beliefs that two-dimensionalism supplies for two related reasons. First, temporalism does not allow an ontology of *dynamic beliefs* that are retained as time passes. Second, temporalism obscures an important distinction between two rules of belief update.

For concreteness, my main target will be the most influential temporalist theory (Lewis 1979). As a stalking horse, I will use Perry's (1979) well-known two-dimensionalist theory. Let's first lay out Lewis and Perry's theories, both of which were motivated by the self-locating beliefs mentioned above.

3 Lewis's Temporalism

Imagine a picture of all the possible worlds, spread out across logical space. Eternalists can think of a belief as locating oneself in a set of these possible worlds. When you believe grass is green, you believe that you have the property of being in a possible world where grass is green. You are locating yourself in logical space. For eternal beliefs the boundaries of where you are locating yourself match the boundaries of the possible worlds. But why should we restrict ourselves to such beliefs? Lewis argues there is no reason.

> We can have beliefs where we can locate ourselves in logical space. Why not also beliefs where we locate ourselves in ordinary time and space? We can self-ascribe properties that correspond to propositions. Why not also properties of the sort that don't correspond to propositions?...Why not?

---

[2] See Kaplan (1989), Stalnaker (1978) for two-dimensional theories of meaning. The framework has been applied to beliefs most vigorously by Chalmers (2002 and many other places). Their arguments are usually based on issues regarding assertion and modality. My arguments are based on mereology (first) and epistemology (second).

> No reason! We can and do have beliefs where we locate ourselves in ordinary time and space. (1979 p. 519)

The problematic cases above were just such beliefs. To allow such beliefs Lewis suggests that 'to believe…is to self-ascribe the corresponding property' (*ibid.* p.518). So to believe that I am making a mess is to self-ascribe the property of making a mess. And to believe that Frege is writing is to self-ascribe the property of being in a world, at a time, when Frege is writing. Call these *attitudes de se*.

Lewis denies that beliefs have an eternal truth value, and holds that they are individuated by cognitive significance. Thus, beliefs will figure in common sense psychology, as they will help explain and predict behaviour. What's important for us is what this leaves out. There is no place in Lewis's theory for a category of eternal beliefs. I will argue that this is a mistake.

4 Perry's Eternalism

Perry (1979) introduces a two-dimensional account. Beliefs have a content and a role.[3]

The content is the eternal belief. When I say 'John Perry is making a mess' and John Perry says 'I am making a mess', the content of the beliefs expressed is

< John Perry, making a mess, t >.

The content has the first feature of propositions – it is eternally true (or false).

But the content misses out a key feature of belief – its role in common sense psychology. One cannot generally tell merely from the content, what should be done about it; we also need to know *the way in which it is believed.* So a second dimension of belief is posited. Perry believes the above content with the *role* expressed by 'I am making a mess'. I believe it with the role expressed by 'You are making a mess'. Perry's belief causes him to bend down and fix the bag of sugar. Mine causes me to tell him he's making a mess. The role for Perry is analogous to all beliefs for Lewis – they figure in common sense psychology and are individuated by cognitive significance. But on Perry's account, each belief consists of a content as well as a role.

Which theory is better? This depends on whether the extra complexity of Perry's theory buys anything. Lewis has a unified account. All objects of belief are self-ascribed properties. Perry has a two-dimensional account. He can do everything Lewis can do, but he has a more complicated way of do-

---

[3] Kaplan (1989), influenced by Perry, also has a well known notion of content. But the issue is complicated because Kaplan is a temporalist, so I focus on Perry. Like him, my focus is on belief rather than assertion.

ing it.[4] I will argue that Perry's theory buys us unified beliefs. For Lewis, the *theory* of belief may be unified, but the *beliefs* are not. For Perry, the *theory* is less unified, but the *beliefs* are more unified. Perry allows us an ontology of *dynamic beliefs* – beliefs which persist through time and are apprehended with different roles. I will then argue that the extra complexity of Perry's theory is independently motivated, and is therefore a virtue.

5 Evans' Argument for Dynamic Beliefs

Let's start with Evans' (1990) arguments for dynamic beliefs, which I find inconclusive, but which will help set up my arguments. Evans argues that the basic unit of belief must be something that is retained over time.

> 'The thought units [beliefs] of the atomist [temporalist] are not coherent, independent thoughts at all, but, so to speak, cross-sections of a persisting belief state which exploits our ability to keep track of a moment as it recedes in time.' (1990 p.86)

If this is right, this would refute not just temporalism, but two-dimensionalism, as two-dimensionalists hold that temporal beliefs are coherent independent thoughts. Why does Evans hold this? His reason is given in the previous sentence, so let's extend the quote. Evans claims that:

> '[1] a capacity to keep track of the passage of time is not an optional addition to, but a precondition of, temporal thought. [2] If this is so, the thought units of the atomist are not coherent, independent thoughts at all, but, so to speak, cross-sections of a persisting belief state which exploits our ability to keep track of a moment as it recedes in time.' (ibid.)

In a moment I will deny that [2] really follows from [1]. But let's first consider [1] - why should we think that a capacity to keep track of time is a precondition of temporal thought?

I can find two arguments in Evans (plus a third passing suggestion we'll come back to). Here is the first.

> 'No one can be ascribed at t a belief with the content 'It is now A', for example, who does not have the propensity as time goes on to form beliefs with the content 'It was A just a moment ago, 'it was A earlier this morning, 'it was A yesterday morning'' (1990 p.86)

I don't think this is true. For a real-life counter-example, Clive Wearing has a memory of less than 5 minutes, due to a virus that damaged his brain in 1985. For a few minutes at a time, he is perfectly normal, except for his lack of memories. If you tell him it is raining outside, he will believe you, and repeat it back if asked what the weather's like. But he has no capacity

---

[4] Lewis: 'Whenever I say someone self-ascribes a property X, let Perry say that the first object of his belief is the pair of himself and the property X. Let Perry say also that the second object is the function that assigns to any subject Y the pair of X and Y' (p.537).

later on to form the belief that it was raining this morning, as by then, he will have forgotten it. Presumably Evans has to say that Wearing does not really believe that it is now raining. This seems implausible.[5]

Evans offers a second argument that a capacity to keep track of the passage of time is a precondition of temporal thought. This is based on an analogy with space. To show that our beliefs are based on our ability to keep track of time, he argues that our beliefs are based on our ability to keep track of space. He gives the example of objects moving, but not so fast that we can't keep track if we watch them. Suppose we start with a belief that one of the objects is valuable. On Perry's conception (that Evans is defending), the belief that the object is valuable persists over time. On the atomistic conception, we have a sequence of different beliefs, and

> 'it ought to be possible to have just one of the members of the sequence no matter which others accompanied it i.e. in the absence of any capacity to keep track of the object. But if that ability is missing, it is not possible for a subject to have a thought about an object in this kind of situation at all.' (1990 p.87)

Let's grant that Evans is right about this case. We won't know which object is valuable unless we remember which object was valuable a moment ago. But it's not clear this proves the point. While we sometimes need to track objects carefully, sometimes we don't, in which case Evans's argument fails to generalize. If the valuable object were the only shiny one, it wouldn't matter if we had failed to keep track of the object.[6] We could still have any of the atomic beliefs expressible at some time as '*that* (shiny) object is valuable'. (This would be analogous to the temporal belief that it is now raining.) Such cases seem to lend support to the idea that we should have an atomic conception of belief just as Evans's example lends support to the dynamic conception.

So Evans' arguments for his view that a capacity to keep track of the passage of time is a precondition of temporal thought [1] are inconclusive. But even if true, [1] does not support the conclusion that 'the thought units of the atomist are not coherent, independent thoughts' [2].[7] Let's grant [1] that a capacity to keep track of the passage of time *is* a precondition of temporal thought. So we grant that

> No one can be ascribed at t a belief with the content 'It is now A', for example, who does not have the propensity as time goes on to form beliefs with the content 'It was A just a moment ago, 'it was A earlier this morning, 'it was A yesterday morning'' (1990 p.86)

---

[5] Evans could perhaps adopt a functionalist or dispositionalist account of belief (Schwitzgebel 2002) and argue that the propensity to form future beliefs is one of the essential dispositions of temporal beliefs. But see fn 8.

[6] Compare Branquinho 1999.

[7] Thanks to Wolfgang Schwarz here.

Nevertheless, 'it is now A' and 'it was A just a moment ago' could be coherent independent thoughts. To see this, suppose that due to idiosyncratic features of human psychology, no-one could be ascribed a belief with the content 'I fear X' who does not have the propensity as time goes on to form beliefs with the content 'I hate X'. This doesn't imply that these are not coherent independent thoughts. So it does not imply that they are just two sub-sections of the same thought. Indeed functionalism and dispositionalism[8] entail that there are such constitutive connections between beliefs, but this does not entail that the beliefs are cross-sections of a single holistic belief state.

Nevertheless, Evans does make an argument in passing that I find much more promising.

> 'One belief cannot give rise to another by any *inference*, since the…belief[9] that would be required to underwrite the inference is not a thinkable one; no sooner does one arrive in a position to grasp the one side of the [belief] than one has lost the capacity to grasp the other'. p.86

I think there are a couple of responses the temporalist could make here. First, they need not say that the later belief is justified by the earlier one. Instead, they could say that both beliefs are justified by some earlier experience, and the persisting memory of that experience. Or perhaps they could say that the later belief is justified by the memory of the earlier belief. But this argument of Evans does draw attention to the fact that rather than an ontology of beliefs that persist through time, the temporalist posits a multitude of beliefs that only last for a limited period of time, before being replaced by new beliefs. This is the major weakness of temporalism, or so I will argue.

6 Dynamic Beliefs

Lewis asked what happens when we replace propositional attitudes by attitudes *de se*.

---

[8] Thus suggesting the functionalist or dispositionalist approach turns out not to have been such a friendly suggestion after all.

[9] I have omitted two references to 'identity beliefs' in this passage. Presumably Evans meant beliefs of the form 'A is identical to B' where A and B are atomic beliefs. But the atomic belief theorist doesn't think there is an *identity* between A and B. In fact he is committed to denying the identity of A and B, which is the source of the disagreement with the dynamic belief theorist. I think Evans should have used some justifying relation that falls short of identity. Thanks to Elliott Sober for spotting this.

> 'Answer: Very little. We replace the space of worlds by the space of centered worlds....All else is as before.'[10] (1979 p.534)

But things are not so simple. *De se* beliefs can change in a way that eternal propositions cannot. The reason is that *de se* facts change in truth-value as time passes, so *de se* beliefs must be adjusted to keep up. The question is whether this should be modelled as a case of belief change. Consider an agent who sincerely utters 'today is Monday' (on Monday) and 'yesterday was Monday' (on Tuesday). Do these sentences express the same belief? Lewis says no. Having the former belief is self-ascribing the property of being temporally located on a Monday, while having the latter is self-ascribing the property of being temporally located on a Tuesday. They are different properties, so they are different beliefs. But surely this is not really a case of belief change. This consideration is the crux of my argument so let's see what we can say to support it.

Consider that 'changing one's beliefs' is more naturally expressed in English as 'changing one's mind'. And surely no-one changes their mind when they change from believing it is Monday to believing it is Tuesday. Lewis's theory gives us the implausible result that we change our minds as the clock reaches midnight. So Lewis's theory is too fine-grained. Instead, we need a theory on which the belief is retained – we need an ontology of dynamic beliefs – and such an ontology is supplied by Perry's content.[11] (Of course, nothing stops us from introducing 'changing one's beliefs' as a technical term and stipulating that our 'beliefs change' as the days pass, but this would not be appealing to someone like Lewis who's trying to vindicate common-sense psychology.)

And as mentioned earlier the problem is not restricted to explicitly temporal beliefs such as 'it is Monday'. Many of our beliefs locate us in time implicitly. We cannot believe 'Frege is writing' without making implicit reference to our temporal position, so for Lewis we cannot retain this belief over time. Consider what Lewis's theory says about the belief(s) expressed by 'Frege is writing' at one time and by 'Frege was writing' at a later time. Has the same belief been expressed? Lewis's theory says no. We are ascribing different properties in the two cases. We are first self-ascribing the

---

[10] To be fair to Lewis, he makes this much quoted comment in the context of discussing *decision* theory. He makes no explicit comment about *confirmation* theory. See http://www.umsu.de/wo/2010/563 for more discussion.

[11] Richard (1981) offers a similar argument for eternalism. But notice we need not just eternalism, but an eternalism that allows for dynamic beliefs (see fn. 12). Kaplan's (1989) discussion of cognitive dynamics presupposes that beliefs are usually retained: 'Suppose that yesterday you said, and believed it, "It is a nice day today." What does it mean to say, today, that you have retained that belief?...Is there some obvious standard adjustment to make to the character, for example, replacing *today* with *yesterday*? If so, then a person like Rip van Winkle, who loses track of time, can't retain any such beliefs. This seems strange.' p.537-538.

property of being in a world at a time when Frege is writing. We are then self-ascribing the property of being in a world at a time before which Frege was writing. They are different properties, so they are different beliefs.

The depth of the problem can be brought out by considering the trouble Frege ran into with indexicals. Frege resorted to the view that all beliefs involving 'I' were incommunicable.

> 'Dr. Gustav Lauben says 'I have been wounded'. Leo Peter hears this and remarks some days later, 'Dr. Gustav Lauben has been wounded'. Does this sentence express the same thought [belief] as the one Dr. Lauben has uttered himself?' (1967 p.24)

Frege concludes that it does not. The reason is that Frege (1892) wanted to individuate beliefs by cognitive significance. Someone could accept 'I have been wounded' without accepting 'Dr. Lauben has been wounded', so these sentences have different cognitive significance, so they must express different beliefs. But Frege also wanted beliefs to have eternal truth-values, so he denied that 'I have been wounded' expresses a single belief when uttered by different people (as the sentence would sometimes be true and sometimes false). With these constraints, communicating the belief expressed by 'I have been wounded' is problematic. It has not been communicated if someone else accepts 'Dr. Lauben has been wounded', nor if someone else accepts 'I have been wounded'. So Frege resorted to incommunicable senses – no-one else could grasp the belief Dr. Lauben expressed with the words 'I am wounded'. This in itself is an unhappy conclusion. But to make things even worse, suppose that, *per impossibile*, someone changed identities. Then they could no longer believe anything they had previously believed using 'I'; the later 'I' would refer to a different person, so the belief would be different. Of course this cannot happen with persons, but it can happen with times.

The analogous view regarding 'now' is that someone cannot express a belief on one day using 'now' and then express the same belief at a later time. The same applies for other terms such as 'today' and 'yesterday'. And implicitly temporal beliefs such as expressed by 'Frege is writing' also cannot be expressed at a later time.[12]

But when it came to time, even Frege could not accept such a view

> If someone wants to say the same today as he expressed yesterday using the word 'today', he must replace this word with 'yesterday'. Although the

[12] Kripke (2008) interprets Frege as saying exactly this; sense is both eternal and atomistic i.e. cannot always be grasped at a later time. Kripke implies that the famous quote of Frege just below in the main text is confused; '[i]f Frege really means that we have expressed literally the same thought again, it is very hard for me to see how to reconcile this assertion with his other doctrines.' p. 204. Kripke argues that the resulting incommunicable senses are independently motivated. My arguments for belief retention also cut against this unusual variant of eternalism. In contrast, Evans (1990) argues that the same sense *is* expressed on different days p. 208.

> thought [belief] is the same its verbal expression must be different. (1967 p.24)

Frege thus seems to reject his early view (1892) that beliefs are individuated by cognitive significance in favour of a view that allows belief retention, and I suggest he would have been right to do so.

Let's press the point a little further. The view which I am attributing to early Frege and Lewis, that we countenance only sense (cognitive significance) and reference in our theory of belief, leaves out dynamic beliefs. To see how bad this is, consider the beliefs expressed by:

1. Snow is white

2. London is in England

These have the same reference (true) and different senses. Compare the beliefs expressed by:

3. Today is Monday (said on the 6th)

and

4. Yesterday was Monday (said on the 7th)

They also have the same reference (true) and different senses. Which means that for (early) Frege and Lewis, 1 and 2 are no more similar than 3 and 4. But this has clearly left something out. It has left out that 3 and 4 express the same belief – a dynamic belief. This completes my main argument against Lewis's view. Let's now consider an objection.

My argument relies on intuitions about belief identity. But an objection to the importance of such intuitions can be extrapolated from Lewis's work. Lewis (1980b) argues that Kaplan's (1989) notion of same-saying is insignificant. We can find an analogous argument against our notion of same-believing. I have changed 'said' to 'believed' in the following quote:

> (1) I believe 'I am hungry'. You simultaneously believe 'You are hungry'. What is believed is the same
>
> (2) I believe 'I am hungry'. You believe 'I am hungry'. What is believed is not the same....
>
> (3) I believe on 6 June 1977 'Today is Monday'. You believe on 7 June 1977 'Yesterday was Monday'. What is believed is the same....
>
> I put it to you that not one of these examples carries conviction. In every case, the proper naïve response is that in some sense what is believed is the same for both sentence-context pairs, whereas in another – equally legitimate sense – what is believed is not the same. (adapted from Lewis 1980b / 1998 p.41)

Let's grant this. Lewis omits the case where it is the same person at two different times:

(4) I believe on 6 June 1977 'Today is Monday'. I believe on 7 June 1977 'Yesterday was Monday'. What is believed is the same.

I put it to you that this example does carry conviction. As argued above, if we deny it is the same belief, we are saying that the agent changed her mind. To re-cap the dialectic, all we need to refute Lewis is one example where a belief is less fine-grained than a self-locating property. That is, where the belief is retained while the self-locating property changes. And 4 seems to me a highly plausible example.

7 Perry's Solution

How does the two-dimensionalist handle the problem of the passage of time? What happens to the old belief that today is Monday as the clock strikes midnight? On a two-dimensional model, the belief has a content that is grasped by a role. The content of the belief has two components – the property of being Monday, and the day (d)

< Monday, d >.

This stays constant. It is eternally true and, we can assume, eternally believed. What changes is the role with which it is believed. On Monday, the day is grasped with the role expressed by 'today'. But roles must change as time passes in order to express the same content. Call the process by which roles change over time *mutation*[13]. Mutation is governed by simple rules such as 'the role expressed by *today is Monday* at t, mutates into the role expressed by *yesterday was Monday* at t + 1'. So the same content is grasped, firstly, with the role expressed by 'today is Monday' and secondly with the role expressed by 'yesterday was Monday'.

The crucial result we need to obtain dynamic beliefs is that 'Today is Monday' said on 6 June and 'Yesterday was Monday' said by the same person on 7 June express the same belief. This is the intuitive result that Lewis's theory denies. To guarantee this result we need a sufficient condition on belief identity. I offer the following:

If sentence 1 uttered at t1 and sentence 2 uttered at t2 express the same content, and the role expressed by sentence 1 has correctly[14] mutated into the role expressed by t2, then both sentences express the same belief.

---

[13] Mutation applies only when nothing that was uncertain is learnt. Think of someone watching the hands of a clock go round in a silent room, with the curtains closed and the phone unplugged. This may be an idealization that is never achieved, but idealization is a standard part of modelling agents (e.g. Bayesianism). Also, we sometimes learn when it is from a position of uncertainty, such as wondering what time it is and looking at your watch. This is not mutation but conditionalization (see below).

[14] By 'correctly' I mean to rule out cases in which the agent has lost track of time. For it is not obvious that Rip van Winkle, who has unknowingly slept for 20 years, retains the belief he

(I offer no necessary condition on sameness of belief. For example, I leave it open whether sentence 1 and sentence 2 express the same belief when uttered by two different people.)

So the two-dimensional theory allows that a belief can be retained over time, even though it is grasped with different roles, is expressed by different sentences, and corresponds to different self-locating properties. I think this ontology of dynamic beliefs is needed to avoid doing violence to our common-sense notions of belief retention and changing our minds, and this is worth the extra complexity of a two-dimensional theory.

Of course, there is nothing to stop someone adapting Lewis's theory to provide for belief retention in some way analogous to that suggested here (e.g. Schwarz (forthcoming); compare Chalmers' (forthcoming) 'enriched propositions'). But this will complicate Lewis's theory, which will undermine the motivation for his view (simplicity). My suggestion is that the resources already provided by two-dimensionalism can be appropriated to provide for belief retention. This completes my first argument against temporalism.

8 Belief Dynamics and Conditionalization

So far I have argued that the extra complexity of two-dimensionalism buys an ontology of dynamic beliefs. But if you think simplicity is very important and/or aren't concerned about dynamic beliefs, you won't be convinced. So I will try to sweeten the deal by arguing that the extra complexity of two-dimensionalism is independently motivated. Once we take confirmation theory into account, contents and roles map onto the two rules of belief update – *conditionalization* and *mutation*. This is evidence that contents and roles cut the world at its joints, or at least that the extra complexity is not gratuitous.

Standard confirmation theory – Bayesianism – admits only one rule of belief change: conditionalization[15]. This says that the degree of certainty in a belief after learning a piece of evidence should equal the earlier *conditional* degree of certainty in the belief, *given the evidence*. For example, suppose your conditional degree of belief that it rains give a thunderclap is 0.9. Now suppose that you do hear a thunderclap. Then your new degree of belief that it rains should be 0.9. Formally, if an agent has prior probabilities $P_0(H_i)$ at t0, and learns E and nothing else between t0 and t1, then her t1 probabilities should be $P_0(H_i|E)$, where $P(E) > 0$. Succinctly, $P_1(H_i) = P_0(H_i|E)$. This model of belief update is widely accepted by confirmation

expressed on going to bed with 'today is Monday' after waking up and holding the belief expressed by 'yesterday was Monday'. See Perry 1993.

[15] Jeffrey (1983) conditionalization has been included in the orthodoxy, but it doesn't affect the problem of *de se* beliefs so I will ignore it.

theorists.[16] But the model does not suffice once *de se* beliefs enter the picture.

Conditionalization only allows belief change when something the agent was uncertain about becomes certain. That is, there must be some evidence E that initially was less than certain, and then becomes certain. But clearly someone who learns nothing of which they were previously uncertain and who grasps a belief with the role expressed by 'today is Monday' should no longer grasp the belief with this role the next day. As we saw above, we need new rules – rules of mutation.

So we now have two rules of belief update – conditionalization and mutation. If we stick with Lewis's 'simple' theory, we have one object of belief that is subject to two types of change. On Perry's more 'complicated' theory, we have two components of belief and each has its rule of update: content is governed only by conditionalization; roles are governed by mutation[17]. So we see that Perry's two-dimensional theory is independently motivated. There are two rules of belief change, so there *should* be two components of belief.[18] Lewis's unified theory merely papers over a crack in the foundations and obscures an important distinction.[19]

(We often apply both rules at the same time of course. Someone watching a long boring film should simultaneously update the content ('the film is long and boring') and the role of his beliefs ('it is now past the time when this movie should have ended'). This kind of case is typical. My argument merely requires that these changes can be broken down into the two components of conditionalization and mutation.)

This completes my second argument against temporalism. The temporalist has to posit two different rules of update that apply to his single type of belief. The two-dimensionalist has two components of belief that match the two types of belief change. So any extra complication in her theory of belief is independently motivated. Before concluding I will mention an important objection that I discuss elsewhere.

The neat bifurcation I defend requires that content only changes by conditionalization. And this requires that mutation doesn't affect content. But many people believe that mutation does affect content. If so, the independent motivation for the two-dimensional theory would disappear; we

---

[16] See Howson and Urbach (1993) or Earman (1992) for influential texts.

[17] I cannot say that roles are governed *only* by mutation. After all, if you discover some new evidence E, the role component of your beliefs will change. But this is parasitic on the change in the content component.

[18] This coheres especially well with Chalmer's (2002) view that primary intensions are functions from centred worlds – which contain times - to truth-values, and secondary intensions are functions from uncentered worlds to truth-values.

[19] Indeed most writers on self-location and confirmation theory have assumed a Lewisian theory.

could then posit one type of belief that is governed by conditionalization, mutation and interactions of the two. Several philosophers have taken this approach and tried to develop such a theory (Halpern 2004, Meacham 2008, Titelbaum 2008, Kim 2009 Schwarz forthcoming), motivated mainly by the arguments of Elga (2000) (Sleeping Beauty) and Arntzenius (2003) (The Prisoner) which purport to show that an agent in certain circumstances should change their mind as time passes despite learning no new evidence that was previously uncertain.

I argue in Bradley (2011) that this is a mistake. I defend the claim that mutation cannot shift a rational agent's degree of belief in any content.[20] If I'm right, then the arguments that mutation can change content fail. So the view that contents should change only due to conditionalization, and not due to the passage of time, remains intact. So contents and roles have different, simple, rules of update. So the two-dimensional theory of belief that posits contents and roles is independently motivated. And whether or not my arguments are successful, there is I think an interesting connection here between philosophy of mind and formal epistemology (Titelbaum (this volume) comes to a similar conclusion).

Epistemologists have spent a great deal of energy arguing about how beliefs should and should not change when new evidence is learnt. Philosophers of mind have spent a great deal of energy arguing about how we should make sense of self-locating beliefs. But self-locating beliefs can change all by themselves, without any new evidence, and this creates a problem of belief retention for temporalism. I have suggested that an ontology of dynamic beliefs that fits naturally with the machinery of two-dimensionalism solves this problem.[21]

References

Arntzenius F. 2003. 'Some problems for Conditionalization and Reflection' *Journal of Philosophy* 100: 356-70

Bradley, D. J. 2011. 'Self-Location is No Problem for Conditionalization' *Synthese* 182: 393-411

Branquinho, J. 1999. 'The Problem of Cognitive Dynamics' *Grazer Philosophische Studien* 56:2-15.

Chalmers, D. 2002. The Components of Content. In *Philosophy of Mind: Classical and Contemporary Readings*. Oxford University Press.

Chalmers, D. 2011. 'Frege's Puzzle and the Objects of Credence', *Mind* 120:587-635.

[20] This is a logically weaker version of Titelbaum's (2008) Relevance-Limiting Thesis.

[21] I thank Dave Chalmers, Branden Fitelson, Chris Meacham, John Perry, Elliott Sober, Mike Titelbaum and Wolfgang Schwarz for helpful comments and discussion.

Earman, J. 1992. 'Bayes of Bust' Cambridge, Mass.: MIT Press

Elga, A. 2000. 'Self-Locating Belief and the Sleeping Beauty Problem', *Analysis.* 60:143-7

Evans, G. 1990. 'Understanding Demonstratives' in *Philosophy of language: the central topics* Ed.s Susana Nuccetelli, Gary Seay

Frege, G. 1892. 'Sinn und Bedeutung' *Zeitschrift fur Philosophie und philosophische Kritik* 100.

Frege, G. 1967. 'The Thought' in P.F. Strawson (Ed.) *Philosophical Logic.* Oxford: Oxford University Press.

Halpern, J. 2004. 'Sleeping Beauty Reconsidered: Conditioning and Reflection in Asynchronous Systems', Proceedings of the Twentieth Conference on Uncertainty in AI, 226-34

Howson, C. & Urbach, P. 1993. *Scientific Reasoning: The Bayesian Approach* 2nd edn, Chicago: Open Court.

Jeffrey, R. C. 1983. The Logic of Decision (2nd Edition). Chicago IL, The University of Chicago Press

Kaplan, D. 1989. 'Demonstratives: An essay on the semantics, logic, metaphysics and epistemology of demonstratives and other indexicals. In J. Almog, J. Perry and H. Wettstein (Eds.), *Themes from Kaplan* pp. 481-566. Oxford: Oxford University Press.

Kaplan, D. 1990. 'Thoughts on Demonstratives' in P. Yourgrau (Ed.) *Demonstratives.* New York: Oxford University Press.

Kripke, S. 2008. 'Frege's Theory of Sense and Reference: Some Exegetical Notes' *Theoria* 74: 181-218.

Lewis, D. 1979. 'Attitudes *De dicto* and *De se*' in D. Lewis (Ed.) *Philosophical Papers*, vol. 1. Oxford University Press, (1983).

Lewis, D. 1980a. 'A Subjectivist's Guide to Objective Chance' in Studies in Inductive Logic and Probability, Vol. 2

Lewis, D. 1980b. 'Index, Context and Content' In S. Kanger and S. Ohman (Eds.) *Philosophy and Grammar*. Dordrecht: Reidel.

Lewis, D. 1994. 'Chance and credence: Humean supervenience debugged' *Mind* 103: 473–90.

Lewis, D. 1998. *Papers in Philosophical Logic*. Cambridge: Cambridge University Press

Meacham, C. 2008. 'Sleeping Beauty and the Dynamics of *De Se* Belief' *Philosophical Studies*

Nuccetelli, S. and Seay, D. 2008. *Philosophy of language: the central topics* Rowman & Littlefield

Perry, J. 1977. 'Frege on Demonstratives' *Philosophical Review* (86) p.474-97

Perry, J. 1979. 'The Problem of the Essential Indexical' *Nous* (13) p.3-21

Perry, J. 1993. 'Rip van Winkle and Other Characters' in *The Problem of the Essential Indexical and Other Essays.* New York: Oxford University Presss.

Salmon, J. 1989. 'Tense and Singular Propositions' in J. Almog, J. Perry and H. Wettstein (Eds.), *Themes from Kaplan* pp. 331-92. Oxford: Oxford University Press.

Titelbaum, M. 2008. 'When are Indexical Beliefs Relevant?' *Philosophical Review* p. 555–605.

12

De Se Epistemology

MICHAEL G. TITELBAUM

As this volume attests, *de se* constructions generate numerous problems in linguistics and the philosophy of language. Among other things, we lack consensus on the *contents* expressed by *de se* utterances. Disagreements persist over the *nature* of those contents—are they properties? propositions? structured propositions?—and over which utterances express the *same* content. Lewis (1979), for example, holds that you and I express the same content when we utter "I'm in New York," while Stalnaker (2008) takes my "I'm in New York" to have the same content as your "You're in New York" (spoken to me).

De se information also generates controversies in decision theory. Piccione and Rubinstein's (1997) paradox of the absentminded driver presents a well-defined decision problem for which it's controversial what strategy the agent should adopt. The paradox concerns a driver who loses track of his location; similar paradoxes can be constructed for agents who lose track of the time or even their identity.

These distinct areas of *de se* controversy intersect in epistemology. Positions on the content of *de se* utterances map onto positions on the content of *de se* beliefs, generating disputes over the objects of doxastic attitudes. Meanwhile, diverging opinions about the absentminded driver map onto diverging answers to the Sleeping Beauty Problem, a puzzle not about strategy but about an agent's degrees of confidence in a particular situation.

Epistemologists have a well-developed theory of how an agent should update her degrees of confidence as she gains information, called Subjective Bayesianism. But traditional Subjective Bayesianism founders when applied to *de se* degrees of belief. A number of alternative updating schemes

Attitudes De Se: Linguistics, Epistemology, Metaphysics.
Neil Feit and Alessandro Capone (eds.).

have been proposed, but they differ on the correct answer to Sleeping Beauty and various other problems. These schemes also differ in their assumptions about the objects to which degrees of belief are assigned.

Perhaps where these two controversies intersect, one can learn something from the other. If we settle disputes about the objects of doxastic attitudes, will that select among updating schemes, solve our Bayesian problems, and clarify decision theory? If we solve puzzle cases about degrees of belief, will our answers favor particular positions on the content of attitudes and utterances?

My main goal in this chapter is to answer "No" to the first question. That answer fits my intuitions—it would be *awfully* strange if the correct theory of content affected how confident agents should be in real-life events and how those agents should act with respect to them. (Lloyd's of London doesn't track developments in semantics journals.) But intuitions about disciplinary boundaries can be unreliable. And in any case I will point at the end of this chapter to a flow in the other direction: The correct answer to an updating problem may be more intelligible on one theory of content than another, and so favor the former over the latter.

So instead of trusting intuitions I will argue that theories of content should not influence updating schemes, by describing an updating scheme that solves degree of belief puzzles while remaining completely neutral about content. A *de se* updating scheme is built up in steps; three of those steps are particularly susceptible to influence from a theory of *de se* content:

1. The step at which the theorist selects objects to which credences will be assigned.
2. The step at which the theorist describes which credence-objects make trouble for traditional Bayesian updating.
3. The step at which the theorist offers his formal updating rules, which may treat certain types of credence-objects differently from others.

This chapter explains how a particular degree of belief updating scheme navigates each of those steps without making *any* controversial commitments about content. I won't present all the details of that scheme—for the full formalism, numerous applications, and arguments that the scheme's results are correct, see (Titelbaum 2013).[1] But I hope to describe enough of the scheme to convince you that questions about how an agent's confi-

[1] The updating scheme discussed here and in (Titelbaum 2013) has been modified from (Titelbaum 2008) in response to criticisms from (Moss 2012).

dences should increase and decrease over time can be answered without answering questions about what those confidences are confidences *in*.

Step One

A Bayesian modeling system represents an agent's degrees of belief over time, then evaluates those degrees of belief for rational consistency. An agent's level of confidence in a particular eventuality is represented by a real number between 0 and 1. (1 represents certainty that the eventuality will occur; 0 represents certainty that it won't.) I will refer to the agent's levels of confidence as "degrees of belief," and the real numbers our models use to represent them as "credences."[2]

A Bayesian model can't just have real numbers floating around; those values must be assigned *to* some sort of objects. Bayesians often assign credences to propositions, which nicely matches the view that propositions are the objects of degrees of belief. After all, if agents adopt doxastic attitudes towards propositions, why not represent those attitudes with numbers assigned to the same propositions? For instance, if John is equally confident that it is cold out as not, it seems natural to represent this degree of belief in the proposition that it's cold out by assigning a credence value of 1/2 to that proposition.

But suppose we want to contrast Jim's high confidence that Bruce Wayne lives in Wayne Manor with his low confidence that Batman lives in Wayne Manor. On some theories of propositions, the proposition that Bruce Wayne lives in Wayne Manor is the same proposition as the proposition that Batman lives in Wayne Manor. So if we are assigning credences to propositions, our model will have one number assigned to the one proposition in play. That seems to misrepresent Jim's two different degrees of belief.[3]

A similar problem arises with *de se* contents. Suppose it's Monday, but I'm uncertain of that. I can be highly confident that it's cold out today without being highly confident that it's cold on Monday. But according to some theories of propositions, on Monday the proposition that it's cold today just is the proposition that it's cold on Monday.

---

[2] Bayesians typically use "degree of belief" and "credence" interchangeably. I prefer to use "degree of belief" for the doxastic attitude in the agent, and "credence" for the real number a model uses to represent the intensity of that degree of belief.

[3] This argument parallels the argument in (Hacking 1967) for using sentences rather than propositions in modeling an agent's degrees of belief on the grounds that an agent may rationally assign different degrees of belief to two sentences that are logically equivalent and therefore express the same proposition.

Here we make the first crucial choice in building our Bayesian updating scheme. It's tempting to wheel in a semantic theory that distinguishes the content expressed by "Bruce Wayne lives in Wayne Manor" from the content expressed by "Batman lives in Wayne Manor." Perhaps we deploy a theory of propositions on which those sentences express different propositions, or we assign credences to a type of content more fine-grained than propositions and more closely aligned with cognitive significance. Notice that if we did that, our Bayesian modeling system would be hostage to the particular semantic theory employed. If someone (perhaps in one of the other chapters in this volume) convinced us that we had the content wrong, we'd have to start modeling again from step one.

But another option is available: We discard the assumption that credences in *models* of degrees of belief must be assigned to the same objects to which the degrees of belief themselves are assigned. Instead of trying to figure out the true objects of doxastic attitudes, I remain neutral on that question by assigning credences to sentences. Whether "Bruce Wayne lives in Wayne Manor" and "Batman lives in Wayne Manor" express different contents or not, those *sentences* are certainly distinct. So if we assign credences to sentences, we will have different credence objects available to represent Jim's two different degrees of belief.[4]

What does it mean to model Jim by assigning a credence of, say, 9/10 to the sentence "Bruce Wayne lives in Wayne Manor"? It does *not* mean that I think linguistic sentences are the true objects of doxastic attitudes. It means that we can ask Jim a question like "What is your current level of confidence that the sentence 'Bruce Wayne lives in Wayne Manor' is true in your current context?" If Jim answers "Oh, about 90%", we represent him in our Bayesian model by assigning a credence value of 9/10 to the sentence "Bruce Wayne lives in Wayne Manor." Presumably if Jim is rational his degree of belief that "Bruce Wayne lives in Wayne Manor" is true matches his degree of belief that Bruce Wayne lives in Wayne Manor. So the credence we assign to the sentence "Bruce Wayne lives in Wayne Manor" matches Jim's degree of belief that Bruce Wayne lives there.[5]

This approach is neutral among theories of content because, whatever you think the true objects of doxastic attitudes are, you'll eventually have to tell a story about how agents use those doxastic attitudes to assess truth-

---

[4] Technically, Bayesians working with propositions assign credence functions over a field built from a starting set Ω. My alternative assigns credences over a set of sentences closed under truth-functional combinations. See (Hájek 2010, Section 1).

[5] Here I'm idealizing away from the fact that agents may inaccurately report their own degrees of belief.

values of linguistic sentences in contexts.[6] Going in the other direction, you'll also have to translate information about an agent's confidence that a sentence is true in a context back into a degree of belief in a real object of mental content. So a Bayesian system that assigns credences to sentences (representing degrees of belief that those sentences are true in contexts) utilizes an element common to all theories of content.

Notice, though, that sentences do not change as the context changes. If I'm interested in John's confidence on Monday that it's cold that day and also his confidence on Tuesday that it's cold *that* day, I'm going to represent each of these degrees of belief by assigning a credence to the sentence "It's cold today." But this won't stop me from modeling situations in which those two confidences differ between those days, because Bayesians employ separate credence functions to represent degrees of belief at separate times. For instance I might label Monday t_1, Tuesday t_2, then represent John's degrees of belief by writing:

$$P_1(\text{It's cold today})=3/4$$
$$P_2(\text{It's cold today})=1/4$$

Again, let me be clear: Just because my Bayesian model assigns credences to the same sentence at t_1 and t_2 in representing John's attitudes towards the temperature, that does not mean that I (or my model) am committed to those sentences' expressing the same *content* at those two times. Since we already have separate credence functions for each time (and this is a device Bayesians used long before *de se* contents were a concern), it's just easier formally not to have distinct credence objects for those two degrees of belief. Choices in constructing a formal model need not track views about identity within the modeled domain.[7]

Step Two

So we model agents' degrees of belief by assigning numerical credence values to sentences. What constraints does rationality place on these cre-

---

[6] In (Titelbaum 2013) I call these linguistic sentences "claims" to distinguish them from formal sentences (strings of symbols) that play a role in Bayesian mathematical models. Our purposes don't require the use of formal sentences, so I'll avoid the "claim" locution and keep referring to natural linguistic "sentences." (Titelbaum 2013) responds to further concerns that sentences have the wrong fineness of grain for capturing cognitive significance.

[7] If an updating scheme that assigns credences to sentences works, one might get an inference-to-the-best-explanation argument for sentences as the true objects of doxastic attitudes. Just as the appearance of electron terms in our most predictive physical theories suggests that electrons exist in the world, the role of sentences in our best updating theories might suggest that sentences are the objects of belief. But I take this to be a very weak argument for a theory of content, even weaker than the argument I will present in this chapter's final section.

dences? Bayesians require rational credences to satisfy Kolmogorov's (1950) probability axioms. But those axioms relate an agent's degrees of belief at a given time to her degrees of belief at the *same* time, and so won't be our focus here. We're more interested in credence *dynamics*—how degrees of belief should change over time.

The traditional Bayesian dynamic rule is updating by conditionalization. Conditionalization relies on the possibility of asking not only for your *unconditional* degree of belief that a sentence is true in a context ("How confident are you that 'It's cold today' is true?"), but also for your *conditional* degree of belief that that sentence is true on the supposition of another. For example I might ask John, "You're not outside right now, but suppose for a moment that 'There are icicles hanging from the trees' is true. Conditional on that supposition, how confident are you of the truth of 'It's cold today'?" We would represent John's response in a Bayesian model as a credence in the latter sentence conditional on the former.

Updating by conditionalization requires unconditional credences at a later time to equal credences from an earlier time conditional on all the information learned between the two times. For example, if after answering my earlier conditional question John looks out the window and sees icicles hanging from the trees, his response to the unconditional question "How confident are you *now* that 'It's cold today' is true?" should be the same as his answer to my earlier conditional question.[8]

Bayesians' static and dynamic credence constraints—the probability axioms and updating by conditionalization—interact to produce interesting results. The most significant for us is that an agent who conditionalizes never loses certainties. That is, once a particular sentence receives a credence of 1, updating by conditionalization retains that maximal credence ever after. To understand why, suppose that instead of letting John look out the window I cover his eyes and lead him outside. He becomes certain that it's cold today. Even if I then ask him to suppose that there are *no* icicles on the trees, he will still be certain that it's cold today.[9] In general, the probability axioms demand that if you're certain of a sentence you continue to be certain of it conditional on any supposition.[10]

But this is *crazy* for sentences like "It's cold today." John may be certain that "It's cold today" is true right now, but then I lead him inside and let him cuddle up for 24 hours. When I then ask how confident he is that

[8] For more on conditionalization see Darren Bradley's contribution to this collection.

[9] Notice that instead of talking about how certain John is that the sentence "It's cold today" is true, I've started talking about how certain John is that it's cold today. I'll often use the latter locution because it's much less cumbersome than the former, but the latter should be read as the former wherever it makes a difference.

[10] Technically, that's any supposition consistent with your current certainties.

"It's cold today" is true in the current context, his certainty a day ago that that sentence was true does not rationally obligate him to be certain that it's true now. Yet that's exactly what an update by conditionalization would require.

It may be objected that the trouble here is not with conditionalization, but with assigning credences to sentences. It's fine for John to be certain while he's standing outside that it's cold today—the objection would run—and for him to retain *that* certainty 24 hours later. It's just that the doxastic object in which John is retaining certainty gets expressed at the later time by the sentence "It was cold yesterday." Certainties *should* be retained (the objector insists) just as conditionalization requires, but the cognitive contents in which they're retained aren't always expressed as the same linguistic sentences over time.

Can we keep conditionalization intact by assigning credences to objects more apt than sentences? While many updating systems have been proposed in the literature to manage degrees of belief in *de se* contents, and many different objects of credence have been tried, none of those proposals has left conditionalization unaltered.[11] Judging by this track record the options seem to be: (1) assign credences to sentences and maintain semantic-theory neutrality, then modify conditionalization; or (2) assign credences to another kind of object (perhaps the kind of object a semantics tells us is the true target of belief), then modify conditionalization anyway. For the sake of simplicity and neutrality, I adopt the first option.

Sticking with sentences as the objects of credences, updating by conditionalization clearly fails for sentences like "It's cold today," so we're going to need a new updating scheme. But before we propose that scheme, let's determine exactly *which* sentences are like "It's cold today" in the relevant fashion. That is, what class of sentences causes trouble for conditionalization?

Once again it's tempting to trot out a position from the philosophy of language. We already divide sentences into indexical/non-indexical, context-sensitive/context-insensitive, *de se*/*de dicto*, centered/uncentered, self-locating/non-self-locating, etc. There are fierce battles about what exactly these distinctions mean, and which sentences fall into which groups. ("S

[11] See, for instance, (Briggs 2010), (Halpern 2005), (Kim 2009), (Meacham 2008), (Meacham 2010), (Moss 2012), and (Schwarz 2012). Bradley (2011) proposes keeping conditionalization, but only for a subset of updates he calls Discovery cases. The only author I know who thinks we can maintain updating by conditionalization in every case just by getting the contents of doxastic attitudes right is Stalnaker (2008). For criticisms of his proposal and suggestions that he hasn't succeeded in maintaining conditionalization after all, see (Weatherson 2011) and (Titelbaum 2013). More generally, Pust (2012) argues that conditionalization can't be correctly applied to *de se* degrees of belief on *any* available theory of content.

knows that P," "It's possible that P," and "Tuna is tasty" are notorious loci of contention.) But do any of these distinctions neatly separate sentences that can cause trouble for conditionalization from sentences that can't?

Instead of invoking a distinction developed for independent reasons, let's focus on the specific problem at hand. Conditionalization runs into trouble because it requires agents to retain certainties. When can it be rational for an agent to stop being certain that a sentence is true? When the agent suspects the sentence's truth-value has changed.[12] So we can distinguish two types of sentences:

- A sentence is **epistemically context-insensitive** for an agent relative to two contexts when the agent is certain in both contexts that the sentence has the same truth-value in one context as it has in the other.
- A sentence is **epistemically context-sensitive** for an agent relative to two contexts when it is not epistemically context-insensitive for that agent relative to those contexts.

A few notes about these definitions: First, notice that a sentence is epistemically context-sensitive or insensitive relative to a particular agent and pair of contexts. A sentence may be epistemically context-sensitive for one agent but not for another (given their background beliefs), and a sentence may be epistemically context-sensitive for an agent relative to two particular contexts but not for that same agent relative to other contexts.

Second, epistemic context-sensitivity is about whether the agent *thinks* a sentence *may* have changed truth-values between two times, not whether the sentence actually *has*. Suppose airplane passenger Anne, headed east, was certain five minutes ago that she was above Missouri, and is now certain that she hasn't crossed a state line since then. Then rationality requires her—in accordance with conditionalization—to remain certain that "I'm over Missouri" is true, even if unbeknownst to her she has actually crossed into Illinois. In the other direction, if Anne suspects she may have crossed the state line it's rational for her to cease being certain of "I'm over Missouri" even if in point of fact she has not. So an agent who suspects that a sentence has changed truth-values may update in a way forbidden by conditionalization.

Third, epistemic context-sensitivity concerns an agent's opinions on whether a sentence's *truth-value* has changed, not whether it expresses a

[12] Agents may also rationally lose certainty when they undergo memory loss or (perhaps) when their evidence is defeated. For discussion of these phenomena and how the updating scheme presented here deals with them, see (Titelbaum 2013).

different *content* from context to context.[13] Once again, this choice utilizes an element common to rival theories of content. Lewis and Stalnaker may debate whether the sentence "I'm in New York" expresses a different *content* when uttered by different people, but if one of those people is in Manhattan and the other in Philadelphia there is no dispute that the utterances have different *truth-values*.

Finally, epistemically context-sensitive sentences are usually epistemically context-sensitive because they contain at least one **epistemically context-sensitive expression**. An expression is epistemically context-insensitive for an agent relative to two contexts when the agent is certain in both contexts that the expression has the same denotation in one context as it has in the other. An expression is epistemically context-sensitive (for an agent relative to contexts) if it's not epistemically context-insensitive. Since these locutions are somewhat cumbersome, from this point on I'll typically speak of sentences or expressions as "context-sensitive" or "context-insensitive," but keep in mind that I mean these phrases in the epistemic senses just defined.

Conditionalization can go awry when agents gain (epistemically) context-sensitive evidence or assign degrees of belief to (epistemically) context-sensitive sentences. If all the relevant sentences in a situation are context-insensitive relative to the agent in question and two times, the agent can safely update her degrees of belief between those times by conditionalization. Bayesians developed conditionalization to help them model agents like scientists, whose evidence and hypotheses presumably don't change truth-values over time. If an agent is certain she's in a situation like that, she should go ahead and conditionalize.

Why is it important to draw the line between troublemakers-for-conditionalization and non-troublemakers in exactly the right place? That importance comes out in the infamous

> **Sleeping Beauty Problem:** A student named Beauty arrives on Sunday to volunteer for an experiment. She will be put to sleep Sunday night, then the experimenters will flip a fair coin. If it comes up heads, they will awaken her on Monday morning, chat with her for a bit, then put her back to sleep. If the coin comes up tails, they will engage in the same Monday process then *erase all her memories of her Monday awakening*, awaken her Tuesday morning, chat with her for a bit, then put her back to sleep.

[13] Here I follow MacFarlane (2005) in using the term "context-sensitive" to designate changes in truth-value. (MacFarlane uses "indexical" to designate changes in content.)

> Beauty is told all of this information, then put to sleep. She awakens Monday morning, but because of the possibility of memory erasure she is uncertain whether it's Monday. At that point, how confident should she be that the coin came up heads?[14]

An answer to the Sleeping Beauty Problem popular among philosophers says that all this business about going to sleep, waking up, memory erasure, etc. is irrelevant to Beauty's degrees of belief concerning the coin. She's certain it's a fair coin, no one has told her how it came out, so when she awakens on Monday morning she should have a 1/2 degree of belief that it came up heads, just as she did on Sunday night.

Elga (2000) adds to the story by imagining that after Beauty awakens on Monday morning and forms a degree of belief in heads, the experimenters tell her that it's Monday. Elga asks what Beauty's degree of belief in heads should be then. According to the popular "halfer" answer just described, information about what day it is *still* shouldn't make any difference; Beauty's degree of belief in heads should remain at 1/2 after she learns it's Monday.[15]

Yet this position runs into a problem. Skipping the details, a straightforward application of conditionalization shows that Beauty's Monday night (after she's been told it's Monday) degree of belief in heads should be greater than her Monday morning (before she's been told it's Monday) degree of belief in heads.[16] So if you think Beauty should update on the information that it's Monday by conditionalizing her degree of belief in heads, you can't maintain the popular (and seemingly reasonable) stay-at-1/2-throughout position.

---

[14] The Sleeping Beauty Problem was introduced to the philosophical literature by Elga (2000) as a modification of Piccione and Rubinstein's absentminded driver paradox.

[15] While Lewis (2001) thought Beauty's degree of belief in heads should be 1/2 when she first awakens, he thought that degree of belief should increase when she learns it's Monday (because of the conditionalization fact I'm about to describe). The rival position (sometimes called "double-halfing") according to which Beauty should keep her degree of belief at 1/2 throughout the experiment (including when she learns it's Monday) is currently much more popular in the literature.

[16] A quick explanation of the details: Beauty is certain on Monday morning that it's either Monday or Tuesday, so her Monday morning degree of belief in heads is a weighted average of her degree of belief in heads conditional on its being Monday and her degree of belief in heads conditional on its being Tuesday. The latter is zero. So Beauty's Monday morning degree of belief in heads conditional on its being Monday is greater than her unconditional degree of belief in heads. If she updates by conditionalizing when she learns that it's Monday, Beauty's Monday night degree of belief in heads equals her Monday morning degree of belief in heads conditional on its being Monday. So if she conditionalizes, Beauty's Monday night degree of belief in heads is greater than her Monday morning degree of belief in heads.

Meacham (2008)[17] notices the trouble sentences like "It's cold today" or "Today is Monday" cause for conditionalization, and identifies the culprit class as centered propositions (a distinction among propositions he takes from Lewis's theory of content). Meacham thinks conditionalization applies to uncentered propositions, but fails when centered propositions get involved. Since the proposition that it's Monday—the proposition Beauty learns between Monday morning and Monday night—is centered, Meacham doesn't require Beauty to update by conditionalization between those two times. So it's consistent with Meacham's position for her to assign a 1/2 degree of belief to heads at both times.

Yet "Today is Monday" is not an epistemically context-sensitive sentence for Beauty between Monday morning and Monday night. Although Beauty doesn't know what day it is on Monday morning, she is certain that whatever day it is, it'll still be the same day after she chats with the experimenters. Similarly, after she learns it's Monday Beauty is certain that it was Monday before she was aware of that fact. So Beauty is certain both on Monday morning and on Monday night that "today" has the same denotation at both times. "Today" is epistemically context-insensitive for Beauty relative to those two times, and "Today is Monday" is as well. By our classification of trouble-spots for conditionalization, Beauty must update by conditionalizing between Monday morning and Monday night, which rules out the stay-at-1/2-throughout position on Sleeping Beauty. Correctly identifying conditionalization's trouble-spots rules out a popular position on a controversial problem.

Step Three

To understand the updating scheme I use to replace conditionalization, consider what you would do if I asked whether the first Saturday after two weeks before tomorrow is one week after the 29th of last month. The first thing you might do to answer this complicated question is translate it into purely "absolute" terms: Tomorrow is the 16th, two weeks before that was the 2nd, this is February 2011 so the first Saturday after the 2nd is.... When faced with a complex situation involving context-sensitivity we often start by re-expressing the problem in context-insensitive, "absolute" terms. We then work through the problem in those terms, and recover any context-sensitive conclusions we need at the very end of the process.

That's the core idea of my updating scheme. When faced with a problem involving both context-sensitive and context-insensitive sentences,

---

[17] Since that article, Meacham has somewhat altered his position on *de se* updating. The new position is presented in Meacham (2010).

we first set aside the context-sensitive sentences and attend exclusively to the context-insensitives. Focusing just on those, we update credences by conditionalization. We can safely do this because we know that (epistemically) context-insensitive sentences cause no problems for conditionalization. Once conditionalization gives us a credence distribution over context-insensitive sentences, we draw any additional conclusions we need about context-sensitive credences.

For example:

> **Jet plane:** At t_1 the pilot of Anne's plane has just announced that they're above Missouri, and Anne's watch reads 3pm. Anne is certain that both the pilot and her watch are infallible. The little screen on the back of the seat in front her also says it's 3pm and shows an icon of an airplane floating above Missouri. Some time later (at t_2) Anne notices that her watch says 3:30pm, but the screen still reads 3pm and shows the plane over Missouri. How confident should Anne be at t_2 that she's still in Missouri?

Here's how our strategy applies to this case: If we were to conditionalize all the sentences figuring in this story, Anne's certainty at t_1 that she's over Missouri would generate a certainty at t_2 that she's over Missouri. But that's not right—there's a serious possibility here that her screen is on the fritz.

So instead of thinking about sentences like "I'm now over Missouri," consider sentences like "When my watch reads 3pm I'm over Missouri" and "When my watch reads 3:30pm I'm over Missouri." If we ignore context-sensitive "now" sentences and focus on context-insensitive "When my watch reads…" sentences, it's rational for Anne to retain at t_2 certainties she had at t_1.[18] So among "When my watch reads…" sentences, we may conditionalize freely. Conditionalization will tell us, for example, that Anne's t_2 degree of belief in "When my watch reads 3:30pm I'm over Missouri" is her t_1 degree of belief that that sentence is true conditional on the context-insensitive sentences she learns between the two times—sentences like "The screen looks the same when my watch reads 3:30pm as when my watch reads 3pm." Though Anne doesn't know at t_1 that her screen is going to go on the fritz, we can ask her at that time how confident she *would* be in the screen's deliverances were it to freeze for half an hour. Whatever confidence she expresses in the screen's *hypothetical* reliability at t_1 is what she

[18] Notice that the presence of "my" and "I" in "When my watch reads 3pm I'm over Missouri" does not make that sentence epistemically context-sensitive. Anne is certain at all times in this story that "I" picks out the same denotation at t_2 as it does at t_1; neither the personal-pronoun expressions nor the overall sentence are context-sensitive in our epistemic sense.

should assign to its *actual* reliability at t_2 when the screen has indeed frozen up.

Finally, once we determine Anne's required t_2 degree of belief in the context-insensitive "When my watch reads 3:30pm I'm over Missouri," we can also determine her degrees of belief in various context-sensitive sentences. For example, at t_2 Anne is certain that "I'm now over Missouri" is true just in case "When my watch reads 3:30pm I'm over Missouri," so we can use her degree of belief in the latter to determine her degree of belief in the former. This completes our strategy of moving to a context-insensitive language, updating by conditionalization, and then drawing conclusions about context-sensitive sentences where necessary.

While this strategy feels intuitive (and mimics how we often think about complex cases involving context-sensitivity), it comes with an important *caveat*. Any time we set aside one set of sentences to work exclusively with another, we need to make sure we haven't set aside crucial information affecting degrees of belief in the sentences that remain.

An analogy: Suppose you've taken bets on a horse race, and are responsible for paying them out accurately. I report the race results to you, but I tell you only the order in which the odd-numbered horses finished. You can't just focus on the odd-numbered horses, calculate the payouts, and leave the even-numbered horses to consider later. Without the even-numbered information, you can't figure out whether any of the odd-numbered horses won, placed, or showed. Information from outside your restricted circle of attention is crucial to determining how things stand within that circle.

Similarly, when we set aside context-sensitive sentences in our strategy's first step, we have to make sure we aren't ignoring context-sensitive information the agent learns that affects her degrees of belief in the context-*in*sensitive sentences that remain.

This isn't a problem in the jet plane story. Anne learns things between t_1 and t_2 that can be expressed in context-sensitive sentences, such as "The screen looks the same now as it did a half-hour ago." But everything she learns has an equivalent context-insensitive formulation, such as "The screen looks the same when my watch reads 3:30pm as when my watch reads 3pm."[19] Since all the context-sensitive sentences that play a crucial role in the story have context-insensitive equivalents for Anne, we needn't worry that when we temporarily ignore context-sensitives we leave out crucial information.

---

[19] I've made the verb tenses in this sentence "eternal" (though somewhat awkward) to keep them from indicating a particular present time.

Going back to the horse-race analogy, imagine you knew as part of your background evidence that every even-numbered horse would come in right behind the horse with a number one lower. Then giving you the order of the odd-numbered horses would tell you everything you needed to know (about both the odd-numbered and even-numbered horses). In fact, with that background any information I give you about even-numbered horses *on top of* the odd-numbered report becomes redundant. Similarly, if an agent has a context-insensitive equivalent for every context-sensitive sentence in a particular situation, context-sensitive information becomes redundant and can safely be ignored in distributing credences over context-insensitives.

Of course we need to specify the notion of "equivalence" in use here, and as we do notions of same-saying and cognitive significance threaten to plunge us back into semantic commitment. But a definition is available that maintains official neutrality:

- Two sentences are **truth-value equivalents** for an agent relative to a context if the agent is certain in that context that the two sentences have the same truth-value (in that context).

This notion of equivalence doesn't employ any deep notions of content; it refers only to truth-values in contexts, which every semantic theory must assign somehow. And it's an *epistemic* definition: it concerns not whether the sentences actually have the same truth-value but whether the agent is *certain* that they do.

Truth-value equivalents were significant in Bayesianism before *de se* contents ever entered the scene. Kolmogorov's probability axioms entail that truth-value equivalents must receive equal unconditional credences at any given time. More broadly, the probability calculus is *extensional* in the sense that if an agent is certain two sentences have the same truth-value the mathematics makes them intersubstitutable.[20]

This notion of equivalence also does the job for our jet plane story. At t_2 Anne is interested in the truth of "I'm now in Missouri," but she's certain that that sentence has the same truth-value as "When my watch reads 3:30pm I'm in Missouri" (because she's certain at t_2 that her watch currently reads 3:30pm). Similarly, the crucial fact Anne has just learned at t_2, "The screen looks the same now as it did a half-hour ago," has the context-insensitive truth-value equivalent "The screen looks the same when my

[20] This is captured in a theorem I call Substitution: If an agent is certain at a time that sentences X and Y have the same truth-value, Y can be freely substituted for X in credence expressions indexed to that time. For example, if $P_1(X \equiv Y)=1$ and $P_1(X \& Z)+P_1(\sim X \& \sim Z)=3/4$, we will also have $P_1(Y \& Z)+P_1(\sim Y \& \sim Z)=3/4$.

watch reads 3:30pm as when my watch reads 3pm." In general, all the important context-sensitive sentences in the jet plane story have context-insensitive truth-value equivalents for Anne at every time during the story, so we need not worry that setting aside the context-sensitives leaves out crucial information.

To summarize, the updating scheme I propose in place of traditional conditionalization works in three stages:

> First: If at every time during a story the agent has context-insensitive truth-value equivalents available for every relevant context-sensitive sentence, we temporarily set the context-sensitive sentences aside.
>
> Second: Having set the context-sensitives aside, we update among the context-insensitive sentences using standard conditionalization.
>
> Third: We then re-introduce the context-sensitive sentences, determining the agent's degrees of belief in them using what we've learned about her degrees of belief in the context-insensitives.

As I said before, (Titelbaum 2013) works out this scheme in much greater, formal detail and applies it to a variety of uncontroversial cases to show that it yields the answers we'd expect.[21]

I'll close this section by highlighting once more how I constructed this updating scheme without committing myself to a particular theory of content. First, instead of assigning credences to entities assumed to be the actual objects of doxastic states, I assigned them to sentences, taking such an assignment to represent the agent's degree of belief that the sentence in question is true in the present context. Second, I identified epistemically context-sensitive sentences as the troublemakers for conditionalization, where "epistemically context-sensitive" was defined in terms of the agent's certainties concerning truth-values of sentences in contexts. Third, I offered a modified updating scheme that allows us to move from epistemically context-sensitive sentences to epistemically context-insensitive ones as long as the former have truth-value equivalents among the latter. "Truth-value equivalent" was also defined in terms of the agent's certainties regarding the truth-values of sentences in contexts, instead of using any idiosyncratic semantic notion of synonymy.

In each of these steps, the crucial move employs the agent's degrees of belief concerning truth-values of sentences in contexts. Any theory of content will allow agents to have such degrees of belief, and will tell a story

[21] I also explain there how to apply the scheme to stories in which the agent lacks a context-insensitive truth-value equivalent for a significant context-sensitive sentence.

about how those degrees of belief relate to degrees of belief in more basic propositions, properties, sets of worlds, or whatever else.[22] Notice also that classing sentences in terms of the agent's degrees of belief about their truth-values fits with another general pattern in Bayesianism. Bayesians typically take constraints on an agent's degrees of belief to be constraints of rational consistency—constraints imposed on the agent's doxastic attitudes by other attitudes she possesses. An updating scheme whose central concepts (epistemic context-sensitivity, truth-value equivalence) concern not the actual truth-values of sentences but instead the agent's *opinions* about those truth-values fits perfectly with a regime of internal consistency constraints.

From Credence to Content?

The updating scheme I've just described shows that it's possible to get correct answers about requirements on an agent's degrees of belief without settling what kind of objects they're degrees of belief *in*. But is there any influence in the other direction? Do some answers to questions about required degrees of belief favor one semantic theory over another?[23]

Let me present a rough argument about a case in which that might occur—recall the Sleeping Beauty Problem from above. Though I won't rehearse the whole argument, my updating scheme entails that when Beauty awakens on Monday (uncertain whether it's Monday or Tuesday), she should have a degree of belief less than 1/2 that the coin came up heads.[24] Since everyone agrees that Beauty's degree of belief in heads should be exactly 1/2 before she goes to sleep Sunday night, this change in confidence seems puzzling.

It's especially puzzling if you maintain a particular principle about the interaction between evidence and degrees of belief. It seems reasonable to

---

[22] For example, if you take degrees of belief to be assigned to propositions, you will want to tell a story about how an agent's degree of belief that the sentence "It's cold today" is true in the present context relates to his degree of belief in the proposition that it's cold today.

[23] Elsewhere in this volume Darren Bradley also argues for a conclusion about contents from a conclusion about updating (or confirmation), though anyone who reads both pieces will see that he and I have much to disagree on!

[24] More precisely, she should have a degree of belief in heads of 1/3. To get an intuitive idea why that number makes sense, here's an argument from (Elga 2000): Imagine the experiment were repeated 1000 times. The coin would come up heads roughly 500 times, and Beauty awakens once if the coin comes up heads. So in 1000 trials there would be 500 awakenings on which the coin had come up heads—call them "heads-awakenings." The coin would come up tails roughly 500 times, and when the coin comes up tails Beauty awakens twice. So there would be 1000 tails-awakenings, for a total of 1500 awakenings on all 1000 trials. When Beauty finds herself on Monday morning in the middle of an awakening, she knows that of all the awakenings she'll experience roughly 1/3 will be heads-awakenings, so she should be 1/3 confident that the coin came up heads. (For further arguments see Bradley's piece.)

say that Beauty's degree of belief in heads shouldn't change unless she receives unexpected evidence. If on Monday morning Beauty is certain, of every piece of evidence she possesses, that on Sunday night she was sure she'd come to possess it, then she shouldn't change her Monday confidence in heads from what it was on Sunday night. This comes from a general idea that one should change one's opinions only if one gets evidence one didn't fully expect to receive; fully-expected evidence should have already been factored into one's doxastic attitudes. If all of Beauty's current (Monday morning) evidence was predictable on Sunday, the fact that she'd be receiving it was already factored into the degree of belief she assigned to heads back on Sunday night.[25]

On a Lewisian semantics, this describes Beauty's situation exactly. Her crucial evidence on Monday morning is captured by the sentence "I'm awake today, and today is Monday or Tuesday." For a Lewisian, this sentence expresses the self-ascription of a property, or perhaps a centered proposition. But crucially, what Beauty believes (and what's expressed by that sentence) on Monday morning is the *same* content she believes if and when she awakens on Tuesday morning, a content she was *certain* on Sunday night she would come to believe at some point during the experiment. So when Beauty awakens on Monday morning, it's no surprise that she's in possession of that evidence; she was certain in advance that she would come to have a belief with such a content. No surprising evidence, so no change of confidence in heads seems warranted.

But our updating scheme tells us Beauty should change her degree of belief in heads. This result fits much better with a non-Lewisian semantics, a picture of content on which "today" evidence says something *different* on Monday than it does on Tuesday. Then Beauty might reason as follows: "I have evidence that I'm awake today. Today is either Monday or Tuesday. So that evidence either says of Monday that I'm awake that day, or it says of Tuesday that I'm awake *that* day. I don't know what the true content of my evidence is. But if my evidence is that I'm awake on Tuesday, *that's* a piece of evidence I wasn't certain in advance I'd receive.[26] And if I'm awake on Tuesday, the chance that the coin came up heads is zero (because on heads I don't get to wake up on Tuesday). So to accommodate the possibility that I've just received evidence of awakening on Tuesday, I should

---

[25] Compare (Meacham 2010, p. 115): "There is something strange about [the 1/3] answer. There wasn't anything surprising about the evidence you got [Monday morning]. Indeed, we can tailor the case so that the scientists will tell you [on Sunday night] precisely what you will experience when you wake up. How can evidence which you know you'll get justify this change in your credences?"

[26] Compare the discussion in (Schulz 2010) of "I'm awake today" as "*potentially* new evidence" for Beauty.

downgrade my confidence in heads, to somewhat less than the 1/2 I previously assigned."[27]

This line of reasoning turns on Beauty's thought that her evidence has a different content if it's Monday than if it's Tuesday—and if it's the latter her evidence indicates something very significant about the outcome of the coin toss. Such a position about the content of Beauty's evidence is incompatible with a Lewisian *de se* story, and more compatible with a semantics like Stalnaker's[28] on which "I'm awake today" has a different content on different days.

The argument I've laid out in this section is very rough, and I'm not sure I would ultimately endorse it. A key sticking point is the precise formulation of the principle concerning degrees of belief and unexpected evidence, and whether such a principle holds true in general. But the argument raises an interesting possibility: We can build a Bayesian updating scheme that answers degree of belief puzzles without making any commitments in the theory of semantics, but when we try to *understand* those answers in terms of information, contents, and evidence some semantic approaches may come out looking more plausible than others.[29]

References

Bradley, D. 2011. 'Self-Location is No Problem for Conditionalization', *Synthese*, 182: 393–411.

Briggs, R. 2010. 'Putting a Value on Beauty', in T. Gendler and J. Hawthorne, eds., *Oxford Studies in Epistemology*, Volume 3 (Oxford: Oxford University Press), 3–34.

Hacking, I. 1967. 'Slightly More Realistic Personal Probability', *Philosophy of Science*, 34: 311–325.

Hájek, A. 2010. 'Interpretations of Probability', in E. Zalta, ed., *The Stanford Encyclopedia of Philosophy*, URL: plato.stanford.edu/archives/spr2010/entries/probability-interpret.

Halpern, J.Y. 2005. 'Sleeping Beauty Reconsidered: Conditioning and Reflection in Asynchronous Systems', in T. Gendler and J. Hawthorne, eds., *Oxford*

[27] On this story, when Beauty is told that today is Monday the possibility that was downgrading her heads confidence disappears, and her confidence in heads springs right back up to 1/2. This accommodates the point made earlier that when Beauty learns it's Monday her degree of belief in heads should increase.

[28] Or Kaplan's—see Bradley's piece in this volume.

[29] I am grateful to Darren Bradley, Matthew Kopec, Josh Sheptow, and Elliott Sober for comments on drafts of this chapter. I am also grateful to the editors for all their work in assembling this collection. Portions of this work were completed under research funding from the Australian National University and the University of Wisconsin-Madison's Graduate School Research Committee.

Studies in Epistemology, Volume 1 (Oxford: Oxford University Press), 111–142.

Kolmogorov, A.N. 1950. *Foundations of the Theory of Probability* (New York: Chelsea Publishing Company).

Kim, N. 2009. 'Sleeping Beauty and Shifted Jeffrey Conditionalization', *Synthese*, 168: 295–312.

Lewis, D. 1979. 'Attitudes *De Dicto* and *De Se*', *Philosophical Review*, 87: 513–545.

Lewis, D. 2001. 'Sleeping Beauty: Reply to Elga', *Analysis*, 61: 171–6.

MacFarlane, J. 2005. 'Making Sense of Relative Truth', *Proceedings of the Aristotelian Society*, 105: 321–39.

Meacham, C.J.G. 2008. 'Sleeping Beauty and the Dynamics of *De Se* Beliefs', *Philosophical Studies*, 138: 245–270.

Meacham, C.J.G. 2010. 'Unraveling the Tangled Web: Continuity, Internalism, Non-Uniqueness, and Self-Locating Beliefs', in T. Gendler and J. Hawthorne, eds., *Oxford Studies in Epistemology*, Volume 3 (Oxford: Oxford University Press), 86–125.

Moss, S. 2012. 'Updating as Communication', *Philosophy and Phenomenological Research*, 85: 225-248.

Parfit, D. 1984. *Reasons and Persons* (Oxford: Oxford University Press).

Piccione, M. and Rubinstein, A. 'On the Interpretation of Decision Problems with Imperfect Recall,' *Games and Economic Behavior*, 20: 3–24.

Pust, J. 2012. 'Conditionalization and Essentially Indexical Credence,' *Journal of Philosophy*, 109: 295-315.

Schulz, M. 2010. 'The Dynamics of Indexical Belief', *Erkenntnis*, 72: 337-351.

Schwarz, W. 2012. 'Changing Minds in a Changing World', *Philosophical Studies*, 159: 239–259.

Stalnaker, R. 2008. *Our Knowledge of the Internal World* (Oxford: Oxford University Press).

Titelbaum, M.G. 2013. *Quitting Certainties: A Bayesian Framework Modeling Degrees of Belief* (Oxford: Oxford University Press).

Titelbaum, M.G. 2008. 'The Relevance of Self-Locating Beliefs', *Philosophical Review*, 117: 555–605.

Weatherson, B. 2011. 'Stalnaker on Sleeping Beauty', *Philosophical Studies*, 155: 445-456.

13

The Role of Motivational Force and Intention in First-Person Beliefs

PIETRO PERCONTI

1 Introduction

Beliefs are directed toward their content, i.e., they are intentional states, and play a causal role in behaviour. In fact, intentionality and the causal role of mental states in behaviour are the two distinctive and fundamental features computational psychology attributes to the human mind. The idea according to which, certain inner episodes are the causes of overt behaviour is crucial for both the folk psychology of desires and beliefs, and the representational computational theory of mind. The ability of mental states to cause actions rests on their local physical properties, or on their "formal characteristics", in Jerry Fodor's terms. However, people's behaviour besides being determined by causes, is also determined by the reasons people have for behaving in a particular way. Beliefs, therefore, have a motivational power, besides a causal role in behaviour.

In what follows I will try to argue that first-person beliefs (henceforth FPBs) have an essentially indexical nature and that only such kinds of beliefs have a genuine motivational force in behaviour. The content of FPBs is referred to their bearer in an essential way. Since these kinds of beliefs instantiate a two-place relation between the bearer and her intentional content, and they are both essentially indexical and endowed with motivational force, therefore, essentiality seems a necessary condition, making beliefs capable of having motivational force.

Attitudes De Se: Linguistics, Epistemology, Metaphysics.
Neil Feit and Alessandro Capone (eds.).

2 Causal *vs.* Motivational Role of Beliefs in Behavior

When a diver jumps off a diving board, the cause of his falling is gravitational force. Is this the only reason behind the fall? Certainly not. The diver falls because she wants to make a good dive or desires to win the diving event. In explaining human behaviour often both causes and reasons come into play. If Romeo kisses Juliet, he does it because he loves her, or whatever. He would have his reasons, of course. The motivational role of beliefs has to do with the reasons for action and the justifications given for a certain behaviour. It seems difficult to explain what takes place between Romeo and Juliet if one sees it as merely a story of causes. If reductionists were right, and it were possible to reduce love to its biological aspect, then we would not need to rely on any reason to fall in love with someone. However, even if the reasons to fall in love do not necessary lead to understanding why people do, individuals have justifications for their love affairs. If chemistry, or any other scientific explanation, were to constitute all we have to know in order to explain why Romeo kisses Juliet or why he falls in love, then there would be nothing else to be taken into account in order to understand love. But, as everyone knows, this is not the case.

If Romeo, after kissing Juliet, commits a crime or a sin and then tries to explain the reasons for his actions before a judge, or a priest, or to his own conscience, as the result of a physical or chemical chain of events, would he thereby provide a justification for his actions? It seems not. To justify is to provide reasons (it makes no difference whether they are true or false), not of showing any sort of physical or chemical cause. The case of love is not an exception. Similar observations can be made for many other facets of human behaviour, like moral judgements or self-consciousness. On the whole, it seems that human actions are not available to a mere causal explanation.

This way of reasoning is based, *inter alia*, on Ludwig Wittgenstein's *Philosophische Untersuchungen* (1953) and on the considerations of his pupils Elisabeth Anscombe (1957) and Georg von Wright (1971). As is well known, Donald Davidson (1963) attempted to provide a persuading argument to settle the dispute between causes and reasons. This contrast is addressed by John McDowell (1994) using the metaphor of the two spaces: the logical space of reasons – an image borrowed by Wilfrid Sellars (1956) – and the "realm of law". The problem arises when, to explain the same phenomenon, causes and reasons are alternative lines of explanation. As long as the causes are called to explain phenomena such as the role of chlorophyll in photosynthesis, and the appeal to reasons is reserved for human actions, scientists can go about their usual business without being bored by those scholars that try to understand the meaning of human events. When causes and reasons are given as two lines of explanation for the same fact, as in the case of the explanations given by cognitive scientists for phenomena such as love, moral sense, and aesthetic judgement, then troubles begin to arise. Are the reasons reducible to causes? Are human beings the only individuals in which both reasons and causes coexist? Is this controversy, after all, just an effect of a hidden Cartesian perspective according to which human beings are the only creatures in the world that have both a body, that is causally determined, and a mind, which lives in the logical space of reasons?

These questions show how deep the concerns arising from the distinction between causes and reasons are. It is a matter of referring to a general philosophical attitude about the role conceptual schemata have in the understanding of the world. While, on one hand, the casual role beliefs have in behaviour is not a logical matter, but an empirical issue; on the other, motivational power is in the end, a linguistic state of affairs. This shows how to understand the different role causes and reasons have in the explanation of behaviour, we would need to clarify what "logical matter" and "empirical issue" mean exactly and which scientific vocabulary is really adequate for our purposes.

In other words, the competition between causes and reasons in the explanation of behaviour is a problem for the issue of naturalism. Naturalizing consciousness, the Self, and the intentionality of mental states, are the hardest challenges for a naturalistic account of the mind. Sometimes, to conceive – into a scientific framework of the world – the reasons people have to behave in such and such a way seems a hopeless daydream. According to Jaegwon Kim, the word "naturalism", refers to a "plethora" of perspectives, such as the attempts to naturalize linguistic meaning, moral and aesthetic judgements, or anything else (Kim 2003: 84). "Naturalism" is a sort of common sense for a part of contemporary philosophy, especially in the American analytical tradition.

According to Hilary Putnam, this attitude depends on the fear of "conceptual pluralism", that is, *prima facie*, "the denial that any one language game is adequate for all our cognitive purposes" (Putnam 2004: 52). Following this line of reasoning, we can say that the language game of "trying causes" is not adequate to someone interested in providing justifications for her own behaviour. Naturalism "with a human face" should be based on the *compatibility* between the two language games mentioned above, while strict naturalists attempt to *reduce* the latter language game to the first one.

3 The Speciality of First-Person Beliefs

The point I would like to make is that FPBs have a special feature. If we take into account the justifications people have for their actions, only FPBs seem endowed with motivational force. Therefore, in order to achieve this power, all the other kinds of beliefs have to be transformed into FPBs. FPBs have an indexical content, i.e., they are indexical beliefs. Indexical expressions or, more simply, indexicals are expressions whose reference shifts over time and location, and from one speaker to another. For example, when you use the word "I", this refers to you; but, if I were to use the personal pronoun "I", it would refer to me instead. The most common indexicals are demonstratives and personal pronouns. However, an indexical component is present in many classes of words, including adjectives, as in the case of "actual".

The kind of indexicality typical of FPBs is that of "pure indexicals" rather than that of "(true) demonstratives". Among pure indexical are included "I", "today", "tomorrow", and the mentioned "actual". Demonstratives include words such as "this", "that", "he", and "her". According to the standard view, their reference is determined in different ways (Kaplan 1989). While in the case of demonstratives the reference depends (more or less) on the speaker's "demonstrations", like pointing gestures or eye gaze, when we use a pure indexical in a given context, its reference does not depend on any sort of speaker action. While pure indexicals like "I", "now", and "here" refer without further ado, other indexical expressions – typically demonstratives – are in need of a demonstration to refer. Pure indexicals are "semantically complete": they are directly referential terms and their reference is determined only in virtue of its conventional meaning and without considering the speaker's intention. On the contrary, the reference of demonstratives depends on the speaker's intention to denote a particular state of affairs. This means, among other things, that demonstrative reference besides being a linguistic event, is a psychological matter.

The fact that in direct reference theory "I" is considered as a pure indexical means, in the words of Esther Romero and Belén Soria (2005), that "when 'I' is uttered, it contributes with an individual to what is said and this individual can only be the speaker". David Kaplan's idea that "I", "now" and "here", are pure indexicals implies that the truth-conditions of the utterance in which these expressions occur involve their referent. As said above, in standard direct reference theory a pure indexical is a referential term that can be considered as semantically complete. Therefore, in the use of a pure indexical like "I", the intention of the speaker would be irrelevant. The linguistic meaning (Kaplan's "character" or Perry's "role") would automatically provide a referent. To refer to oneself, an individual does not have to necessarily point at her body, or to allude to herself in any other way. The reference of "I" in a given context is always the speaker, like the reference of "tomorrow" in a given context is always the day after the day of the utterance.

We are facing two ideas. On the one hand, the fact that FPBs are essentially indexical means that the replacement of the indexical component included in these beliefs, does not guarantee the explanation of the action we are observing. On the other hand, the essentiality of FPBs seems to be that of pure indexicals rather than that of demonstratives. Given a context, the reference of a pure indexical would be automatic and the intention of the speaker would be irrelevant. It would be expected that the motivational force of FPBs depends on the automaticity of their reference. However, it is matter of explaining what the word "automaticity" here means exactly. The automaticity of FPBs, in fact, can be interpreted in two different ways. A FPB can refer in an automatic way because it is not in need of any intention or because its reference does not depend on any attribution of a property. According to the first interpretation, the reference of FPBs is not a psychological matter. The second interpretation, on the contrary, leaves open the possibility that the reference of FPBs depends on cognitive functions, which do not consist in the mastering of any concept or property.

I would like to argue that this latter possibility is exactly the case. The reference of FPBs depends on a specific mode of presentation of first-person bodily perspective, which is specifically realized in the human brain. As we will see in what follows (par. 6), the brain represents the body in a direct and specific way, without any attribution of a property to oneself or the mastery of a self-concept. In other terms, the word "I" and similar pure indexicals are the linguistic counterpart of the cognitive processes the human brain uses to shape bodily self-representation.

"Intention" is not the name of a danger for the semantics of FPBs. In a sense, it is in play even in the case of the reference of (pure) indexicals. We might wonder whether the difference between demonstratives and pure indexicals is really as well founded as one would imagine. The sharpness of that difference, in fact, is controversial, because it is not able to account for all the uses of the classes of expressions one would like to account for. While, on one hand, there are cases in which demonstratives do their job without any demonstration, on the other, there are cases in which it seems that pure indexicals need a demonstration.

Demonstratives without demonstrations are able to refer successfully, without any ambiguity, when in the context in which they occur there are facts that are extremely relevant. Suppose you are walking with a friend on an empty street when suddenly, a terrible rumble occurs. Your friend says to you: "That was really soft!". Which is the referent of the demonstrative "that"? I think that the best candidate for this role is "rumble". When in the context in which a demonstrative occurs there is an exceptionally relevant fact, this attracts the reference of the demonstrative in a quasi-automatic way. In these cases demonstratives are similar to pure indexicals.

On the other hand, there are uses of (pure) indexicals in which demonstrations are not irrelevant. It is the very idea of a *pure* indexical that is contentious. The analysis of written notes (on a *post-it*, for example) and recorded messages, suggests that sometimes strange sentences, like "I am not here", can be used in an appropriate way (Predelli 2010; Predelli 1998; Corazza *et al.* 2002; Sidelle 1991). This leads also to rejecting the existence of *pure* indexicals. The beginning of a standard conversation on the intercom is another way to show the role of "demonstrations" in (pure) indexical reference. We ask:

(1) Who is it?

And the answer given by someone we know very well usually is:

(2) It's me.

Although answer (2) is not really informative, it is successful in typical circumstances. Why? The reason why (2) can be the right answer to give over the intercom is that with the use of the personal pronoun "me", along with the Kaplan character, a clear demonstration is associated, i.e. the timbre of the voice. It is thanks to the vocal timbre that the speaker is actually recognized.

Now, the "pure indexicals" theorist could probably maintain that in this case we only have the appearance of the use of the personal pronoun "me", while the entire job is actually done by the timbre of the voice. This objection, however, does not work. Suppose your intercom interlocutor says: "Strawberry jam". Perhaps he would also be recognized in this case. But, would he have said the same as: "It's me"? The answer, of course, is: "No". The words "me" and "strawberry jam", after all, do not mean the same thing. And personal pronouns are not used only to allow the recognition of speakers.

These kinds of examples show that to associate pure indexicals with a demonstration is sometimes relevant. In a similar way, demonstratives sometimes refer without any demonstration. Perhaps the difference between pure indexicals and demonstratives can be sharply drawn only in the more common cases. The role of intention in indexical reference is more important than generally believed. It is, therefore, useful to consider the role the speaker's intention, and in general, mind reading, plays in indexical competence.

4 Indexical Competence and Mindreading

In the last twenty years there has been considerable debate about our ordinary capacity to understand the mind. This is not surprising, considering that in everyday dealings we constantly appeal to our and other people's mind. Every individual aged four and older, even without any training in psychology, is a perfect mind reader. The word "mind-reading" refers to the ability to interpret and predict – on the basis of the attribution of psychological states – the behaviour of other individuals. Reading the minds of others is an activity every human being is engaged in, most of the time, for the ordinary purposes of everyday life.

"Mind-reading" is not the only expression used to refer to this capacity. Other expressions are: theory of mind, folk psychology, and social cognition. The reason why I prefer to use "mind-reading" is that this expression conveys, more than the other expressions on the list, the idea that the attribution of psychological states is an activity based on the interpretation of people's intentions. Reading other people's mind, as well as our own, is a matter of producing correct behavioural predictions by supplying the most appropriate interpretation of observed behaviour, so that one might find oneself in the best possible condition to accomplish predicted future tasks.

Mind reading plays an important role in linguistic competence, especially in the indexical one. On one hand, drawing attention to the role of mind reading in indexical competence is a move towards providing a psychologically plausible linguistic theory. On the other hand, stressing the indexical competence component involved in mind reading can be considered a move towards providing a theory of mind. This is not equivalent to saying that mind reading *is* a linguistic activity. Mind reading has a clear *non*-linguistic component, which consists in giving a linguistic form to a *non*-linguistic intention. Let us take into consideration certain arguments in favour of the thesis that mind reading, interpreted in the above-mentioned way, plays a role in indexical competence.

4.1 Idiosyncratic (and Non-Idiosyncratic) Use of Language

Imagine yourself to be at the entrance of a nursery school in Florence, Italy, at the time when parents pick up their children from school, and that one of the mothers present says to another mother: "That child is the ugliest of the lot" ("Codesto bambino è proprio il più brutto"). Near the two mothers – call them "S" and "H" (Speaker and Hearer) – there are several children including H's own child. According to the Italian language (especially the variety of it spoken in Tuscany), we must use "codesto" for referring to things which are near the hearer, "questo" for referring to things which are near the speaker, and "quello" for referring to things which are far from both the hearer and the speaker (Fig. 1). While the Italian system of demonstratives has three terms, the English system has only two (Fig. 2). In the case of a three-term system, the interlocutors have to take into consideration more elements than in the two-term case, and this fact makes more evident the role of the taking of perspective involved in the part of linguistic competence we are studying.

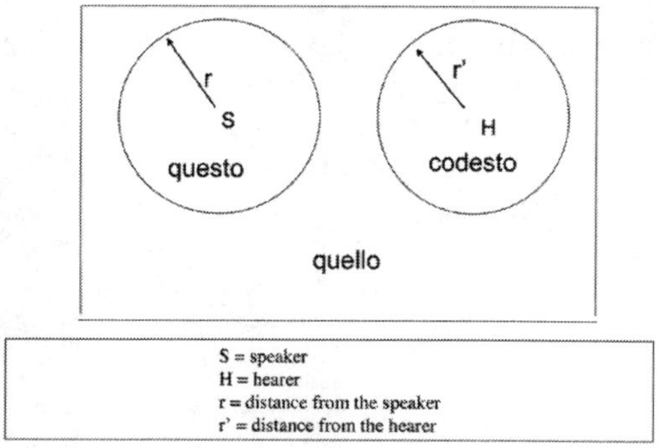

Fig. 1. The Italian system of demonstratives

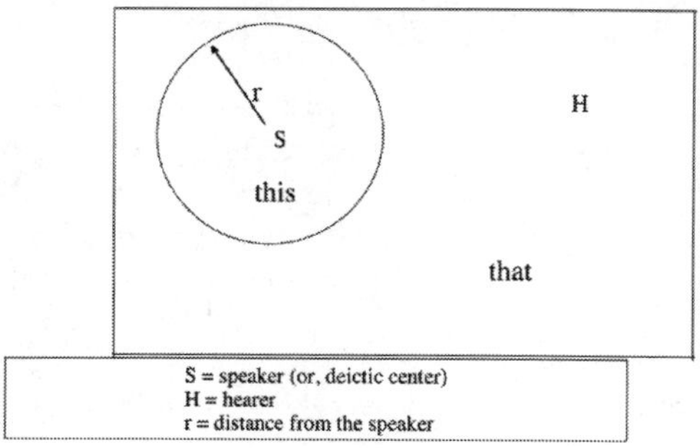

Fig. 2. The English system of demonstratives

In our example S does not intend to upset H with what she says. In fact, she is not referring to H's son, but to another child who is much closer to H than H's son. What if H thinks that her son isn't far from her and the phrase "That (codesto) child" refers to him?

Although in the language spoken by S and H there are rules, which are meant to deal with this kind of problem, there are also situations in which words are used in an idiosyncratic way. The situation considered involves the idiosyncratic use of words because in this case the ability to interpret other people's minds is particularly relevant. It is interesting to note, in fact, that, if S thinks that H uses the demonstrative "codesto" in an idiosyncratic manner or that H has an idiosyncratic view of the surrounding space, then, if S doesn't want to upset H, she has to take into consideration H's perception of the surrounding space and her use of language. Suppose H has a "Napoleonic" (i.e., extremely large) perception of her surrounding space. To achieve her communicative purposes, S should take into consideration the "Napoleonic idea" of the surrounding space held by H.

Indeed, the perception of the region of space, which is considered to be far from the hearer, depends neither on objective criteria (there are no chalk lines on the ground that could guide us) nor on the speaker's opinions. In general, the competence in the use of demonstratives in Italian, for how it is spoken in Tuscany, does not presuppose only the capacity to distinguish between three different regions of space, but also the ability to assume the point of view of the hearer. This is particularly clear in Italian, because this system of demonstratives is particularly complex, but the same thing happens when demonstratives are used in many other languages (Diessel 1999).

Furthermore, the putting oneself in someone else's shoes is not only required in the case of the idiosyncratic use of language, but also in standard circumstances. Imagine you are talking to someone and you have to choose the right article between "the" and "a" for the noun "man". If you are telling a story in which there is a man that is doing so and so, then you have to use the article "a". However, you have to refer to that man using "the", "that man", or "he" in the following references. In fact, at this point your interlocutor knows the individual you are talking about. Ron Smyth (1995) studies what cognitive pathways children use when they are engaged in the resolution of an anaphora. Anaphoric reference is more complex than simple deictic reference. Suppose a child says to another: "Ralph told William that Bonnie bored him (= Ralph)". This utterance can be understood in two different ways, according to whether we interpret the personal pronoun 'him' as referring to Ralph or to William. If we want to understand the meaning of the sentence above, we need to construct a model of the situation in which the sentence is uttered and infer that it is more probable that Ralph intended to say something informative to William, namely, that Bonnie bored Ralph, rather than to state something that William should have known by direct experience, i.e., that Bonnie bored William. Therefore, to understand the sentence above, a third party must first of all imagine himself to be in the situation in which Ralph was when he said such-and-such, and then imagine himself to be in the situation in which William was when he heard Ralph saying such-and-such. According to Smyth, the ability to carry out this double change of framework is one of the conditions, which must be satisfied for the understanding of assertions such as the one we have considered above. In fact, the number of mistakes made by children in interpreting assertions like "Ralph told William that Bonnie bored him" decreases as they grow older, and the difficulty of changing framework also decreases.

As a rule, in the choice of the right article or personal pronoun the speaker has to keep track of conversational information oriented to the listener. He has to make conjectures about his interlocutor's knowledge to choose the right article, and "making conjectures" about someone else's knowledge is a way of trying to read his mind.

4.2 Typical Development

Many psychologists, including Paul Bloom (2004; 2007), have convincingly suggested that understanding the thoughts of others is broadly involved in children's word learning. According to this perspective, word learning is a kind of intentional inference. Mind reading develops earlier than word acquisition and children use their understanding of other minds to figure out what other individuals are referring to when they use words. This is a controversial issue, which generally depends on what one exactly means by the expression "mind-reading". If by ''theory of mind' one means the kind of ability exhibited by the false belief tasks (Wimmer & Perner 1983), then it is clear that word acquisition develops before children are able to solve false belief tasks. However, mind reading is a capacity that comes in degrees. When children are able to pass the false belief task, at the age of four, their mind reading is completely developed. However, the roots of this capacity can be traced to the first year of life (Perner & Ruffman 2005; Csibra & Southgate 2006; Surian *et. al.* 2007; Reddy 2010). There are several abilities that prepare and mediate the fully mature stage of mind reading, including shared attention and gaze following, pretence, and imitation.

Among the precursors of the mind-reading capacity manifested at the age-four-stage, to be able to follow pointing gestures is particularly noteworthy. There are two types of pointing gestures in infants: proto-declarative and proto-imperative (Bates *et al.* 1975). While proto-imperative pointing is aimed to obtain an object, proto-declarative pointing is purely used to remark on an object or an event in the world. The aim of the proto-declarative pointing is to make another person attend to what the infant is thinking about. This suggests that proto-declarative pointing requires the ability to individuate features of other people's inner life, since this kind of gesture seems to involve the child representing the psychological state of thinking or attending to. Normal children produce the pointing gesture when they are 9-14 months old. Moreover, the proto-imperative gesture normally is produced and understood earlier than the proto-declarative function of the same gesture (Camaioni *et al.* 2004). Pointing can be considered as a sort of proto-indexical signal performed earlier than the indexical competence that later becomes an ingredient of mature linguistic competence.

There is evidence that suggests that becoming competent in using personal pronouns depends on the capacity to understand both mental and spatial perspectives of other people. With regard to the *acquisition* of the personal pronouns "I" and "you", Katherine Loveland (1984) first found that this competence depends on the capacity to take other individuals' perspective. Until children have not realized the consequences of taking the spatial perspective of someone else, they are not able to master the personal pronouns "I" and "you". This suggests that, in order to use personal pronouns correctly, children must be able to take perceptual roles. But they also must be able to take on the conceptual perspectives of other individuals.

4.3 The Communication Disorders of Autism

The evidence offered by typical development suggests that when a child in standard circumstances shows his indexical competence, he is using his ability to read his mind as well as that of others. But what happens when either mind reading or indexical competence is lost? The conjecture I have put forth seems to suggest that when one of the two above mentioned abilities is lost the other will endure the same fate. As we shall see in what follows, this is precisely what happens.

The case we are now going to examine is that of people affected by autism. As is well known, this syndrome is characterised by the inability to engage in mind reading. Individuals affected by autism are, in Simon Baron-Cohen's words, "mentally blind". Autism involves a difficulty in interpreting people's behaviour as causally linked to mental states. Since Baron-Cohen's, Alan Leslie's and Uta Frith's (1985) seminal paper, in which the experimental model of "false belief" was applied to the study of autistic children, the conjecture according to which mind-reading is at the heart of autism has been confirmed many times. At the same time, the theory-of-mind hypothesis of autism has been further integrated by other research directions, including the role played by the mirror-neuron system in social interactions, face recognition, imitation, just to name a few (Tager-Flusberg 2007).

While not as popular a theme as that concerning problems in mind-reading, anomalies in the use of indexicals by autistic individuals have been pointed out since the autistic pathology was first described. In his 1943 paper Leo Kanner saw in the inversion of first- and second-singular personal pronouns one of the characteristic traits of the autistic syndrome. Fay and Schuler (1980) refer to the inversion of pronouns as a "patognomic sign" of autism in children. However, the inversion of pronouns is only one aspect of the linguistic deficiencies associated with autism. Since linguistic development is closely linked to the development of mind-reading abilities (Astington & Baird 2005), then language capacity is impaired in this syndrome. Individuals affected by such a pathology are impaired in their performance with regard to all indexical expressions, e.g., demonstratives and tenses. Moreover, the inversion of pronouns is not the only case in which the use of pronouns is impaired. Children affected by autism use proper names in cases in which normal children of the same age use pronouns; and when they eventually learn to use pronouns they are prone to losing this competence. Mental state terms (e.g., think, know, pretend) are underrepresented in the vocabulary of children with autism (Tager-Flusberg 2000).

Furthermore, autistic children have difficulties in performing other communicative acts in which the ability to consider a point of view different from one's own is involved. An example of this is represented by narrative discourse, i.e., the set of linguistic activities exemplified by: the telling of fiction stories, scripts (as one does after waking up in the morning), and the passing on of information. The lack of ability in taking into account the point of view of the hearer is also at the root of the anomalies affecting the intonation of speech in autistic children. It is because autistic children do not realize what might surprise, interest or frighten the interlocutor, that they are unable to modulate the intonation of their speech in such a way as to influence the state of mind of the interlocutor.

4.4 Some Evidence from Animals' Minds

To study mind reading and indexical acquisition in children is not a straightforward task. However, a similar operation in comparative psychology is more complicated. In the comparative psychology of mind reading the key question is whether the ability to reason about mental states is a uniquely human trait. From the time when Premack and Woodruff's seminal paper was published (1978), the controversy is now based on new experimental tests. Most of them are devoted to the question concerning whether chimpanzees and other primates understand the connection between "seeing" and "knowing". While Michael Tomasello claims that chimpanzees are endowed with at least parts of a theory of mind (Tomasello *et al.* 2003), according to Daniel Povinelli, if chimpanzees do have some kind of mind-reading ability, it must be radically different from our own (Penn & Povinelli 2007). There is evidence in favour of the thesis that "our closest living relatives" are able to monitor and use the gaze of others. However, non-human primates are not able to appreciate all the psychological aspects of seeing. They can reason about behaviour, but not about concepts that refer to unobservable entities or processes, like ghosts, God, and minds. Twenty five years of mind-reading research confirms what Premack himself stated in 1988, i.e., that great apes are in an intermediate position between humans and the other species of the animal kingdom. Almost all other species are unable to attribute mental states to others to make sense of and predict their behaviour; human beings aged four and older attribute mental states with the only limitation represented by a certain number of sub-clauses (John thinks that Mary believes that Bill desires …); and non-human primates attribute mental states too, but in a limited way.

What about indexical signals performed by other animals and especially by the great apes? I speculate that the above-mentioned situation Premack argues for psychological attribution is also present when we study indexical competence. Taking these concerns into consideration, in another paper (Perconti 2002), I examined extensively the issue of context-dependence in animal communication and in human language. The comparison shows a complicated network of similarities and differences which reveals a much more sophisticated use of context in human language. Nevertheless, animal signals depend on context in many ways too. For instance, the meaning of the signal depends on the animal to which the signal is directed. According to Leger's description (1993), the sources of contextual information which regard the receiver are of four types: 1) the animal's age and degree of development; 2) its psychological conditions; 3) the behaviour in which the receiver is engaged at the time of the communicative interaction; 4) the memory of the consequences that a given signal has had in the past, and the relationship between the receiver and the sender of the signal. Among sources, which are external to the receiver, particularly relevant are those that depend on the subject emitting the signal, for example the behaviour in which the subject is engaged in at the time of communication. Other contextual information concerns the place in which the communicative interaction occurs, the distance between the subjects involved and the events that take place in the meantime. Moreover, each of these elements varies according to the different systems of communication of the species.

This type of context-dependence of the meaning of animals' signals is based on psychological and social aspects of the communicative act. On the contrary, the type of context-dependence exhibited by human indexicals is a genuine semantic fact. It is a matter of how this kind of expression works and not of the behavioural and environmental modifications their use could produce or experience. For this reason we can consider the variety of uses of context studied by Leger as 'extra-semantic uses' of context, while those which are typical of indexicals as 'semantic uses of context' (Perry, 2003).

Probably the 'best candidate' for the role of indexical in animal communication is the referential pointing that has been documented in the four species of great apes, e.g. in chimpanzees (Fouts *et al.* 1982), in orangutans (Miles 1990; Call & Tomasello 1994), in bonobos (Savage-Rumbaugh *et al.* 1986) and in gorillas (Patterson 1978). Pointing gestures by apes in captivity is referential and intentional. It is referential since it singles out a specific item and it is intentional insofar as it is sensitive to the "audience effect" (Call & Tomasello 1994) and to the state of visual attention in an observer (Leavens, Hostetter, Wesley, & Hopkins 2004). Moreover, the gestures are intentional also because they are accompanied by high rates of gaze alternation (Leavens, Hopkins & Thomas 2004).

The question that arises at this point is what functions gestural communication in nonhuman primates serve. It is questionable whether pointing gestures in humans and in other primates are used in the same way (Povinelli, Bering, & Giambrone 2003). For instance, we can observe an interesting circumstance. Apes in captivity, who regularly interact with humans clearly point, but in the wild they do not. Evidence of pointing by wild apes exists, but it is rare and anecdotal (Inoue-Nakamura & Matsuzawa 1997; Veà & Sabater-Pi 1998; Bard 1992). One can make the hypothesis that the greater production and comprehension capacities of pointing in subjects trained by humans to use some language or at least exposed intensely to contact with humans, is caused by captivity (Call & Tomasello 1994).

Furthermore, as in the case of human gestures, we can suppose that nonhuman primates' pointing can be used either in a proto-declarative or in a proto-imperative way. As we have seen, there is evidence that protodeclarative pointing gestures in children by about the end of the second year can be considered as a behaviour that can influence the internal attentional states of communicative partners. On the contrary, in the case of chimpanzees there is no evidence that they use pointing gestures in a protodeclarative way. There is not much evidence that they comprehend such gestures as a simple cue to direct their behaviour (Povinelli *et al.* 2003). It is interesting that domestic dogs comprehend the underlying referential aspects of the pointing gesture better than apes do. Probably this kind of social learning among domestic dogs depends on the fact that they have coexisted with human beings for the last 100,000 years.

Why is it that apes in the wild do not point in the same way they do in captivity? There are two possible answers to this question. On one hand, we can simply suppose that pointing emerges in a particular kind of context, where a signaller is dependent upon another being to retrieve items for it, i.e., such as the context in which apes are in, in captivity (Leavens, personal communication). Another possibility is that the pointing gestures performed by apes in the wild is proto-imperative and that great apes can only learn to point in a proto-declarative way when they are in captivity, living in an environment characterized by the presence of humans. Unlike proto-imperatives, which may only involve an expression of the animal's needs, proto-declarative gestures involve joint attention, that is, sharing with another person interest in an object or an event, and entail an incipient understanding of intentionality or goal-directedness in the behaviour of others.

All these considerations draw a parallel between other animal's capacities to read into other minds and their capacities to use indexical signals. In both cases, great apes occupy an intermediate position between humans and other animals. Great apes can read other minds, but not in the sophisticated way that happens in humans. On the other hand, great apes use indexical signals, specifically pointing gestures, but in the wild they only make use of the proto-imperative function of this gesture. This probably depends on the fact that the development of mind reading in great apes is sufficient enough to permit no more than the proto-imperative use of indexical signals, which does not require highly sophisticated mental attribution and perspective taking. Indeed the absence of a sophisticated capacity to attribute mental states to others in order to predict their behaviour, rules out the possibility of mastering genuine indexical signals as the proto-declarative pointing gestures.

5 *De Se* Beliefs and the Problem of Essentiality

The findings mentioned above show how the role of the intentions of the speaker as well as the ability to interpret one's own mind and that of others, are more pervasive phenomena in indexical competence than have been expected. From this perspective, indexical reference seems to have to deal with cognitive issues, at least as it concerns logical questions. We might ask whether the "essentiality" is a feature of the same kind of indexicality, that is, if it is a typical feature of *de se* beliefs. In other words, are all kinds of *de se* beliefs essentially indexical? According to Wayne A. Davis (this volume), "the problem of *de se* attitudes *is* the problem of the essential indexical" (my italics). I would argue that this identification is misplaced. It is possible, in fact, to have a belief about oneself in an attributive way. According to David Hunter (2009), the idea that indexical beliefs are essential to understanding human action can be interpreted in two different ways. John Perry's (1979, 2000, 2002) seminal suggestion, according to which "in the absence of the first-person belief the explanation of the event would lose its 'force'", is challenged by the more radical interpretation by Eric Kraemer (1985) and David Velleman (2007). In their perspective "first-person beliefs make a difference to what happens, and not just to the rational or intentional character of what happens" (Hunter 2009).

Why do FPBs have this amazing feature? To settle this dispute, we may say that it is nothing but a misunderstanding, which depends on the failure to distinguish between causes and reasons. As said above, beliefs have both a causal role on behaviour and a motivational force. Therefore, they make the difference in what is happening, as causes, *and* for the reason why something happens, as reasons.

Another possibility is to assume that the motivational force of FPBs depends on their kind of reference. Is the direct attribution of indexical beliefs the rationale of their characteristic behaviour? I think that this is not the case. Arthur Falk (2004: 265) is right when he asserts that sometimes "direct attribution sounds like a name for a mystery". The point is that "to attribute a property" (even to oneself) is a matter of establishing a relation between a given individual and a property, and the very nature of this action includes the possibility of error. While attributions (about other people or oneself) can be incorrect, in order to explain an action performed by a subject it is necessary to suppose a transparent relationship, from a semantic point of view, between the bearer of the belief and the intentional content. In the case of indexical beliefs we should definitely do without the idea of "attribution of a property". Indexical beliefs do not refer to their bearer through the satisfaction of any property, but thanks to a linguistic rule that ensures the coincidence between the content of the belief and its bearer. It is in virtue of this coincidence that people can provide a justification for *their* actions.

6 Cognitive Aspects of Indexical Beliefs

Gareth Evans (1982) drew a distinction between knowledge that is dependent on identification and knowledge that is free from identification. The best example of identification-free knowledge is that of demonstrative propositions, like: "This is red". Demonstrative identification, in fact, does not pass through the recognition of any property. It is this feature that generates the immunity to error through misidentification of the I-thoughts. To say something about other people or about the world we need some piece of evidence. On the contrary, statements about our own beliefs or our own feelings do not need any evidence. According to Evans, the immunity from self-misidentification is better in the case of demonstrative identification than that of I-thoughts. While it is uncontroversial that I may be wrong about how the world goes, or in my inferences about what happens in the heads of other people, it is doubtful that I might actually be wrong about the contents of my own mind. This immunity, however, is not absolute (Shoemaker 1968; Davidson 1984). In some cases we may be wrong even on the content of beliefs about ourselves. First, the authority of the first person is higher for certain attitudes, such as beliefs and desires, and less for others, such as intention or memory. Moreover, in many cases evidence that is available to others, or even to ourselves at a later time, can modify the opinion that an individual has about himself. After all, the authority of the first person is based simply on an asymmetry between the speaker and the listener in interpreting the words of a conversation. While the listener interprets the speaker on a wide range of facts, the speaker does not interpret his own words. According to Davidson, the authority of the first person is not a logical question, but it is based on the different strategies for attention allocation between the speaker and the listener. Since the speaker cannot continually ask himself whether he really means what he is saying, he must consider true what he is actually saying, while the listener engaged in the process of interpreting the speaker may have some doubt about the content of what he is listening to.

Davidson then builds the asymmetry between the representations that concern themselves, and those concerning others or the rest of the world, on a cognitive resource such as attention. As mentioned above, my claim is that reference of FPBs depends on a specific mode of representation of the first-person bodily perspective. It seems that the human brain represents the body in a specific way, without any attribution of a property to oneself or the mastery of a self-concept. There is a huge amount of research on the neural basis of categorization. Neural networks, which are responsible for self-recognition and bodily self-representation, have different architectures. The localization of the Self in the brain remains controversial. Some evidence, however, is quite strong. The feeling of body ownership, for example, is no longer a mystery, it is but a neural function consisting in the integration of bodily sensations. According to Frederique De Vignemont, "The sense of ownership thus derives from a sensori-motor map that defines the spatial boundaries of one's own body. These boundaries are flexible, depending on the integration of afferent and efferent information. By its relationship with the body schema, the sense of ownership of one's own body is linked to the sense of agency of one's own actions. These two aspects of self-consciousness are both grounded in action" (De Vignemont 2007: 445).

On the whole, the findings of cognitive neuroscience provide a comprehensive picture of the functional architecture of the feeling of body ownership. In the pre-motor cortex the main centre for multimodal integration of the tactile, proprioceptive, vestibular, and sensorimotor information is found. The body schema — a spatial and multimodal representation aimed for motor control — is responsible for the sense of body ownership. According to Henrik Ehrsson, Charles Spence and Richard Passingham, the feeling of ownership of limbs would be the result of integration in the premotor cortex of three streams of information: from proprioception, sensorimotor response and sight. Moreover, the role of the vestibular system is evidenced by the so-called "Pinocchio experiment". In this particular type of proprioceptive illusion, psychologists induce illusory arm extension by tendon vibration. If a blindfolded individual holds his nose and, and at the same time, is subjected to a stimulation of wrist tendons, he will experience his nose as getting longer (Lackner, 1988).

The neural architecture of body ownership and other evidence coming from (mirror)self-recognition and out-of-body experiences show how neural networks which encode the sense of ownership of one's own body are different from these which are responsible for the categorization of other people and objects (Metzinger 2005). Although categorization is essential to many cognitive processes, identifying the neural substrates underlying categorization is a real challenge. The processes of object recognition and categorization are widely distributed in the brain (Riesenhuber 2009; Pulvermüller 2010). However, brain areas mainly involved in linguistic and conceptual categorization are different from these dedicated to encoding body self-identification. This suggests that self-reference is a cognitive function specifically realized in the brain and characterized by non-conceptual bodily representations.

7 Indexical Beliefs and Consciousness

The essentiality of *de se* beliefs is not to be confused with self-consciousness. One could think that "demonstrative and *de se* beliefs involve a demonstrative mode of awareness" (Hunter, 2009), since first-person beliefs can make the difference in an explanation of agency only if they make a difference in an agent's dispositions. But this does not mean that self-consciousness causes the behaviour. We simply cannot understand it without an essential relationship between an agent and the content of her belief. Self-consciousness itself is neither a necessary nor sufficient condition to cause the overt behaviour. There are, in fact, many actions that happen without consciousness, and many conscious states that do not produce any action.

The fact that a FPB is essentially referred to its bearer does not mean she has to be conscious both of the cognitive state and of the reference. It is not necessary to imagine an individual as conscious to understand how her (indexical) beliefs work (see also Feit 2008: 92-93). The fact that indexical beliefs refer in an "essential" way to their bearer is a condition that gives them a special motivational force. However, this does not mean that the bearer of the beliefs must necessarily be aware of this circumstance. Consciousness and self-consciousness are the logical space for the justification of actions.

My account of the relationship between self-consciousness and FPBs is based on the distinction drawn by Alvin Goldman (2006) between two levels of mind reading. One of these is represented by a low level simulation concerning the understanding of the aim of an action, understanding that is controlled by the mirror system in the brain; and the other consists of a high level simulation taking place in cognitive processes such as that of taking a different point of view from one's own, and the so-called "counterfactual imagination". But these states of mind are systematically formulated in the form of first-person beliefs (for instance: "If I were in your shoes, then I would behave in such and such way").

We need to notice that usually, low level simulations take place unconsciously, whereas high-level simulations give rise to the feeling of awareness. However, what is most important in this is that high level simulations make use of the same cognitive resources, such as counterfactual imagination, that are in play in self-consciousness. When we develop inner speech, silently drifting in our stream of consciousness, we reason in the same way as when we simulate another individual in order to explain and predict her actions. High-level simulation is an activity of projection which, to take place, must have an inner space upon which to be based and from which to operate. Self-consciousness is the inner space from which high level simulation proceeds in its behavioural predictions, and in understanding the reasons behind the actions of others as well as our own. To explain behavioural prediction in competitive situations and in playing games, the simulationist's approach must be able to distinguish between what I would do in counterfactual circumstances, and what, instead, I would expect the individual I am simulating would do. The idea that reflexive reasoning, i.e., the conceptual and linguistic side of self-consciousness which is systematically formulated in the form of first-person beliefs, could work as a base for high level simulation, and as inner space for behavioural explanations, is a way of making it possible for simulationism to tackle one of its most difficult problems. It is also a way of shedding some light on the mysterious relationship between self-consciousness, mindreading, and first-person beliefs.

References

Anscombe, E., 1957. *Intention*. Oxford: Basil Blackwell.

Astington, J., & Baird, J. (eds.). 2005. *Why language matters for theory of mind.* Oxford: Oxford University Press.

Bard, K. A., 1992. "Intentional behaviour and intentional communication in young free-ranging orangutans". Child Development, 63, 1186-1197.

Baron-Cohen, S., Leslie, A., Frith, U., 1985. "Does the autistic child have a 'theory of mind'?". *Cognition* 21, 37-46.

Bates, E., Camaioni, L., Volterra, V., 1975. "The acquisition of performatives prior to speech". *Merrill-Palmer Quarterly*, 21, 205-226.

Bloom, P., 2004. *Descartes' Baby: How the science of child development explains what makes us human.* New York: Basic Books.

Bloom, P., 2007. "More than words: A reply to Malt and Sloman". Cognition 105, 649-655.

Call, J., Tomasello, M., 1994. "Production and comprehension of referential pointing by orangutans (Pongo Pygmaeus)". *Journal of Comparative Psychology* 108, 4, 307-317.

Camaioni, L., Perucchini, P., Bellagamba, F., Colonnesi, C., 2004. "The role of declarative pointing in developing a theory of mind". *Infancy* 5, 3, 291-308.

Corazza, E., Fish, W., Gorvet, J., 2002. "Who is I?". *Philosophical Studies* 107, 1-21.

Csibra, G., Southgate, V., 2006. "Evidence for infants' understanding of false beliefs should not be dismissed". *Trends in Cognitive Sciences* 10, 4-5.

Davidson, D., 1963. "Actions, Reasons and Causes", *Journal of Philosophy* 60; reprinted in *Subjective, Intersubjective, Objective*. Oxford: Oxford University Press, 2001.

Davidson, D., 1980. *Essays on Actions and Events*. Oxford: Clarendon Press, 3-19.

Davidson, D., 1984. *Inquiries into Truth and Interpretation*. Oxford University Press: Oxford.

De Vignemont, F., 2007. "Habeas Corpus: The Sense of Ownership of One's Own Body". *Mind and Language* 22 (4).

Diessel, H., 1999. *Demostratives. Form, Function, and Grammaticalization*. Amsterdam and Philadelphia: Benjamins.

Evans , G., 1982. *The Varieties of References*. Oxford: Oxford University Press.

Falk, A., E., 2004. *Desire and Belief.* Hamilton Books (revised edition).

Feit, N., 2008. *Belief about the Self.* Oxford: Oxford University Press.

Fouts, R. S., Hirsch, A. D., Fouts, D. H., 1982. “Cultural transmission of a human language in a chimpanzee mother-infant relationship”. In Fitzgerald. H., Mullins J., Cage P. (eds.). Child nurturance: Studies of developmental in nonhuman primates. New York: Plenum Press, 159-193.

Goldman, A., I., 2006. *Simulating Minds: The Philosophy, Psychology, and Neuroscience of Mindreading.* Oxford: Oxford University Press.

Hunter, D. A., 2009. “Demonstrative Belief and Dispositions”. *Journal of Philosophical Research*

Leavens, D. A., Hostetter, A. B., Wesley, M. J., Hopkins, W. D., 2004. “Tactical use of unimodal and bimodal communication by chimpanzees, Pan troglodytes”. *Animal Behaviour* 67, 467-476.

Leger, D. W., 1993. “Contextual sources of information and responses to animal communication signals”. *Psychological Bullettin* 113, 2, 295-304.

Kanner, L., 1943. “Autistic disturbances of affective contact”. *Nervous Child* 2, 217-250.

Kaplan, D., 1989. "Demonstratives." In Almog, J., Perry, J., Wettstein, H. (eds.). *Themes from Kaplan.* Oxford: Oxford University Press, 481-563.

Kim, J., 2003. “The American origins of philosophical naturalism”. *Journal of Philosophical Research*, APA Centennial Volume, 83-98.

Kraemer, E.R., 1985. “Beliefs, Dispositions and Demonstratives”. *Australasian Journal of Philosophy* 63, 167-76.

Lackner, J.R., 1988. “Some proprioceptive influences on the perceptual re- presentation of body shape and orientation”. *Brain* 111, 281-297.

Loveland, K. A., 1984. “Learning about points of views: spatial perspective and the acquisition of ‘I/you’”. *Journal of Child Language* 11, 535-556.

McDowell, J., 1994. *Mind and World.* Cambridge, Mass.: Harvard University Press; reissued with a new introduction, 1996.

Metzinger, T., 2005. “Out-of-body experiences as the origin of the concept of a «soul»”. *Mind & Matter* 3, 1, 57-84.

Miles, H. L., 1990. “The cognitive foundations for reference in a signing orangutan”. In Parker, S.T., Gibson, K.R. (eds.). *Language and intelligence in monkeys and apes: Comparative developmental perspectives* . Cambridge: Cambridge University Press, 511-536.

Inoue-Nakamura, N., Matsuzawa, T., 1997. “Development of stone tool use by wild chimpanzees (Pan troglodytes)”. *Journal of Comparative Psychology* 111, 159-173.

Nunberg, G., 1993, “Indexicality and Deixis”. *Linguistics and Philosophy* 16, 1.

Patterson, F. 1978. Linguistic capabilities of a lowland gorilla. In Peng F. (ed.). *Sign language and language acquisition in man and ape*. Boulder: Westview Press, 161-201.

Penn, D.C., Povinelli, D.J., 2007. “On the lack of evidence that chimpanzees possess anything remotely resembling a ‘theory of mind’”. *Philosophical Transactions of the Royal Society* B, 362, 731-744.

Perconti, P., 2002. “Context-dependence in human language and animal communication systems”. *Foundations of Science* 7, 3, 341-362.

Perner, J., Ruffman, T., 2005. "Infants' insight into the mind: How deep?". *Science* 308, 214-216.

Perry, J., 2000. *The Problem of the Essential Indexical and Other Essays*. Expanded Edition: Stanford, CSLI Publications (or.: 1979).

Perry, J., 2002. *Identity, personal identity and the self.* Indianapolis and Cambridge: Hackett.

Povinelli, D.J., Bering, J., Giambrone, S., 2003. "Chimpanzee 'pointing': Another error of the argument by analogy?". In Kita S. (ed.). *Pointing: Where language culture and cognition meet.* Lawrence Erlbaum, 35-68.

Predelli, S., 1998. "I am not here now". *Analysis* 58 (2), 107-115.

Predelli, S., 2010. *I Am Still Not Here Now*. Erkenntnis.

Premack, D.G., Woodruff, G., 1978. "Does the chimpanzee have a theory of mind?". *Behavioral and Brain Sciences* 1, 1978, 515-526.

Pulvermüller, F., 2010. "Brain-language research: Where is the progress?". *Biolinguistics* 4 (2-3), 255-288.

Putnam, H., 2004. "The Content and Appeal of 'Naturalism'". In De Caro, M., Macarthur, D. (eds.), *Naturalism in question.* Cambridge, Mass: Harvard University Press, 59-70.

Reddy, V., 2010. "Engaging Minds in the first year: The developing awareness of attention and intention" In Bremner G., Wachs, T. (eds). *Handbook of Infant Development.* 2nd Edition. Chichester: Wiley-Blackwell.

Riesenhuber, M., 2009. "Object categorization in man, monkey, and machine: some answers and some open questions". In Dickinson, S.J., Leonardis, A., Schiele, B., Tarr, M.J. (eds.). *Object Categorization. Computer and Human Vision Perspectives.* Cambridge: Cambridge University Press.

Romero, E., Soria, B., 2005. "'I' as a Pure indexical and metonymy as language reduction", en Modeling and Using Context: 5th Int. and Interdisciplinary conference, CONTEXT 2005, Springer-Verlag, LNAI.

Savage-Rumbaugh, E. S., McDonald, K., Sevcik, R. A., Hopkins, W. D., Rubert, E., 1986. "Spontaneous symbol acquisition and communicative use by pygmy chimpanzees (Pan paniscus)". *Journal of Experimental Psychology: General* 115, 211-235.

Sellars, W., 1956. "Empiricism and the Philosophy of Mind". In Feigl, H., Scriven, M. (eds.). *The Foundations of Science and the Concepts of Psychoanalysis, Minnesota Studies in the Philosophy of Science*, vol. I, reprinted in *Science, Perception and Reality*, Routledge & Kegan Paul Ltd; London, and The Humanities Press: New York; 1963, 127–96.

Shoemaker, S., 1968. "Self-reference and Self-awareness". *Journal of Philosophy* 65, 555-67.

Sidelle, A., 1991. "The Answering Machine Paradox". *Canadian Journal of Philosophy* 81 (4), 525-539.

Smyth, R., 1995. "Conceptual perspective-taking and children's interpretation of pronouns in reported speech". *Journal of Child Language* 22, 171-187.

Surian, L., Caldi, S., Sperber, D., 2007. "Attribution of beliefs by 13-month-old infants". *Psychological Science* 18, 7, 580-58.

Tager-Flusberg, H., 2000. "Understanding the language and communicative impairments in autism". In Glidden, L-M. (ed.). *International Review of Research on Mental Retardation*, Vol. 20, San Diego: Academic Press, 185-205.

Tager-Flusberg, H., 2007. "Evaluating the theory of mind hypothesis of autism. Current Directions". *Psychological Science* 16, 316-320.

Tomasello, M., Call, J., Hare, B., 2003. "Chimpanzees versus humans: it's not that simple". *Trends in Cognitive Science* 7, 239-240.

Vea, J. J., Sabater-Pi, J., 1998. "Spontaneous pointing behaviour in the wild pygmy chimpanzee (Pan paniscus)". *Folia Primatologica*, 69, 289-290.

Velleman, D., 2007. *Practical Reflection.* Stanford, CSLI Publications.

von Wright, G., 1971. *Explanation and Understanding.* Ithaca: Cornell University Press.

Wimmer, H., Perner, J., 1983. "Belief about belief". *Cognition* 13, 103-128.

Wittgenstein, L., 1953. "Philosophical Investigations". In Anscombe, G.E.M., Rhees, R. (eds.). Oxford: Basil Blackwell.

14

Time and Person in Thought

MICHAEL NELSON

The accuracy of much of our belief and speech is contextual in the broad sense that its correctness is dependent on the circumstances of the thinking and speaking. My thinking that I am writing is correct and your thinking that you are writing is not. The difference seems to trace to the contextual difference that I thought my thought and you thought yours. Similarly, my saying today, "It is sunny," is correct while my uttering the same words yesterday incorrect. Again, the difference seems to trace to the contextual difference about the time the utterances occurred and the location the reports concerned.

My primary focus will be on first-personal and temporal thought. I argue that there are important differences between the nature of the contextualization in these two cases. First-personal thinking involves a context-sensitive element that remains constant across different thinkers, accounting for the similarity in the different acts of thinking. When tokened by those different thinkers, that context-sensitive element determines an impersonal proposition about that thinker herself and hence a different proposition for each thinker. So, the proposition I entertain when I think to myself, "I am writing," is a proposition directly about me and distinct from the proposition Bill entertains when he thinks to himself, "I am writing." If the proposition [Bill is writing] is true relative to Bill, if that even makes sense, then it is true relative to everyone; its truth is indifferent to any "person parameter" that may be assigned it. I argue that temporal thought, on the other hand, is contextually invariant, in the sense that the proposition I entertained when yesterday I thought to myself, "It's sunny," is the same proposition I entertain today when I think to myself, "It's sunny." The day of the thinking

Attitudes De Se: Linguistics, Epistemology, Metaphysics.
Neil Feit and Alessandro Capone (eds.).

does not affect the proposition entertained. Instead, this proposition's truth value is sensitive to the time at which it is assessed. One and the same proposition is true with respect to today and false with respect to yesterday. In this way, time is a meaningful parameter of truth and persons are not. This difference affects the nature of the dependence on the circumstance of thinking of first-personal and temporal forms of thought.

I am thus taking a stand on the issue of contextualism versus relativism, which has received a fair amount of press of late. We intuit a variation in the truth value of a single sentence *s*. The contextualist claims that that is to be explained in terms of the context-sensitivity of *s*'s linguistic meaning. *s* expresses different propositions, some with different truth values, in different contexts.[1] Temporal adverbs like 'yesterday' provide a fairly noncontroversial example of context-sensitivity. The relativist, on the other hand, accounts for the same phenomena by claiming that *s* expresses the same proposition in every context, ignoring the possible effects of other contextual factors. But that proposition is not true or false absolutely. It is true at some points and false at others. The standard view of alethic modals is relativistic. A nonmodalized sentence like 'Bill is sitting' expresses a world-neutral proposition. Because that proposition is true at some worlds and false at others, 'It is necessary that Bill is sitting' is false.

Formally, contexts and indices play similar roles. In each case they are sequences of parameter values—say, a person, a time, a place, a world, an evaluative standard—that function as points at which we can relativize some aspect of a sentence's semantic value. But they relativize different

---

[1] For the purposes of this paper I operate with a single version of the contextualist strategy according to which a sentence expresses different propositions in different contexts. But much of what I say carries over to both ambiguity and implicature strategies. Ambiguity strategies find that the sentence form is associated with a multitude of different linguistic meanings and context selects the operative meaning. Implicature strategies find that utterances of the sentence pragmatically implicate different propositions, even though the sentence itself expresses the same proposition across all contexts, at least with respect to the parameter in question. What unites these strategies, and differentiates them from the relativist strategy described below, is that they uncover different propositions communicated by the different utterances and claim that those different propositions have different truth values, accounting for the original intuition that the different utterances have different truth values. I will thus use the standard contextualist account as a model for all of these views. While I am a contextualist about first-personal thought, which is my main focus, I find an implicature account more appealing for the other phenomenon I discuss in passing and for which I defend a contextualist account in the text. The differences between contextualism proper and ambiguity and implicature accounts is not pertinent to the main aims of this paper and so I cast them all under the same umbrella here. It is a different set of considerations that decide between the ambiguity, contextualist, and implicature theorists than decide the case between the contextualist and relativist and the other two views will be, by and large, in the same boat with respect to the disagreement with relativism.

semantic aspects. Contexts relativize what a sentence expresses and indices relativize the truth value of what sentences express.

Relativists offer linguistic and psychological evidence in favor of their views. For example, some offer the phenomena of faultless disagreement, in which two parties genuinely disagree about a matter but neither is making a mistake, as evidence favoring relativism over contextualism.[2] In the late seventies and early eighties, David Lewis (Lewis 1979) offered psychological evidence that he claimed favored a position similar to relativism about first-person thought. And recent defenses of contextualism involve syntactic arguments claimed to support contextualist accounts of a variety of linguistic expressions. Also in the early eighties, Mark Richard (Richard 1981, 1982) offered psychological evidence that he claimed favored contextualism about temporal thought. I think that these arguments underdetermine the choice between contextualism and relativism. I argue for a paradigm shift in our approach to these issues. I argue for a strong connection between meaning, what is said, and truth conditions and the nature and constitution of reality. This connection allows us, then, to bring metaphysical considerations to bear on the debate. I argue that this promises to shed new and brighter light on the issues. In brief, I argue that a given parameter is a parameter of truth only if reality is constituted relative to that parameter. This follows from the above connection between meaning and the constitution of reality. Truth relativism about a given parameter entails a form of relativism about how things are. The relativist incurs a metaphysical burden of the constitution of reality, how things are, being relative to parameters of truth. Turning, then, to metaphysics, there are reasons to think that the constitution of reality is perspectival with respect to time but not persons and so we should be relativists about temporal thought and speech and contextualist about first-personal thought and speech. I suggest that these considerations can be extended to show that only times and worlds are parameters of truth.

The structure of the paper is as follows. In section 1 I discuss first-personal thought. I use Lewis as a representative relativist about the first-person and John Perry as a contextualist. I argue that the considerations each side uses to support their position, largely psychological in character, fail to settle the matter. I discuss temporal thought in section 2. I survey the primary arguments for and against contextualism about temporal thought and again find them wanting. In section 3 I extend the response strategies developed in the earlier sections to more recent arguments, focusing on the faultless disagreement argument for relativism. In section 4 I present an argument linking the relativist/contextualist debate to metaphysical theses

[2] See for example (Kölbel 2003, 2008). I discuss the argument in section 3 below.

about the constitution of reality. In section 5 I argue that reality is fundamentally perspectival with respect to time but not persons, which, in light of the conclusions from section 4, supports relativism about temporal thought and contextualism about first-personal thought.

1 First-Personal Thought

One can have a thought that just happens to be about oneself. One may see what is in fact one's own reflection in a mirror without realizing it as such. In such a case one has third-personal beliefs that happen to be about oneself. First-personal beliefs are importantly different. When one feels hungry and thinks to oneself on that basis, "I am hungry," one's belief doesn't just happen to be about oneself. One's belief is immune to error through misidentification, in the sense that one cannot be correct that someone is hungry on that basis but mistaken about who it is that is hungry. (Shoemaker 1968) Furthermore, when I identify the person that I am as myself, my thought about, say, my disheveled appearance has very different effects on my behavior and roles in my psychological life than the third-personal judgment to the same effect, even though the judgment does not exhibit immunity to error through misidentification. If I am motivated to look nice, the first-personal thought will lead me to reach up and straighten my hair while the other will not. Our topic, then, is what precisely this difference between first-personal and third-personal thought comes to and what these differences shows about the nature of attitudes like belief, the objects of the attitudes, and the nature of truth.

David Lewis famously argued that propositions, conceived as sets of possible worlds, are not the objects of the attitudes. Lewis argued that having a first-personal thought about oneself should be construed as self-ascribing a property. In this case, the object of thought is not a proposition, something true or false, but a property, something had by individuals.[3] John Perry, first in (Perry 1977), argued that the objects of first-personal thought are impersonal propositions about the thinker, a proposition that anyone else can grasp and that is true or false absolutely, but that there is an independent level of thought—in the case of beliefs, what Perry calls in (Perry 1979) *belief states* as opposed to *belief contents*—that comes in both first- and third-personal flavors. While we can all grasp the proposition [JP is disheveled], only JP can believe that proposition in virtue of being in a first-personal belief state. While we can all be in a first-personal belief state to

[3] While Lewis only targets the view that the objects of the attitudes are propositions in the sense of sets of possible worlds (Lewis 1979, 134–135), I think that his arguments are no less plausible when applied to any account of the objects of first-personal attitudes that construes them as both impersonal and absolutely true or false.

the effect that one is disheveled, each of us thereby believes a different proposition; and finally, while JP all the while believed the proposition [JP is disheveled] after stepping on the bus and seeing his reflection, it is only after he realized that he had been viewing himself that he came to believe that proposition in virtue of being in a first-personal belief state. So, for Perry, ordinary, impersonal propositions are the uniform objects of thought; the difference between first- and third-personal thinking about oneself is accounted for at the level of differences in belief states.

While Perry's view is evidently an instance of the contextualist strategy characterized above, it is less apparent that Lewis's view is an instance of the relativist strategy. However, Lewis's thesis that properties are the objects of first-personal thought is isomorphic to a position according to which relativized structured propositions are the objects of the attitudes that are true or false at agents. Suppose that there is a concept **FIRST-PERSON** that is directly about an individual without being attached to any particular person. This concept retains its identity and content under different assignments of objects, where those assignments are extra-contentful, somewhat analogously to a free variable in standard quantificational logic. Then the thought that contains the concept **FIRST-PERSON** and the property **wrote this paper** is a thought that is true or false only under an assignment of an object to **FIRST-PERSON** and its truth value shifts across different assignments. One and the same thought is true relative to an assignment of me as the subject of the concept and false relative to an assignment of you as the subject. It is important that we conceive, however, the "assignment" in this case functioning as an index of truth, relativizing the truth or falsity prediction to the same content. Such a view promises to make sense of the rather mysterious primitive in Lewis's view of self-ascribing a property: Self-ascription of a property is just entertaining a proposition with that property and the self concept.

Lewis and Perry consider the case of Hume and Heimson.[4] Both Hume and Heimson have beliefs that they would express by uttering the words 'I am Hume.' Hume is right and Heimson is crazy. This may lead one to conclude that they think different thoughts. If they believed the same thing, one

---

[4] Perhaps Lewis's most famous case is that of the two gods who believe all and only true impersonal propositions but are nonetheless ignorant about who they are. The case strikes me as problematic. Lewis imagines the two gods acting in the world that they have complete impersonal omniscience of: One throws down manna from the tallest mountain and the other throws down thunderbolts from the coldest mountain. But action is impossible without first-personal thought. So, the gods either do not act or they must have *some* idea who they are, lest none of their thoughts and intentions of, say, manna dropping direct and cause their behavior. In any case, more familiar cases like the Hume/Heimson case seem to be less problematic.

and the same thing would be both true and not true, which cannot be. This, then, is our first argument against relativism.

Lewis responded by denying that what is believed is true or false. He then offered a counterargument from interalism about the mental that Hume's and Heimson's beliefs are the same. The first is his defense of relativism and the second his argument against contextualism and in favor of relativism. Let's take each in turn.

To believe of oneself that one is Hume is, Lewis claims, to self-ascribe the property **being identical to Hume**. Ascriptions of properties are not true or false *simpliciter*; they are, like open sentences, only true or false of an object or sequence of objects. The property **being identical to Hume** is true of Hume and false of Heimson (and everyone but Hume). So, conceiving of the property **being identical to Hume** as the object of both Hume's and Heimson's beliefs is compatible with Hume's belief being true and Heimson's false, provided we embrace the following principle: *x*'s self-ascription of the property **F** is true just in case *x* instantiates *F*. If we adopt the relativized proposition version of Lewis's view, we can similarly escape the objection. In that case, we embrace the following principle: *x*'s self-thought consisting of the concept **FIRST-PERSON** and the property **F** is true just in case that relativized proposition is true relative to an assignment of *x* as subject of the first-person concept.

Each principle renders the view that Heimson and Hume think the same thing when they say to themselves, "I am Hume," consistent with the fact that Hume is correct and Heimson is not. This seems to me a powerful response to the argument. I now turn to Lewis's positive argument for relativism.

Suppose that Heimson and Hume both think to themselves,

"I am being attacked by a bear." Both will behave much the same way: They will run and for the same reason. Suppose that each thinks to himself, "I need to brush my hair," and each has the same idea about what constitutes good hygiene and motive for good hygiene. Again, both will behave in similar ways (provided they are presented with the same sort of hair-brushing devices). We explain their behaviors by citing the psychological states that caused them and those states, in virtue of their contents, should rationalize that behavior. But then the contents of their states are the same, as the explanation of their similar behavior is the same. Contextualism entails that they believe different propositions, in light of the different contextual differences between their identities. So, contextualism should be rejected. This, in brief, is the argument from internalism in favor of relativism about first-personal thought.

The contextualist can respond to the argument from internalism by appealing to Perry's distinction between cognitive states and cognitive contents. Every thinking event has two aspects: First, the cognitive state, which is the internally individuated aspect of the episode, and, second, the cognitive content, which is the proposition the agent entertains in virtue of being in the state she is in the circumstances she finds herself. Cognitive states are individuated in terms of narrow functional roles; roughly, in terms of their inferential relations to one another and causal relations between sensory input and muscle movements.[5] Perry thinks of cognitive states as structured, composed of notions of objects and ideas of properties and relations.[6] Suppose I have two unrelated notions of Sam. Believing of Sam that he is funny under one of those notions and believing of Sam that he is not funny under the other notion is not rationally inconsistent. Similarly, it does not rationally license the inference that someone is funny and not funny. When those notions come to be linked, that inference is licensed and so, being reluctant to make it, there is rational pressure, not present when my ideas were unlinked, to revise either my belief that Sam is funny or my belief that he is not funny. Notions and ideas are thus implicated in the explanation and predictions of behavior and rational assessment of attitudes.

Let's return to Hume and Heimson and the argument from internalism. In virtue of their different circumstances—in particular, the fact that Hume is Hume and Heimson is Heimson—the content of Hume's belief is distinct from the content of Heimson's, the first being about Hume and the second about Heimson. Still, our contextualist agrees that *something* important is the same about Heimson and Hume's mental states; she just denies that that something is content. Our contextualist accepts the existence of internally individuated cognitive states and Hume and Heimson are in the same type of cognitive state. Cognitive states are important to psychology, as they help us use the propositional attitudes of an agent to explain, predicate, and rationally assess behaviors. The internalist intuitions, then, are to be explained in terms of these cognitive states. Lewis is right that psychology requires something internally individuated but wrong that the objects of the attitudes is so individuated.

Perry's account is more complex than Lewis's, in that he posits a distinction between content and state where Lewis doesn't. But some further complexity is needed to do justice to the phenomena. Do Heimson and Hume believe the same thing? Ordinary intuition is equivocal. Lewis does a nice job of highlighting the side that says yes. One way of highlighting the

---

5 Cognitive states are both holistic and idiosyncratic. They must be to do the work of accounting for all differences in cognitive value. This makes them particularly ill-suited to serve the role of contents of the cognitive states, which should be both shareable and often shared.

6 Notions and ideas are first introduced in (Crimmins and Perry, 1989). See also (Perry 2002, chapter 10).

other side is to focus on the fact that Hume is right and Heimson is wrong, which I believe Lewis accommodates. But there are other reasons to think that they do not believe the same thing. When you say to me, "I am going to dinner," I believe what you said. But I don't then self-ascribe the property **going to dinner**. Instead, I believe an objective proposition about you. I don't believe what you say by coming to believe that *I* am going to dinner but instead by coming to believe that *you* are going to dinner. I am not suggesting that the relativist is unable to account for this. Of course she can, but to do so she must introduce her own complexity, offering an account of successful communication and intuitions concerning when two people "believe the same thing" in terms of sufficient similarity between distinct content. Both sides must recognize something in common and something different between Hume's and Heimson's belief. The contextualist and the relativist offer different accounts of what is the same and what is different, but both sides need to recognize some complexity mirrored by the other side. The difference is not that one view is simpler than the other; it is instead where the variety is located.

I have compared two competing accounts of first-personal thought and argued that the psychological data presented as favoring one side over the other are inconclusive. In the next section I discuss Perry's account of self-thought in more detail. I return, in sections 4–5, to this debate, arguing that we have metaphysical grounds for preferring a contextualist account of first-personal thought.

1.1 Perry on Forms of Self-Knowledge

In (Perry 1998, 2002), Perry distinguishes three kinds of self-knowledge. He calls the first agent-relative knowledge, the second self-attached knowledge, and the third knowledge of the person one happens to be. The second is the familiar kind of self-knowledge where the agent conceives of herself in a first-person way as having a given property or bearing a given relation. The third is the kind of self-knowledge involved in cases of mistaken identity, where the object whose identity one is mistaken about is oneself. I argue that Perry's catalog is both long by one and short by one. Agent-relative knowledge is not, I argue, a genuine form of self-knowledge. And the list does not include the philosophically important notion of knowledge of oneself as an object in the world, which I argue is distinct from all of the forms of self-knowledge Perry articulates.

Perry claims that agent-relative knowledge is a kind of knowledge that concerns oneself but does not involve a self-notion. When we gain information about our immediate environment and act on that information, we have a form of self-knowledge but, typically at least, the self-notion is not involved. So, this form of knowledge involves neither the employment of the self-notion nor an explicit representation in thought of the person one is, thus distinguishing it from the other two forms of self-knowledge. It is nonetheless knowledge about the self as it "embodies knowledge of the relations things stand in to the agent; the thoughts are true because of facts about the agent" (Perry 1998, 329). The self is an unarticulated constituent of this form of knowledge.

We need to begin by clarifying the notion of an unarticulated constituent and then evaluating the grounds for the thesis that perceptual knowledge that guides behavior does indeed have the self as an unarticulated constituent.

The notion of unarticulated constituents first appeared in (Perry 1989). While Perry employs the notion frequently, there remains some unclarity in how to understand the notion. I present two interpretations. According to the first, an unarticulated constituent is a constituent of a proposition expressed by an utterance that is not contributed by any syntactic element, however deeply buried in logical form, of the sentence uttered. As an example, Perry claims that there is no syntactic element corresponding to a location in the sentence 'It is raining' and yet typical utterances of that sentence express propositions with a fairly determinate location specification as a constituent. Unarticulated constituents are related to the relevance theorist's notion of free enrichment. (See (Sperber and Wilson 1986) and (Carston 2002).) The notion of an unarticulated constituent applies to cases of thinking as opposed to speaking as follows. A thought has an unarticulated constituent when there is a constituent of the proposition entertained that is not contributed by and does not correspond to any notion or idea in the cognitive state in virtue of which the agent entertains that proposition.

A competing understanding of the notion of an unarticulated constituent conceives of the constituent in question not as an element of the proposition expressed or entertained but rather as a parameter relative to which that proposition has a truth value. On this version of the view, all utterances of the sentence 'It is raining' express the same proposition, but a given utterance also contributes a location specification against which that proposition is to be evaluated and in virtue of which the utterance is correct or incorrect. And similarly for the thought version of the view. On this account, accepting that a given parameter is an unarticulated constituent is accepting a version of truth relativism about that parameter. This seems to be how François Recanati (Recanati 2007) interprets Perry's view that the self is an unarticulated constituent in agent-relative knowledge.

While I suspect that Perry intended the first interpretation,[7] the text is not explicit. In order to remain neutral between the two conceptions of unar-

[7] Perry has confirmed this in conversation.

ticulated constituency distinguished above, I shall operate with a very broad conception of implicit components of a judgment that include components the agent is not in a position to articulate, constituents of the thought grasped that do not correspond to any ideas or notions constitutive of the agent's judgment, and constituents at which the thought grasped is evaluated for truth and falsity. I argue that Perry fails to provide compelling reason to think that the self is implicit, even in the broad sense above, in cases of immediate perception-based action. I thus think that the form of knowledge Perry labels as agent-relative self-knowledge is not a genuine form of *self*-knowledge.

I see an apple in front of me and, wanting a bite, reach my hand out, seize the apple, and bring it to my mouth. Perry claims that there are identities that "one need not keep track of" in thought as they are "architectural" relations between the eyes and arms" of the agent (Perry 2002, 208). I agree and so grant that facts about who is perceiving, thinking, and acting and her relationship to objects in the world enter into the full account of the success of the action, even if those facts are not consciously and explicitly being considered by the agent herself at the time of perceiving, thinking, and acting. But I deny that the thoughts guiding her behavior are therefore a form of self-knowledge and that those thoughts are "true because of facts about the agent."

We should distinguish preconditions for making a given judgment and factors implicit, in the above sense, to that judgment. I claim that relations between the object perceived and acted on and the agent are preconditions, not implicit factors, of the judgments that cause the behavior.

Consider the perceptual judgment one would express by saying, "There is an apple there." Perry claims that, while nothing refers to the agent herself, the information ``that the apple was a certain distance and direction" from the agent is part of the judgment, for otherwise the perceptual judgment would not guide behavior the way that it evidently does (328). "The complex movement of arm, hand, fingers, neck and jaw was successful in getting the apple into my mouth because of the distance and direction the apple was from *me*. What I learned from perception, then, must have been the distance and direction of the apple from *me*" (327). Perry maintains that, in this case, the agent is an unarticulated constituent of the perceptual judgment, akin to the relativization to time zone in a judgment that it is 3pm, to the Northern Hemisphere in a judgment that December is a winter month, and to a locale in a judgment that it is raining. Reflection shows, however, that the role of the agent is very different than the role of time zones, hemispheres, and locales in the other judgments. The apple's being a certain distance and direction from the agent is a precondition of making the perceptual judgment that there is an apple there, in the manner judged, not an implicit constituent of the judgment, as they are in the other cases. Facts about the perceived object's relation to the agent are relevant, as preconditions, for the agent's being in a position to form the perceptual judgment she does. Those facts do not, however, function as either constituents or parameters of truth of the perceptual judgment.

Perry argues that the judgment one would express by saying, "That's an apple," is ill-suited to guide one's apple-eating behavior. The content of that judgment is constituted by the particular apple being perceived and the property of appleness. But one can grasp that content—one can make a judgment with that content—without being in a position to have that judgment guide one's behavior in such a way that results in eating the apple. The content of the demonstrative just is the particular apple itself and the property of appleness, which is a content that one can grasp by, say, remembering the apple one has demonstrated or perhaps by having been told about the apple by someone else, assuming communication transfers demonstrative identification, without being anywhere near the apple at the time of judging. In such cases, the judgment does not lead one to reach out one's hand and successfully bring the apple to one's mouth. These judgments, unlike the perceptual judgment I make in front of the apple, do not guide successful apple eating behavior. So more must be involved in the perceptual judgment. Perry seems to conclude that the full articulation of the perceptual judgment is "That's an apple *in front of me*." But then the judgment makes implicit reference to the agent insofar is it guides behavior.

I agree with Perry that the judgment that that is an apple is unsuited to guide behavior in the way that my perceptual judgment of the presence of the apple before does. I can grasp that content that that is an apple in a demonstrative way and yet, not being currently perceptually related to the apple or its location, not make a judgment that guides my apple-eating behavior in the way my actual judgment does. But the analogous argument is less effective with the judgment expressed by "There is an apple there." I am in a position to demonstratively identify the location of the apple—to refer to the place as "there" in my thought—only when I am currently in perceptual contact with that location. So, it is a precondition for thinking of a spatial location in a demonstrative way that one is currently perceptually related to that location. While the content of that judgment—the thought that there is an apple at location *l*—may well be graspable in other ways that do not require current perceptual contact with location *l*, that content cannot be grasped in a *demonstrative* way without being currently in perceptual contact with that location. A perceptual judgment will evidently involve a demonstrative identification of the spatial location. So it is a precondition for making the judgment—i.e., for grasping that content about the apple's location in a demonstrative way—that one be perceptually related to the location. But then one's relation to the location is a precondition, not an implicit constituent, of making the judgment one does.

I conclude that there is a thoroughly agent-free account of perceptual judgments that guide ordinary behaviors like eating apples, grasping cups of coffee, and petting cats. These judgments are not, in any interesting sense, forms of self-knowledge and the self is not an implicit constituent of them. Instead, they are judgments that involve demonstrative identifications of proximate spatial locations. This leaves Perry's category of agent-relative self-knowledge empty.

There is also an important variety of self-knowledge distinct from any the Perry discusses. This is knowledge of oneself as an object in the world. This kind of knowledge requires a first-personal conception of oneself that is linked with an objective representation of oneself. The failure to recognize this form of self-knowledge leads Perry and many of his followers to place too high a condition on self-attached knowledge and possession of a self notion. Nonhuman animals capable of purposeful behavior have, I believe, self-attached knowledge. They possess a self notion that they employ in thought about what to do. They also, at times at least, have knowledge of the being that they happen to be, as when a dog sees its own reflection in the mirror or perhaps when a cat plays with its tail. What they lack, and what normal functioning adult humans possess is the capacity to identify those two sorts of representations as representations of the same object. Only humans, as far as we know, conceive of themselves as a subject in the world and so conceive of themselves, under a self notion, as a self among others. This is a distinctive and important form of self-knowledge. It is perhaps composed of elements of the other two forms of self-knowledge Perry articulates—namely, the self-notion of self-attached knowledge and the objective representation of knowledge of the person one happens to be—but it involves a further cognitive capacity that goes beyond either category.

2 Temporal Thought

I turn now to temporal thought. I present the debate between relativists and contextualists about temporal thought. I argue that the evidence, largely linguistic and psychological in character, for and against the opposing positions from the existent literature leave the issue unsettled. My conclusion complements the discussion of self-thought from section 1 and motivates a search for new considerations to settle the issue, which I turn to in sections 4 and 5.

David Kaplan (Kaplan 1977) argued for relativism about tenses on the basis of the existence of temporal modifiers like `tomorrow' that shift the truth value of a sentence. Kaplan assumed that these temporal modifiers are operators and that they operate on propositions. He then reasoned that the propositions operated on must be neutral with respect to the feature shifted. For suppose that the sentence 'George is sitting' expressed a temporally saturated proposition—something to the effect that George sits at *t*. Then a temporal operator would be otiose, never shifting the truth value. For if it is ever true that George sits at *t*, then, assuming a determinate future and past, it is always true, even tomorrow, that George sits at *t*. So, for a temporal modifier to meaningfully operate on the truth of the proposition, it must operate on temporally neutral propositions. But temporally neutral propositions have their truth value relative to a time and have different truth values at different times. So, the existence of temporal modifiers supports relativism.

There are several problems with this argument. First, it overgeneralizes. 'There is no beer over here' may be true even though 'There is no beer' is false. Does this show that 'There is no beer' expresses a location neutral proposition that has a truth value only relative to a location? That seems hard to believe. Much better, it seems, to view 'at *l*' as modifying something other than the entire sentence, functioning more as an adjunct than an operator. Second, and relatedly, the argument simply assumes that expressions like 'tomorrow' express, first, operators and, second, propositional operators. But there are other options. For example, Nathan Salmon (Salmon 1989, 2003) argues that 'tomorrow' is a non-propositional operator that operates on an extra level of content. In that case the content of the sentence can be temporally specific, as there is an additional temporally neutral level of meaning for the operator to affect. Furthermore, Jeffrey King (King 2003), following the extensive literature from linguistics on the semantics and syntax of nature language tense, has argued that tenses are quantificational and temporal modifiers are not operators at all.

Whereas the relativist thinks that a simple sentence like 'George is sitting' expresses, across every context, the same temporally neutral proposition that has different truth values at different times, the contextualist maintains that an utterance of 'George is sitting' at *t* expresses the temporally specific proposition [George sits at *t*], which is true or false absolutely. There are two sets of arguments for contextualism found in the literature. The first originates in Gareth Evans's argument against tense logic (Evans 1985), and is echoed by Hugh Mellor (Mellor 1981, 1998) and Kit Fine (Fine 2005), among others. The second originates in G.E. Moore (Moore 1966) and William and Martha Kneale (Kneale and Kneale 1970) and is developed by Mark Richard (Richard 1981, 1982, 2003) and Nathan Salmon (Salmon 1989, 2003), among others. I discuss both and develop relativist responses. The responses bear a similarity to the responses developed above in section 1 on behalf of the relativist about first-personal thought. This suggests a uniform strategy of rebutting such arguments for and against relativism. I extend this strategy in the section 3 when discussing faultless disagreement.

The first argument turns on an alleged connection between semantic theory and utterances of sentences. In Evans's own words: ``I do not believe that a theory without implications for the correctness and incorrectness of utterances can lay claim to the title of a semantic theory, and it is not clear what is the connection between 'true *t*' [Evans's abbreviation for truth at-a-time] and such an evaluation of utterances" (Evans 1985, 345). Consider two utterances of the sentence 'George is speaking'. Let the first—call it U_1—occur at a time—t_1—when George is speaking and the second—call it U_2—occur at a time—t_2—when he isn't. Then U_1 is correct and U_2 is incorrect. But, the argument continues, this conflicts with the dictates of relativism.

Kit Fine (Fine 2005) articulates the following assumptions as supporting the argument.[8]

> **Link**: An utterance is correct if and only if what it states is verified by the facts.
>
> **TV1**: U_1 is correct.
>
> **TV2**: U_2 is incorrect.
>
> **Content1**: U_1 semantically encodes the proposition [George is speaking].
>
> **Content2**: U_2 semantically encodes the proposition [George is speaking].
>
> **TV Stability**: If an utterance is correct, then it is always true.
>
> **Content Stability**: If an utterance semantically encodes the proposition *p*, then it always semantically encodes *p*.

Fine claims to derive a contradiction from these claims. If both U_1 and U_2 semantically encode the same thing and so, by Content Stability, always semantically encode the same thing, then it would seem that admitting that one is correct and the other not requires that one and the same proposition is true and false, which is a contradiction. So, we should reject the relativist's assumption that the two utterances semantically encode the same proposition, opting instead for the contextualist thesis that the two utterances semantically encode different temporally specific propositions, the first absolutely true and the second absolutely false.

---

[8] The target of Fine's argument is presentism as opposed to relativism. But the argument is equally an argument against relativism and I find his presentation of the basic principles driving the argument to be particularly insightful.

The relativist can respond by offering a more complicated account of the relationship between assessments of semantic contents and assessments of utterances. A semantic theory assigns a content to a sentence-in-context. The relativist can accept that (semantic) correctness and incorrectness of an utterance is absolute even though the propositions utterances semantically encode are sometimes nonabsolutely true or false by adopting the following principle.

> **Utterance Correctness**: For all utterances *u* and times *t*, if *u* occurs at *t*, *u* is correct just in case (i) *u* semantically encodes *p* and (ii) *p* is true at *t*.

Given Utterance Correctness, we can say that U_1 from above is semantically correct and that U_2 is semantically incorrect, even though both utterances semantically encode the same proposition—the temporally-neutral, irreducibly present-tensed proposition [George is-presently speaking]. This is because that proposition has different truth values at different times, being true at t_1 and false at t_2. The semantic correctness of an utterance is inherited from the truth value of the proposition it encodes at the time of the utterance. The derivation of the contradiction presented above rests on a simple connection between utterance correctness and propositional truth, which the version of relativism being sketched here denies.

Utterances, as concrete events, are ``anchored to" their time of occurrence. While contextualist might think that this shows that the time of utterance affects the content semantically encoded, relativists can account for this fact by saying that utterances aren't evaluated at other times but have their point of evaluation fixed on the time of their occurrence. What is said, or the content an utterance semantically encodes, is evaluable at other points of evaluation, as it is temporally neutral, but the utterance itself has its anchor set by the circumstantial fact of its time of occurrence. I conclude that relativism is not threatened by the considerations raised by Evans's link between semantics and utterance evaluation. The relativist can make room for absolute correctness for utterances, inherited from relative truth for propositions those utterances semantically encode, provided she adopt some connecting principle like Utterance Correctness above.

The second argument for contextualism about temporal thought I shall consider concerns propositional attitude reports. In Richard's words: ``The evidence against temporally neuter objects is simply that diachronic agreement and disagreement seems to be, of necessity, a matter of agreement or disagreement about something temporally specific" (Richard 2003, 40). The argument runs as follows. Propositions are the objects of belief. Suppose that they are temporally neutral. Then Janet's believing in 1996 that Clinton is president combined with Janet's believing in 2005 everything that she believed in 1996, which is what it is for Janet to have not changed her mind about anything she believed in 1996, seems to entail that Janet believes in 2005 that Clinton is president. But this is the wrong result. What Janet believes in 2005 in virtue of believing in 2005 everything she believed in 1996 is that Clinton was president in 1996! So, the objects of belief are not temporally neutral and what Janet believed in 1996 is not the irreducibly present-tensed, temporally neutral proposition [Clinton is-presently president]. Instead, what Janet believed in 1996 and still believes in 2005 is the temporally saturated proposition [Clinton is president in 1996]. Relativism is inconsistent with the facts about continued belief and should, for that reason, be rejected.

The relativist can respond by distinguishing between Janet's continuing to believe in 2005 what she believed in 1996, on the one hand, and her believing in 2005 everything that she believed in 1996, on the other. The argument assumes, quite naturally it must be admitted, that they come to the same thing; the argument assumes that continued belief is believing the same thing across time. It starts with the intuitive idea that Janet continues to believe in 2005 what she believed in 1996. Such a thing should be possible without insane results, like having Janet still think that Clinton is still president in 2005. However, assuming that continued belief involves believing the same thing and the relativist thesis that the content of Janet's belief in 1996 is the temporally neutral proposition [Clinton is-presently president], that is just the result we get. My relativist responds by rejecting the natural assumption identifying continued belief with believing-true the same propositions. Insofar as Janet continues to believe in 2005 what she believed in 1996, the contents of her beliefs shift across time when those contents are temporally neutral propositions concerning temporary matters. Absent the assumption that continued belief is belief in the same proposition, the argument loses its force. For if we start not with the idea that Janet continues to believe in 2005 what she believe in 1996—not, that is, with intuitive ideas about continued belief and changing one's mind—but instead simply with the claim that she believes-true all the same proposition in 2005 that she believed-true in 1996, then the result that she believes-true the temporally neutral proposition [Clinton is-presently president] in 2005 is hardly objectionable. Sure, that's her state of mind if she believes-true all the same propositions. That is only problematic, it seems to me, if that's what it is for Janet to have not changed her mind. Drained of any connection to intuitive notion of continued belief and changing one's mind, the result is not counterintuitive. So, I maintain at its heart, the primary data driving Richard's argument are intuitions concerning continued belief across time and changing one's mind. Richard derives his result that relativism has problematic consequences regarding Janet's states of mind by assuming that continued belief is belief in the same proposition.

If continued belief is not believing-true the same propositions, then what is it? Like utterances, judgments, considered as events, occur in time. My judging that I am sitting concerns the current time, not because it contains the current time as a constituent of its content but rather because my judgment aims at or targets the present. Its correctness conditions, then, are anchored to the present. Even my present beliefs about what I was doing in the past and will be doing in the future are anchored in the present, even though they concern the past and future respectively. The times they concern are in part determined by the relation of those times to the present time at which my believings occur. The content of my judgment, however, is not anchored to the present time. To ask whether my belief (considered as a state) is true, it is not sufficient to simply look to its content; we need to also know when the belief is held, in order to have the belief's content anchored to a time and thus evaluate that content. (This is an extension of the observations I made above about the connection between assessments of semantic contents and assessments of utterance.)

These considerations ground a more complex account of continued belief and change of mind than the simple account assumed in Richard's argument. Janet's 1996 belief concerns the happenings in 1996. As time passes, to persist in her belief, she must continue to have a belief that concerns the happenings of 1996. She must, that is, have a belief with the same correctness conditions as her 1996 belief. If the original belief is temporal and she is aware of the passing of time, this requires believing a distinct proposition—the proposition [Clinton was president]—to be the content of her continued belief. This shifting in content is required to persist in having a belief with the same correctness conditions, which is what it is to continue in one's belief.[9]

I conclude that evidence concerning assessments of utterances and continued belief does not support contextualism. More generally, I argue that

[9] Complications arise. Sometimes the bare past-tense is not sufficient for continued belief. I have persisted in my belief that I ate breakfast yesterday. This is not just to believe today that I ate breakfast *sometime in the past.* The particular occasion of breakfast eating is more determinately conceived. I'm not sure that it must be completely determinately conceived. Perhaps I retain over time some conception of that particular breakfast eating event without keeping track of precisely how much time has passed. While I needn't be in a position to precisely identify the relevant period in order to count as continuing to believe what I believed before, I must have some at least rough conception of the time in question that goes beyond the bare past-tense. The sharper my conception, the firmer the intuition that I have continued to believe as I have before. I don't pretend to have given an adequate account of continued belief. My main aim it to suggest that one cannot simply assume the simple view according to which continued belief just amounts to believing the same thing.

the sort of psychological and linguistic evidence considered in this section fail to settle the issue splitting the contextualist and the relativist about temporal thought.

3 Faultless Disagreement

George judges that durian tastes good and Bill that it is disgusting. It may well be that neither is making a mistake. Neither would be better representing reality by changing his mind. That's just how things are; George likes the taste of durian and Bill doesn't. This may suggest that taste judgments are irreducibly subjective. What George judges is that durian tastes good *to George* and what Bill judges is that durian does not taste good *to Bill.* Neither is then making a mistake because both judgments are true. Tastes vary across people and taste judgments incorporate the subjective dependence into their content. This is the contextualist view of taste judgments.

Contextualism respects the sense that neither George nor Bill are at fault in their judgments. But it does so at the expensive of the intuition that George and Bill disagree. On the most straightforward version of the faultless disagreement argument, two parties disagree when one judges true a proposition that the other judges false (or the other judges true a negation of that proposition). Contextualism entails that the proposition Bill judges true is not the negation of the proposition George judges true. So, if contextualism is true, they do not disagree, which seems the wrong result.[10]

The relativist claims that the content of George's judgment is the proposition [Durian tastes good] and the content of Bill's judgment is the proposition [Not [Durian tastes good]]. The one is the negation of the other, so there is a clear sense in which George and Bill disagree. Neither is at fault, however, as those propositions aren't true or false *simpliciter* but only relative to a standard of taste. Relative to George's standard of taste, the first is true and the second false; relative to Bill's standard of taste, the second is false and the first is true. The world as it is in itself does not recommend one standard over the other. Similar arguments can be constructed for relativist accounts of epistemic modals, knowledge attributions, certain gradable adjectives like `tall', `rich', etc.. So, the relativist account should be pre-

[10] This argument bears similarities to Lewis's argument for relativism about first-personal thought, arguments from successful communication and accepting what another says, suggest in end of section 1 above, against a relativist view about first-personal thought, and Richard's argument against relativism of temporal thought. That the same basic principles concerning sameness of content generate arguments both for and against relativist and contextualist accounts suggests to me that the arguments must be flawed. That similar response strategies are available to opponents (on both sides of the contextualist/relativist divide) of these arguments strengthens that suggestion.

ferred over the contextualist account, as only the former respects both disagreement and faultlessness intuitions.

The case of George and Bill needs to be spelled out more fully. Let's turn from judgments to speech acts and imagine George and Bill addressing one another.[11] There are many ways the dialogue may unfold and not all of them elicit the intuition that there is faultless disagreement. For example, we can imagine George and Bill discussing what they should serve at their party. "Hey," says George, "let's get durian. Durian tastes good. Everyone likes durian. It's a party favorite." Bill responds, "Actually, durian is disgusting. Most people find it offensive." If we imagine the further context in the above way, there is a strong inclination to find disagreement but little inclination to say that neither party is at at fault. If we imagine George being perfectly sincere and literal, then he is simply wrong and Bill is right. Even if 'everyone' in Bill's utterance, "Everyone likes durian," is hyperbolic, he is still wrong in his claim, as a sizable group do not like durian. In this case, the contextualist seems to get the right results straightaway; namely, George says that durian tastes good to most people and Bill rejects that very content. Bill is right and George wrong.

Suppose now that George clarifies what he meant. "But remember, we are only having over the Johnsons and the whole family loves it." In this case it is plausible that George intended by his earlier utterance, "Durian tastes good," that durian tastes good to the Johnsons and that the intended domain of 'everyone' in his utterance of 'Everyone likes durian' was that group of people. In this case, the intuition that there was disagreement gives way to the claim that there was instead misunderstanding. George was only speaking of the Johnsons and Bill took him to mean everyone in the world. They were simply talking past one another. The most plausible way of imagining the conversation continuing is with Bill's saying, "Oh, now I see what you meant. You're right. Let's get durian." (Or perhaps we can imagine Bill taking issue at the new factual claim that the group of people they have invited all or mostly like durian, in which case again it is highly plausible that one side of this new dispute is right and the other wrong.)[12]

---

[11] In (Schaffer 2011), Jonathan Schaffer claims that it is *only* when we imagine the parties in dialogue with one another that we elicit the intuition that there is disagreement. If both parties are simply sitting alone in their own room thinking about their own likes, Schaffer suggests, we have no qualms in saying that they do not disagree. While I agree with Schaffer that the intuition is more forceful when we imagine the parties addressing one another, I think that we can still elicit the intuition even when we imagine the parties thinking on their own. After all, George cannot rationally simply take over Bill's state of mind, in the sense of entering the same type of cognitive state as Bill, without first revising his earlier stance, when both George and Bill are at best only implicitly representing their own tastes in their judgments.

[12] These points follow (Schaffer 2011).

The intuition that neither party is at fault is most easily elicited when both parties are simply thinking of their own differing tastes, in which case there is no disagreement. And the intuition that the parties disagree is most easily elicited when both parties are thinking of the taste of the same particular group, in which case one side is wrong and the other right. Proponents of the faultless disagreement argument, then, need to take care that they are describing a *single* case in which there is both faultlessness and disagreement, as the contextualist can easily account for faultlessness of one kind of case and the disagreement in another. One case in which both intuitions are elicited are ones in which both parties "dig in their heals" without appealing to the tastes of a particular, independently identified group of agents (which renders the disagreement factual, with one party right and the other wrong) and without offering any further reasons for their judgment (which again holds the promise of factual resolution, as when, for example, one party says that a particular wine is good because of the subtle hints of cherries, when there is simply no cherry in the wine). We should imagine, then, Bill saying to George, "Durian tastes good. I love it," George responding, "No it doesn't. It tastes like gym socks," and Bill replying, "No, it is good." George's not responding, "Well, you may like it but to me it tastes like bad," or Bill replying, "Well, you may not like it but I do," seems to suggest that neither was simply reporting their own tastes but aiming to say something more general. There is something the one party seems to accept that the other party rejects. But it does not seem to be a factual matter, settled by how the world is, as they do not seem to have in mind any particular group's taste as the target. A case like this holds the promise of eliciting both faultlessness intuitions and disagreement intuitions at once.

The argument against contextualism assumes that the sense in which George and Bill disagreement is best explained by positing a proposition that is the content of Bill's judgment that durian is tasty the negation of which is the content of George's judgment that durian is not tasty. The contextualist should reject that assumption. There are several alternative accounts of the sense of disagreement. One sees George and Bill making a semantic mistake, as when a child responds, "No, I'm hungry," to his mother's saying, "I'm full." The child imagines what *he* would be saying if he uttered his mother's words and rejects that. But what he is rejecting is not what his mother said. In the case of the first-person pronoun, we all know it is just confusion, but that's because the indexicality is overt. With cases like taste predicates and epistemic modals, the mistake in thinking that there is real disagreement is hidden as the indexicality is hidden. We have already seen above, particularly in our discussion of first-personal thoughts and the sense that Hume and Heimson believe the same thing, that our intuitions of "sameness of thought" and "sameness of what is said" are unreliable guides to sameness of content. Intuition reliably picks up that, in some cases, there is something that George takes one attitude towards and Bill the opposite. But it does not reveal that that something is the contents of their attitudes. A contextualist may say that George accepts a sentence that Bill accepts the negation of. The contextualist can continue that both George and Bill are in psychological states such that the one cannot rationally enter the same type of psychological state as the other without first abandoning his earlier state. This provides a contextualist account of the sense that George and Bill "disagree" about the taste of durian. They don't disagree in the contents they believe-true. Instead, they disagree about their psychological states. This account of the sense of disagreement comports well with the fact that the sense of faultlessness or disagreement seems to quickly dissipates, as noted above, once the parties begin offering reasons for their judgments.

4 Meaning, Truth, and Reality

I have suggested that the arguments surveyed above based primarily on linguistic and psychological considerations for settling the issue between contextualism and relativism do not convince. I am inclined to view the differences between a contextualist and relativist account of a given phenomenon as genuine and important. So I would like to find further considerations that will help decide the matter.

Scott Soames, in (Soames 2011), offers the following argument against relativism. His primary focus is truth relativism about possible worlds. But the argument extends to other proposed parameters of truth. The argument turns on a link between meaning and truth. What it is for a sentence to have a meaning, in the most basic case of a context-invariant, simple atomic sentence of the form *Fa*, is for it to represent a particular object as being a certain way. But a thing is a certain way *simpliciter*; that is, a thing simply instantiates (or does not instantiate, as the case may be) a property.[13] This leads, then, to an atomic sentence *Fa* being true or false *simpliciter*. The same is true for atomic propositions. An atomic proposition represents a thing as being a certain way and it either is or is not that way *simpliciter*. As a thing's being a certain way is an absolute matter, so is the truth or falsity of corresponding atomic propositions. The truth values of more complex sentences should be built from, in some way or another, the truth values of the atomic sentences and propositions. This leads in turn to the idea that the most basic notion of truth is truth *simpliciter*, not truth relative to some parameter.

[13] More precisely, we should say that a sequence of objects stand in a relation (or fail to stand in that relation) *simpliciter*. For simplicity, I focus on the case of monadic properties in the text.

It is fairly clear how truth functional connectives and quantification works on this picture. In the first case, we analyze the truth of complexes like conjunctions in terms of the truth values of their parts and ultimately the truth values of the atomic propositions that serve as their basic building blocks. If those atomic propositions have absolute truth values, so do the complexes. Similarly, for quantificational propositions. While the truth definition is not ultimately compositional, we define the truth of a quantificational proposition in terms of a thing simply instantiating a property. So, the truth and falsity of these complexes, then, will be absolute and not relative precisely because the basic notion grounding their truth—namely, a thing or sequence of things instantiating a property or bearing a relation—is absolute. Modality may seem to be a counterexample, as the standard Kripkean semantics for quantified modal languages employs a relativistic notion of truth at a world and a thing being a certain way at a world. But Soames suggests that we help ourselves to that account insofar as we explicate the notion of a thing's being a certain way (or a sequence of things bearing a certain relation) at a possible world w as follows: x is Φ at w just in case, were w actual, then x would have been Φ. In this way, Soames argues that a possible worlds semantics of modal languages does not commit one to taking as basic the notion of truth at a world. The fundamental truth property is an absolute, monadic property that propositions simply have or don't have. This is because the metaphysical correlate—a thing's being a certain way or instantiating a property—is an absolute matter. The absoluteness of the instantiation relation then transfers to absolute truth of propositions. To think otherwise is to break the connection between truth and meaning.

I am drawn towards possible worlds and time relativism. And I think that the basic principles driving Soames's argument actually support rather than refute that position. I also think that those same principle rule out any other form of relativism. I think the first because I maintain that there are compelling reasons to think that the notion of a thing's instantiating a property *is* fundamentally a relative matter, being relative to a world and a time. I think the second because I think that other proposed parameters of truth do not relativize the instantiation relation. In both cases, however, I maintain that Soames's focus on the connection between meaning, truth conditions, and the constitution of reality promises to break the stalemate between the contextualist and the relativists, even if it does not settle the issue in quite the way Soames claims. In my view, Soames simply takes for granted absolutism about the constitution of reality and derives absolutism about truth from it. In the following section I will question this assumption, explicitly arguing that the constitution of reality is perspectival with respect to time and use Soames's principles to argue for relativism about temporal thought and speech.

While my primary focus will be defending relativism about time, let me begin by arguing that Soames's explication of the notion of truth at a world has unfortunate consequences, suggesting that his account of truth at a world is to be rejected. Soames's account of truth at a world is equivalent to Alvin Plantinga's account, in (Plantinga 1974, 1983), which has been subject to powerful criticism ((Adams 1981) and (Fine 1985)). In particular, it does not offer an adequate account of the intuitive idea that some things that actually exist might not have existed and so some negative singular existential sentences of the form $\neg\exists x(x=a)$ which are actually false could have been true. The issues here are complex and it is beyond the scope of this paper to fully settle the matter. The following will have to suffice.

Let a name a contingently existing, actual individual. Then $\neg\exists x(x=a)$ is true at a nonactual world w accessible from the actual world w^*. Grant that the notion of a nonactual world's being possibly actual makes sense.[14] Then Soames's explication entails that, had w been actual, the proposition expressed by $\neg\exists x(x=a)$ would have been true. Soames would admit that that proposition is singular with respect to the object named by a.[15] But had w been actual, that object would not have existed and so it is not true that a singular proposition about it would have been true, as there would not, in that case, have been any such proposition. Soames's explication of the notion of truth-at a world conflates, then, the distinction between truth-in, or internal truth, and truth-at, or external truth, that Adams and Fine argue is

[14] I doubt that it does. Counterfactual talk and talk of how things could have been makes sense when applied to ordinary objects like people, cats, chairs, and tables. That talk is regimented using the resources of possible worlds. Whether or not that regimentation is reductive, it is problematic to then turn around and use the resources of the object language and the metalanguage together, which is just what the phrase 'were w actual' does. More to the point, the phrase suggests that the actuality of a world is contingent in the same way that the blueness of my pants or the hairiness of my leg are contingent. But the "contingency" of the actuality of a world is a cross-model matter, as one world is actual in one model and nonactual in another model. The contingency of the blueness of my pants, on the other hand, is an intra-model matter, as my pants are blue in one world of a model and not blue in another world of that same model. This makes suspicious talk of a nonactual world being possibly actual, as it collapses intra-model, cross world comparisons with a cross model comparison.

[15] I think that Plantinga is best understood as denying that negative existentials like $\neg\exists x(x=a)$ express propositions singular with respect to the referent of the singular term a, despite his claim, in (Plantinga 1983), to the contrary. Instead, Plantinga is best understood as claiming that such a sentence expresses a proposition that contains as a constituent an individual essences of that referent, where an individual essence of an object necessarily exists, even if it is uninstantiated. The proposition expressed by $\neg\exists x(x=a)$ can then be thought of, roughly, as the proposition that individual essence **I** is not instantiated, where **I** is an individual essence of the referent of a.

essential to an adequate understanding of modal discourse about contingently existing objects.[16]

While these considerations are not conclusive, they suggest problems with Soames's explication of the notion of truth at a world, or of an object's being a certain way at a world. I don't take the failure of the accounts considered to prove this, but I suggest that a better account of the matter takes as basic the relativization to a world. A thing's simply being a certain way is itself explicated as that thing being that way *at the actual world*; the basic notion is a thing's being a certain way at a world. How a thing is, then, is, at the most metaphysically basic and fundamental level, world relative. Reality is irreducibly perspectival with respect to worlds. The most basic instantiation relation is a world relative one.

Grant my claim that instantiation is fundamentally world relative. Then we can invert the connections between meaning, truth, and the constitution of reality that Soames articulates into an argument *for* world relativism. Because the most basic notion of a thing's being a certain way is world relative, the most basic notion of an atomic proposition's being true is also world relative. And because of the connection between truth and meaning, we should in turn expect the meaning of atomic, context-invariant sentences of the form *Fa* to express propositions that are true or false only relative to a world.

Soames presents his argument as a general argument against relativism. I have argued that it fails as such, insofar as there is reason to deny absolutism about the constitution of reality. But I have furthermore suggested that the basic principles Soames invokes promise to refocus the debate between contextualism and relativism. We should look not at linguistic, semantic, or psychological data to decide whether a factor of meaning functions as a contextual parameter or an index of truth. We should look instead at whether or not that factor is plausibly a parameter at which the basic notion of a thing's being a certain way is relative. If it is not, that factor serves as a contextual factor, relativizing the proposition sentences express, for the reasons

---

[16] Soames thinks that nonactual individuals are in the range of the most unrestricted of quantifiers. So, had *w* been actual, there still would have been something, in the most unrestricted sense of 'something', that is the referent of *a*. When we intuit that $\neg\exists x(x=a)$ expresses something that would have been true, it is because we are implicitly restricting the range of the quantifier $\exists$ to individuals that exist "in" the world in question. Because Soames quantifies over entities that do not actually exist, then, he can escape this problem in a way distinct from Plantinga's solution, which requires taking an individual essence to be ontologically more basic than the individual that it is an essence of. While I cannot adequately defend the claim here, I think both Plantinga's and Soames's account of contingent existents is problematic and thus I reject Soames's explication of the notion of truth at a world. I discuss the matter in more depth in (Nelson 2009).

Soames gives. If, on the other hand, reflection reveals that a thing's being a certain way is relative to that parameter, then that relativization should be reflected in the truth of the propositions sentences express, for those same reasons run in the other direction.

In the following section I use this framework to argue that self thought is best conceived in contextualist terms and temporal thought in relativist terms, as there are reasons to think that the constitution of reality is perspectival with respect to time but not persons. While I do not argue the general case here, I think that these considerations suggest that truth is *only* relative to a time and a world and thus more exotic forms of relativism, according to which propositions are true relative to a standard, a set of assumptions, a point of view, or someone's knowledge, are false.

5 Is Reality Fundamentally Tensed? Is Reality Fundamentally Personed?

In this section I argue that there are metaphysical grounds for claiming that the constitution of reality is fundamentally relative to a time. I argue that the best account of qualitative change across time requires as much. Parallel reasons support the claim that the constitution of reality is fundamentally relative to a world, in light of the most promising analysis of contingency, but I only discuss the case for time. I then argue that there are reasons to reject that reality is perspectival with respect to persons. Given the principles connecting meaning and the constitution of reality discussed in the previous section, these claims support relativism about temporal thought and speech and contextualism about first-personal thought and speech.

Things change. That much is evident. But a proper explication of change is controversial. Take a paradigm case of qualitative change across time in intrinsic property.[17] Right now I am sitting and soon I will stand up and walk to the kitchen. So, I am sitting and I am standing. But nothing both sits and stands. So, change is impossible, as it would involve one and the same object having a property and its complement.

Something has gone horribly wrong and it seems clear what. The temporal modifier mysteriously dropped out in the derivation of the contradiction. We started by noting that I *am-presently* sitting and *will be* standing. We then quickly moved to saying simply that I sit and stand. Contradiction? Not so fast. I am *presently* sitting and I *will* not be sitting *in the future*. No contradiction. The appearance of contradiction depends upon ignoring time, one wants to say. While this is surely correct, it ends just where it should

[17] David Lewis, in (Lewis 1986), famously presented a special version of the puzzle of change—what he called the problem of temporary intrinsics—which I here follow. Lewis took the puzzle to support the doctrine of temporal parts, which I discuss below.

begin. For, we should ask, what do temporal modifiers modify? There seem only three choices.

First, a temporal modifier might modify the subject. I—the trans-temporal persister—am sitting only in virtue of having a temporal part—I-now—that sits *simpliciter* and I will not be sitting in virtue of having a distinct temporal part—I-in-the-future—that does not sit *simpliciter*. Persisting objects have their properties at a time indirectly, in virtue of the properties had by their temporal parts, and are derivative on their temporal parts. This is the doctrine of temporal parts (DTP for short).[18] A proponent of DTP can think that the fundamental prediction relation is tenseless. Let 'BE' be untensed. Then, on standard versions of DTP, [I am sitting at 2:00pm EST on 20 February 2010] is best thought of as [I-at-2:00pm-EST-on-20-February-2010 BE sitting], as the primary bearers of properties—momentary object—have their qualities *simpliciter* and absolutely, not varying the qualities they instantiate across time. The temporality of predication is absorbed, on this view, into what entity is the fundamental bearer of the property.[19]

Second, the temporal modifiers might be thought to modify the predicate.[20] Call this *Relationalism*. I have the property being a sitter-now and I have the property being a non-sitter-in-the-future. The latter is not a true complement of the former, any more than my bearing the father-of relation to some people and not others is contradictory. This view is best thought of as involving tenseless predication at the most fundamental level and so [I am sitting at 2:00pm EST on 20 February 2010] has the deeper form [I BE sitting-at-2:00pm-EST-on-20-February-2010].

Both views are most naturally conjoined with a view according to which predication is ultimately tenseless. This is because the temporal modification, in each case, is taken up into the items of the predication: The subject, in the case of DTP, and the predicate, in the case of Relationalism. There is thus no more work for tense to do in resolving any threat of contradiction. What seemed like a threat of contradiction—my both sitting and standing—is resolved by the proponent of DTP into predications of incompatible properties to numerically distinct objects and, by the Relationalist,

[18] This view is defended in (Armstrong 1980), (Lewis 1986), and (Quine 1963).

[19] The stage theory, defended by (Hawley 2001) and (Sider 1996, 2001), is a close cousin of DPT. The primary bearers of properties are also momentary objects, on this view, that have their qualities *simpliciter* and absolutely. But the persisting object, on this view, just is the momentary object. Past- and future-tensed predications are true of it in virtue of its bearing counterpart-theoretic relations to certain numerically distinct momentary objects simply having the property at earlier or later times. I don't distinguish the position in the text because it will be subject to the same complaint I raise against DTP.

[20] This view is defended in (Mellor 1981).

as predications of ultimately compatible properties to the same object, as those properties are really incompatible relations but to different times.

The following principle seems essential to genuine change: At the most basic level, one and the same object sheds and gains incompatible properties.[21] Although I will not defend the principle here,[22] I will assume it and assume that it provides compelling reasons to reject the above two views. This brings us to the third possibility of what the temporal modifier modifies.

According to the third view, temporal modifiers modify the entire sentence. 'I am sitting' expresses a temporally neutral and irreducibly present-tensed proposition to the effect that I [presently] sit. This proposition is true now and false in the future. Metaphysically, the instantiation relation between an individual and a property (even an intrinsic property) is relative to a time.[23] I instantiate the property **sitting** relative to the present time and I do not instantiate that very same property relative to a future time. Unlike DTP, the basic bearer of a persisting object's properties is the object itself and, unlike Relationalism, the properties that thing instantiates are, in the case in which it undergoes change, genuinely contradictory. The threat of contradiction is avoided by noting that the self-same object that is sitting and standing instantiates the first property at one time and the second at another time. Call this Relativizationism.

Relativizationism is attractive. But it threatens to collapse into one of two views. The first is Relationalism. I shall argue that if the *tensed* or A-theory of time is true, then this collapse can be averted. Detensers maintain that tense is not a fundamental feature of reality whereas tensers claim that it is. The issue is metaphysical, not semantical, concerning whether or not the most basic facts that obtain are tensed facts. Tensed facts, claim the detenser, supervene on tenseless facts and so tensed facts are not basic. Being present is not an objective, fundamental feature of time, but is given a reductive account in terms of simultaneity with an utterance, thought, or other event. The tenser insists, on the other hand, that reality is fundamentally tensed; tense does not reduce to anything more basic and does consist solely

---

[21] This principle is inspired by Sally Haslanger's *Incompatibility Condition* and *Proper Subject Condition* (Haslanger 2003, 316–317).

[22] But see (Haslanger 1989a,b, 1994, 2003), (Hinchliff 1996), and (Zimmerman 1996, 1998).

[23] Sally Haslanger (Haslanger 1989a,b, 1994, 2003), Mark Johnston (Johnston 1987), and Peter van Inwagen (van Inwagen 1990) have proposed similar views. Both Johnston and van Inwagen explicitly state that the instantiation relation that obtains between an object and a property is a three-place relation, taking a time as a third relatum. Haslanger and Forbes also have a three-place instantiation relation, although they do not take it as a primitive the way Johnston and van Inwagen do.

of our perspectival grasp and consciousness of reality. If the tensed theory of time is correct, then tensed predications are irreducible. I argue below that Relativizationism collapses to Relationalism only if the detensed theory is true; if the tensed theory is true, then the two views can be kept distinct. However, the tensed theory of time in turn threatens to entail the thesis of presentism—the thesis, roughly, that absolutely everything that exists is present and how things are *simpliciter* is how they are presently—which promises a fourth account of qualitative change incompatible with Relativizationism. In either case, Relativizationism seems to be an unstable position. I first spell out more fully why Relativizationism threatens to collapse into either Relationalism or presentism and then argue that there is a stable, consistent, and attractive position of nonpresentist, tensed Relativizationism. The view has the consequence that the constitution of reality is fundamentally perspectival with respect to a time, thus supporting my contention about relativism about temporal thought and speech.

Mark Hinchliff makes a powerful case that Relativizationism is Relationalism in disguise.

> As appealing as the relativization strategy is, it fails to accommodate our intuition that shapes are properties. Relativized properties are not properties, because a thing cannot just have them. So what are they? They are nothing new; they are relations in disguise. Mellor's straight-at relation which the candle bears to t can be disguised as the relativized property of being straight which the candle instantiates at t by noting that the candle cannot instantiate the relation *simpliciter* but only relative to a time. The same conjuring trick can disguise any relation. The earlier-than relation can be disguised as the relativized property of being past which a thing can have at a time but cannot just have. The far-from relation can even be disguised as the spatially relativized property of being far, which a thing can have at a place but cannot just have. The relativization reply may conceal what it denies, but it still denies our intuition that shapes are properties not relations. ((Hinchliff 1996), 122; three footnotes omitted)

Hinchliff argues that presentism is required to make proper sense of change. Part of his case for this turns on his claim, defended in the above quote, that Relativizationism is not a genuine alternative to Relationalism.

If tense is not a fundamental feature of reality, then Relativizationism collapses into Relationalism. I agree with Hinchliff on that point and for the reasons he gives. The claim that the instantiation relation is a three-place relation is just a disguised way of saying that what we thought were monadic properties are really relations to times. But if tenses are fundamental features of reality, then relativizing is distinct from relationalizing. The Relativizationist says that I instantiate the irreducibly present-tensed property of sitting relative to t^*, the present time. The Relationalist paraphrases this as follows: The two-place sitting relation obtains between me and t^*. But this second eliminates the tense. So, if the Relativizationist is a tenser, the Relationalist reduction can be resisted on the grounds that it eliminates the tense. So, as long as tense is an ineliminable feature of reality, Hinchliff's argument against Relativization can be resisted.

There are powerful reasons to think that a tensed theory of time entails presentism and presentism promises a fourth account of the puzzle of change incompatible the Relativizationist's account. This is the threat of collapse facing the Relativizationist from the other direction.

I start with the last claim. If presentism is true, then how a thing is *simpliciter* is how it is presently. So I am just sitting *simpliciter*. My past and future standings are hypothetical. I am (presently) a past and future stander not in virtue of my standing in some past time but primitively. It is a fundamental fact about me that it was/will be the case that I am standing.[24] This is a consequence of the claim that the past- and future-tense operators are basic operators, not being analyzed in terms of the sentences they operate on being true at some nonpresent region of reality. The presentist maintains that reality is exhausted by how things presently are. There is no need for relativization, on this view, as the past and future happenings are not on an ontological par with the present. So, if presentism is true, Relativizationism is false.

I have argued that the Relativizationist needs the tensed theory of time, lest her position collapse into Relationalism, and we have just seen that she also needs to reject presentism. This brings us to the first claim two paragraphs back: Does the tensed theory of time entail presentism? I shall look at two arguments that it does, the first from Mark Hinchliff and the second from Dean Zimmerman, and argue that they can be resisted. There is room, I argue, for a well-motivated and coherent nonpresentist tensed theory of time.

Hinchliff argues that the tensed theory of time entails presentism as follows. "If M can have a tense only at a time, then any statement about M's having a tense is incomplete unless it specifies a time at which M is said to have the tense. Statements about the A series must include a time specification" (Hinchliff 1988, 16). Tensed predications seem to be incomplete without a time specification. From the point of nowhen, it seems that I am neither sitting nor not sitting. The tenser has two options concerning how the time specification is provided: Either tenselessly, in which case it would

24 This follows (Prior 1967).

seem there are not after all irreducibly tensed predications—for surely that M is present at *t* is tenselessly true if true—which would refute the tenser's own position, or tensedly, in which case the predication is once again incomplete without a time specification and a vicious regress ensues.[25] The tenser can resolve this problem, however, by accepting the presentist thesis. For then present-tensed predications *are* complete in themselves and *do not* require further temporal specification because how reality is *simpliciter* just is how it presently is. In that case, the God's-eye view on reality is the view from the present and so the predication of present-sitting to me is simply true. So, the argument concludes, only the presentist thesis that how a thing is *simpliciter* is how it is presently can provide the tenser with an adequate account of temporal predication.

The nonpresentist must admit that M's being present, past, or future is incomplete. Only the presentist can say that it is complete, as that requires that how reality is *simpliciter* is how it presently is. And there are problems providing a completer, as the completing time specification must either be provided tensedly, in which case the same problem arises, or tenselessly, leading to a detensed theory. But there is an alternative. The nonpresentist tenser can reject the assumption that predications are complete. That assumption is based on absolutism, that there is a perspectival-less obtaining, which a relativist rejects. So, if we reject the requirement that the full specification of the facts be "complete," in the sense that they absolutely either obtain or do not obtain from a perspectival-less position, then we can offer a nonpresentist tensed response to the argument. But then it is not true that the tensed theory requires presentism.

Dean Zimmerman offers a complementary argument that the tensed theory entails presentism. The argument is complex and I cannot here do justice to the intricacies. Zimmerman notes that a detenser can "take tense seriously," in the sense that she can agree that there are tensed sentences for which there are no tenseless sentences that mean just the same thing, but there are no basic tensed facts. Tenses are, in that case, semantically basic but metaphysically dependent. Tensers must distinguish their view from this view. To do so, Zimmerman argues that the tenser must claim that being present marks an ontic divide. Only with presentism can the tenser carve out a metaphysically significant thesis that the "serious" detenser would reject. In that way, Zimmerman argues, a nonpresentist tensed theory of time is unstable, being unable to distinguish itself from its detenser opponent while rejecting the presentist thesis.

---

[25] Hinchliff maintains, and I agree, that this is a way of understanding McTaggart's argument (McTaggart 1908) against the tensed theory of time, or what he calls the A-theory.

The tenser maintains that tense is a fundamental feature of reality. She thinks this because she thinks that it is required for genuine change. And she thinks that because she thinks that only a tensed fact can, in a nonderivative way, obtain at one time and not at another, which is what change requires. If a fact is tenseless, then it is the sort of thing that obtains at every time if it obtains at any. This is most clear for dated facts. A dated fact is specific as to the time it concerns. But what happened at that time does not shift across time (ignoring views of the future according to which there is deep metaphysical unsettledness), its obtaining does not vary across times. The same is true of nondated tenseless facts, if any there be. If George simply is-tenselessly sitting, then what sense does it make to say that that fact obtains at one time and not at another? So, for one and the same fact to obtain at one time and not at another, that fact must be irreducibly tensed. But then tense is an objective feature of reality, which is inconsistent with a detensed theory of time. I think that this provides the wedge the nonpresentist tenser can use to pry a space between the reductionism of the detensed theory and the extremes of presentism.

Zimmerman considers similar strategies for distinguishing the nonpresentist tensed theory of time, appealing to temporary exemplification. But he turns that into a view about the truth of proposition—a thesis of temporary truth—and worries that it requires nondeflationary theories of truth.[26] Atomic propositions are true or false in virtue of the obtaining of facts. Zimmerman suggests that "our eternalist A-theorist [nonpresent tensed theorist, in my terms] sets aside tensed truth, and instead emphasizes the non-relational exemplification of monadic properties by individuals that change with respect to those properties" (*ibid.*, 343). After a detailed discussion, Zimmerman argues that this suggestion collapses into a claim about the nature of truth. Whether or not that is true, the view I suggested in the previous paragraph does not face this problem. Facts are distinct from propositions and we can remain the entire time at the level of facts by focusing on what is required for one and the same fact to obtain at one time and not at another, concluding that that fact must be an irreducibly tensed fact. The notion of truth is not implicated in this talk and so there is no fear that, when push comes to shove, we are floating only a semantic thesis. So, I conclude that there is a viable nonpresentist tensed theory.

My proposed nonpresentist tensed theory of time avoids problems with presentism.[27] The presentist does not take presentness seriously in the right

---

[26] (Zimmerman 2005, 433–434).

[27] The problem I discuss, at least in the form that I discuss it, is distinct from the more familiar objections raised against presentism, which include the grounding problem, in its many

way. While the presentist claims that presentness marks the extent of reality, both what there is and how it is, there is a deeper sense in which presentness is basic that the presentist cannot accommodate. I quote St. Augustine. "For if there are times past and future, I wish to know where they are. But if I have not yet succeeded in this, I still know that wherever they are, they are not there as future or past, but as present" (Augustine 397, Bk 11 Chpt 18). Augustine's insight is that presentness is more basic than pastness and futurity, which is incompatible with presentism.

The presentist thinks that it is a basic feature of the present that George Bush was president. The presentist refuses to analyze this in terms of the present-tensed fact of George Bush's being president obtaining at a past time. Past- and future-tensed facts are primitive. This claim is at the heart of the presentist's unique solution to the puzzle of change. But then the presentist is not truly respecting the priority of presentness. Augustine's insight was that presently past facts obtain in virtue of, in the basic level, there being a "portion of reality" where the past "resides" as present. On my relativizationist view, there is a set of irreducibly present-tensed facts corresponding to each past time. The presently past truths, which include the truth that Bush was president and that Aristotle philosophized, are true in virtue of those facts and their relation to the present; namely, those past facts bearing certain causal relations to present facts. But they are, in their most fundamental form, present-tensed. All of these sets of facts are equally constitutive of reality. But the obtaining of any of these facts is irreducibly relative to a time. The sum total of all of the facts that constitute reality, then, are an incoherent mess, because both the (present-tensed!) fact of my sitting and the (present-tensed!) fact of my standing are equally constitutive of reality, from a perspectival-less standpoint. It is just that none of these facts obtain in a nonrelative way. This makes the view importantly different from the presentist view, which treats past- and future-tensed facts as irreducibly past- or future-tensed. And I maintain that the position is genuinely a version of the tensed theory of time because the most basic facts that obtain are present-tensed facts, not just dated or tenseless facts.

I don't pretend to have shown all competing views to my nonpresentist tensed view are false. But I do think that it is the best theory of persistence through change on offer. Supposing it accepted, then the constitution of reality is ultimately and fundamentally relative to a time. With the arguments from section 4, that entails truth relativists about temporal thought and speech. Atomic propositions are not true or false absolutely, as the contextualist insists, but only at a time. For otherwise the connection between

---

guises (see for example (Crisp 2007)), and the problem of cross-temporal relations that seem to go beyond how things presently are at any one time (see for example (Crisp 2005)).

the constitution of reality (which we have argued to be nonabsolute and only relative to a time; how a thing is at the most basic level is relative to a time) and the truth of an atomic proposition is ruined.

We are now in a position to quickly argue against truth relativism about persons. If first-personal thought is to be analyzed in terms of propositions that are true or false only at persons, then, as I have argued in section 4, we are committed to thinking that the constitution of reality is ultimately and fundamentally relative to a person. But that is both metaphysically unmotivated and independently implausible. It is unmotivated because there is no phenomena like persistence through qualitative change or contingency of how one is that is best analyzed relativistically. There are no metaphysical grounds for thinking that the constitution of reality is ultimately perspectival with respect to a person. It is implausible because it is not even clear what content to give to the claim that the a given fact obtains at one person but not at another.

The same form of argument can be made against other forms of truth relativism on the market. It is implausible, of questionable intelligibility, to claim that the constitution of reality is relative to a standard of taste, body of evidence or knowledge, or comparison class. A fact does not obtain with respect to one, say, standard of taste but not another. But then we should reject accounts that make the truth of propositions fundamentally relative to such parameters; we should reject, that is, relativist accounts of taste predicates, knowledge attributions, epistemic modals, and comparative adjectives, for example.

I have argued that debates between relativist and contextualist accounts of some expression, type of linguistic construction, or type of thought by turning metaphysical: We should ask whether or not there are metaphysical phenomena whose best explication requires that the constitution of reality is relative to the corresponding parameter in dispute. In the case of times and worlds, I argue that there are: Qualitative change and contingency are best accounted for, I have suggested, in terms of conceiving of how a thing is as being fundamentally relative to a time and a world. In the case of persons, standards of taste, and comparison classes, on the other hand, there are no reason to think that the constitution of reality is relative to such a parameter. But then we should prefer a contextualist account of the corresponding linguistic phenomena. The guiding thread linking the metaphysical considerations explored in section 5 to the theses of relativism and contextualism that have been the main focus of this paper is the idea that there is a constitutive connection between meaning, truth, and the constitution of reality. We should only countenance, then, indices of truth—parameters relative to which a proposition is true or false—only when we are willing to conceive of how a thing is and, more generally, a fact's obtaining as being relative to that same parameter.

References

St. Augustine, 397, *Confessions*, H. Chadwick (tr.), 1991. (Oxford: Oxford University Press).

David Armstrong. 1980. 'Identity Through Time'. In P. van Inwagen (ed.), *Time and Cause: Essays Presented to Richard Taylor*. (Dordrecht: Reidel), 67–78.

Robyn Carston. 2002. *Thoughts and Utterances: The Pragmatics of Explicit Communication*. (Oxford: Blackwell).

Mark Crimmins and John Perry. 1989. 'The Prince and the Phone Booth: Reporting Puzzling Beliefs'. Reprinted in J. Perry, 2000, *The Problem of the Essential Indexical and Other Essays, Expanded Edition*. (Stanford, CA: CSLI Publications), 207–232.

Thomas Crisp. 2005. 'Presentism and Cross-Time Relations', *American Philosophical Quarterly* 42: 5–17

Thomas Crisp. 2007. 'Presentism and Grounding' *Noûs* 41: 89–109

Gareth Evans. 1985. 'Does Tense Logic Rest Upon a Mistake?' In G. Evans, *Collected Papers*. (Oxford: Clarendon Press), 343–363.

Kit Fine. 1985. 'Plantinga on the Reduction of Possibilist Discourse'. In J. Tomberlin and P. van Inwagen, (eds.), *Alvin Plantinga*. (Dordrecht: Reidel), 145–186.

Kit Fine. 2005. 'Tense and Reality'. In K. Fine, *Modality and Tense: Philosophical Papers*. (Oxford: Clarendon Press), 261–320.

G.W. Fitch. 1998. 'Temporalism Revisited'. *Philosophical Studies* 92: 251–256.

G.W. Fitch. 1999. 'Tense and Contents'. *Philosophical Studies* 94: 151–158.

Sally Haslanger. 1989. 'Endurance and Temporary Intrinsics'. *Analysis* 49: 119–125.

Sally Haslanger. 1989. 'Persistence, Change, and Explanation'. *Philosophical Studies* 56: 1–28.

Sally Haslanger. 1994. 'Humean Supervenience and Enduring Things'. *Australasian Journal of Philosophy* 72: 339–359.

Sally Haslanger. 2003. 'Persistence Through Time'. In M. Loux and D. Zimmerman (eds.), *The Oxford Handbook of Metaphysics* (Oxford: Oxford University Press), 315–354.

Katherine Hawley. 2001. *How Things Persist*. (Oxford: Oxford University Press).

Mark Hinchliff. 1988. *A Defense of Presentism*. Ph.D dissertation, Princeton University.

Mark Hinchliff. 1996. 'The Puzzle of Change'. *Philosophical Perspectives* 10: 119–136.

Mark Johnston. 1987. 'Is There a Problem about Persistence?' *Proceedings of the Aristotelian Society* Supp. Vol. 61: 107–135.

David Kaplan. 1977. 'Demonstratives'. In J. Almog, J. Perry, and H. Wettstein (eds.). 1989. *Themes from Kaplan*. (Oxford: Oxford University Press), 481–564.

Jeffrey King. 2003. 'Tense, Modality, and Semantic Value'. *Philosophical Perspectives* 17: 195–225.

William Kneale and Martha Kneale. 1970. 'Propositions and Time'. In A. Ambrose and M. Lazerowitz (eds.), *G.E. Moore: Essays in Retrospect*. (New York: Humanities Press), 228–241.

Max Kölbel. 2003. 'Faultless Disagreement'. *Proceedings of the Aristotelian Society* 104: 53–73.

Max Kölbel. 2008. 'Motivations for Relativism'. In M. García-Carpintero and M. Kölbel (eds.), *Relative Truth*. (Oxford: Oxford University Press), 1–40.

David Lewis. 1979. 'Attitudes *De Dicto* and *De Se*'. *Philosophical Review* 88: 513–543.

David Lewis. 1986. *On the Plurality of Worlds*. (Oxford: Blackwell).

J.M.E. McTaggart. 1908. 'The Unreality of Time'. *Mind* 18: 457–484.

Hugh Mellor. 1981. *Real Time*. (Cambridge: Cambridge University Press).

G.E. Moore. 1966. 'Facts and Propositions'. In G.E. Moore, *Philosophical Papers*. (New York: Collier), 60–88.

Michael Nelson. 2009. 'The Contingency of Existence'. In L. M. Jorgensen and S. Newlands, (eds.), *Metaphysics and the Good: Themes from the Philosophy of Robert Merrihew Adams*. (New York: Oxford University Press), 95–155.

John Perry. 1977. 'Frege on Demonstratives'. Reprinted in J. Perry, 2000, *The Problem of the Essential Indexical and Other Essays, Expanded Edition*. (Stanford, CA: CSLI Publications), 1–26

John Perry. 1979. 'The Problem of the Essential Indexical'. Reprinted in J. Perry, 2000, *The Problem of the Essential Indexical and Other Essays, Expanded Edition*. (Stanford, CA: CSLI Publications), 27—44

John Perry. 1986. 'Thought Without Representation'. Reprinted in J. Perry, 2000, *The Problem of the Essential Indexical and Other Essays, Expanded Edition*. (Stanford, CA: CSLI Publications), 171–188.

John Perry. 1998. 'Myself and I'. Reprinted in J. Perry, 2000, *The Problem of the Essential Indexical and Other Essays, Expanded Edition*. (Stanford, CA: CSLI Publications), 325–340.

John Perry. 2002. *Identity, Personal Identity, and the Self*. (Indianapolis, IN: Hackett).

Alvin Plantinga. 1974. *The Nature of Necessity*. (Oxford: Oxford University Press).

Alvin Plantinga. 1983. 'On Existentialism'. *Philosophical Studies* 44: 1–20.

Arthur Prior. 1959. 'Thanks Goodness That's Over' *Philosophy* 34: 12-17.

Arthur Prior. 1967. *Past, Present and Future*. (Oxford: Oxford University Press).

Arthur Prior. 1970. 'The Notion of the Present'. *Stadium Generale* 23: 245–248.

W.V. Quine. 1963. 'Identity, Ostension, and Hypostasis'. In W.V. Quine *From a Logical Point of View* 2nd edn., rev. (Evanston, Illinois: Harper & Row), 65–79.

François Recanati. 2007. *Perspectival Thought: A Plea for (Moderate) Relativism*. (Oxford: Oxford University Press).

Mark Richard. 1981. 'Temporalism and Eternalism'. *Philosophical Studies* 39: 1–13.

Mark Richard. 1982. 'Tense, Propositions and Meanings'. *Philosophical Studies* 41: 337–351.

Mark Richard. 2003. 'Introduction to Part I'. In A. Jokic and Q. Smith (eds.), *Time, Tense, and Reference*. (Cambridge, Massachusetts: MIT Press), 25–45.

Nathan Salmon. 1989. 'Tense and Singular Propositions'. In J. Almog, J. Perry, and H. Wettstein (eds.), *Themes from Kaplan*. (Oxford: Oxford University Press), 331–392.

Nathan Salmon. 2003. 'Tense and Intension'. In A. Jokic and Q. Smith (eds.), *Time, Tense, and Reference*. (Cambridge, Massachusetts: MIT Press), 107–154.

Jonathan Schaffer. 2011. 'Perspective in Taste Predicates and Epistemic Modals'. In A. Egan and B. Weatherson (eds.), *Epistemic Modality*. (Oxford: Oxford University Press), 179–226.

Sydney Shoemaker. 1968. 'Self-Reference and Self-Awareness'. *Journal of Philosophy*,65: 555–67.

Theodore Sider. 1996. 'All the World's a Stage'. *Australasian Journal of Philosophy* 74: 433–453.

Theodore Sider. 2001. *Four-Dimensionalism: An Ontology of Persistence and Time*. (Oxford: Oxford University Press).

Scott Soames. 2011. 'True at'. *Analysis Reviews* 71: 124–133.

Dan Sperber and Deirdre Wilson. 1986. *Relevance: Communication and Cognition*. (Oxford: Blackwell).

Peter van Inwagen. 1990. 'Four-Dimensional Objects'. *Noûs* 24: 245–255.

Dean Zimmerman. 1996. 'Persistence and Presentism'. *Philosophical Papers* 35: 115–126.

Dean Zimmerman. 1998. 'Temporary Intrinsics and Presentism'. In P. van Inwagen and D. Zimmerman (eds.), *Metaphysics: The Big Questions*. (Oxford: Blackwell), 206–221.

Dean Zimmerman. 2005. 'The A-theory of Time, the B-theory of Time, and 'Taking Tense Seriously''. *Dialectica* 59: 401–457.

15

Self-Locating Beliefs

JOHN PERRY

1 Introduction

Canonical belief reports have the form:

At t, A believes that S

The belief reported is true, if the statement "S", made by the same person who made the report at the same time as the report was made, was or would have been true. If you say, "My eldest brother believes that I am a fool," the belief you report your eldest brother to have is true just in case your statement "I am a fool" is true; that is, if you are a fool.

These facts suggest a simple account of belief. Belief is a "propositional attitude"; it consists of an agent at a time having a relation, belief, to a proposition. In the report, the proposition is identified by the content sentence—"I am a fool" in our example. The clause in which the content sentence is embedded—"that I am a fool", in our example—is a singular term that refers to this proposition. The proposition is an abstract object that encodes the truth-conditions of the content sentence, as uttered by the reporter. The canonical report gives us everything we need: an agent, a time, the attitude and the proposition. I'll call this "The Fregean View," since it is in the spirit of the view he held at the time he wrote "Über Sinn und Bedeutung" (1892).

An alternative is that believing is basically a matter of having mental representations of a certain sort. On the traditional picture, mental representations are structures of ideas, which come in various types: beliefs, desires, intentions and so forth. On the second view, belief is a relation to such men-

Attitudes De Se: Linguistics, Epistemology, Metaphysics.
Neil Feit and Alessandro Capone (eds.).

tal representations. I'll call this "The Fodorian View," since it is in the spirit of at least one of Fodor's most influential views, the one espoused in "Propositional Attitudes" in his seminal book *Representations* (1981).

A third view naturally suggests itself, a combined or hybrid view. Belief involves a person having a mental representation, and in virtue of that, having a relation to a proposition. Belief is a bit like saying. When we say something, we utter a sentence that has a certain meaning. In virtue of the meaning of the sentence we utter, or at least partly in virtue of it, we *say* something; what we say is a proposition, the *content* of our statement. Our ordinary indirect discourse concept of saying tracks the propositions we express, not the sentences we use to express them. But we couldn't very well express any propositions, without uttering sentences, and the meanings of the sentences we utter help determine which propositions we express. Similarly, on the hybrid view, our reports of what people believe track the propositions they believe, not the mental representations in virtue of which they believe them. But we couldn't have beliefs without mental representations, and how the mental representations represent things, plays a major role in determining what we believe.

This view also treats belief as a relation that a person has to a proposition at a time, but this relation is the product of (i) the agent having a belief, an internal mental representation, and (ii) that representation having, in virtue of what the ideas that compose it are *of*, a certain proposition as its content. The hybrid view comes in simple and more complex versions, depending on what one thinks that the *of* relation between ideas and things in the world comes to.

Russell held a simple version of the hybrid view. We have simple ideas, which he calls "logically proper names." These are *of* or *mean* objects with which the believer is acquainted. The proposition believed was a complex with these objects as constituents. The objects in question were sense-data, the properties of sense-data, relations among sense-data, and, perhaps, the self.

On Russell's view, complex relations of the sort we have to more ordinary objects, like the things we see, the people we know, or the places where we grew up, or the properties of the surfaces of objects that determine which sensations we have, are not involved in determining what our ideas are *of*. Hence they play no role in determining the constituents of the propositions we believe.[1] These relations, and the objects with which they

[1] They are constituents of propositions we "believe to be true." For example, the proposition that Bismarck was a gifted diplomat has Bismarck and the property of being a gifted diplomat as constituents. One might have good reasons for believing there was such a proposition, and that it was true. But one would not *understand* the proposition, since one would not be acquainted with its constituents. One cannot believe it, but one can believe that there is such a proposition and that it is true. See (Russell, 1912).

connect us, come in only on the far side of the propositions we believe, as it were. The objects are only known "by description," which means they are not constituents of the propositions we believe, but things whose existence is implied by the things we believe.

My own view is a version of what we might call the complex version of the hybrid view. The constituents of the propositions we believe are ordinary objects, and their properties. Our ideas are *of* such things. So the *of* relation, between ideas and things, is much more complicated, and much more contingent, than Russell conceived of it. It depends on the complicated circumstances that connect my ideas—the inner workings of my brain—with the objects in the external world. You and I can have very similar ideas of very different objects, because of the difference in our circumstances. I can have very different ideas of the same object, connected to it by very different circumstances. And I can have ideas that are of the sort that could be connected with objects, but in fact are not. I will assume a picture of mental representations that is doubtless much too simple. There are predicative ideas—which I simply call 'ideas'—that are of properties and relations. And there are ideas of particular things, which I call 'notions'. A simple belief has a structure like **I(a,b,...n)** where **I** is an idea suited to be of an n-ary relation and **a,b,...n** are notions. The belief is true if there is an n-ary relation that **I** is of, and there are object that **a,b,...n** are of, and they stand in that relation.

In this paper I defend a complex version of the hybrid view. The complicated relations we stand in to ordinary external objects determine which of those objects our ideas are of, and the propositions we believe have those objects as constituents. I said above that the hybrid view holds that what one believes is the product of (i) the agent having a belief, an internal mental representation, and (ii) that representation having, in virtue of what the ideas that compose it are *of*, a certain proposition as its content. The complex version of the hybrid view, however, divides the second factor into two components: (a) which ideas are involved in the representation and how they are structured (b) how those ideas are connected to the world, and thus which things (if any) they are *of*. From now on, when I talk about the hybird view, I'll mean the complex version of the hybrid view.

I argue that this complex view provides the best account of an important and pervasive phenomenon I call "self-locating belief." A couple of clarifications, then I'll explain what I mean by "self-locating beliefs." As I use the term "proposition," propositions are *not* representations. They are abstract objects. They can't be seen or heard, so they are not linguistic or pictorial representations. They are not located in the heads of people, so they can't very well be the effects of perceptions and inferences, or the causes of inferences or actions, which is what mental representations do. Propositions are abstract objects that encode truth-conditions, that philosophers use for theoretical purposes, systematizing uniformities that are registered in ordinary language by the systematic use of sentences, on their own and as parts of content-clauses, to describe the world, describe utterances, and describe minds. I call this the classificatory view of propositions.

I believe this is now a pretty common use of "proposition," but it has not always been. The term has been used for sentences and in particular mental sentences, and so for representations. Russell was not always careful to keep mental representations and the propositions that were very intimately connected with them, on his view, separate, using the term "proposition" for both. If we conflate these uses, thinking of propositions as both mental representations and as propositions, it is easy to get confused. This confusion may make the first of the three views I described, the Fregean view, seem more plausible than it is. If we have the classificatory view of propositions, it seems to me very hard to make much sense of the Fregean view.

In line with the complex view, by a "belief" I will mean a state of an agent's mind, something that has causes and effects, is based in the brain, and thus has a location, however dispersed, inside the agent's head. As noted, beliefs have contents, and are most often described in terms of their contents. The term "belief" is sometimes used for the contents of belief, as when someone says, "Bachman and Santorum share the belief that Iran is a grave threat to the U.S." What this means, in my terminology, is that Bachman and Santorum each have a belief, and that their beliefs share a content. The content in question, that Iran is a grave threat to the U.S., is a proposition, an abstract object, not located anywhere, much less distributed around some Republican's brain.

A belief is *self-locating* if the truth of the belief constrains the location of the belief and the believer. Suppose you have read about Gilmore Lake in the Desolation Wilderness, and believe it is small, clear and blue. Hiking in the Wilderness, you see the lake for the first time, not knowing which lake it is, and think, "That is a small, clear, blue lake." Intuitively, the truth of your first belief doesn't put any constraints on your location at the time you have it, or at least not any very significant ones. You presumably need to exist after the geologic era in which the lake was formed, somewhere in the universe that could have been reached by information about it by that time. But the second belief seems like it would not be true, unless you were looking at the lake. It is the sort of belief that is about the very object the person who has the belief is seeing. The belief itself is connected to the agent's perception of the object.

These are clearly two beliefs, with different properties; they were formed at different times, on the basis of a different kind of evidence; they are different in type, one seeming to involve a name in an important way, the other a perception in an important way. On the complex version of the hybrid view, there is a distinction to be drawn between the truth-conditions of a belief and its content—this is what the next section is about. Given this distinction, the two beliefs can be supposed to have the same content, the proposition that Gilmore Lake is small, clear and blue, but different truth-conditions, due to differences in the sort of mental representations involved.

2 Truth-conditions and contents

If we adopt the complex view, we need to distinguish between the truth-conditions of a belief and its content. Suppose we have a simple belief, consisting of a notion of a thing, and an idea of a property that sort of thing might have. Call the belief **b**, and say that **b = I(n)** meaning that **b** is a structure of the belief sort, consisting of the predicative idea **I** and the notion **n**. Then it seems:

b is true iff:

(i) There is some cognizer C, to whom **b**, **I**, and **n** all belong;
(ii) There is a property *P*, of which **I** is an idea;
(iii) There is an object *a*, of which **n** is a notion;
(iv) *a* has property *P*.

The content of **b** is the proposition that a certain object, the one of which **n** is a notion, has a certain property, the one of which **I** is an idea. The truth-conditions, however, are conditions on **b** itself. For this reason I call these "reflexive" or "belief-bound" truth-conditions. A belief may have belief-bound truth-conditions, but not have a content, since some of the ideas and notions in it may not be of anything. For example, many people have beliefs that they might express with "Nessie lives in Loch Ness." It seems probable, at least on the evidence I have seen, that these beliefs have truth-conditions, but not content, since there is no monster suitably connected to their notions of Nessie, to serve as what those notions are of.

To get from the reflexive truth-conditions of a belief to the other interesting properties, and especially its content as ordinarily conceived, we need to fix additional facts about the belief in addition to its basic structure. These facts are of several interconnecting types:

i. Phenomenological facts: what it's like to have the ideas involved;
ii. Facts about the origin of the ideas; where they came from;
iii. Facts about the current status of the ideas;
iv. Facts about the cognizer;
v. Facts about connections of the ideas to external objects;
vi. Facts about what the ideas are of.

Consider a belief we might suppose President Obama to have, with the content that Michele Bachmann was born in Iowa. It's likely that Obama first acquired a notion of Bachmann by reading about her, or hearing about her in a conversation. If he acquired the idea by reading a newspaper, then he no doubt saw the name "Michele Bachman" as a part of a larger text. That use of the name "Michele Bachman" was of Michele Bachman because of the intentions of the person who wrote the sentence that was printed in the newspaper, and facts about where he or she has acquired the name, and so on, according to whatever the right story is about names and whom they refer to. The notion Obama formed was *of* the same person that the name he read referred to. Since that time he has, I assume, met her on a number of occasions, seen her on television, read more about her, and heard more about her in conversations. His idea of the relation of being born in, and his notion of the state of Iowa, he no doubt had long before he heard of Bachmann.

Obama's idea of Bachman is presumably a component of many beliefs he has about her, and also of conjectures, suspicions, open questions, hopes, fears and other cognitions of his. I'll speak loosely of the "mental file" constituted by a notion and the ideas associated with it in various ways.

The reflexive truth-conditions of a belief are clearly not the content of the belief. The content is what we get, once we fix the facts of type (vi). (I'll call these the referential facts, rather than the "of-facts," since the latter sounds awkward.) As we have supposed them to be, the content of **b** is the proposition that Michele Bachmann is from Iowa. The reflexive truth-conditions of **b** are about **b** itself, not about Michele Bachmann. The content of **b** is about Michele Bachman, not about **b** itself.

We can talk about the reflexive *content* of **b**, by considering a proposition that encodes the reflexive truth-conditions. Then we can contrast this with the *referential* content of **b**, as the proposition that encodes *what else* has to be the case for **b** to be true, given its reflexive truth-conditions plus the referential facts. We can think of this as generalizing the theory of content that is implicit in the way we use sentences to describe the world, and to both express and report beliefs. Our ordinary concept of what a person believes is the same as, or at least closely related to, the referential content of the person's beliefs.

So, given a belief **b** = **I(n)**:

(a) The reflexive content of **b** is the proposition that

- (i) There is some cognizer C, to whom **b**, **I**, and **n** all belong;
- (ii) There is a property P, of which **I** is an idea;
- (iii) There is an object *a*, of which **n** is a notion;
- (iv) *a* has property P.

(b) The referential content of **b** *given that:*
  (i) **I** is of property P, and
  (ii) **n** is of object *a*
 is the proposition *that a is P*.

Note that, intelligent as he is, Obama probably does not *believe* the reflexive content of his belief. The reflexive content of **b** is not something that is the *referential* content of any belief Obama has. It is, perhaps, the referential content of a belief you now have about Obama, involving ideas of his ideas, which you formed in reading this section.

2.1 Frege Cases

A Frege case involves two beliefs that are about the same object, and to the effect that it has the same property, but are importantly different in some cognitively significant way. Cicero and Tully and the not very diligent student, and London and Londres and Kripke's (1979) Pierre, are classic examples. Suppose Elwood believes that Cicero, who he has learned about in his philosophy class, was an orator, but doesn't believe that Tully, who he has heard of in his classics class, was an orator. It seems that there are different truth-conditions, corresponding to the belief he has and the belief he doesn't have. On the simple view, difference in truth-conditions means difference in content; so there must be two propositions, one of which Elwood believes and the other of which he does not believe. These propositions cannot be "singular propositions," that is, propositions that are individuated by objects and the properties they are required to have, since there is only one object, Cicero, involved.

On the complex view, however, one can say that there are two beliefs with different reflexive contents, but both beliefs have the same referential content, the singular proposition that Cicero was a Roman orator. Elwood has two ways of believing the same singular proposition, since he has two ideas that are, as it turns out, of the same thing, one acquired in his philosophy class and one acquired in his classics class. He has a belief with the content that Cicero was an orator, which has the first of them as a component, but does not have such a belief with the second as a component.

2.2 Austin Cases

A David Austin case also involves a believer with two beliefs with the same referential content, but importantly different properties (Austin, 1990). In my version of Austin's most powerful example, Elwood looks through an apparatus with a tube for each eye. He sees a small black circle when he closes his left eye, which he names Righty. He sees a small black circle when he closes his right eye, which he calls Lefty. With both eyes open, he seems to see two circles, in a somewhat blurry way. He realizes that Righty may be Lefty, but he has no way of knowing. In fact, Righty is Lefty. The two tubes are aimed at the same circle. It seems that Elwood has two beliefs with the content, that a certain object, which he has given two names, is a small black circle. But these are different beliefs. They were acquired at different times. They cause different behaviors; one leads Elwood to say, "Righty is a small black circle," while the other one leads him to say that "Lefty is a small black circle." Again, on the simple view we have to find two contents, while on the complex view we have two beliefs and two ideas to work with. Elwood has two beliefs, involving different notions of the same object, with different reflexive contents but the same referential content. He believes the same thing, in two similar but different ways.

These cases provide considerations in favor of the complex view, although perhaps not completely determinative ones. Now I turn to self-locating beliefs, explaining what they are, and how the complex view handles them.

3 Self-Locating Beliefs

Let's return to your hike in California's Desolation Wilderness. You come to the top of a hill and see Gilmore Lake in the valley below. Although one of the larger lakes in the Desolation Wilderness, it is small as lakes go. It is also blue and clear. You form a belief that you would express by saying, "That is a small, clear, blue lake." Given your background beliefs and the way your perceptual system works, the belief is caused by the visual sensations that you had as you topped the hill. Your belief also has effects. You desire to fish, swim, and refill your canteen. Your belief, combined with these desires, motivates you to walk down the hill towards the lake. It is like something to have this kind of belief; you've likely had beliefs like it, about other lakes. The belief has a structure; there is your idea of the lake, connected with your perception of it, an idea that also plays a role in your intention to take a swim in the lake. And there are other ideas, of being a lake, being small, being blue, being clear, that are involved in this belief, but also in many others, about quite different things.

In this case, you have a notion of Gilmore Lake with certain important properties. It is connected in important ways to your perception of the lake. The perception gave rise to the idea. It remains connected to it as you examine the lake. As you walk towards it, swim in it and so on, you will attach information gained perceptually to the mental file based on this notion. I'll simply say the notion is attached to a stream of perceptions. In such a case, the notion is *of* the object the perceptions are of, the object you were seeing. You saw Gilmore Lake, so your idea is *of* Gilmore Lake.

Given the nature of your idea of Gilmore Lake, the idea itself, the brain in which it resides, and hence the possessor of the brain, have to be in important causal and geographical relations to Gilmore Lake. It has to be causing the perception to which the idea is attached, and so you have to be in a position to see it.

This belief is self-locating, then, in two senses. First, the truth of the belief constrains the belief *itself* to be in certain causal and geographical relations to Gilmore Lake. Secondly, the self to which the belief belongs, you in this case, are similarly constrained. The truth of the belief requires not merely that there be a clear blue lake, but that the belief itself belong to an agent that is seeing that lake. The belief has to be in your brain, where it can be affected by your perceptions, and, in conjunction with your desires, affect your bodily movements.

Your perception-based notion of Gilmore Lake, and the belief of which it is a part, are the sorts of cognitions that various might people might have. You or I or anyone else might have a belief like this when seeing Gilmore Lake from the hill you are on, or when coming to the top of another hill in the Desolation Wilderness and seeing Susie Lake, or coming to the top of other hills around the world, and seeing other lakes. One might also come to have a belief of this sort in a variety of situations in which it wouldn't be true: there is a large lake that appears closer than it really is; there is a greenish-brown lake that only appears to be blue from a distance on clear days; there is no lake, but only a mirage; and so on.

This type of belief has several important aspects, closely related but distinguishable. First, it has a structure; it involves a notion of a particular geographical feature, that you acquired as you came over the hill and saw Gilmore Lake, being associated with a number of predicative ideas you have had for a long time, your ideas of being a lake, being blue, being small and being clear.

Second, the belief has a causal role, in David Lewis's sense (Lewis, 1966). It is the type of belief that a person typically acquires when he tops a hill and sees a small, clear blue lake in the valley below. It is also the type of belief that typically motivates the agent who has a desire to swim or fish, or refill his canteen, to walk down the hill into the valley and towards the lake.

Third, it is like something to have this sort of belief; there is a bit of phenomenology associated with it; that's why you can understand what I am getting at when I describe your having one. You know what it's like to come over a hill and see a lake in the distance, perhaps not being certain that it is a lake or a mirage at first, and then forming the belief that it is a lake, and then noting that it is small, compared at least to Lake Tahoe or even Fallen Leaf Lake, that it is blue and that it is clear. You know this sort of belief can lead to feelings of relief if you are tired and have been looking for a place to stop where you can get a drink and perhaps take a swim.

On the complex view, the truth-conditions of beliefs of this sort fit with their other properties. Recall that in general a belief **b** like this will have reflexive truth-conditions of this form:

b is true iff:
(i) There is some cognizer C, to whom **b**, **I**, and **n** all belong;
(ii) There is a property *P*, of which **I** is an idea;
(iii) There is an object *a*, of which **n** is a notion;
(iv) *a* has property *P*.

These are the "barebones" truth-conditions, that assume nothing special about **b**. Each time we add some information about **b**, fixing some of its properties, we generate a new question: what *else* has to be the case for **b** to be true? What is special about self-locating beliefs of this sort pertains to clause (iii). What is required for a notion to be *of* an object depends on the kind of notion it is. The notion you have is tied to perception; it was formed as the result of perception; it's the kind of idea one acquires when one perceives; it remains connected to the perceptions you have, as you approach the lake and add to and perhaps modify your beliefs about it. The object the notion is *of*, is the one that the perception which gave rise to that notion, was *of*. So when we add this fact to our bare bone truth-conditions, *what else* has to be the case? The object, that **n** is *of*, must be a perception of the cognizer, which gave rise to **n**. So, the cognizer must be appropriate situated, and the belief **b** is self-locating.

Now recall that, as you are hiking up the hill, you already have a notion of Gilmore Lake, one you acquired when you read about the Desolation Wilderness in a guidebook before your visit. And you have a belief, involving this notion, based on what the guidebook says, that Gilmore Lake is small, clear and blue. That notion is quite different from the one you acquired as you came over the hill. It's different phenomenologically. Forming an idea of a lake by reading about it is quite different than forming an idea of a lake by seeing it. Even when you are no longer reading about it, when you think about the lake you'll most likely to be able to identify the idea involved as one you formed by reading rather than perceptually. It is associated with a name, "Gilmore Lake," but not with a memory of seeing of a lake. The file associated with the notion, since it is based on reading the guidebook and perhaps looking at the maps therein, will have a different "shape and feel" to one formed on the basis of perception.

Each of your two notions of Gilmore Lake is of that lake because of the process that led to its formation. The notion you acquired from the guidebook is *of* the lake that was referred to by the referring expressions in the text you read, and so only indirectly connected to the lake. The notion you acquired from coming over the hill and seeing Gilmore Lake is of what the perception that gave rise to it is of, and so much more directly connected to the lake. In fact one thing, Gilmore Lake, plays both roles. It is the thing you read about, and it is the thing you see.

The reflexive truth conditions of the two beliefs are different simply because they are two beliefs. When we add facts about the nature of the notion involved, the incremental truth conditions, given those facts, remain quite different; in the one case there must be a lake you read about, in the other case a lake you are seeing. However, once we add the facts about what the notions are of, and ask what *else* has to be the case for the beliefs to be true given all of that, we get the same result. The referential contents are the same, that Gilmore Lake is a small, blue, clear lake.

This is both a Frege case and an Austin case. It is a Frege case because you have a belief that you are seeing Gilmore Lake; you have this belief via your perception based notion of Gilmore Lake. But you don't believe the same proposition via another notion, the notion of Gilmore Lake you acquired from reading. It is an Austin case, because you have two beliefs with the same content, that Gilmore Lake is small, clear and blue, that have different causes and different effects.

As noted, in conjunction with desires and other "pro-attitudes," the belief motivates actions. If you are thirsty and want a swim, other things being equal, you will walk towards the lake. This action will increase the chances of satisfying your desires if the belief is true. However, we need the right choice of truth-conditions to see the connection. The fact that you are thirsty and want a swim, and Gilmore Lake is a small, clear, blue lake do not make sense of your actions. What is needed is that there is a small clear blue lake in front of you. For your walking to get you closer to it, it must be appropriately related relative to you, and your belief guarantees this. The level of truth-conditions that makes this clear is what we might call the "agent-bound" truth-conditions. We fix the fact that you are the agent, and that **I** is of the property of being small clear blue lake. What else does the world have to be like, for **b** to be true? You must be perceiving a small, blue, clear lake in front of you. Given that you want to swim, walking forward, towards the lake you see, makes sense.

If we were to describe this episode in the normal way, we would not mention the belief as such, and would focus on the agent-bound or subject matter contents. We might say that you learned *that there was a small clear blue lake down the hill from you*, or simply that you came to believe that Gilmore Lake was small, clear and blue (even though you didn't realize it was Gilmore Lake). We would be likely to describe it the first way, if we were explaining the impact the episode has on you—why you heaved a sigh of relief, and started to walk briskly towards the lake. The second way might be appropriate if we were using you as an authority on Gilmore Lake, because we know it was the lake you just saw. You believe it is a small, clear, blue lake, so it probably is. On the complex view, the contents we ascribe to a given belief are relative to our interests in describing the belief, and in particular whether we want to explain what the belief motivates the believer to do, or what the truth of the belief means for our own view of the world.

In such ordinary talk, the belief itself comes in only as implicitly quantified over. We are saying, more or less, that you have a belief, the agent-bound content of which is that there is a lake before you, or that you have a belief, the subject matter content of which is that Gilmore Lake is small blue and clear. It cannot be said, in favor of the complex view, that it falls out directly from the way we talk about beliefs. It can be said in its favor that it makes sense of how we do so.

4 Epistemic and Pragmatic Roles

Without self-locating beliefs, intentional action makes no sense. Action always takes the form of a physical movement of an agent at a time having a result in a larger situation. Intentional action involves purposefully making a movement as a way of bringing about a desired result in a larger situation. The larger situation consists of relations the agent and various of his effectors have to objects around him, and the further properties of those objects, including their relations to other things, and so on. For a belief, in combination with a desire, to motivate an action, it should be the sort of belief the truth of which guarantees, or at least makes probable, that the situation is one in which that movement will have that result.

The centrality of this pattern is more basic than human cognition. Think of a toad flicking out its tongue to catch a fly, or a bass spotting a minnow, darting towards it and devouring it, or a hen spotting a kernel of corn, walking to it, and pecking. In each case, the success of the action depends on the distance and direction of the object perceived relative to the agent and its operative parts, as well as further properties of the object—in these cases, that it is the sort of thing the creature in question eats.

The job of perception is to provide information about the aspects of an animal's situation that may vary from time to time, and which call for different actions for survival, or procreation or pleasure, or whatever it is exactly that Mother Nature is after. Permanent features of the environment can be taken care of by basic architectural features of the animal. The chicken has everything it needs to get the kernel of corn into its gullet, except information about where such a kernel is to be found. Perceptions of the relevant kinds should occur, in normal conditions, only when kernels are to be found in various relations to the chicken, and, in normal chickens, cause behavior that will get them into the chicken's gullet.

I use "role" as a way of describing relational facts. Often an object is the default thing whose relation to other things is in question for a certain stretch of discourse—it is the subject of the discourse, but may not be referred to in any of the normal grammatical ways. In such cases I'll say the subject is "indexed" rather than referred to. Suppose you are filling out a form. The answers may all take the form of specifying objects that stand in certain relations to you. *You* are the subject, the object taken as given. The form is an index that stands for you; all the answers to provide are *about* you. Entries like "address," "telephone number," "place of birth," and the like are questions about which objects stand in certain relations to you, that is play certain roles relative to you—play certain roles in your life. The words on the form specify the role; you are to identify the object that plays it relative to you: *your* address, *your* telephone numbers, and so on. Another example. You get an invitation to a party. The party is the subject. The invitation is the index; it stands for the party. The words on the invitation tells which objects play crucial roles *relative to that party*: type of party, date of party, host of party, and so forth. Spreadsheets and other tabular forms of presenting information can be seen in these terms: the left-most column provides an index, identifying the subject of the information to the right; the rest of the columns correspond to roles; the cells tell the occupant of the role relative to the indexed object.

We can think of perception as a way of giving animals information about which kinds of objects play important roles in their lives at a given moment. What is in front of us? What are we holding? What are we hearing? What sort of thing is on our tongue? The perceiver is the index for information perception provides. If you wake up in the Sierras and see a bear, you learn that there is a bear in front of *you*. If you see a bear chasing someone across the way, your perception has to tell you whom the bear is chasing. But if you see a bear in front of you, perception doesn't have to tell you whom it is in front of. Your perceptions provide information that is indexed to you.

This isn't exactly a necessary truth. Suppose our defense department decides to let raw recruits defuse bombs, under the guidance of well and expensively trained experts, who are some distance from the bomb and well-protected. Transmitters and receivers are set up so that, after throwing a switch in his goggles, the expert has the visual sensations and visual perceptual experience of the recruit, and can tell him just what he should do. The expert is getting information perceptually, more or less, about what things are like in front of the recruit, not in front of himself.

Our lives depend heavily on two kinds of linkage, index links and role links. In normal perception, the perceiver is the index for a number of different relations. He is the perceiver, the cognizer who will form beliefs as a result of the perceptions, the agent who will form intentions act on the basis of the beliefs. He is also the person whose eyes the objects seen are in front of. These index links are architectural. We have imagined technology breaking the last link. Imaginative philosophers have gone further along these lines (Dennett, 1978).

Some of the role links we depend on are also built into the way we are built and the way we fit into normal environments. I see a computer screen before me, and what I see and don't see motivates me to move my fingers across a computer keyboard. The computer whose screen I see is normally the one that I affect by moving my fingers and pressing keys. If I am using a desktop computer with a detachable keyboard, it won't be hard for some prankster to disrupt this role-link. It's harder with laptops.

A car is a symphony of convenient role-linking. The car I sit in, the one I see the road ahead of, the one I steer with the wheel I grasp, the one I accelerate with one pedal and brake with another, are all the same. As I write, even the geniuses in Detroit have not managed to screw up this brilliant architecture; but it could be done, and someone is no doubt working on it.

When indices and roles are linked architecturally, or by pervasive features of the natural environment, or by convenient technology, or some combination of these things, we normally will not need to think about them. That is, we won't need to have beliefs consisting of role-ideas and the idea of being the same thing. It doesn't occur to me to worry about whether the car I am steering is the one I am sitting in—at least, if it does occur to me, it is while doing philosophy and not while driving. I do have the capacity to think such thoughts, however. Most likely, chickens don't have the capacity to worry about whether the kernels they see are the same ones they will eat if they head in the right direction and peck, much less to worry about whether the same chicken that now perceives will be the one who pecks later.

Certain relations and roles are *epistemic*; they are ways of getting information about the objects that stand in them, or are closely connected to such ways. Objects that are in front of me are ones that I can usually see, and find out more about by looking more closely, or moving around them, or reaching out and touching them, or talking to them, if they are the sort of things one can talk to. Certain roles are *pragmatic*; they are connected with certain actions I might take to have an effect on them, or prevent them from having an effect on me. The roles most closely tied to our perceptual systems are often both epistemic and pragmatic. The thing in my hand I can feel, I can usually find out more about it by looking at it; I can throw it; I can put it in my mouth and eat it; it may be able to sting me if I don't drop it quickly.

The lives of primitive animals, and the more primitive parts of the lives of humans, center on picking up information about objects playing important roles in our lives, and acting in ways that make sense given what we find out about them. I see a piece of fruit in a bowl before me. I go closer, pick it up, examine it, check its color, squeeze it perhaps, decide that it is an apple, red enough to be ripe, firm enough to be not too ripe, and I eat it. I see a black and white animal in the distance. I walk a bit closer to see if it is cat or a dog or a skunk. As I approach I sniff. It looks like a skunk and smells like a skunk. So I turn around and vacate the area. Mostly I don't need to do a lot of thinking about the links between these roles—whether the animal I see is the one I smell, whether the area I am in is the one the animal I see is in, and so on.

On the other hand, humans have the capacity to wonder whether the same object plays two roles, consider evidence for and against it, and make mistakes about it. When I recognize someone at tonight's party that I met at last night's party, I am role-linking. I am linking the role of being the person I met yesterday, and now remember, with the role of being the person I now see. Doing this requires a somewhat more complicated cognitive system than simply seeing apples and eating them, or smelling skunks and heading the other direction.

4.1 Direct and Indirect Epistemic Roles

Perception is the most direct epistemic role that external objects can play in our lives. But reading about objects, or talking about them, or looking at a picture of them, is also a way of finding out about them. These are what I'll call "indirect" epistemic roles. That an object is playing an indirect epistemic role in my life—I am reading about it, say—imposes some constraints are our relative locations. I must be someplace in space and time where I can perceive of a name that has been given to the object, and used in texts that can perceive. So we shouldn't say that beliefs we form as we read about objects are completely not self-locating; they are, I'll say, "weakly self-locating."

4.2 Attached and Detached Notions

Among notions, I distinguish between attached notions, or "buffers," and detached notions. Buffers are attached to epistemic and/or pragmatic roles; they are associated with perceptions or plans. But, like your notion of Gilmore Lake after you walk away from it, they can become detached. You still have beliefs, think thoughts, make inferences, and form intentions involving these notions. But they are not associated with perceptions that provide information about the objects, or with intentions to affect the objects, in virtue of their current relation to you.

What's the point of detached notions? They allow us to retain knowledge of things, for later use. You meet someone at a party. You talk to her, learn her name, her interests, and the like. If you see her again a day or a month later, and recognize her, your interactions will be informed not only by the things you learn about her on that occasion, but also what you learned earlier. Also in the meantime you can use the detached notion to reason with, and maybe figure out more about her, like what might be a good thing to say next time you meet.

Suppose you go beyond this. You look up her name in the phone book. Now your notion has become attached to a perception of a representation of her. I'll call this being "indirectly attached." Suppose you find her address and write her a letter (to consider a rather old-fashioned possibility). This involves her playing what we might call an indirect pragmatic role in your life, being the person to whom a letter will be delivered, in virtue of the name and address you write on it. So again we can say that while you are doing all of this your notion of her is indirectly attached.

4.3 Linking, Merging, and Messes

Upon arriving home after your hike in the Wilderness, you spend some time with maps and guidebooks figuring out which lake you visited. You combine what you learn with what you remember, and figure out that it was Gilmore Lake that you visited.

We can imagine this takes a little time. Before lunch you look at a map. You know that you went by Fallen Leaf Lake up the Mount Tallac trail. You aren't very sure what you did after that. It was a nice day and you knew you could find your way back since Lake Tahoe and Fallen Leaf Lake were often visible. (I'm not recommending this approach to hiking.) But now that you look at the map, you are pretty sure that it was Gilmore Lake. Your two notions become linked, but not fully merged. If you come back after lunch and find out you were wrong, you can undo the inferences you made based on the presumed identity. But at some point in the afternoon, after reading the guidebook, surfing the internet, and the like, the notions become fully merged. Now all the beliefs you have about Gilmore Lake, whether acquired through reading, or perception, or looking at photos or maps, involve the same notion.

Suppose, however, that in spite of all your work, you are wrong. Suppose it was really Susie Lake you visited. Then we would have what I call a "mess." Is your merged idea really of Gilmore Lake? Or Susie Lake? Or both? or neither? This is a case where there is no fact of the matter, but there are facts about the matter. By this I mean that there is no automatic answer in such cases, but if we add details it may become clear what we should say. Suppose you go on to read more and more about Gilmore Lake, and the next spring hike up to see it again. It doesn't seem quite the way you remember it. You are not sure it is the lake you saw the time before. Here it seems that you believe a lot of things about Gilmore Lake; you believed that you had seen it before; you came to doubt this. You can truthfully say, "That's Gilmore Lake, the lake I thought I had visited, but now I'm not so sure." Perhaps your merged notion went through a period when it wasn't definitely of either Susie Lake or Gilmore Lake; but by this time it has acquired the status of being fully of Gilmore Lake.

This sort of indeterminacy may bother some. You have a belief the whole time. Surely, one might think, there must be *something* that you believe. On the simple view, that seems to be required. If having a belief is having a relation of belief to a proposition, there can't very well be a belief without a believed proposition.

This seems quite wrong-headed to me. Our ability to classify what is going on in someone's head—the way their brain has sifted and stored the data of experience, the structures that are engaged by perception and motivate action—with sentences that describe the external world, is quite amazing. It all depends on functional connections between internal states and external objects, that is, that the *of* relation leads from one idea to one appropriate object. It's not all that surprising that ideas sometimes fail to live up to the logical requirements our system of reporting rests on. It seems to me an advantage of the complex theory that it allows for this; we can have beliefs, with no clear answer to the question of what is believed. Logically speaking, not all is lost in such cases. We can have reflexive contents, without having referential contents.

In human life there is a huge commerce in detached information about things, presented in forms in which it is easily attachable. That's what books and libraries and now websites are all full of, and what conversations mainly deal in. This information typically tells you what things are like, pretty independently of where you are in relation to them, using names and descriptions. One has to be in a position to perceive the representation—to hear the conversation, or read the book, or see the picture—but not the object itself. To use the information to augment one's pre-existing files, one has to get oneself into at least an indirect epistemic relation to the object. For the information to guide an action one must get oneself into a pragmatic relation to the object. This is impossible with Aristotle, but can be managed with Gilmore Lake, by driving back to the Wilderness and going back along the Mt. Tallac trail.

As the example of Aristotle shows, we enjoy the commerce in such information even when there is no possibility of applying it directly to the object. The one-off applications, in reading and writing, in conversations and even in mid-terms, are sufficiently rewarding to keep the practice going, even in such cases. Indeed, the one-off applications—reading and talking about people and places and things that are not present, or no longer exist, or perhaps never did exist—often provide a much pleasanter way to spend a day that actually interacting with live, present, existents.

5 Beliefs about oneself

Suppose our chicken sees a kernel of corn, approaches it, pecks at it, eats it. The chicken picks up some important information about an object that plays certain important roles in its life. It perceives something a certain distance and direction in front of it, with properties that suggest edibility. It then takes actions that make sense, given that information; it moves its legs in a way that brings it towards the thing it sees, perhaps picking up more information about edibility as it goes. It then pecks and swallows, moving its head, beak, and gullet in a way that brings that thing to its gizzard. This works because the thing seen, the thing approached, and the thing pecked and swallowed are the same; if the thing seen is edible, the thing pecked will be too. The chicken has a temporary perceptual buffer, and no need for a detached notion.

There is another object, the identity of which is important to the success of the chicken's adventure: the chicken itself. There is one thing, the chicken, such that (i) *it* has the perception; (ii) the perception gives information about *it* in the sense of which sorts of objects occupy various roles in *its* life; (iii) the perception directly controls *its* walking and pecking; and (iv) the walking and pecking secure food for *it*, at least when things go right.

The chicken doesn't have the job of keeping track of things to make sure that the chicken that sees the corn is the same one that eventually eats it. It's taken care of by what I called architectural index-linking; perhaps I should call it "the physical unity of apperception." There is no reason to posit a notion of itself in the chicken, attached or detached; *all* the information it gets has to do with how things are in relation to *it*. Insofar as the chicken has a representation of itself, it is its whole cognitive system. The whole cognitive system has the job of providing information about the chicken, in the way that the whole invitation had the job of providing information about the party, which wasn't explicitly mentioned.

In such a case we would say something like "The chicken knows that there is a kernel in front of it." We need to use *it* in our report of the content, to keep track of what the chicken is getting information about. But the chicken does not need a representation of itself. The chicken is an unarticulated constituent of the contents we use to keep track of its mental states. I also call this "primitive self-knowledge"; the chicken has to know where things are relative to *it*, but it doesn't need a self-notion to do so.

Much the same goes on with humans much of the time. When I see a sandwich, reach out and pick it up, put it my mouth and chew it up, and swallow, I don't need to worry about whether the person who saw the sandwich, the person who grabs it, the person who is hungry, and the person who gets nourished are the same. There is a pre-established harmony, a physical unity of apperception, a system of architecturally linked indices, that takes care of things; that is, primitive self-knowledge suffices.

We on the other hand see ourselves as one person among many, who has the same sorts of properties and stands in the same sorts of relations as other people. We not only have beliefs concerning ourselves, we have beliefs about ourselves, involving our self-notions. This allows us to predicate the same properties to ourselves that we predicate to others.

Self-knowledge, ordinarily conceived, of the sort adult humans have, but chickens (at least as far as I can tell) don't have and don't need, is an interesting special case of role-based knowledge. The truth conditions of a self-belief **b** are:

If **b** = **I(n)**,
b is true, given that **n** is a self-notion, iff:
(i) There is some cognizer C, to whom **b**, **I**, and **n** all belong;
(ii) There is a property *P*, of which **I** is an idea;
(iii) There is an object *a*, of which **n** is a notion;
(iv) *a* = C,
(v) *a* has property *P*

We each play an important role in our own lives, the role of *self*. This is the role that corresponds to the relation of identity. It is both an epistemic and pragmatic role. There are certain ways of knowing about a person, that are normally (and in some cases, necessarily) ways of knowing about oneself. If I have a sensation of hunger, I learn that I am hungry; you can learn that I am hungry, but not in that way. If I see a tree, I learn that there is a tree in front of me. The self-notion is thus a *buffer*, tied to an epistemic and pragmatic role of great importance.

But what is the point of having such a self-notion, if our role-based organization of information already constitutes a way of having information about ourselves? Because we have access to other pools of information about ourselves, which is of the same form, employing the same predicates, as information about others. Such information typically involves modes of access that are not normally self-informative, in addition to those that are. We need a single notion to pool what we learn about ourselves in normally self-informative ways, and what we learn about ourselves in other ways—say by looking at old photographs of ourselves, or hearing what others remember about us, or have noticed about us, or have decreed that we shall do. We gain information about ourselves in indirect ways, hearing our names in conversations, reading our names in class-schedules, and so on.

Because there is only one person that ever plays the role of self for a given person, the self-buffer can serve the purpose of a detached notion, without ever being detached from our ordinary ways of knowing about ourselves. That is, one can accumulate information gained in self-informative ways, being assured it is all about the same person, something one cannot do with other roles, like being the person one is looking at, or being the person on the phone, since one person may play such a role at one time, and another person at another time.

Self-locating knowledge and the physical unity of apperception is basic to all animal cognition, or proto-cognition. But ordinary self-knowledge, as important as it is to us, is not nearly so essential, even in the lives of most humans throughout our history, as other cases of self-locating knowledge, of the sort required by any chicken or termite or slug.

6 Self-Attribution and De Se Belief

It is a source of pride that my article "Frege on Demonstratives" (1977) played an important part in inspiring the late great philosopher, and friend, David Lewis to significantly alter his views, in a characteristically original and bold fashion, in order to accommodate self-locating belief (Lewis, 1979). He used the term "de se belief" for both the phenomenon and his theory of it. I want to end this essay by calling attention to some differences between his theory and mine.

Lewis developed his theory as a modification to his counterpart theory (Lewis, 1968). In counterpart theory, the actual world is our world, the only world we are in; we are all "world-bound" individuals. Other possible worlds are as real as ours; they are actual for their inhabitants, in the same way that ours in actual for us. Although all individuals, in all worlds, are world-bound, they are more or less similar to individuals in other worlds. When I say that if I hadn't gotten a fellowship to graduate school, I would have been a lawyer, the claim I am really making is something like this: in the world most like ours (relative to the relevant standards of similarity for worlds), in which the individual most like me (relative to the relevant standards of similarity for individuals) didn't get a fellowship to graduate school, that person became a lawyer.

For Lewis, propositions are sets of worlds, and properties are functions from worlds to sets of individuals. On his earlier view, belief is a relation between an individual at a time and a proposition. So, in terms of the framework of the first section of this essay, he held a Fregean view, although of course his propositions were much different metaphysically than Frege's *Gedanken*. His theory of de se belief takes belief instead to be a relation to properties of individuals at times. Belief consists of an agent "self-attributing" a property at a time, or, on his preferred way of looking at it, a person-stage self-attributing a property, *simpliciter*. The belief is true if the agent doing the attributing has the property at the time of the self-attribution. My current belief that I am a human has as its object not the proposition that John Perry is a human, but the property of being a human. This belief locates me in logical space, that is, it is true if I am an inhabitant of a world in which I am a human. My belief that Obama is President in 2012 is a self-attribution of the property of being in a world in which Obama is President in 2012. The beliefs that I had thought of as self-locating, are simply the special case in which the truth of the belief does not only require that I be in worlds of a certain sort, but that I be at certain places, or occupy certain further roles, within those worlds.

I don't much care for Lewis's metaphysics. As far as I can see, he simply thought that the one and only world is a very complicated place, with lots of causally insulated universes comprising it. I have yet to see a compelling reason for thinking there are *any* universes other than the one I am in, much less as many as Lewis's theory requires. Even if there are that many causally insulated universes, I can't see why something being possible in our universe should amount to its happening in some other universe. If perchance there is no universe in which someone a lot like me didn't get a fellowship and became a lawyer instead, that wouldn't mean that it wasn't a possibility for me. Of course Lewis heard all of this, and was unmoved, at least in this world.

Be that as it may, many philosophers who share my skepticism for Lewis's "modal realism" and counterpart theory, adapt many of the ideas he developed to more plausible conceptions of what possible worlds are. In particular, Neil Feit, a co-editor of this volume, has written a very fine book developing such a view (Feit, 2008). And Lewis emphasized that his theory of de se belief does not really depend on his rather radical metaphysics. So this is not the difference I have in mind.

One difference is that on Lewis's counterpart theory, even adapted to a less radical metaphysics, there is no room for singular propositions in the way they are usually thought of. Consider the proposition that Obama is inaugurated in January 2013. Conceived as a singular proposition, within a possible worlds framework, this would be the set of worlds in which a certain individual, Obama, is inaugurated in January 2013. This requires that Obama be a trans-world individual, not one bound to our world. So this proposition just isn't available.

On my view, ordinary self-knowledge (or self-belief)—the sort expressed with the word 'I'—involves belief in singular propositions. Ordinary self-knowledge is distinguished from knowledge that merely *concerns* the self. A baby or an animal might have knowledge that concerns itself, in the sense described in the last section, without having ordinary self-knowledge of the sort that more grown-up humans have. Ordinary self-knowledge is a special case of knowledge about objects via important epistemic and pragmatic roles they play in our lives. Knowledge that concerns oneself is simply a matter of having beliefs, or doxastic states, the reflexive truth-conditions of which are conditions on oneself.

I think what Lewis calls "self-attribution" has to be taken as belief that concerns oneself. It is not clear to me what his account of ordinary self-knowledge is.

On my view, our system of propositional attitudes is grounded in the phenomenon of agents having role-based representations of the external world; that is, agents having beliefs *about* objects that play various key roles in their lives. To understand the internal causal roles of such attitudes, we need to attend to the role-based representations. To understand the role of such beliefs in communication and action, we need to attend to the way the same objects can occupy different roles for different people, or the same person at different times, or the same person relative to different stages of a plan of action. On this view, belief about objects—the sort of belief we characterize with singular propositions—is an important part of the story about how beliefs are supposed to work, without which an account of the causal role of beliefs, and the ways in which their contents are based on their causal roles, is pretty hopeless.

This two-sided nature of belief is based on the two-sided nature of all representation, rather than being something special about belief, involving a special activity of self-attribution; that is, that is the distinction between reflexive and referential content. To understand how representations represent in virtue of constraints about how the world works, we need to attend to reflexive content. To use the information thus provided in dealing with objects in our lives, we need to attend to referential content.[2]

There are other problems with Lewis's account which I won't go into here; I tried to explain them some time ago (1986b). They need to be revisited within the context of the current version of my theory, but I don't have time or space to complete that task now and here.

References

Austin, David F., 1990. *What's the Meaning of 'This'?* Ithaca, NY: Cornell University Press.

Crimmins, Mark and John Perry, 1989. 'The Prince and the Phone Booth: Reporting Puzzling Beliefs.' *Journal of Philosophy* 86: 685-711. Reprinted in Perry2001a, Chapter 12.

Crimmins, Mark, 1992. *Talk About Beliefs*. Cambridge, Mass.: Bradford/MIT.

Dennett, Dan. 1978. 'Where Am I?' In *Brainstorms: Philosophical Essays on Mind and Psychology*, Cambridge, Bradford Books.

Feit, Neil. 2008. *Belief about the Self.* New York: Oxford University Press.

---

2 The development of the views put forward in this essay began with (Perry, 1977) and (Perry, 1979), and then were developed further in the various articles collected in (Perry, 2000), the articles with David Israel and Syun Tutiya, and most recently in (Perry, 2012) and (Korta and Perry, 2012).

Fodor, Jerry A., 1981. *Representations: Philosophical Essays on the foundations of cognitive science*. Cambridge: Bradford/MIT.

Frege, Gottlob, 1892. 'Über Sinn und Bedeutung.' Zeitschrift für Philosophische Kritik, NF 100, pp. 25-30.

Frege, Gottlob, 1960a. 'On Sense and Reference.' Translation of Frege, 1892 by Max Black, in Frege 1960b: 56-78.

Frege, Gottlob, 1960b. *Translations From the Philosophical Writings of Gottlob Frege*. Edited and translated by Peter Geach and Max Black. Oxford: Basil Blackwell.

Frege, Gottlob, 1967a. 'The Thought: A Logical Inquiry.' In *Philosophical Logic*, ed. P. F. Strawson. Oxford: Oxford University Press: 17–38. This translation, by A.M. and Marcelle Quinton, originally appeared in *Mind* 65 (1956): 289-311. The original, 'Der Gedanke. Eine logische Untersuchung,' appeared in Beiträge zur Philosophie des deutschen Idealismus I (1918): 58-77.

Israel, David and John Perry, 1990. 'What is Information?' In *Information, Language and Cognition*, edited by Philip Hanson, Vancouver: University of British Columbia Press: 1-19.

Israel, David and John Perry, 1991. 'Information and Architecture.' In *Situation Theory and Its Applications*, vol. 2, edited by Jon Barwise, Jean Mark Gawron, Gordon Plotkin and Syun Tutiya, Stanford University: Center for the Study of Language and Information: 147-60.

Israel, David, John Perry and Syun Tutiya, 1993. 'Executions, Motivations and Accomplishments.' *The Philosophical Review*: 515-40.

Kaplan, David, 1989a. 'Demonstratives.' In J. Almog, J. Perry, and H. Wettstein (eds.). 1989. *Themes from Kaplan*. (Oxford: Oxford University Press), 481-564.

Korta, Kepa and John Perry, 2012. *Critical Pragmatics*. Cambridge: Cambridge University Press.

Kripke, Saul, 1979. 'A Puzzle about Belief.' In *Meaning and Use*, ed. A. Margalit, 239-83. Dordrecht: Reidel.

Lewis, David, 1966. 'An Argument for the Identity Theory.' *Journal of Philosophy*: 63: 17-25.

Lewis, David, 1972. 'Psychophysical and Theoretical Identifications.' *Australasian Journal of Philosophy* 50: 249-258.

Lewis, David, 1979. 'Attitudes De Dicto and De Se.' *Philosophical Review* 88: 513-543.

Lewis, David, 1968. 'Counterpart Theory and Quantified Modal Logic.' *Journal of Philosophy* 65 (5): 113-126.

Perry, John, 1977. 'Frege on Demonstratives.' *Philosophical Review*, 86(4): 474-97. Reprinted in Perry, 2000a, Chapter 1.

Perry, John, 1979. 'The Problem of the Essential Indexical.' *Nous* 13(1)1: 3-21. Reprinted in Perry, 2000a, Chapter 2.

Perry, John, 1997b. 'Indexicals and Demonstratives.' In Robert Hale and Crispin Wright (eds.) *Companion to the Philosophy of Language*. Oxford: Blackwell: 586-612.

Perry, John, 1998a. 'Myself and I.' In Marcelo Stamm, ed., *Philosophie in Synthetisher Absicht. A festschrift for Dieter Heinrich*, Stuttgart: Klett-Cotta: 83-103. Reprinted in Perry 2000a, Chapter 19.

Perry, John, 2000. *The Problem of the Essential Indexical*, Expanded edition. Stanford: CSLI Publications.

Perry, John, 2002. *Identity, Personal Identity and the Self.* Indianapolis: Hackett Publishing.

Perry, John. 2012. *Reference and Reflexivity*, 2nd edition. Stanford: CSLI Publications.

Russell, Bertrand, 1912. *Problems of Philosophy*. London: Williams and Norgate. 1997 Reprint, Oxford: Oxford University Press.

Stalnaker, Robert, 1981. 'Indexical Belief.' *Synthese* 49: 129-151.

Stalnaker, Robert, 1984. *Inquiry*. Cambridge, MA: MIT/Bradford.

Index